O. Palmer Robertson taught for twenty years at Reformed Theological Seminary, Westminster Theological Seminary, and Covenant Theological Seminary. He is currently pastor of Wallace Memorial Presbyterian Church in Hyattsville, Maryland. His previous books include *The Christ of the Covenants*.

THE NEW INTERNATIONAL COMMENTARY ON THE OLD TESTAMENT

R. K. HARRISON, *General Editor*

The Books of
NAHUM, HABAKKUK, and ZEPHANIAH

by
O. PALMER ROBERTSON

WILLIAM B. EERDMANS PUBLISHING COMPANY
GRAND RAPIDS, MICHIGAN

To my beloved
"The heart of her husband trusts in her"
—**Proverbs 31:11**

Copyright © 1990 by Wm. B. Eerdmans Publishing Co.
255 Jefferson Ave. S.E., Grand Rapids, Mich. 49503

Library of Congress Cataloging-in-Publication Data

Robertson, O. Palmer
The books of Nahum, Habakkuk, and Zephaniah /
by O. Palmer Robertson.
p. cm.
— (The New international commentary on the Old Testament)
Includes bibliographical references.
ISBN 0-8028-2374-2
1. Bible. O.T. Nahum — Commentaries. 2. Bible. O.T. Habakkuk—
Commentaries. 3. Bible. O.T. Zephaniah — Commentaries.
I. Title. II. Series.
BS1625.3.R63   1990
224′.9—dc20
89-28141
CIP

CONTENTS

AUTHOR'S PREFACE

The design of the *New International Commentary on the Old Testament* challenges the commentator to combine the carefulness of an exegete with the concern of a pastor. This design intends to provide a resource for pastors and teachers of the Word in a useful and practical form.

The first beneficiary of such a procedure naturally will be the author himself. What a privilege it has been to wrestle with the writings of these seventh-century B.C. prophets in terms of their significance for today.

The close-knit bond between prophecy and history becomes particularly apparent through the study of these three books. Their brevity demands a context. As the place in history of these messages is explored, it becomes more and more apparent that biblical history itself embodies prophecy. Not only does biblical prophecy arise out of the concrete circumstances of history; biblical history itself functions as prophecy. The events that occurred to Judah and its neighbors spoke in anticipation of world-shaking circumstances that were yet to come.

This perspective on the events of Judah's history provides the needed link for seeing the current implications of the message of these ancient seers. For if successive divine judgments on ungodly nations have a prophetic dimension, then people and nations of today must take heed (Nah. 1:2). If God has promised that his own people "shall live" despite the crumbling of mighty nations all about them, then those who keep trusting in the Lord may continue in hope despite all calamities (Hab. 2:4). If God has promised that he would manifest himself in the form of the "victorious hero" who saves because of his determined love, then every successive generation must center its hope on the coming of the Lord in his great Day (Zeph. 3:17).

May the Lord of the Scriptures now be pleased to bless these comments on a relatively neglected portion of his Word with a fresh outpouring of his Spirit. May all preachers and teachers committed to the Christ of Scripture find renewed reason for making their contributions toward the fulfillment of the prophecy that the earth shall be filled with the knowledge of the glory of the Lord as the waters cover the sea (Hab. 2:14).

O. Palmer Robertson
Washington, D.C.
May 1, 1986

ABBREVIATIONS

AB	Anchor Bible
ANET	J. B. Pritchard, ed., *Ancient Near Eastern Texts.* 3rd ed. Princeton: Princeton University Press, 1969
ASTI	*Annual of the Swedish Theological Institute*
AV	Authorized (King James) Version
BDB	F. Brown, S. R. Driver, and C. A. Briggs, *A Hebrew and English Lexicon of the Old Testament.* Repr. Oxford: Clarendon, 1962
BHS	K. Elliger and W. Rudolph, eds., *Biblia Hebraica Stuttgartensia.* Stuttgart: Deutsche Bibelstiftung, 1967–77
Bib	*Biblica*
BibOr	Biblica et orientalia
BKAT	Biblischer Kommentar: Altes Testament
BSac	*Bibliotheca Sacra*
BZAW	Beihefte zur *Zeitschrift für die alttestamentliche Wissenschaft*
CBQ	*Catholic Biblical Quarterly*
CBQMS	Catholic Biblical Quarterly Monograph Series
DOTT	D. W. Thomas, ed., *Documents from Old Testament Times.* Repr. New York: Harper & Row, 1961
EvQ	*Evangelical Quarterly*
ExpTim	*Expository Times*
Fest.	Festschrift
GKC	E. Kautzsch and A. E. Cowley, *Gesenius' Hebrew Grammar.* 2nd ed. Oxford: Clarendon, 1910
HAT	Handbuch zum Alten Testament
HUCA	*Hebrew Union College Annual*
ICC	International Critical Commentary
IDB(S)	G. A. Buttrick, et al., eds., *Interpreter's Dictionary of the Bible.* 4 vols. Nashville: Abingdon, 1962. *Supplementary Volume.* Ed. K. Crim, et al. 1976

IEJ	*Israel Exploration Journal*
JBL	*Journal of Biblical Literature*
JETS	*Journal of the Evangelical Theological Society*
JNES	*Journal of Near Eastern Studies*
JSS	*Journal of Semitic Studies*
JTS	*Journal of Theological Studies*
KAT	Kommentar zum Alten Testament
KB	L. Koehler and W. Baumgartner, *Lexicon in Veteris Testamenti Libros.* Leiden: Brill, 1958
lit.	literally
LXX	Septuagint
ms(s).	manuscript(s)
MT	Massoretic Text
NASB	New American Standard Bible
NICNT	New International Commentary on the New Testament
NICOT	New International Commentary on the Old Testament
NIV	New International Version
OTL	Old Testament Library
OTS	*Oudtestamentische Studiën*
RevQ	*Revue de Qumran*
SBL	Society of Biblical Literature
T.B.	Babylonian Talmud
TDNT	G. Kittel and G. Friedrich, eds., *Theological Dictionary of the New Testament.* 10 vols. Tr. and ed. G. W. Bromiley. Grand Rapids: Eerdmans, 1964–76
TDOT	G. J. Botterweck and H. Ringgren, eds., *Theological Dictionary of the Old Testament.* Vols. 1–. Tr. D. E. Green, et al. Grand Rapids: Eerdmans, 1974–
VT	*Vetus Testamentum*
VTSup	Supplements to *Vetus Testamentum*
WTJ	*Westminster Theological Journal*
ZAW	*Zeitschrift für die alttestamentliche Wissenschaft*
ZPEB	M. Tenney, et al., eds., *Zondervan Pictoral Encyclopedia of the Bible.* 5 vols. Grand Rapids: Zondervan, 1975

INTRODUCTION

I. REDEMPTIVE-HISTORICAL SETTING

If Moses and Joshua provided the direction for Israel in their possession of the land, then the writing prophets provided the direction for Israel through their loss of the land. An appreciation for the richness of the biblical-theological significance of the land imagery in Scripture may enhance this aspect of the ministry of Israel's writing prophets, including Nahum, Habakkuk, and Zephaniah.

Abraham had been promised a land not because he had none, but because this gift of God communicated the hope of restoration to paradise. He wandered in the land all his lifetime, waiting to possess the promise until the day of his death. When the land was finally claimed, it was described in idyllic terms: it was a land "flowing with milk and honey" (Exod. 3:8, 17; etc.). Like a paradise restored, its possession symbolized the consummation of God's redemptive purposes.

But what then could banishment from the land mean to God's people? They had become "Not-My-People" (cf. Hos. 1:9). They no longer possessed the symbol of the blessings of redemption. What could be more drastic? Who could explain such an experience? This task was given to Israel's writing prophets. As the God-inspired interpreters of the breakup of nations, they offered the framework for a faith that would provide the key to life in the midst of cataclysmic circumstances.

In many respects, the exile of Israel from the land was a redemptive event far more complex than the call of Abraham. God's purposes of redemption focused originally on a single individual. But now an entire nation manifesting a diversified response to the challenges of faith became the center of redemptive acts of judgment and salvation. As God worked out his purposes, mighty world powers marshalled troops that strode across continents

1

seeking the fulfillment of their ambitious goals. They too had a role to play in the ongoing drama of redemption.

The struggle of the life of faith originally demonstrated by a single wandering patriarch had become international in scope. Instead of claiming the promise of the land in opposition to other localized peoples, the people of God must now exercise faith in the face of an international power struggle seeking to control the Palestinian land bridge that joined three continents.

It is remarkable to see how faith triumphs (or how nonfaith fails to triumph) in a scene involving all the intrigue of international politics. Particularly when the struggle climaxes as it does in the 7th century B.C., the faith of the kings of Judah in the covenant promises of God determines the course of individuals and nations more than all the resources of the mightiest of monarchs in their hours of greatest strength.

Central to this entire cosmic drama is *faith;* and it is the prophets of Israel who interpret and apply the demands of faith to their own generation. The ministries of Nahum, Habakkuk, and Zephaniah fit within this scheme of God's redemptive purposes. Their ministries focus on the nation of Judah, since God had given her a central role as his chosen servant. But it is always Judah as his emissary to bring the message of redemption and judgment to the nations that provides the basis for God's concentration on this tiny nation among the giants of the globe.

In viewing the history of the world of the 7th century B.C. from a redemptive-historical perspective, key eras may be noted which crystallize the role of redemption on the international scene.

A. THE TRIUMPHS OF FAITH IN THE DAYS OF HEZEKIAH (715–687 B.C.)

A head-on confrontation of the principal players begins the 7th century B.C. Sennacherib of Assyria (705–681) stands at the gates of Jerusalem in 701. Hezekiah of Judah had taken massive steps of faith by repudiating Assyria's dominance and preparing for the retaliation that was sure to come (2 K. 18; 2 Chr. 32; Isa. 36–37). One of these works of faith was the construction of Hezekiah's tunnel, still today "justly recognized as one of the great engineering feats of antiquity."[1] Starting from both ends, workers hewed through solid rock for a total length of 600 yards; the tunnel dropped a mere 7 feet 2 inches as it proceeded on its serpentine route. Though overwhelmed at the sight

---

1. C. F. Pfeiffer, ed., *The Biblical World: A Dictionary of Biblical Archaeology* (Grand Rapids: Baker, 1966), p. 530.

of the terrifying Assyrian troops when they did arrive, the Israelites at least could laugh among themselves at the taunts of Sennacherib's emissary that they would die of thirst if they resisted him (cf. 2 Chr. 32:11).

But this manifestation of faith in the supremacy of the one true God by Hezekiah hardly compares with the work that the Lord himself was going to do in response to the faith of his servant. The Assyrian army encamped outside Jerusalem was destroyed overnight, and Sennacherib was forced to return to Assyria (Isa. 37:36–38; 2 K. 19:35–37; 2 Chr. 32:20–21). Not only the scriptural records but also the Assyrian annals attest to the work of God, despite Sennacherib's attempts to conceal his calamity. As preserved on the Oriental Institute Prism of Sennacherib, the monarch boasts:

> In my third campaign I marched against Hatti [Syro-Palestine]. Luli, king of Sidon, whom the terror-inspiring glamour of my lordship had overwhelmed, fled far overseas and perished. . . .
>
> . . . Sidqia, however, king of Ashkelon, who did not bow to my yoke, I deported and sent to Assyria, his family-gods, himself, his wife, his children, his brothers, all the male descendants of his family. . . .
>
> . . . In the mêlée of the battle, I personally captured alive the Egyptian charioteers with the(ir) princes and (also) the charioteers of the king of Ethiopia. . . .
>
> As to Hezekiah, the Jew, he did not submit to my yoke, I laid siege to 46 of his strong cities. . . . Himself I made a prisoner in Jerusalem, his royal residence, like a bird in a cage. . . . Hezekiah himself, whom the terror-inspiring splendor of my lordship had overwhelmed. . . . In order to deliver the tribute and to do obeisance as a slave he sent his (personal) messenger.[2]

An examination of Sennacherib's record reveals several noteworthy points:

(1) Sennacherib deported the king of Ashkelon—who had resisted Assyrian authority—with his family and replaced him with a loyal substitute.

(2) Sennacherib makes no similar claim respecting Hezekiah, and history shows that Hezekiah continued on the throne, contrary to Sennacherib's normal pattern.

(3) The biblical record includes a reference to the assault of Tirhakah (or Taharqa), the Cushite king of Egypt, against Sennacherib (2 K. 19:9). This notation corresponds to Sennacherib's own reference to the intrusion of Egypt during this campaign, and provides one more indicator of the way in

---

2. *ANET,* pp. 287–88.

which the Lord ordered the movements of nations to serve his redemptive-historical ends.[3]

(4) The vivid imagery of Hezekiah's being made a prisoner in his own royal city of Jerusalem "like a bird in a cage" only underscores the fact that the city was not taken but only placed under siege.

(5) A relief on the wall of Sennacherib's palace in Assyria shows the king sitting on a portable throne outside Lachish. As D. J. Wiseman has noted, "the prominence given by the sculptures of Sennacherib to this event underlines his failure to capture Jerusalem, despite the emphasis given to the siege of the capital of Judah in his written records."[4]

(6) The final humiliation of Sennacherib as recorded in Scripture corresponds basically to the records of Assyria and Babylon. According to Scripture, the haughty king suffered the double humiliation of being slain by his own sons—in the house of his own gods! (2 K. 19:36–37). Correspondingly, the cylinder of Ashurbanipal, grandson to Sennacherib, reads: "As a posthumous offering at this time I smashed the rest of the people alive by the very figures of the protective deities between which they had smashed Sennacherib, my own grandfather. Their cut up flesh I fed to the dogs, swine, jackels, birds, vultures, to the birds of the sky, and to the fishes of the deep pools."[5] No mention is made specifically of Sennacherib's being slain in the house of his gods. But the mention of the "figures of the protective deities," referring to the colossal winged bulls with human heads which guarded the main doorways of the Assyrian palaces and temples, suits well the biblical testimony. A brief note in the Babylonian Chronicle provides further confirmation: "In the month of Tebitu, the 20th day, his son killed Sennacherib, king of Assyria, during a rebellion."[6]

So in the midst of the marchings of a mighty tyrant, the interceptions of a second world empire, and the internecine intrigues of a royal family, the covenant God of Israel was showing himself faithful to the promises made to David and his sons. Hezekiah's faith in the sovereign purposes of God was stronger than human armies. God's purposes to provide a way of redemption from sin proved stronger than the purposeful strivings of human beings.

---

3. More recent studies confirm that Tirhakah was old enough by 701 B.C. to have commanded the Egyptian army in Palestine. Cf. B. Oded, in *Israelite and Judaean History,* ed. J. H. Hayes and J. M. Miller, OTL (Philadelphia: Westminster, 1977), p. 448.

4. D. J. Wiseman, in *DOTT,* p. 69.

5. *DOTT,* p. 72.

6. *ANET,* p. 302.

B. THE DARK DAYS OF UNBELIEF UNDER MANASSEH (687–642 B.C.) AND AMON (642–640 B.C.)

King Manasseh must be held personally responsible for introducing the abominations of sacred prostitution and human sacrifice within the cult of Israel (2 K. 21:6–9; 2 Chr. 33:6–9), no matter what pressures may have been placed on him from without. By these pollutions, he sealed Israel's fate in spite of subsequent repentances.

Despite his wickedness, Manasseh survived the rulership of three Assyrian monarchs: Sennacherib (705–681), Esarhaddon (681–669), and Ashurbanipal (669–627), but not without a price. The records of Esarhaddon report on the submission of Manasseh: "I called up the kings of the country Hatti [Syro-Palestine] and (of the region) on the other side of the river (Euphrates) (to wit): Ba'lu, king of Tyre, Manasseh *(Me-na-si-i)*, king of Judah *(Ia-ú-di)*. . . . all these I sent out and made them transport under terrible difficulties, to Nineveh, the town (where I exercise) my rulership, as building material for my palace: big logs, long beams (and) thin boards . . . products of . . . Lebanon *(Lab-na-na)* mountains, which had grown for a long time into tall and strong timber."[7]

During this time, the determination of Assyria to subdue Egypt reached its fever pitch. As a consequence, aggressive Assyrian military and political power was felt in Palestine throughout this period. So it is not surprising to see Manasseh listed among those forced by Ashurbanipal to aid him in his incursions into the depths of Egypt: "In my first campaign I marched against Egypt (Magan) and Ethiopia. . . . During my march (to Egypt) 22 kings from the seashore, the islands and the mainland. . . . Manasseh *(Mi-in-si-e)*, king of Judah *(Ia-ú-di)* . . . servants who belong to me, brought heavy gifts . . . to me and kissed my feet. I made these kings accompany my army over the land— as well as (over) the sea-route with their armed forces and their ships."[8] Whether Israel's troops were forced to accompany the king for the entire 400-mile trip down the Nile to Thebes is not indicated. The Assyrian monument proceeds to relate how Tirhakah "heard in Memphis of the defeat of his army" so that "he left Memphis and fled, to save his life, into the town Ni' (Thebes)." Ashurbanipal notes: "This town (too) I seized and led my army into it to repose (there). . . . With many prisoners and heavy booty I returned safely to Nineveh." The tale of this unbelievable conquest was well known to the inhabitants of Judah, as seen by the prophecy of Nahum. He boldly asks the As-

---

7. *ANET*, p. 291.
8. *ANET*, p. 294.

syrians themselves if their situation for defense is better than that of No (the Ni' of Ashurbanipal's inscription) (Nah. 3:8–10).

Quite intriguing is the fact that Assyrian presence in Israel reaches its zenith at the time when the monarch of Israel shows little or no faith in the one true living God. From a purely secular perspective, Assyria had to invade and subdue Egypt if they intended to maintain control of Syro-Palestine. As impossible as the task might have seemed, the effort had to be made. Otherwise Assyrian aspirations for world domination had to be surrendered. But one can hardly overlook the fact that the time of Assyrian expansionism corresponded with the dark days of unbelief under Manasseh. The God of all nations would not allow the people bearing his name to deny him with impunity.

Another chapter in the life of Manasseh is reported by the writer of Chronicles. According to this account, Manasseh was carried away to Babylon by the captain of the host of the king of Assyria, where he repented, humbled himself, prayed to the Lord, and was brought again to Jerusalem. Upon his return, he instituted certain building projects and initiated a number of religious reforms (2 Chr. 33:11–20).

While no direct testimony outside Scripture confirms this distinctive record of the Chronicler, certain circumstantial considerations support the account. Widespread unrest throughout the Assyrian empire was generated by a revolt in 652 led by Shamash-shum-ukin, the older brother of Ashurbanipal and ruler of Babylon.[9] Perhaps Manasseh had been bold enough to revolt while Assyria's attention was directed eastward, particularly in the light of the growing strength of Psammetichus I (or Psamtik; 663–609), son of Neco, whom the Assyrians had treated mercifully.[10] A subsequent excursion westward by Ashurbanipal might have been the occasion of Manasseh's humiliation, temporary exile, and ultimate return to Palestine.[11] Apparently between the subduing of his brother in 648 and the humbling of Elam farther to the east in 639, Ashurbanipal mounted an assault to the west in order to subdue those who had revolted along with the Arabs.[12] Although Judah is not specifically mentioned, the Assyrian texts do mention the subduing of Edom, Ammon, and Moab.[13] As for the rebellious king of Arabia, Ashurbanipal

---

9. J. Bright, *A History of Israel,* 3rd ed. (Philadelphia: Westminster, 1981), p. 313.

10. *ANET,* p. 295.

11. Bright, *History of Israel,* p. 314.

12. G. Roux, *Ancient Iraq* (Baltimore: Penguin, repr. 1976), pp. 302–3.

13. *ANET,* p. 298.

declares triumphantly: "I put a pillory (on) his (neck) together with a bear (and) a dog and made him stand on guard (duty) at the gate in Nineveh."[14]

Manasseh might have been there too! If Manasseh's exile came after Ashurbanipal's suppressing of his brother's revolt in 648, the Judean king would have been over sixty years of age at the time, having known nothing but life on the throne since he was twelve years of age (2 Chr. 33:1). The shock of such a sudden and complete humiliation might have brought about the piety that may have marked perhaps the last five years of his fifty-five-year reign.

Just such an historical circumstance provides an appropriate setting for the prophecy of Nahum. With the return east and the triumph over the Elamite capital of Susa in 639, the Assyrian empire could not have looked stronger. From Egypt to Elam they dominated all the nations of the world. Yet Nahum does not hesitate to declare their doom. The reform of Manasseh, small though it might have been in comparison with the long years he had spent laying a solid foundation for an enduring apostasy, may explain why Nahum says little or nothing about the guilt of God's people. The further Nahum is dated beyond the death of Ashurbanipal in 627, the less impact is felt from a key feature of his prophecy:

> Thus says Yahweh:
>   Though they be complete
>   and also numerous,
>   Yet they shall be mowed down
>   And he shall pass over. (Nah. 1:12)

In introducing this analysis of Nineveh's condition in his own day, Nahum employs the customary, solemn "Thus says Yahweh" for the first and only time. He lays the strongest possible stress on the fact that despite all appearances of full strength in Assyria, God shall see to it that they fall. Only faith in the sovereignty of the God of redemption could generate belief in this message concerning Nineveh's fall under such circumstances. But if the hand of God may be seen coordinating the hour of greatest strength for God's chastening instrument with the deepest depravity of his people, then faith may also believe in the coming destruction of his enemies even when they currently appear to be in full force.

Manasseh was succeeded by his son Amon, who reigned only two years before he was assassinated by the servants of his own house (2 K. 21:19–23; 2 Chr. 33:20–24). The rareness of this kind of violence against the

---

14. Ibid.

throne in the southern kingdom attests to the grace of God in honoring the promise to the line of David. While ten different dynasties consumed one another in the approximately 200-year history of the northern kingdom, only the one dynasty of David reigned in Judah for almost 350 years.

Scripture does not discuss the reason for Amon's assassination. Possibly at Egypt's instigation an anti-Assyrian party removed Amon when they detected his return to the earlier policies of his father Manasseh.[15] In any case, the "people of the land" immediately took over, executed Amon's assassins, and placed his own eight-year-old son Josiah on the throne (2 K. 21:24; 2 Chr. 33:25). These "people of the land" may have been "a privileged social and political class or an aristocratic institution of landowners which was active on the legal and military level and which had political influence."[16] At any rate, they seemed to have a loyalty to the provisions concerning throne succession as found in the Davidic covenant. Their swift action preserved the throne of David intact despite the possibility of international intrigue.

C. REFORMATION UNDER JOSIAH (640–609 B.C.)

Josiah began his public career at eight years of age with the trauma of being told that his twenty-four-year-old father had been murdered, that the assassins had been executed, and that he was to be king. No doubt the acts of intrigue generated much hustling and bustling about the halls of the royal palace in those days.

Nothing is known of the early years of Josiah's reign. But he must have been impressed very early with an awareness of God's covenant fidelity throughout the centuries. He was a son of David, a direct descendant of the one chosen by God to reign in this very place three hundred years previously! Neither the pharaohs of Egypt nor the monarchs of Assyria could boast of a God so faithful and so powerful. By the time he was sixteen years of age, Josiah "began to seek after the God of David his father" (2 Chr. 34:3). In this passage distinctive to the Chronicler, the exilic author employs one of his keywords to describe the early religious experience of the youthful king: he began to "seek" the Lord (2 Chr. 34:3; cf. the programmatic statement of 2 Chr. 7:14). Following this early inclination, Josiah at twenty years of age began to purge Judah and Jerusalem of the pagan images which Manasseh had introduced (2 Chr. 34:3–7). He extended his reform into the Assyrian-

---

15. B. Oded, in *Israelite and Judaean History*, p. 456.
16. Ibid., p. 457. See his discussion for bibliographical references.

dominated territory of the northern kingdom of Israel, including cities located in the territory of Manasseh, Ephraim, Simeon, and even Naphtali (2 Chr. 34:6). The precise timing of the early beginning of Josiah's purge is significant for three reasons:

(1) This early purge occurs in the twelfth year of his reign, which would be 628 B.C. The significance of this date is that it apparently falls *before* the death of Ashurbanipal, which is now confirmed to have occurred in 627.[17] The mighty tyrant who had cowed Manasseh into aiding him with his assault against Egypt still lived. Yet Josiah presumed to move into the northern part of Palestine and exercise his prerogative as Israel's messianic-king figure. For a young man only twenty years of age, this action could be inspired only by folly or by faith in the rightness of the Lord's cause.

(2) This early purge of Josiah preceded the call and ministry of Jeremiah and apparently of Zephaniah as well. As a young lad without prophetic backing, Josiah had the courage, the faith, and the strength of will to overthrow a religious, social, and political tradition that had regulated the whole life of his populace for the previous sixty years.

(3) This early purge preceded the discovery of the "law book" in the temple by six or seven years. Even without this authoritative justification for his actions, the king introduced his radical program of reform.

With the death of Ashurbanipal in 627, an era came to an end. For the previous one hundred years, the might of Assyria had dominated the life of the people of Palestine. After a brief interlude under Ashur-etil-ilani (627–623), his weak-willed brother Sin-shar-ishkun (623–612) presided over the kingdom's rapid demise. Within little more than ten years of his accession to the throne, Nineveh the great had fallen. No sooner had Ashurbanipal died than did Babylon assert its independence under the leadership of Nabopolassar (626–605), the first king of the Neo-Babylonian empire. A revived Media under Cyaxares (625–585) emerged to become more than merely a troublesome thorn in Assyria's side.

The net result of this development of new political threats from the east meant that the west could function relatively free of the fear of immediate Assyrian reprisal. While this new relief must not be seen as a primary factor in Josiah's reform movement, it did provide a climate most favorable to the king's intentions. If the weakness of Manasseh's faith had corresponded to the time of Assyrian strength under Ashurbanipal, the strength of Josiah's faith corresponded with a time of unprecedented weakness for Assyria.

17. J. Bright, *Jeremiah,* AB (Garden City, NY: Doubleday, 1965), p. xxxvi.

It was in this context that the "book of the law" that had been "given by Moses" was discovered in 622 (2 K. 22:8; 2 Chr. 34:14–15). Now the reform of Josiah took a significant leap forward. The book of Kings stresses the destruction of false-worship centers and the extension of the reform to Bethel in the territory of the northern kingdom (2 K. 23). The book of Chronicles pays special attention to the cultic celebration of the Passover, noting the prominent role of priests, Levites, and singers (2 Chr. 35).

The powerful prophetic ministry of Zephaniah appears to have arisen just at this point.[18] Josiah made his public commitment to institute a mode of life for his kingdom based on the pattern established in the "book of the covenant." He found just the support he needed in the ministry of the prophet Zephaniah. With language steeped in the covenantal formulations of the book of Deuteronomy, Zephaniah presents a picture of covenantal judgment without rival anywhere in Scripture for its stark depiction of the terrors of the coming consummation. At the same time, his penetration into the love of God reaches dimensions that stagger the imagination. Even in the context of coming devastation because of sin, the redeeming love of God for his people shall prevail.

Scripture provides little information concerning the international scene between the time of Josiah's reform in 622 and his death in 609. But the following skeleton of events may be constructed from various documents external to Scripture:

(1) A series of attacks and counterattacks defined the relation of the Assyrians to the Babylonians during this period.[19] In the meantime, Psammetichus I of Egypt (663–609) aligned himself with a weakening Assyria, perhaps sensing that the emerging state of Babylon was to them a greater threat than their previous conqueror.[20]

(2) Cyaxares, king of the Medes, took Asshur, the ancient capital of Assyria, in 614. This event further confirmed the weakened character of the Assyrian empire.

(3) The Medes and Babylonians joined forces and assaulted Nineveh itself in 612. The city fell after a three-month siege, with the Assyrian king Sin-shar-ishkun apparently perishing in the flames. An account of the fall is found in the Babylonian Chronicle: "The king of Akkad [Babylonia] cal[led up] his army and [Cyaxar]es the king . . . marched towards the King of Akkad

---

18. See further the section below on the date and authorship of Zephaniah.
19. Roux, *Ancient Iraq,* p. 340.
20. Bright, *History of Israel,* p. 316.

. . . they marched (upstream) on the embankment of the Tigris and . . . [pitched camp] against Nineveh . . . they made a great attack against the city. . . . The city [they turned] into ruin-hills. . . . Cyaxares and his army returned to his country. . . . Ashuruballit . . . sat down in Harran upon the throne to become king of Assyria."[21] From this account, it becomes evident that the Babylonians assumed the supremacy over this area about the Tigris while the Medes returned eastward. At the same time, a remnant of loyal Assyrian subjects established a new king and capital at Harran, approximately 150 miles west of Nineveh.

(4) Two years later, in 610, Babylon defeated the remaining Assyrian forces once more at Harran, although Assyrian resistance was not altogether eliminated. Pharaoh Neco II (609–594) continued the policy of his father Psammetichus and determined to provide further aid to the remaining troops of Assyria. If Harran could be regained, perhaps Assyria could continue as a buffer state between Egypt and Babylon.[22]

It was at this point that King Josiah made his fatal move. Perhaps he saw the march of Egyptian forces through his territory as an affront to his expanded sovereignty. Perhaps he felt it absolutely necessary to resist any strengthening of the hand of an Assyria that had oppressed his nation for so long. In any case, Josiah strategically intercepted the Egyptian army at the pass of Megiddo in 609. Neco attempted to dissuade him. According to the Chronicler, the words of Neco were the "mouth of God" to Josiah, but he would not heed them (2 Chr. 35:21–22). Having been fatally wounded, Josiah retreated to Jerusalem, where he died.

Appropriately, all Judah and Jerusalem mourned for Josiah according to the lamentation composed by Jeremiah (2 Chr. 35:24–25). His senseless death marked the end of an era. It was the last glimmer of hope for Judah. The mourning for Josiah became a statute in Israel (2 Chr. 35:25), and was remembered vividly almost a hundred years later in the time of Israel's restoration (cf. Zech. 12:10–11). This act of mourning over the last of the faithful king-messiahs of Israel eventually was treated prophetically in Scripture. It became a picture of the ultimate lamentation of Israel as it grieved over the sufferings of its true messianic king (John 19:37; cf. Rev. 1:7).

21. *ANET,* pp. 304–5.
22. The testimony of the monuments coincides with the statement of Scripture in 2 K. 23:29, understanding that the verse should be translated "Pharaoh Neco, king of Egypt, went *up to [ʿal]* the king of Assyria," instead of the AV "*against* the king of Assyria."

D. FINAL DESTRUCTION UNDER THE SONS AND GRANDSON OF JOSIAH (609–587 B.C.)

From the point of Josiah's death, the end came quickly. In rapid succession, three of Josiah's sons and one of his grandsons ruled in Jerusalem until the fateful collapse of the kingdom to the Babylonians in 587. Why the reforms of good King Josiah did not reach into his own family is not explained explicitly in Scripture. But an analysis of the evidence concerning his household circumstances may supply some understanding of the problem.

Josiah began to reign when he was eight years of age and continued on the throne until he was thirty-nine (2 K. 22:1). Since his second oldest son Jehoahaz (by his wife Hamutal) was twenty-three when he succeeded his father (2 K. 23:31), Josiah must have been sixteen when Jehoahaz was born. But then Scripture notes that when his oldest son Jehoiakim (by another wife named Zebidah) succeeded his brother three months later, Jehoiakim was twenty-five (2 K. 23:36). So Josiah's first son was born to him when he was fourteen, meaning that he was married by the time he was thirteen. In sum, Josiah took the throne when he was eight years of age, must have been married at least by the time he was thirteen, must have been in a polygamous situation by the time he was fifteen, and was a father of at least two sons by two different wives by the time he was sixteen.

It seems likely that the "people of the land" may have sponsored the early marriages of Josiah out of a zeal to maintain the line of David. After the assassination of Josiah's father Amon, they may have been very anxious to guarantee a Davidic successor to the young king. Possibly Hamutal, mother of Jehoahaz, had been the first wife of Josiah, and their marriage had been arranged even before he was thirteen years old. When this marriage failed to produce a son, Josiah, then thirteen, may have been provided with Zebidah, mother of Jehoiakim. This possible sequence of events might explain why Jehoahaz, born two years later than Jehoiakim, was the first of the sons to hold the throne. At any rate, a domestic scene involving a sixteen-year-old lad with two wives and two sons might provide a basis for explaining why Josiah's sons were not affected by their father's reforms.

Although the "people of the land" acted swiftly in the establishment of Jehoahaz as king immediately on the death of Josiah (2 Chr. 36:1), their control of the situation was destined to be short-lived. Egypt proceeded on its line of march to Harran that it might attempt once more in cooperation with the remnants of the Assyrian army to repulse the advances of Nabopolassar of Babylon. The Babylonian Chronicle records the confrontation on the banks of the Euphrates north of Palestine: "In the [seventeenth year (of

Nabopolassar, which would be 609 B.C.)] . . . Ashur-uballit, king of Assyria, a great Egyptian army . . . crossed the river, and marched against the city of Harran to conquer it . . . they slew the garrison which the Babylonian king had stationed there . . . and he besieged the city of Harran . . . but although he did not take it, they withdrew."[23]

Returning from this frustrating failure to win a decisive victory over Babylon, Neco paused in Riblah north of Damascus to lick his wounds. Apparently in an effort to consolidate his control over Syria and Palestine, he summoned Jehoahaz, deposed him, and designated his older brother Eliakim as his successor, changing his name to Jehoiakim. Jehoahaz was carried in chains to Egypt, where he died in fulfillment of the prophecy of Jeremiah (cf. Jer. 22:10–11).

It is not clear why Neco favored Eliakim over Jehoahaz. On the one hand, perhaps it was simply that he intended to assert his will in appointing a man who would be beholden to him. On the other hand, the choice of Jehoahaz by the "people of the land" may have represented their expectation that he would follow the same anti-Egyptian tendencies maintained by his father Josiah. In any case, the people of Israel had exercised their will for the last time in determining who would rule over them.

Jehoiakim early manifested a character that was particularly odious to Jeremiah (cf. Jer. 22:13–23). While the Lord required justice and uprightness, Jehoiakim had insisted on a luxurious cedared palace, far exceeding the dwelling of his pious father Josiah. Because he actually could not afford such luxury, Jehoiakim had forced the citizenry to labor on his extravaganza without pay. The much more upright Josiah had been content simply with food and drink, feeling that the maintenance of justice among the people was more important than palatial structures. So Jeremiah denounced the king by announcing that Jehoiakim would be humiliated in his death in contrast with the honors heaped on his father. The prophet promised the king "the burial of an ass" (Jer. 22:19).

This historical circumstance that prevailed between 609 and 605 fits well the message of the prophecy of Habakkuk. The prophet begins with a severe complaint because of pervading violence among God's people. He is concerned particularly because the *torah* seems helpless, which indicates that he is talking about violence among God's own people (Hab. 1:4). With the example of a king like Jehoiakim lived out before the people, it would be surprising for the citizens to do otherwise. Jehoiakim's return to the idolatries of Manasseh would have provided broad theological support for disregard-

23. *DOTT,* p. 77.

ing the *torah* of Yahweh. The Lord responds through his prophet Habakkuk by indicating that he would deal with the situation in a way that the people would not believe even if it were told them (1:5). He would raise up the Babylonians, a fierce people that march throughout the whole earth seizing territory not theirs (1:6).

In analyzing the internal evidence from Habakkuk that might aid in locating the place of the book in redemptive history, several factors must be balanced. The judgment on Judah must fall soon enough to be observed by Habakkuk's contemporaries, since the word of the Lord says this judgment would come "in your days" (1:5). The Babylonians apparently made their presence felt enough to be designated as a "fierce and impetuous people who march throughout the earth" (1:6).

By the time Jehoiakim sat on the throne, Nabopolassar had marched to Harran and stood off an assault of the combined forces of Assyria and Egypt. Yet before the battle of Carchemish in 605, Babylonia's dominance in Syro-Palestine had not been clearly established. It was, after all, Neco of Egypt who had appointed Jehoiakim as his puppet king. But within ten years, Nebuchadrezzar (or Nebuchadnezzar), successor to Nabonidus, would be carrying away captives from Judah (in 597); and within twenty years the un-believable devastation of the city of David would be an accomplished fact (587).

In this hour of Israel's greatest crisis, the prophet Habakkuk declares essentially a single message: the person of faith ". . . *shall live*" (Hab. 2:4). Even as Judah is primed to experience the ultimate of God's judgments, a sinful person may be "justified by faith," and so know that he is accepted by God despite his and the nation's transgression of covenant law. Even as the mighty empires of the world are crumbling all about, the person of faith "shall live." He shall survive, he shall receive the blessings of the covenant, if only he will continue to believe no matter how bleak may appear the events of history. It is a message for the ages. If under these circumstances the covenant promises of God hold true to the one who believes, God's work of redemption can never fail.

Although the Babylonian army under the aged Nabopolassar (626–605) had managed to hold their ground at Harran against the combined Assyrian/Egyptian assault in 609, it did not prove capable of crossing the Euphrates westward and taking the strategic city of Carchemish. But in 605 the picture changed dramatically. As crown prince and eldest son of Nabopolassar, Nebuchadrezzar made his decisive move. He crossed the Euphrates and assaulted Carchemish. The Babylonian Chronicle records the dramatic moment:

In the twenty-first year [of Nabopolassar, which would be 605] the king of Babylon stayed in his own country while the crown-prince Nebuchadrezzar, his eldest son, took personal command of his troops and marched to Carchemish which lay on the bank of the river Euphrates. He crossed the river (to go) against the Egyptian army which was situated in Carchemish and . . . they fought with each other and the Egyptian army withdrew before him. He defeated them (smashing) them out of existence. As for the remnant of the Egyptian army which had escaped from the defeat so (hastily) that no weapon had touched them, the Babylonian army overtook and defeated them in the district of Hamath, so that not a single man [escaped] to his own country. At that time Nebuchadrezzar conquered the whole of the land of Hatti.[24]

Once the Egyptian resistance had been broken, Babylon could not be stopped. The author of Kings reflects the completeness of Egypt's defeat: "The king of Egypt came not again any more out of his land; for the king of Babylon had taken, from the brook of Egypt unto the river Euphrates, all that pertained to the king of Egypt" (2 K. 24:7).

After a few years of subservience to Babylon, Jehoiakim joined in a revolt against Nebuchadrezzar. In December of 598, the king of Babylon began his march back to Palestine. Having arrived, he besieged Jerusalem, and in March of 597 he took the city and captured the king. This king would have been Jehoiachin, a lad of eighteen years of age, since his father Jehoiakim had died while Nebuchadrezzar was already on the march.

Jehoiachin is included with the kings condemned by Jeremiah (Jer. 22). The prophet indicates that Jehoiachin and his mother would be given over to Nebuchadrezzar and hurled into a foreign land never to return (vv. 26–27). This young king is described as a broken pot, as though childless, none of whose descendants would sit on the throne of David (vv. 28–30).

This grandson of Josiah actually represents the farthest point of genealogical succession for the line of David. Although Zedekiah, a third son of Josiah, replaced Jehoiachin his nephew, serious questions were raised by his contemporaries about the validity of his succession.[25] Texts in Babylon continue to mention the exiled Jehoiachin as "king of Judah," and expectation was high that Jehoiachin would be released despite the prophecies of Jeremiah to the contrary (Jer. 28:4). Although the actual destruction of Jerusalem came ten years later in 587, in a real sense the succession

24. *DOTT,* pp. 78–79.
25. Bright, *History of Israel,* p. 328.

to the line of David ended with the deportation of Jehoiachin, grandson to Josiah.

This perspective on the continuing significance of Jehoiachin despite his exile makes even more important the peculiar turnabout of affairs in Babylon. In the thirty-seventh (!) year of his exile, when Jehoiachin would have been fifty-five years of age, the new king of Babylon lifted him from his prison and gave him a seat of honor which he retained until his death. Jehoiachin received a daily allowance, and for the rest of his life ate at the king's table (2 K. 25:27–30). Something more than a token messianism resides in this concluding observation concerning the monarchy in Israel. After such a thorough justification for the exile of God's covenant people, the writer of Kings certainly had a reason for recording the turn of fortunes of this son of the Davidic line.

From a new covenant perspective, the significance of these events becomes apparent. That Jehoiachin (Jeconiah/Coniah, Jer. 22:24; 24:1; cf. Matt. 1:11) appears in the genealogy of Jesus Christ may appear puzzling in the light of Jeremiah's prophecy:

> Thus says the Lord,
> Write this man down childless,
> A man who will not prosper in his days;
> For no man of his descendants will prosper
> Sitting on the throne of David
> Or ruling again in Judah. (Jer. 22:30)

Perhaps a solution to this problem may be found in the fact that none of the immediate offspring of Jehoiachin sat on the throne of Judah. As a matter of fact, except for Jehoiachin's uncle Zedekiah, the throne of David remained vacant for the next six hundred years, almost twice the time Davidic succession had been maintained. Not until the appearance of great David's greater Son did the true throne of David, located at the right hand of God, find a worthy occupant.

It was this Son of David that Jeremiah also expected. Following the condemnations of Jehoahaz (Shallum; Jer. 22:10–12), Jehoiakim (vv. 13–23), and Jehoiachin (Jeconiah/Coniah; vv. 24–30), Jeremiah declares in his very next prophecy that expectations must remain high about the divine messiah that was sure to come:

> Behold, the days are coming, declares the Lord
> When I shall raise up for David a righteous Branch;
> And he will reign as king and act wisely,
> And do justice and righteousness in the land.
> In his days Judah will be saved,

And Israel will dwell securely;
And this is his name by which he will be called,
The Lord our righteousness. (Jer. 23:5–6)

The 7th century B.C. was indeed a time of the tramping and tromping of nations. But to the eye of faith guided by the words of God's prophets of old, a clearer vision may be gained concerning God's purposes of redemption as they are being realized in history. The message of these prophets continues to speak with revelational clarity even today.

II. THEOLOGICAL PERSPECTIVE

Because Nahum, Habakkuk, and Zephaniah all ministered essentially to the same constituency and labored within thirty years of one another, it may be helpful to discuss their theological perspective as a whole. Individualized distinctives are clearly present. But many overriding themes are common to all three, and may be understood better in the light of the united testimony.

A. MESSIANISM IN THE SEVENTH-CENTURY B.C. PROPHETS

The most distinctive thing about the messianism of Nahum, Habakkuk, and Zephaniah is the absence of virtually a trace of messianism.[1] The expectation of an anointed king who would be the savior of Israel is developed explicitly in the eighth-century B.C. prophecies of Hosea (3:4–5), Isaiah (7:10–14; 9:6–7; 11:1–10), and Micah (5:2–4). How then could this expectation drop totally out of the picture one hundred years later?

Postdating all messianism in the eighth-century prophets to a point after the Exile is too facile a solution. It fails to deal adequately with the hard evidence of the texts of the prophets in the only form in which they exist. It also ignores the contextual considerations which bind these prophecies to the history of the 8th century.

Delusion with the historical experience of kingship in Israel appears to offer a realistic resolution to this problem. All three of these prophets labored after the depravities of Manasseh had sealed the fate of the nation's future. No repentance could remove the stench of the abominations that had been practiced by Israel for over fifty years (cf. 2 K. 21:10–15; 22:14–20).

---

1. Although Jeremiah also ministered partially in the 7th century B.C., his messianic message seems to occur after the end of this century. Cf. Jer. 22–23.

It had been thought that Jerusalem was inviolable. The covenant promise to David asserted that the dwelling place of God's name would remain forever (1 K. 11:13, 36; 14:21; 15:4; 2 K. 19:34; 20:6; 21:7). The collapse of the siege of Sennacherib outside the gate of Jerusalem in 701 and his doubly humiliating death at the hands of his sons in the house of his gods proved the point. Samaria might fall, but never Jerusalem.

Jeremiah also had to contend with this deeply embedded belief in the inviolability of the city of David. "The temple of the Lord, the temple of the Lord, the temple of the Lord is this" had become a popular incantation that was believed would protect the city from every threat (Jer. 7:4). Yet the seventh-century prophets knew full well the misappropriation of God's promise that lay at the root of such a perspective. Zephaniah declared in no uncertain terms that God's purging judgments would move through Jerusalem from gate to gate, from district to district, until every nook and cranny had been scrutinized with the searching lights of God's impartial administration of justice (Zeph. 1:9–12). Habakkuk's whole being trembled uncontrollably at the vision of devastation for God's own people (Hab. 3:16–17). God's answer to his complaint about violence in Judah began with a summons to "be astonished" and "wonder" at a work no one would believe even if they were told (Hab. 1:5–6). The ferocious Babylonians would sweep through Judah like the wild wind and leave nothing standing (Hab. 1:10–11).

If it was actually possible that the city of David could be devastated, what about the line of David? Could this second major provision of the Davidic covenant also suffer rude violence? Not only was it possible; it was certain. Even the "sons of the king" were not immune from the final sanctions imposed on covenant violators (Zeph. 1:8). They too would become the sacrifices of the awesome covenant meal which would give final expression to the wrath of God.

So where in this context was to be found the hope of the Davidic messiah? The disillusion of the seventh-century prophets with the promised royal line kept them from finding any hope in the descendants of David. Yet they did not grieve as those who had no hope. They had full confidence that the redemptive purposes of God would be realized (cf. Nah. 1:14; Hab. 2:4; 3:18–19; Zeph. 3:9–20).

In a sense it may be said that these seventh-century prophets were throwbacks to the times of Samuel. They fully recognized that Israel needed a king, a messiah, a savior. But they could see none other than God himself fulfilling that role. Who but God alone could provide a propitiatory sacrifice worthy of removing the deep, dark stain of Israel's sin? Who but God alone had the force at his disposal to repulse his people's mighty enemies? Who but God alone had the wisdom essential for governing a people such as Israel?

So these prophets of the time of deterioration return to the original scheme of things. The Lord himself is the one who takes vengeance on his enemies (Nah. 1:2). The Lord himself is the one coming in splendor, with rays flashing from his hands, moving swiftly from Sinai to the conquest of the land (Hab. 3:3–7). The Lord himself is "the King of Israel in your midst" (Zeph. 3:15), a "Mighty Hero who saves" (Zeph. 3:17). Those very functions that once had been assigned to the scion of the line of David now revert to the person of God the Lord himself.

This reorientation of the seventh-century prophets should not be perceived as a lack of faith on their part. These three brave men were absolutely right in seeing that only God could fulfill the role assigned to Israel's messiah. They interpreted the signs of their times correctly. It was the God of the covenant that brought the Davidic line to its termination point in the context of the old covenant formularies. Only the false prophets kept recalling the old expectations without understanding the reality of what God was doing in their own day (Jer. 28:1–4).

Neither should the perspective of Nahum, Habakkuk, and Zephaniah be perceived as a finalized elaboration of God's covenant word incapable of subsequent modification. Characteristic of all old covenant revelation is its limited, conditional shape that perforce cannot say everything all at once. So it should not be surprising at all to find messianism uniformly in all the prophets after these three expanding on Israel's messianic hope in unmistakable terms. For Jeremiah, the coming messiah is a "righteous branch for David" who will "reign as king" and be known as "the Lord our righteousness" (Jer. 23:5–6). For Ezekiel, he is the "one shepherd," God's "servant David" who will feed them (Ezek. 34:23). For Haggai, it is David's descendant Zerubbabel whom God will treat as his own signet ring (Hag. 2:23). For Zechariah, he is priest crowned king, whose name is "Branch" (Zech. 6:11–13); the coming king riding on a donkey, with his dominion stretching "from the river to the ends of the earth" (Zech. 9:9–10). In Malachi, he is the Lord, the messenger of the covenant, who will purify the sons of Levi (Mal. 3:1–3).

But in the last hours before the Exile it is as though the Lord interrupts the movement toward messiah to declare clearly that he alone can be king in Israel. None but God himself can be the savior, the deliverer of his people from their sins. By the exclusive emphasis of these three seventh-century prophets on God's distinctive role as savior in the vacuum created by the absence of a viable Davidic option, one more solid reality of history points to the necessity of a divine messiah. No other solution would have been adequate for the dilemma perceived by Samuel even at the beginning point of Israel's monarchy. Israel needs a king; but God must be king in Israel. The idea of calling a specific individual the "son" of God in distinction from a general corporate appellation (2 Sam. 7:14; Ps. 2:7) points in the same direction, for a "son" is equal to his father. The explicit address of the occupant of David's throne as "God" echoes the same theme (Ps. 45:7 [Eng. 6]), as does the name given the virgin-born child: "God-with-us" (Isa. 7:14) and "Mighty God" (Isa. 9:5 [Eng. 6]).

So it may well be that Nahum, Habakkuk, and Zephaniah did not have the complete picture of the Way and the One who would redeem his people Israel. But their unique ministry, even in the absence of "messianism" as it is commonly perceived, supplied a vital contribution to the ongoing revelation of the God-man who would be Savior and king, even the Lord, Jesus the Christ.

B. THE CENTRALITY OF GOD

The questionable role of messianism in these three prophets leaves ample room for the object which indeed is so central to the message of each of them. Simply put, their message is theocentric. God himself occupies their every thought and provides the framework by which they perceive all reality. Nahum begins with a presentation of the central attributes of God as they related to the circumstances of his day. Yahweh is a jealous God who takes vengeance, takes vengeance, takes vengeance (Nah. 1:2). It is he himself who moves to assault the fortress of Nineveh, for he is against them (Nah. 2:14 [Eng. 13]; 3:5). God is the one who raises up the Babylonians as his chastening instrument even for his beloved Judah (Hab. 1:6). Yet in the end the prophet acknowledges that the only possession of worth in life is the reality of God (Hab. 3:17–19). The day of judgment distinctively is the Day of Yahweh, the Day that he enforces his unique sovereignty as the Lord of the covenant (Zeph. 1:7, 14). He himself personally takes on the role of Savior, of Warrior, of King who exults in his personal love for his people (Zeph. 3:15–17).

So for the seventh-century prophets, there is no other but God alone. Perhaps the anticipation of the loss of all things in their lifetime was a major factor in their development of this permeating God-centeredness. Yet it is clear that they were not confused with the idea of a beatific vision of God that saw him in the abstract, separated from the creation he had made. They are too much men of the covenant to overlook or to minimize the reality of the material world. It is the God of the world and the promises of his word that alone are central to their life-view.

Out of this centrality of God himself, Nahum, Habakkuk, and Zephaniah develop certain emphases that bring to bear the reality of deity on the age in which they lived. Four themes in particular may be noted: the justice of God, the judgment of God, the covenant of God, and the salvation of God.

1. The Justice of God

One aspect of God's justice becomes plain as the messages of these three prophets are considered together. God's justice is marvelously impartial. He will in no wise clear the guilty, whoever they may be. He sees Nineveh and all the atrocities it has committed (Nah. 1; 3). He sees also all the nations surrounding Judah—to the west, the east, the south, and the north (Zeph. 2). All of these peoples will have to give account, both corporately and individually, of their violations of the law of God.

But the Lord also sees Judah. When Habakkuk gives expression to his complaint over the sin of Judah, God announces the awful reality of the judgment coming on his own people. They shall be subjected to the brutalities of the Babylonian instrument just as any other heathen nation (Hab. 1). God is righteous within Judah, and so pronounces a woe over their rebelliousness (Zeph. 3).

The timing of God's institution of justice may remain a mystery beyond human wisdom. But the message is clear. Eventually he shall bring every work into judgment whether it be good or evil. This message is sorely needed in the world today. How many different peoples of the earth somehow regard themselves as the favored of the Lord, exempt at least from the extremities of his judgment that shall be brought on the "others." The long-suffering of God, far from leading to repentance, leads them to presumption. Unrepentant sinners, beware!

2. The Judgment of God

The message that can be disputed but cannot be missed is that God's judgment is retributive and not always restorative in nature. That is, God at times may bring judgment as a way of chastening human beings to bring them to himself. But in the end, his judgment has a character of rightness that has no further end beyond expressing the reality that a person or a nation shall receive from God's hand exactly what he deserves. If by brutality, immorality, and irreligion he has wrought havoc on the order intended by God the creator, he can expect nothing less than the wrath and the curse of the Almighty.

The restorative dimension of God's justice is implied in the book of Nahum, although it is not explicitly developed. Judah may celebrate its feasts and keep its vows because the wicked one shall never pass through it again (Nah. 2:1 [Eng. 1:15]). The statement implies that Assyria had been a rod of God's chastisement on his people for their sin. Habakkuk's continuing survival despite judgment presents him as a token remnant that shall remain despite the chastening of the Lord (Hab. 2:4; 3:16–19). Since his vision is destined for the ages to come, it may be presumed that many others also shall "live by faith" despite the crumbling of their world about them. Zephaniah's "Perhaps!" (Zeph. 2:3) may appear to be a faint wisp of hope for those who seek the Lord in face of the burning wrath of God. But it is nonetheless there and provides encouragement to any sinner who truly has been moved (by God's Spirit) to seek the Lord. Far more explicit as a sign of hope, and therefore more encouraging, is this prophet's bold announcement: "The Lord has taken away his judgments against you . . . God delights in his love for you" (Zeph. 3:15–17). Not even in the glorious revelations of the new covenant can be found a fuller word of comfort.

Yet the balance must be maintained. Chastening judgments from which recovery is possible will not go on forever. The time must come for the end, and it comes on some nations and peoples in every generation. With the ministry of Jonah in the 8th century, Nineveh repented and was restored to the favor of God, much to the chagrin of the prophet himself. But one hundred years later, the iniquity of the Ninevites had become full, and Nahum offers them no message of hope. As they have maltreated others, God shall maltreat them.

The same may be said of Habakkuk's message for Babylon (Hab. 2:5–20). The equitable law of an eye for an eye and a tooth for a tooth shall come to expression on a national scale. The pillager shall be pillaged, the shameless defamed, and the worshiper of powerless idols left powerless.

The meaning of the Day of the Lord in Zephaniah relates closely to this same principle. As the Day in which God shall enforce his covenant both in its creational and its redemptive expressions, a just repayment for all deeds done in the body shall be effected. Involved in this divine expression of ultimate uprightness must be a final destruction of the wicked. No hint of restoration is found in this imagery (Zeph. 1:2–18).

No message could be more repulsive to the modern mind than the idea of retributive justice. But this truth finds open exposition in the messages of these seventh-century prophets. The historical events that befell Judah, Assyria, Egypt, and Babylon attest to the truthfulness of their declaration. It finds no contradiction in the Scriptures of the new covenant, but only repeated reinforcement (2 Thess. 1:6–10; 2 Cor. 5:10).

3. The Covenant of God

Of the over two hundred times that the term *covenant* appears in the OT, not one of these occurrences is found in the prophecies of Nahum, Habakkuk, or Zephaniah. Yet it cannot be supposed that the concept of covenant has fallen into ill repute, since it plays such a critical role in the prophecy of their contemporary, Jeremiah. This absence of the term may be compared to the strange paucity of the word *covenant* in the NT, which is a phenomenon that has not yet received adequate explanation.

It may be that the breakup of nations and the dispersion of Israel explains the minimal usage of the term *covenant* at this point in redemptive history. To be sure, Israel's role as God's covenant nation was not yet finished in the 7th century. But something very drastic was happening by their being cast out among the nations of the world. The perimeters of God's "kingdom of priests" would have to be drawn along different lines. The problem is vividly displayed in a small note in the book of Esther. When the second decree of the king went forth to all his 127 provinces scattered over three continents, Scripture states that "many peoples of other nationalities became Jews!" (Esth. 8:17). Now how is "covenant nation" to be defined?

For at least fifteen hundred years beginning with the time of Abraham, the idea of "covenant" had been associated particularly with Israel. Even from a new covenant perspective, one of the distinctive blessings of the Jews is that the covenants belong to them (Rom. 9:4). So it may be that the decline in the usage of this term in these seventh-century prophets might have something to do with the usage of the term in its specific relation to the nation of Israel. Once the idea of the new covenant had been formulated in Jeremiah and Ezekiel, the term was revived fully as a priceless tool for linking the old covenant with the new.

From another perspective, the absence of the term *covenant* in these prophets must not be overplayed. For the *concept* of "covenant" is certainly present. Particularly in Zephaniah the whole framework for understanding his development of the idea of the Day of the Lord relates to his rehearsal of the features of the successive covenants. He begins with Noah, and notes the destruction of fish, birds, beast, and man (Zeph. 1:1, 3; cf. Gen. 6:20). Although Zephaniah adds "fish" to his list and reverses the order of things mentioned, the allusion is unmistakable. Next he speaks of a prepared sacrifice with consecrated guests, in which final judgment is expressed in the devouring of the flesh of the cursed (cf. Zeph. 1:7). This language echoes the picture of covenantal consecration which begins in Gen. 15 and runs through the whole OT. Finally, he depicts the arrival of the dread Day of Yahweh in terms drawn directly from the account of the theophanic manifestation at Sinai (Zeph. 1:15). In this light, it seems that Zephaniah understood the Day of Yahweh in covenantal terms. For on this day of the Lord's manifestation of his sovereignty, he brought to bear on all transgressors the sentence assigned by the covenant.

Other aspects of the covenant idea may be implied in the Lord's bringing to judgment a heathen nation like Assyria. Foreign nations also were bound to discharge their national obligations in a way reflecting their creational bond. Failure meant the activation of the curse. In the book of Habakkuk, the imputation of righteousness by faith alone accords with the covenantal formulation of Gen. 15:6. The "life" that Habakkuk promises represents nothing other than the richest blessings of the covenant.

So these three seventh-century prophets do not stand as oddities outside the mainstream of covenantal thinking in the OT. Instead, they appear as prophets of the Lord forced to expand the concepts of covenantal reality beyond the strictures dictated by previous circumstances.

4. The Salvation of God

Judgment and salvation are closely linked in the theology of these prophets. Salvation for God's people comes directly in association with the judgment of God's enemies. Nahum's "glad tidings" may be published in Judah only because Nineveh has been destroyed (Nah. 2:1 [Eng. 1:15]). Habakkuk's sober joy emerges as a matured fruit of his contemplation on the series of judgments that shall fall first on God's own people and then on the heathen nations. He must "wait quietly for the day of distress," and yet he may rejoice in the God of his salvation (Hab. 3:16–19). Zephaniah too must "wait" while the Lord's indignation is poured out, for then he shall purify his people (Zeph. 3:8–9). Salvation for him also comes through judgment.

The salvation of God ultimately shall include Gentiles as well as Jews. Particularly Zephaniah underscores this point (Zeph. 3:9–10). But the universalism of salvation is also implied in Habakkuk's emphasis on faith and faith alone as the criterion that determines who shall survive in the "midst of the years" (Hab. 2:2–4; 3:2). Between the judgment executed on the people of Israel and the judgment executed on the heathen nations, the justified by faith shall live by faith. Echoing the original message to Abraham the "father of nations," this word of acceptance by faith alone has international implications.

The love of God for a sinful people functions as the key factor in the salvational activity of God. Alternating between contented contemplation of

24

the objects of his love and shouts of joy at the pleasure they bring, the Lord of love remains in the midst of his people until he has saved them wholly (Zeph. 3:17). This salvation shall involve a regathering of his own people and a restoration of their fortunes in a way reminiscent of paradise (Zeph. 3:19–20; Nah. 2:1 [Eng. 1:15]). Although Habakkuk places the promised blessing of a fruitful land in a negative form (Hab. 3:17), his comments show the framework of reality with which he is dealing. Joined with the message of his contemporary Zephaniah (cf. Zeph. 3:20), it becomes a message of hope.

In sum, the salvational message of these prophets who must witness the breakup of nations centers on the possession of God himself. Since everything else has been taken from them, they must look to him alone. All other blessings may be removed; yet they still will possess the ultimate blessing. All other things can have meaning only as they possess God himself and are possessed by him.

III. SHAPE OF THE PROPHECIES

Until the recent emergence of canonical criticism, study of the shape of prophecy concentrated on forms within the prophetic material which might lay behind the finalized text. But now a greater balance has been achieved. Attention is directed also to the prophetic word according to the shape in which it now appears.[1]

Indeed, it may be possible at times to detect a preliterary form underlying a particular prophetic oracle, and thereby to gain insight into its message as well as its function in the community of God's people. But at the same time, there is something healthy about the more recent commitment to deal seriously with the text of Scripture as it presents itself to the current reader. Its finalized form speaks directly to the message that is being conveyed.

In the prophecies of Nahum, Habakkuk, and Zephaniah, a number of characteristics, types, and forms emerge which determine the shape of the

---

1. Cf. the full exploration of the subject in B. S. Childs, *Introduction to the Old Testament as Scripture* (Philadelphia: Fortress, 1979). Childs is sometimes surprising in his conclusions on the basis of canonical criticism. He says the misunderstanding created by the historical-critical method "arises from assuming that each prophetic passage must be interpreted from a specific historical setting." He then suggests that the canonical process "has disregarded historical differences and organized the material theologically" (p. 460). Yet if a major distinctive of Israel's theology is its historical orientation, how then could historical differences be ignored and a true representation of the theology be achieved at the same time?

material. In many cases the form is unique to the author himself and enhances significantly the communication of his message.

By way of introduction, some comments will be offered concerning styles, structures, and poetic parallelisms. Fuller analyses will be reserved for the body of the commentary.

A. STYLES

Comments such as "forceful," "clear," or "awkward" with reference to the style of an author are frequently very subjective in nature. Yet some reflection on the literary impact of these prophecies may have a useful place.

The book of Nahum runs the risk of being monotonous because of the singularity of the author's purpose and theme. He is intent on saying only one thing: Nineveh shall fall. But the variety of methods which he employs in saying this one thing are quite remarkable and lend great force to his message. He repeats the phrase "God of vengeance" three times at the beginning of his first prophecy (Nah. 1:2). The adjectives "emptied, desolate, and waste" combine characteristics of assonance as well as synonymity in the original text (Nah. 2:11 [Eng. 10]). The sting found in his addressing the doomed city as a "charming madame, a harlot of the harlots" (Nah. 3:4) can hardly be missed. Perhaps most striking is his combining the sensations of sight and sound which rise to a climactic crescendo as he depicts the advance of the attack on Nineveh:

> Crack
>   of whip
> And rumble
>   of wheel
> Steed
>   rearing
> And chariot
>   lurching
>
> Horseman
>   charging
> with flash
>   of sword
> and glitter
>   of spear. (Nah. 3:2–3)

By his vivid use of images, the prophet's vision transfers directly into the imagination of the reader.

Habakkuk also has developed his own distinctive style. A by-product of the audacity of his address to God is the directness of his speech in questioning the Almighty (Hab. 1:2, 3, 12, 17). A fuller explication of his use of assonance, alliteration, double entendre, and possibly even rhyme is found in the introductory remarks to Hab. 2:6–20. In ch. 3, his collage of previous images depicting older theophanies is noteworthy, as well as his vivid picture of God's approach from Sinai to Palestine. The description of rays emanating from God's clenched fist and the trembling solar plexus of the prophet illustrate the vividness of his language.

Zephaniah shows a distinctive ability to play on words. He notes those who swear *to* the Lord while swearing *by* Milcom (Zeph. 1:5). He makes use of the geographical situation of Jerusalem by describing it as the "Pounding Place" (1:11). He interchanges various words each of which apparently uses the root for "stubble" in order to describe the readiness of the nation for consumption in the fire of God's anger (2:1).

Zephaniah's style is dictated in part by his extensive dependence on the phraseology of the book of Deuteronomy (Zeph. 1:13–18; 3:17–20). His ability to incorporate this material into his work without losing his own distinctive flow of argument is noteworthy. The piling up of borrowed images, particularly as they describe the coming Day of Yahweh, is quite effective:

A Day
    of adversity and distress;
A Day
    of destruction and desolation;
A Day
    of darkness and thick darkness;
A Day
    of cloud and thick cloud
A Day
    of trumpet blast and battle shout. (Zeph. 1:15–16)

A great deal of variety and creativity marks the style of each of these three prophets. Each has developed his own distinctive approach to the use of language in the communication of his message.

B. STRUCTURES

Habakkuk is perhaps the most distinctive of these three prophets in terms of the variety and uniqueness of the structures he employs. In the first section of the book, his message comes as a "dialogue of protest." In this form the prophet interacts with God himself concerning the perplexing problems with which he is forced to wrestle. More similar in form to the Song of Songs than the book of Job, Habakkuk's alternating speakers are not introduced by any designation in the text itself. Yet they may be readily determined by the context. This distinctive form in Habakkuk engages the reader in the prophet's progress through the maturing of his faith.

The five "woes" of Hab. 2 employ a form common to other prophets in Israel. But the inclusion of a complete psalm readied for corporate celebration in Hab. 3 is a distinctive structure in this book. As the psalm reaches its final resolution, it moves into a regularity of cadence. Five stanzas in a row employ the common *a-b-b-a* parallelism of Hebrew poetic structure.

Much discussion has dealt with the possibility of an acrostic poem in Nah. 1. The pursuit of an alphabetic structure apparently began with a certain Pastor Frohnmeyer of Württemberg, Germany, whose suggestion appeared in a footnote of Franz Delitzsch's commentary on the Psalms in 1867. Before the turn of the century, Gunkel and then Bickell had extended the acrostic form in Nah. 1 to include the whole chapter. Wellhausen responded by insisting that the acrostic could be extended only through vv. 2–8. The chapter gives evidence of some remnants of acrostic structure, but not enough to be conclusive. The matter is discussed more fully in the commentary proper.[2]

A more radical proposal concerning Nahum's form suggests that the book is a prophetic liturgy composed for celebration in the cultus of Israel after Nineveh had fallen.[3] This liturgy has been seen by some as a cultic depiction of Israel's struggle with Assyria against the backdrop of the primeval struggle between cosmic adversaries in the Babylonian New Year's festival.[4] But evidence derived from the prophecy of Nahum itself "lends little support to the theory that Nahum was a cultic functionary."[5]

---

2. For a brief sketch of the history of the discussion, see Maier, p. 21. For a thorough analysis of the possibilities, see the older article of G. B. Gray, "The Alphabetic Poem in Nahum," *The Expositor* 8 (1898) 207–20. A sane evaluation may be found in O. T. Allis, "Nahum, Nineveh, Elkosh," *EvQ* 27 (1955) 67–80. Allis allows for the possibility of acrostic material, but regards the elements of assonance and alliteration to be far more significant. A more recent treatment in the light of a current theory of Hebrew meter is found in D. L. Christensen, "The Acrostic of Nahum Reconsidered," *ZAW* 87 (1975) 17–30.

3. See P. Haupt, "The Book of Nahum," *JBL* 26 (1907) 1–53.

4. See A. Haldar, *Studies in the Book of Nahum* (Uppsala: Almqvist and Wiksell, 1947).

5. R. K. Harrison, *Introduction to the Old Testament* (Grand Rapids: Eerdmans, 1969), p. 929. Cf. R. H. Pfeiffer, *Introduction to the Old Testament*, rev.

More obvious is a structure in Nahum built on a series of rhetorical questions found in the third chapter (vv. 7, 8, 19). By employing this device, the prophet has engaged his readers actively in responding to his message.

Zephaniah follows the more traditional balance of prophetic oracles. He begins with an oracle of judgment against Judah (ch. 1). Then he delivers a series of oracles against the nations (ch. 2). Finally, he proclaims the hope of the future by an oracle of salvation (ch. 3).

C. POETICAL PARALLELISM

All three of these books are filled with numerous varieties of poetic parallelism. In the commentary below, these constructions have generally been marked in the translation by paralleling indentation of the various members, and by marking the lines with the same letters of the alphabet. A glance at the various portions of the translation will show just how thoroughly this element permeates the form of these seventh-century prophets.

IV. DATE AND AUTHORSHIP

Already in this introduction the ministries of Nahum, Habakkuk, and Zephaniah have been set in the context of redemptive history of the 7th century B.C. Yet more specific comments regarding the dating of these prophecies may be helpful. In addition, some effort must be made to glean whatever scant picture may be possible concerning the life, the personality, the dynamic that made the man behind the message.

A skeletal history of the significant events relating to the life and ministry of these three men is as follows:

701 B.C.   Hezekiah's faith repels the assault of Sennacherib of Assyria
687 B.C.   Manasseh begins his half-century "reign of decline"
648 B.C.   Ashurbanipal of Assyria subdues his brother in Babylon to the east, while Manasseh (apparently) joins a revolt in the west
ca. 645 B.C. Ashurbanipal subdues the rebels in the west. Manasseh is exiled, repents, and returns

---

ed. (New York: Harper and Brothers, 1948), p. 600, who says the proposals about a prophetic liturgy are not to be taken too seriously. J. A. Soggin, *Introduction to the Old Testament,* rev. ed., tr. John Bowden, OTL (Philadelphia: Westminster, 1980), p. 276, comments that "given the present state of the sources" there is not enough evidence to support the idea of a background in a mythological struggle. Cf. Childs, *Introduction,* p. 441.

MINISTRY OF NAHUM, who declares Nineveh's fall even while Assyria is still in full strength

642 B.C.   End of the half-century rule of Manasseh, during which time Judah had gone beyond the point of no return
640 B.C.   Assassination of Amon and establishment of eight-year-old Josiah as king
632 B.C.   Josiah at age sixteen begins to seek the Lord
628 B.C.   Josiah's first public reform movement
627 B.C.   Murder of Ashurbanipal, the last great Assyrian monarch
622 B.C.   Josiah's discovery of Moses' law book and the beginning of his thoroughgoing reform

MINISTRY OF ZEPHANIAH, who provides the needed prophetic support for Josiah's reform

612 B.C.   Fall of the Assyrian capital of Nineveh to the combined forces of the Medes and the Babylonians; the Assyrians retreat and regroup in Harran
609 B.C.   Tragic death of Josiah and immediate moral decline under Jehoahaz and Jehoiakim

MINISTRY OF HABAKKUK, who denounces Judah's sin, announces their judgment within his day by an emerging Babylon, and promises reciprocal judgment on Babylon for their excesses

605 B.C.   Babylonian dominance in Syro-Palestine established at Carchemish by their defeat of the combined Egyptian-Assyrian forces
597 B.C.   Jehoiachin, grandson to Josiah, exiled by Nebuchadrezzar
587 B.C.   Final destruction of the city of David
539 B.C.   Cyrus of Persia destroys Babylon; Israel's return begins.

A half century of prophetic silence corresponded to the apostate decline under Manasseh, so far as the production of canonical material is concerned. This vacuum, this famine of the word of God, may be seen as a judgment of the Lord on Judah for their consent to Manasseh's depravity. Perhaps God's servants the prophets were silenced and suppressed during this time by official resistance to the word of the Lord.

A. NAHUM

Quite possibly Nahum was the man who broke this silence. It is generally agreed that his prophecy dates between the fall of Thebes of Egypt about

664 B.C. and the fall of Nineveh in 612.[1] This firm conclusion is based on Nahum's allusion to the fall of No-Amon, which is Thebes (Nah. 3:8), and his anticipation of the fall of Nineveh, which is the central subject of his prophecy.

A precise date between these brackets is more difficult to locate. But the time should combine at least the following two features: (1) Ashurbanipal would probably still be reigning, since Nahum characterizes Nineveh as being in "full strength" (Nah. 1:12). His rule ended in 627. (2) Judah may be in a period of reform, since Nahum says little to denounce their sin. This circumstance would fit the last years of Manasseh in which he made an effort at reform (ca. 650–642) or the time of Josiah's reforms (ca. 628–609).

This combination of circumstances points to the time of Manasseh's reform at the end of his life (ca. 650–642) or the early days of Josiah's reform (ca. 628–622). It is more difficult to think in terms of the days of Josiah's later reform, since by that time (622) the weakening of Assyrian strength had become more obvious. The last days of Manasseh appear to be the most likely time for the prophecy of Nahum, although this date cannot be affirmed with certainty.

Nothing is known about the person of Nahum, except that he must have been a very bold prophet to deliver this scathing denunciation of the Assyrians while they were still in full strength. His name means "comforter," but no evidence exists to link the meaning of his name with his character. The title of the book declares him to be the "Elkoshite," which generally is taken to refer to the village in which he lived. The absence of positive identification of Nahum's hometown "only shows the perplexity of tradition in face of the historical ignorance of the facts."[2]

---

1. O. Eissfeldt, *The Old Testament, An Introduction,* tr. P. R. Ackroyd (New York: Harper & Row, 1965), p. 415, says: "In any event it appears clear that we are dealing with genuine threats belonging before the catastrophe, and not with a triumphant retrospect upon events already in the past." A. Weiser, *The Old Testament: Its Formation and Development,* tr. Dorothea M. Barton (New York: Association Press, 1961), p. 258, agrees. Cf. Harrison, *Introduction,* p. 928. Childs, *Introduction,* p. 443, relativizes the whole matter by observing that whatever theories of postexilic editing may be proposed, the final canonical function addresses Nineveh before its fall. R. H. Pfeiffer, *Introduction,* p. 594, is concerned particularly with the alphabetic poem of the first chapter. He concludes that ca. 300 B.C. a redactor provided this introduction from a poem which he vaguely remembered: "It is clear that he did not copy the alphabetic psalm from a manuscript but wrote it down as best he could from memory." This stumbling redactor not only had forgotten the second part of the poem but was also "unconscious of the alphabetic arrangement of the lines." Pfeiffer's imaginative explanation as to why a supposedly alphabetic poem does not appear as an alphabetic poem has not proved convincing.

2. Weiser, *Introduction,* p. 256.

Specific locations in Assyria, Galilee, and Judea for Nahum's Elkosh have been proposed over the centuries. Al-Qush, a little village located about twenty-five miles north of the ancient site of Nineveh, contains a place that has been designated as the tomb of Nahum, but apparently only since the 16th century.[3] In the 5th century, Jerome in his prologue to the prophet Nahum located the village of "Helkesei" (Elkosh) in Galilee, but did not provide adequate information for a more particular location. "Capernaum," which could mean "village of Nahum," has a traditional connection with the prophet dating back to the 14th century, but any connection of "Capernaum" with "Elkosh" remains vague.[4] The Judean location is indicated by some church fathers, including Pseudo-Epiphanius.[5] But the tradition is so vague and inconsistent that it cannot be given a great deal of weight.

In the end, it must be acknowledged that little if anything is known of the person of Nahum. In common with the other two prophets of his day, he appears only as a "voice."

B. ZEPHANIAH

Of the three books under consideration, only Zephaniah dates his own prophecy by connecting his ministry with the times of the kings of Judah. Stating the evidence negatively, nothing convincingly opposes the location of Zephaniah's ministry in the days of Josiah as indicated by the title.

One factor having some significance is the oracle against Assyria in 2:13–15. Because these words would have little significance if Assyria already had fallen, they should be dated at least before Nineveh's collapse in 612 B.C.[6]

Is it possible to date Zephaniah's ministry more precisely within the reign of Josiah? Can one determine whether he prophesied before or after the radical reform instituted as a result of the discovery of the law book in 622 B.C.? More recent opinion generally favors a date before the discovery of the law book.[7] This conclusion is based largely on the corrupt conditions presumed in 1:4–6, 8–9; 3:1–4.

---

3. Maier, p. 21.
4. Ibid., p. 25.
5. Weiser, *Introduction,* p. 256. The reference in Pseudo- Epiphanius is found in *De Vitis Prophetarum* 17. The city apparently is located near the modern Beit Jibrin, about twenty-five miles southwest of Jerusalem.
6. A. Kapelrud, *The Message of the Prophet Zephaniah* (Oslo: Universitetsforlaget, 1975), p. 42.
7. W. Rudolph, p. 255; S. R. Driver, *An Introduction to the Literature of the*

However, a dating after the discovery of the law book has been defended by older works, and the argument cannot be discounted too easily.[8] As a matter of fact, it is rather unrealistic to suppose that the corrupt traditions engraved in Israel's life-style over the previous fifty years of Manasseh's reign could have been eliminated overnight. More probably a prolonged contest would have developed out of the study of the law book. In such a circumstance, the ministry of a prophet like Zephaniah would have been invaluable as an aid to young King Josiah.

The most convincing factor that points to the period immediately after the discovery of the law book is the parallelism between the phraseology of Zephaniah's prophecy and the phraseology of the book of Deuteronomy. This material is so extensive and so similar that it virtually requires that Zephaniah had access to the "book of the law" as the basis for much of his prophecy.[9]

From an alternative perspective, the idea that Zephaniah may have participated in the development of a pseudo-Mosaic tract to aid in Josiah's reform proves too much. For if Zephaniah had been prophesying before 622 in terminology identical to the language of the law book of Deuteronomy, then the "pious fraud" veiling the forgery of Deuteronomy in the name of Moses would have been uncovered.

Suggestions of a date later than the time of Josiah are not convincing.[10] The complete exclusion of prophecies of hope before the reality of judgment is a purely subjective conclusion that does not enjoy the general favor it held some years earlier.

We know as little about the person of Zephaniah as we do about his contemporary Nahum. His name is borne by three other individuals mentioned in Scripture. But none of their circumstances corresponds with what may be deduced about the Zephaniah of this book.[11]

Distinctive to Zephaniah among all the prophetic books of the OT is

---

Old Testament, 9th ed. (1913), p. 103; J. M. P. Smith, pp. 168–69; E. J. Young, *An Introduction to the Old Testament* (Grand Rapids: Eerdmans, 1960), p. 290.

8. Cf. the discussion of C. F. Keil, 2:118–20, 125.

9. For the details of the comparison, see the commentary below on Zeph. 1:1.

10. J. P. Hyatt, "The Date and Background of Zephaniah," *JNES* 7 (1948) 25, argues for a date in the days of Jehoiakim (609–598 B.C.). Bright, *History of Israel*, p. 320n.29, judges such arguments to be unconvincing. L. P. Smith and E. R. Lacheman, "The Authorship of the Book of Zephaniah," *JNES* 9 (1950) 142, argue that the book is pseudepigraphic and ought to be read against the background of the circumstances of 200 B.C. But the discovery of a fragment of a Qumran commentary on Zephaniah (4QpZeph) argues rather strongly against such a supposition.

11. Cf. 1 Chr. 6:36–38; Jer. 21:1; Zech. 6:10.

the tracing of his genealogy through four generations. The possibility that his "Hezekiah" of the fourth generation is the good king who preceded Josiah by a half century is a very real one. If this were the case, then Zephaniah would be of royal descent. This position might add some force of regal authority as additional support for the young king attempting to lead a radical reform.

But as in the case of Nahum, this man Zephaniah also appears only as a "voice." His bold word from the Lord has no authority other than the force inherent in the truth itself.

C. HABAKKUK

The precise dating of Habakkuk's prophecy hinges on the interpretation given to the progression of the argument of the book. The complaint that begins the book finds resolution by the time it closes. The dialogue between God and the prophet preserves uniquely a series of troubled complaints from a servant of the Lord. The Lord's gentle responses finally bring Habakkuk to a fuller extension of his faith. But what precisely is the historical circumstance with which the prophet wrestles?

Happily a firm starting point for the historical context of this maturation in faith is supplied by the reference to the "Kasdim" in the first chapter (Hab. 1:6). This term occurs about 70 times in Scripture, always in reference to the "Chaldeans" (Babylonians). Although the word has been interpreted in this verse as referring to the Persians, the Greeks, the Selucids, a mythological demonic power, and an unidentified conquering nation, the normal meaning is unambiguous.[12] The "Kasdim" are the Neo-Babylonians, whose empire began with the accession of Nabopolassar in 626 B.C. As G. Fohrer appropriately notes: "This interpretation must be adhered to, even though it has clearly at times . . . appeared too simple and been denied."[13]

The reference to God's "raising up" this fierce nation (Hab. 1:6) indicates that at the time of this prophecy the Babylonians had not yet realized their zenith of power. So Habakkuk's message must be set prior to the end of the 7th century. For by that time the Neo-Babylonian empire dominated the world.

The precise time in the process of Babylon's ascendancy to which Habakkuk refers depends on the context envisioned in this dialogue with the

12. G. Fohrer, *Introduction to the Old Testament,* tr. D. Green (Nashville: Abingdon, 1968), pp. 454–55.
13. Ibid.

Almighty. More particularly, the question turns on the identification of the "wicked" who are oppressing the "righteous" (Hab. 1:4). Are the "wicked" to be understood as evil inhabitants from among the citizenry of Judah itself? Or are they to be understood as the Assyrians, who were Babylon's principal rivals?

Considering the context in which Habbakuk sets his first complaint, it appears much more appropriate to regard the "wicked" who oppress the "righteous" as the corrupted citizens of Judah itself. It is the *torah* that they ignore, and *justice* that is perverted. These terms suggest internal oppression through the legal system of the day. Observance of *torah* and justice in a heathen community would be more than could be expected.

Appeal to Habakkuk's second complaint (1:12–17) consistently characterizes the argument of those who interpret the "wicked" of the first complaint as the Assyrian oppressors.[14] It is pointed out that the figure described in these verses exercises his brutality on an international scale. These wicked ones make men "like the fish of the sea" (1:14), and "continually slay nations without sparing" (1:17). Because the "wicked" in Judah of the 7th century never expanded their domain beyond their own borders, they could hardly fit this description, it is argued.

It should not be disputed that the oppressor of Habakkuk 1:12–17 exercises his brutality across the length and breadth of the nations, and so could not describe Judah of the 7th century. Yet it must be asked, where now is Habakkuk in the progress of his dialogue with the Almighty? Has he not advanced beyond the point at which he began his disputation?

The prophet had begun his complaint by citing abuse of *torah* and justice (1:4). The Lord had responded by announcing that he was raising up the Babylonians to deal with the problem. As many as twenty different characterizations pointing up the effectiveness of this instrument for judgment had been depicted vividly before the eyes of the prophet (1:5–11).

But how does Habakkuk respond to this revelation he has just received? Does he respond with skepticism? Does he doubt that the Almighty will do by the hand of the Babylonians what he had just revealed that he intended to do? Is he still wrestling with the same problem he presented in his first complaint? It does not seem likely. More probably the prophet now has a new problem. God has appointed the Babylonians to judge and correct the "wicked" against whom the prophet had complained. Habakkuk indicates acceptance of this fact (v. 12). But will God then allow the Babylonians to swal-

14. Eissfeldt, *Introduction,* p. 420; Fohrer, *Introduction,* p. 455; Weiser, *Introduction,* p. 263.

low up "those more righteous than they?" (v. 13). If those swallowing up the righteous are the same Assyrians with which he was concerned in his first complaint, then Habakkuk still is precisely where he was in his opening complaint. The Lord's revelation concerning his destruction of the oppressor of his first complaint (1:5–11) has fallen on deaf ears, and so Habakkuk still would be asking the same question with which he began.

But if the oppressor of 1:4 refers to the wicked of *Judah* instead, then the Lord's announcement in 1:5–11 resolves the first complaint of the prophet. God shall raise up the Chaldeans to deal with this problem. The Babylonians shall overrun the wicked in Judah.

But this revelation has the effect of creating a new problem. How can the Lord chastise his people with an instrument more wicked than they (1:13)? The Lord's next response explains that the Babylonians in their turn also would receive their judgment at his hand (2:6–20).

How do these two alternatives in identifying the "wicked" either with Assyria or the evil in Judah affect the question of the dating of the book of Habakkuk? Primarily, they provide differing perspectives on the level to which the Babylonian menace has progressed by this point in history. On the one hand, if Assyria is the enemy of the Lord in 1:2–4 which shall be judged by the Babylonians, then clearly Habakkuk's prophecy must come before the fall of Assyria's capital to the Babylonians in 612. A date between the emergence of Babylon as a contending world power in 626 and the fall of Nineveh in 612 would fit the circumstances.[15]

On the other hand, if the wicked within Judah are the enemies of the Lord in 1:2–4, then the dating of this prophecy could be somewhat later than the fall of Nineveh in 612. From the picture presented in Habakkuk's prophecy, it appears that the Babylonian empire had begun to make its power felt among the nations. This circumstance would have developed only after the appearance of the first of the Neo-Babylonian monarchs, beginning with Nabopolassar in 626. At the same time, the original complaint of Habakkuk concerning prevailing injustice in Judah would not appear very apropos during the time that the social reforms of Josiah were in effect (628–609).

For these reasons, it would appear most appropriate to date Habakkuk's prophecy after the period of Josiah's reign which ended in 609. The early years of Jehoiakim, in which he led a return to the corrupt practices of Manasseh's day, would fit the circumstances of Habakkuk's succession of complaints. The "unbelievable" characterization of the Lord's revelation to him (Hab. 1:5) would appear to set this prophecy before the clear estab-

15. Weiser, *Introduction,* p. 263.

lishment of Babylon's dominance over Syro-Palestine at the battle of Carchemish in 605.

The net result of this analysis places the prophecy of Habakkuk in the days of the reign of Jehoiakim, probably between the years of 608 and 605. This view in its essence has been adopted by a number of scholars.[16] It appears to satisfy all the various aspects that need to be considered.

Perhaps the most radical alternative proposal concerning the dating of Habakkuk begins by emending the text of 1:6 so that it reads *kittîm* (Kittim or Cypriots) rather than *kaśdîm* (Chaldeans).[17] Under this construction, the book is dated about 330 B.C., and the "Kittim" are interpreted as the Greeks under Alexander during his campaign in Asia.[18] It is, however, "quite arbitrary" to emend the text from *kaśdîm* (Babylonians) to *kittîm* (Greeks), since no external evidence supports this modification.[19] Quite interestingly, the Qumran commentary on Habakkuk interprets the verse as referring to Kittim, apparently applying the term to the Romans of their own day; but they *retain* the reading *kaśdîm* in their representation of the text of Scripture. The fact that the Qumran scribes felt compelled to retain *kaśdîm* while interpreting its meaning as Kittim would appear to indicate that they had no textual tradition supporting the reading *kittîm*.

As in the case of Nahum and Zephaniah, nothing concrete is known of the life of the prophet Habakkuk. His book indicates that he was a prophet with a heart that interceded for God's people. His opening "How long?" reveals that for some time he had been pleading with the Lord over this crisis (Hab. 1:2).

The suggestion that Habakkuk was a member of a temple choir[20] or a cult-prophet on the basis of the dialogue in ch. 1 and the subscription to his

---

16. Fohrer, *Introduction*, p. 455, cites Rothstein (1896), Humbert (1941), and Nielsen (1953) as holding this view. Cf. C. von Orelli, p. 241; Young, *Introduction*, pp. 287–88 (who cites Jehoiakim's time as one of two viable options); G. L. Archer, *A Survey of Old Testament Introduction* (Chicago: Moody, 1964), p. 344; and Bright, *History of Israel*, p. 333, who places Habakkuk "probably . . . in Jehoiakim's reign as the Babylonian invasion struck."

17. One position more radical is that of O. Happel, *Das Buch des Propheten Habackuk* (Würzburg, 1900), who dates Habakkuk in the time of Antiochus Epiphanes, ca. 170 B.C. The Qumran scroll of Habakkuk (1QpHab) makes this suggestion rather unlikely.

18. Cf. C. C. Torrey, "Alexander the Great in the Old Testament Prophecies," in *"Von Alten Testament,"* Fest. K. Marti, ed. K. Budde, BZAW 41 (Berlin: Töpelmann, 1925), pp. 281–86.

19. Fohrer, *Introduction*, p. 454.

20. T. Laetsch, p. 313.

psalm in ch. 3 is not very convincing.[21] Legend has placed him in the den of lions with Daniel, but the supposition has no basis in fact.[22]

For the third time Scripture underscores the fact that each of these prophets of the 7th century functions only as a "voice." In an era when mighty nations clash, the divine response comes in the form of words from men unknown among the nations of the world. Mightier than human armies is the prophetic word of God.

V. UNITY AND AUTHENTICITY

If the objective testimony of extant manuscript evidence were given a fuller place in evaluating the unity and authenticity of these three prophecies, little question would remain about the genuineness of the material. So far as I know, the books are intact in the various manuscripts that are available, with the single exception of the omission of the psalm of Habakkuk from the manuscript of the Qumran commentary (1QpHab). This testimony ought to be given its proper recognition as a starting point for discussion concerning unity and authenticity.

With respect to the absence of the psalm of Habakkuk from the Qumran scroll, it ought to be noted that this chapter is found in the LXX, a roughly contemporary document. It could be that the Qumran manuscript was never finished, particularly in the light of some significant evidence that the last three verses of the second chapter were completed by a second hand.[1] At the same time, the omission may simply represent a process of selectivity that is manifested elsewhere in the Qumran scrolls.

The tendency of scholarship to give significant weight to subjective judgments about authenticity continues, although an increasing awareness of the problems of subjectivism has developed of late. Primarily these judgments are based on stylistic, form-critical, and content-oriented considerations.

With respect to style, A. Weiser notes that "it is not possible to doubt"

---

21. Rudolph, p. 194, concludes that the idea that Habakkuk was a cult-prophet is imaginary.

22. See the apocryphal addition to Daniel, called Bel and the Dragon, vv. 33ff. But cf. Harrison, *Introduction,* p. 931.

1. Cf. W. H. Brownlee, *The Midrash Pesher of Habakkuk,* SBL Monograph 24 (Missoula, MT: Scholars Press, 1979), p. 219. Brownlee indicates that this "latter hand" had carefully corrected the entire ms., which he considers an indicator that the work was completed. Yet it may have been for any number of reasons that this second scribe did not progress any further than the end of ch. 2.

the authenticity of Nah. 2 and 3. Because of the "compelling emotion" and "a most impressive kaleidoscopic agitation," this material must be Nahum's.[2] But the same author regards Nah. 1 as more doubtful in its authenticity, since it "does not exhibit the same depth of feeling as the denunciation of Nineveh."[3] Precisely how Weiser discovered that the true Nahum was a man consistently marked by "kaleidoscopic agitation" is not clear.

In similar fashion, S. R. Driver questions the genuineness of Zeph. 3:14–17 because of the "buoyant tone" which stands in marked contrast to the "sombre, quiet strain" of Zeph. 3:11–13.[4] Again, it is not clear how it can be determined that a prophet who lived 2,500 years ago and about whom little or nothing is known had a capability for only one mood even when responding to a variety of circumstances.

Somewhat more objective is the argument concerning authenticity based on form-critical considerations. Following this line, serious questions have been raised about the genuineness of the "alphabetic poem" of Nah. 1 and the completed psalm of Hab. 3.

A fuller exploration of these questions may be found in the commentary proper. But with respect to the possible acrostic in Nah. 1, the first factor that should be noted is the coherence and variety of poetic parallelism currently represented in the verses under consideration. Included in 1:2–9 are parallel structures according to the pattern of *a-b-b-a, a-b-a-b, a-b-c-c-b-a, a-b-c-b-c,* and *a-b-b-b.* It would be quite remarkable if a later author could incorporate the fragment of an alphabetic poem, break up its original order, and establish a new poetic structure—all the while maintaining a powerful, coherent piece of literature.

With respect to the genuineness of Hab. 3, the substance of the material provides strong evidence for its connection with the first two chapters. A psalm to be celebrated in worship is a fitting extension to the summons for all the earth to keep a worshipful silence in the Lord's holy temple (Hab. 2:20). The third chapter begins with a note that the prophet has "heard" the "report" of the Lord, which corresponds perfectly with his "waiting" to "see" what the Lord would answer him (Hab. 2:1). The final resolution of ch. 3 in which the prophet declares his acceptance of the Lord's program for the ages provides an appropriate resolution of the contention between God and the prophet that formed the body of the earlier chapters. For a more detailed treatment of this inner connection, see the commentary below.

2. Weiser, *Introduction,* p. 30.
3. Ibid.
4. Driver, *Introduction,* p. 342.

Even in this area of judgment about authenticity on the basis of form analysis, subjectivism still appears as a major factor. O. Eissfeldt notes that the tone of the "acrostic" in Nah. 1 suits the rest of the book. But apparently basing his analysis on the presence of the distinctive acrostic form, he concludes that the chapter may well be a poem inserted later.[5] Yet who is to say that Nahum himself is not likely to have used an acrostic form at one time and a structure based on parallelism at another? It may be true that poetic structure is more likely to circulate independently of a fixed context. But it should be remembered that roughly 75% of the material of these three prophets is poetic in style. Is this bulk of material therefore to be judged as secondary?

Conclusions concerning authenticity also are frequently based on an analysis of the suitableness of the content of the prophetic message. In this regard, the genuineness of Zeph. 3:14–20 is most often denied because of the elevated expression of hope which it is assumed cannot belong to a preexilic prophet. Once more, subjectivism prevails.

Happily the pendulum is swinging back to a position which allows that a message of hope is appropriate for the preexilic prophets. With respect to this section of Zephaniah, Kapelrud declares: "Words of promise and hope are also found, and we have no right to delete them from the text because of their content."[6] He then objects to the textual notes of a recent edition of the Hebrew Bible, observing that "opinions on this question should not have been found in the text apparatus."[7]

In sum, the materials of the books of Nahum, Habakkuk, and Zephaniah present themselves as authentic words of the seventh-century prophets and should be treated as such unless further evidence points in another direction. As of the present, no evidence has been advanced that provides adequate ground for denying the integrity of this material.

VI. TEXT

Distinctive to these three prophets is the preservation of portions of commentaries from Qumran on each of these books. Although the material is extremely fragmentary in the case of Zephaniah, the manuscripts are significant in attesting to the importance of these short works to a community existing 100 years before Christ.[1]

5. Eissfeldt, *Introduction,* p. 416.
6. Kapelrud, *Message of the Prophet Zephaniah,* p. 37.
7. Ibid., p. 40.
1. For a presentation of these texts, and a comparison with the Massoretic

The existence of these manuscripts from Qumran raises the question of the relationship of the MT, the LXX, and the Qumran texts to one another. It is too early to render judgments concerning the relative worth of the theory of families of "local" texts for the OT in comparison to the theory of multiple texts related more directly to socio-religious groupings.[2] But the following general observations may be noted:

The fullest of the Qumran manuscripts on these three prophets is the commentary on Habakkuk (1QpHab). The principal variants between the MT and 1QpHab have been numbered at about fifty. Roughly one-third of those variants have to do with articles and conjunctions.

In evaluating a comparison of these readings, Millar Burrows notes that with only a few exceptions of minor significance the ancient versions including the LXX support the MT over the Qumran readings.[3] William Brownlee, another author who has made extensive comparisons between the MT and 1QpHab, concludes that although he does not judge the MT to be always correct, he suggests that in all cases of doubt the safer criterion would be to follow the Massoretic reading.[4]

Brownlee also notes that deliberate alteration may have played a part in the formation of some of the variants in 1QpHab, although a number of divergent texts may have been available from which the "reading most advantageous to the purpose at hand" might have been chosen.[5] While the variants of 1QpHab may establish the antiquity of optional readings other than those represented in the MT, it more often "substantiates the antiquity of the readings" of the Massoretes.[6]

Since the turn of the century, the special problems associated with the usage of the LXX as a source for the reconstruction of the Hebrew text of the

counterpart, see M. P. Horgan, *Pesharim: Qumran Interpretations of Biblical Books,* CBQMS 8 (Washington: Catholic Biblical Association, 1979). Horgan lists the relevant bibliography and includes a discussion of the significance of the Qumran *pesharim.*

2. Cf. the varying theories as represented by F. M. Cross and S. Talmon in their jointly edited work, *Qumran and the History of the Biblical Text* (Cambridge: Harvard University Press, 1975).

3. Millar Burrows, *The Dead Sea Scrolls* (New York: Viking, 1955), p. 318. He cites K. Elliger, who, "after a painstaking examination of the variants, concludes that the commentary has very little value for restoring a more correct text."

4. W. H. Brownlee, *The Text of Habakkuk in the Ancient Commentary from Qumran,* JBL Monograph 11 (Philadelphia: SBL, 1959), pp. 113, 117–18.

5. Ibid., pp. 117–18. Cf. S. Talmon, "Aspects of the Textual Transmission of the Bible in the Light of Qumran Manuscripts," *Textus* 4 (1964) 130–32.

6. Brownlee, *Text,* p. 118.

OT have been generally recognized.[7] The difficulty of working through the maze of Greek texts to determine the best text which might be compared with the Massoretic tradition must be faced. In addition, the subjectivism and uncertainty associated with any retroversive "text" derived by translation from a Greek manuscript into Hebrew must be fully recognized.[8] Although some of the LXX readings may support the text of Qumran over against the MT, that fact alone does not automatically mean that the LXX reading is to be regarded as the preferred text.[9] In general, the text of these three prophetic books is well preserved in the Massoretic tradition.

VII. CANON

All three of these prophetic books begin with a claim to divine origin which accords with the establishment of the prophetic office in Israel as the continuing means by which the Lord would communicate his truth to his people (cf. Deut. 18:15–22). Nahum's book is described as a "vision" (Nah. 1:1). Habakkuk's oracle is a message which he "saw" (Hab. 1:1). Zephaniah's message is the "word of the Lord" which "came" to him (Zeph. 1:1). In each case, these designations point to the receptivity of the prophets in terms of the origination of their message.[1] Rather than claiming to have produced their own words, the prophets emphasize that the word they declare comes from the Lord.

These men of God also spoke in accord with the criterion for truth that had been established by the previous covenantal documents sealed by the oath of the Lord. In declaring judgment on covenantal violators among all nations without discrimination, they supported the reality of the one true God of the universe as manifested in Israel. In offering hope of salvation through faith in the sovereign working of the God of Israel, their message

7. Cf. F. M. Cross, *The Ancient Library of Qumran and Modern Biblical Studies,* rev. ed. (repr. Grand Rapids: Baker, 1980), pp. 173ff. E. Würthwein, *The Text of the Old Testament: An Introduction to the Biblia Hebraica,* tr. E. Rhodes (Grand Rapids: Eerdmans, 1979), pp. 63–64, notes that today it is generally recognized that the LXX was not a "precise scholarly translation."

8. Cf. M. H. Goshen-Gottstein, "Theory and Practice of Textual Criticism. The Text-Critical Use of the Septuagint," *Textus* 3 (1963) 132.

9. Cf. the analysis of J. Weingreen, *Introduction to the Critical Study of the Text of the Hebrew Bible* (Oxford: Oxford University Press, 1982), p. 30.

1. Cf. B. B. Warfield, "The Biblical Idea of Revelation," in *The Inspiration and Authority of the Bible* (Philadelphia: Presbyterian and Reformed, 1967), pp. 87–91.

conformed to the scriptural declaration of hope for people from all the nations. These prophets present themselves as having spoken their message before the events occurred that they described, and history consistently has appeared as confirming rather than as contradicting their words. The permanent place of these prophecies in the history of redemption is settled by allusion as well as by specific citation of the core of their messages in the authoritative Scriptures of the new covenant.

These three books always have had their place among the twelve Minor Prophets in both the Jewish and the Christian canon. Their role of bearing God's authoritative word among the nations is firmly fixed. The work of the Spirit of God in the hearts of believers confirms the divine origin of their message.

VIII. ANALYSIS OF CONTENTS

Nahum

SUPERSCRIPTION (1:1)
I. PUBLIC ANNOUNCEMENT OF NINEVEH'S JUDGMENT (1:2–14)
A. THE AWESOME TERROR OF GOD'S JUDGMENT (1:2–6)
   1. His Person as Judge (1:2–3)
   2. His Action as Judge (1:4–5)
   3. Your Stance Before Him as Judge (1:6)
B. THE SPECIFIC TARGET OF GOD'S JUDGMENT (1:7–11)
   1. Judgment in a Context of God's Care for His Own (1:7)
   2. Judgment Directed Specifically against Seventh-Century B.C. Assyria (1:8–11)
C. THE IMMINENT CHARACTER OF GOD'S JUDGMENT (1:12–14)
   1. Judgment Now Despite Assyrian Strength (1:12a)
   2. Judgment Now as Relief from Judah's Suffering (1:12b–13)
   3. Judgment Now as the Lord Has Decreed (1:14)
II. DRAMATIC DEPICTION OF NINEVEH'S JUDGMENT (2:1–14 [ENG. 1:15–2:13])
Introduction: The Announcement of Accomplished Judgment Means Joyful News for Judah (2:1 [Eng. 1:15])
A. THE CITY IS TAKEN (2:2–8 [ENG. 1–7])
   1. Announcement of the Coming Siege (2:2–3 [Eng. 1–2])

      2. Approach of the Assaulters (2:4–5 [Eng. 3–4])
      3. Resistance of the Inhabitants (2:6 [Eng. 5])
      4. Entry Is Gained (2:7 [Eng. 6])
      5. The City Falls (2:8 [Eng. 7])
   B. THE CITY IS PLUNDERED (2:9–11 [ENG. 8–10])
   C. THE CITY IS HUMBLED (2:12–14 [ENG. 11–13])
      1. A Mockery Song of the City (2:12 [Eng. 11])
      2. The Brutality of the City (2:13 [Eng. 12])
      3. The Lord Speaks Against the City (2:14 [Eng. 13])

III. THE SURETY OF NINEVEH'S JUDGMENT (3:1–19)
   A. SURE BECAUSE OF THEIR SIN (3:1–7)
      1. The Sins of the City (3:1, 4)
      2. The Assault on the City (3:2–3)
      3. The Lord Against the City (3:5–7)
   B. SURE JUST AS NO-AMON (THEBES) (3:8–13)
      1. Thebes Devastated Despite Her Many Advantages (3:8–10)
      2. Nineveh May Expect the Same (3:11–13)
   C. SURE DESPITE THEIR STRENGTH (3:14–19)
      1. The Utter Futility of Human Resources (3:14–18)
      2. The Final Tragedy of Persistent Sin (3:19)

HABAKKUK

SUPERSCRIPTION (1:1)

I. THE DIALOGUE OF PROTEST (1:2–17)
   A. THE PROPHETIC SPOKESMAN COMPLAINS AGAINST
      UNANSWERED PRAYER FOR RELIEF FROM INJUSTICE
      (1:2–4)
   B. THE LORD UNVEILS HIS AWESOME INSTRUMENT OF
      RETRIBUTION (1:5–11)
      1. Preparation for the Unveiling of God's Instrument of Retribution (1:5)
      2. Identification of God's Specific Instrument of Retribution (1:6a)
      3. Characterization of God's Instrument of Judgment (1:6b–11)
   C. THE PROPHETIC SPOKESMAN CHALLENGES THE
      LORD'S PROGRAM FOR PUNISHMENT (1:12–17)
      1. Confidence in God (1:12)
      2. Questioning God (1:13–17)

ZEPHANIAH

IX. SELECT BIBLIOGRAPHY

A. GENERAL WORKS

Ahlström, G. W., *Joel and the Temple Cult of Jerusalem.* VTSup 21. Leiden: Brill, 1971.

Archer, G. L., *A Survey of Old Testament Introduction.* Chicago: Moody, 1964.

Bentzen, A., *Introduction to the Old Testament.* 6th ed. Copenhagen: Gad, 1961.

Bright, J., *A History of Israel.* 3rd ed. Philadelphia: Westminster, 1981.

Burrows, M., *The Dead Sea Scrolls.* New York: Viking, 1955.

Calvin, J., *Commentaries on the Twelve Minor Prophets.* Tr. John Owen. Vols. 3–4. Repr. Grand Rapids: Eerdmans, 1950.

Černý, L., *The Day of Yahweh and Some Relevant Problems.* Prague: University of Karlova, 1948.

Childs, B. S., *Introduction to the Old Testament as Scripture.* Philadelphia: Fortress, 1979.

Cohen, A., *The Twelve Prophets*. Soncino Bible. Bournemouth, Hants.: Soncino, 1948.

Cross, F. M., Jr., *The Ancient Library of Qumran and Modern Biblical Studies*. Rev. ed. Repr. Grand Rapids: Baker, 1980.

Cross, F. M. and S. Talmon, eds., *Qumran and the History of the Biblical Text*. Cambridge: Harvard University Press, 1975.

Cross, F. M. and D. N. Freedman, "Josiah's Revolt Against Assyria," *JNES* 12 (1953) 56-58.

Driver, S. R., *An Introduction to the Literature of the Old Testament*. 9th ed. Edinburgh: T. & T. Clark, 1913.

_____, *The Minor Prophets*. Vol. 2. Century Bible. New York: Oxford University Press, 1906.

Dupont-Sommer, A., *The Jewish Sect of Qumran and the Essenes*. Tr. R. D. Barnett (London: Valentine & Mitchell, 1954).

Eissfeldt, O., *The Old Testament: An Introduction*. Tr. P. R. Ackroyd. New York: Harper & Row, 1965.

Goshen-Gottstein, M. H., "Theory and Practice of Textual Criticism. The Text-Critical Use of the Septuagint." In *Textus. Annual of the Hebrew University Bible Project* 3 (1963) 130–58.

Harrison, R. K., *Introduction to the Old Testament*. Grand Rapids: Eerdmans, 1969.

Hayes, J. H., and J. M. Miller, eds., *Israelite and Judaean History*. OTL. Philadelphia: Westminster, 1977.

Henry, M., *A Commentary on the Holy Bible: With Practical Reminders & Observations*. Vol. 4. New York and London: Funk and Wagnalls, n.d.

Hillers, D. R., *Treaty-Curses and the Old Testament Prophets*. BibOr 16. Rome: Pontifical Biblical Institute, 1964.

Horgan, M. P., *Pesharim: Qumran Interpretations of Biblical Books*. CBQMS 8. Washington: Catholic Biblical Association of America, 1979.

Keil, C. F., *The Twelve Minor Prophets*. Biblical Commentary on the Old Testament. Vol. 2. Tr. James Martin. Repr. Grand Rapids: Eerdmans, 1977.

Laetsch, T., *Bible Commentary: The Minor Prophets*. St. Louis: Concordia, 1956.

Mendenhall, G. E., *Law and Covenant in Israel and the Ancient Near East*. Pittsburgh: Biblical Colloquium, 1955.

Orelli, C. von, *The Twelve Minor Prophets*. Tr. J. S. Banks. Repr. Minneapolis: Klock & Klock, 1977.

Pfeiffer, C. F., ed., *The Biblical World. A Dictionary of Biblical Archaeology.* Grand Rapids: Baker, 1966.

Pfeiffer, R. H., *Introduction to the Old Testament.* Rev. ed. New York: Harper and Brothers, 1948.

Pritchard, J. B., ed., *Ancient Near Eastern Texts Relating to the Old Testament.* 3rd ed. Princeton: Princeton University Press, 1969.

Pusey, E. B., *The Minor Prophets: A Commentary.* 2nd ed. Repr. Grand Rapids: Baker, 1966.

Rad, G. von, and G. Delling, *"hēméra."* In *TDNT.* 2:943–53.

Roberts, B. J., *The Old Testament Text and Versions.* Cardiff: University of Wales Press, 1951.

Roux, G., *Ancient Iraq.* Repr. Baltimore: Penguin, 1976.

Rudolph, W., *Micha–Nahum–Habakuk–Zephanja.* KAT 13/3. 2nd ed. Gütersloh: Gerd Mohn, 1975.

Smith, G. A., *The Book of the Twelve Prophets.* 2nd ed. Expositor's Bible. Garden City, NY: Doubleday, Doran, and Co., 1929.

Smith, J. M. P., W. H. Ward, and J. A. Bewer, *Micah, Zephaniah, Nahum, Habakkuk, Obadiah and Joel.* ICC. Edinburgh: T. & T. Clark, 1911.

Soggin, J. A., *Introduction to the Old Testament.* Rev. ed. Tr. John Bowden. OTL. Philadelphia: Westminster, 1980.

Talmon, S., "Aspects of the Textual Transmission of the Bible in the Light of Qumran Manuscripts." In *Textus. Annual of the Hebrew University Bible Project* 4 (1964) 95–132.

Thomas, D. W., ed., *Documents from Old Testament Times.* New York: Harper & Row, 1961.

Torrey, C. C., "Alexander the Great in the Old Testament Prophecies." In *"Von Alten Testament."* Fest. K. Marti. Ed. K. Budde. BZAW 41. Berlin: Töpelmann, 1925. Pp. 281–86.

Vermes, G., *The Dead Sea Scrolls: Qumran in Perspective.* Rev. ed. Philadelphia: Fortress, 1977.

Warfield, B. B., "The Biblical Idea of Revelation." In *The Inspiration and Authority of the Bible.* Philadelphia: Presbyterian and Reformed, 1967. Pp. 71–102.

Weingreen, J., *Introduction to the Critical Study of the Text of the Hebrew Bible.* Oxford: Oxford University Press, 1982.

Weiser, Artur, *The Old Testament: Its Formation and Development.* Tr. Dorothea M. Barton. New York: Association Press, 1961.

Weiss, Meir, "The Origin of the Day of the Lord Reconsidered," *HUCA* 37 (1966) 29–60.

Wiseman, D. J., *Chronicles of the Chaldean Kings (626–556 B.C.) in the British Museum.* London: British Museum, 1956.

Würthwein, E., *The Text of the Old Testament: An Introduction to the Biblia Hebraica.* Tr. E. Rhodes. Grand Rapids: Eerdmans, 1979.

Young, E. J., *An Introduction to the Old Testament.* Grand Rapids: Eerdmans, 1960.

B. NAHUM

Allegro, J. M., "Further Light on the History of the Qumran Sect," *JBL* 75 (1956) 89–95.

_____, "More unpublished pieces of a Qumran commentary on Nahum (4QpNah)," *JSS* 7 (1962) 304–8.

Allis, O. T., "Nahum, Nineveh, Elkosh," *EvQ* 27 (1955) 67–80.

Arnold, W. R., "The Composition of Nahum 1:2–2:3," *ZAW* 21 (1901) 225–65.

de Boer, P. A. H., "An Inquiry into the Meaning of the Term *Massa,*" *OTS* 5 (1948) 197–214.

Cathcart, K. J., *Nahum in the Light of Northwest Semitic.* BibOr 26. Rome: Pontifical Biblical Institute, 1973.

_____, "Treaty Curses and the Book of Nahum," *CBQ* 35 (1973) 179–87.

Christensen, D. L., "The Acrostic of Nahum Reconsidered," *ZAW* 87 (1975) 17–30.

Dahood, M. J., "Causal *Beth* and the Root NKR in Nahum 3,4," *Bib* 52 (1971) 395–96.

DeVries, S. J., "The Acrostic of Nahum in the Jerusalem Liturgy, " *VT* 16 (1966) 476–81.

Driver, G. R., "Farewell to Queen Huzzab!" *JTS* 15 (1964) 296–98.

Gaster, T. H., "Two Notes on Nahum," *JBL* 63 (1944) 51–52.

Glasson, T. F., "The Final Question—in Nahum and Jonah," *ExpTim* 81 (1969) 54–55.

Gray, G. B., "The Alphabetic Poem in Nahum," *The Expositor* 8 (1898) 207–20.

Green, W. H., Review of "Nahum's Prophecy Concerning Nineveh Explained and Illustrated from Assyrian Monuments" by Otto Strauss, *Biblical Repertory* 27 (1855) 102–32.

Haldar, A., *Studies in the Book of Nahum.* Uppsala: Almqvist and Wiksell, 1947.

Haupt, P., "The Book of Nahum," *JBL* 26 (1907) 1–53.

Hoenig, S. B., "The Pesher Nahum 'Talmud' (Nahum 3:4)," *JBL* 86 (1967) 441–45.

Keller, C. A., "Die theologische Bewältigung der geschichtlichen Wirklichkeit in der Prophetie Nahums," *VT* 22 (1972) 399–419.

Kitchen, K. A., "Thebes." In *ZPEB* 5 (Grand Rapids, 1975) 714–17.

Lambdin, T. O., "Thebes." In *IDB,* IV (Nashville, 1962), 615–17.

Maier, W. A., *The Book of Nahum.* St. Louis: Concordia, 1959.

Rowley, H. H., "4QpNahum and the Teacher of Righteousness," *JBL* 75 (1956) 188–93.

Saggs, H. W. F., "Nahum and the Fall of Nineveh," *JTS* 20 (1969) 220–25.

Thomson, W. M., *The Land and the Book.* Hartford, 1910.

Van der Woude, A. S. "The Book of Nahum: A Letter Written in Exile," *OTS* 20 (1977) 108–26.

Yadin, Y., "Pesher Nahum Reconsidered," *IEJ* 21 (1971) 1–12.

C. HABAKKUK

Albright, W. F., "The Psalm of Habakkuk." In *Studies in Old Testament Prophecy Presented to T. H. Robinson.* Ed. H. H. Rowley. Edinburgh: T. & T. Clark, 1950. Pp. 1–18.

Brownlee, W. H. "The Composition of Habakkuk." In *Hommages à André Dupont-Sommer.* Ed. Nigel Arigad. Paris: Librairie de Adrien-Maisonneuve, 1971. Pp. 255–75.

_____, *The Midrash Pesher of Habakkuk.* SBL Monograph 24. Missoula, MT: Scholars Press, 1979.

_____, "The Placarded Revelation of Habakkuk," *JBL* 82 (1963) 319–25.

_____, *The Text of Habakkuk in the Ancient Commentary from Qumran.* JBL Monograph 11. Philadelphia: SBL, 1959.

Burrows, M., *The Dead Sea Scrolls of St. Mark's Monastery.* Vol. 1: *The Isaiah Manuscript and the Habakkuk Commentary.* New Haven: American Schools of Oriental Research, 1950.

Cassuto, U., "Chapter iii of Habakkuk and the Ras Shamra Texts." In *Biblical and Oriental Studies.* Vol. 2: *Bible and Ancient Oriental Texts.* Tr. Israel Abrahams. Jerusalem: Magnes, 1975. Pp. 3–15.

Crenshaw, J. L., *"Weḏōrēk ʿal-bāmŏtê ʾāreṣ,"* *CBQ* 34 (1972) 39–53.

Delcor, M., "La geste de Yahvé au temps de l'Exode et l'esperance du psalmiste en Habacuc III," in *Miscellanea Biblica.* Montserrat: B. Ubach, 1953. Pp. 287–302.

Eaton, J. H., "Origin and Meaning of Habakkuk 3," *ZAW* 76 (1964) 144–71.

Gaster, T. H. "Habakkuk 3:4," *JBL* 62 (1943) 345.

Irwin, W. A., "The Mythological Background of Habakkuk 3," *JNES* 15 (1956) 47–50.

_____, "The Psalm of Habakkuk," *JNES* 1 (1942) 10–40.

Johnson, S. Lewis, Jr., "The Gospel That Paul Preached," *BSac* 128 (1971) 327–40.

Lloyd-Jones, D. M., *From Fear to Faith; Studies in the Book of Habakkuk.* London: Inter-Varsity, 1953.

Marbury, E., *Obadiah and Habakkuk.* Repr. Evansville, IN: Sovereign Grace Publishers, 1960.

Margulis, B., "The Psalm of Habakkuk: A Reconstruction and Interpretation," *ZAW* 82 (1970) 409–42.

Silberman, L. K., "Unriddling the Riddle. A Study in the Structure and Language of the Habakkuk Pesher," *RevQ* 3/11 (1961) 323–64.

Southwell, P. J. M., "A Note on Habakkuk 2:4," *JTS* 19 (1968) 614–17.

Walker, H. H. and N. W. Lund, "The Literary Structure of Habakkuk," *JBL* 53 (1934) 355–70.

Young, E. J., "The Teacher of Righteousness and Jesus Christ: Some Reflections Upon the Dead Sea Scrolls," *WTJ* 18 (1956) 121–45.

D. ZEPHANIAH

Anderson, G. W., "The Idea of the Remnant in the Book of Zephaniah," *ASTI* 11. Fest. Gillis Gerleman (Leiden, 1978) 11–14.

Ball, I. J., Jr., *A Rhetorical Study of Zephaniah.* Berkeley, CA: Graduate Theological Union, 1972.

Bennett, W. H., "Sir J. G. Frazer on 'Those that leap over (or on) the threshold' (Zeph. 1:9)," *ExpTim* 30 (1918–19) 379–80.

DeRoche, M., "Zephaniah 1:2, 3: The 'Sweeping' of Creation" *VT* 30 (1980) 104–9.

_____, "Contra Creation, Covenant and Conquest (Jer. 8:13)," *VT* 30 (1980) 280–90.

Gaster, T. H., "Two Textual Emendations: Num. 24:8, Zeph. 3:17," *ExpTim* 78 (1967) 267.

Gerleman, Gillis. *Zephania textkritisch und literarisch untersucht.* Lund: Gleerup, 1942.

Gray, J., "A Metaphor from Building in Zephaniah 2:1," *VT* 3 (1953) 404–7.

Hyatt, J. P., "The Date and Background of Zephaniah" *JNES* 7 (1948) 25–29.

Kapelrud, A., *The Message of the Prophet Zephaniah.* Oslo: Universitetsforlaget, 1975.

Kselman, J. S., "A Note on Jeremiah 49:20 and Zephaniah 2:6, 7," *CBQ* 32 (1970) 579–81.

Sabottka, L. *Zephanja: Versuch einer Neuübersetzung mit philologischen Kommentar.* BibOr 25. Rome: Pontifical Biblical Institute, 1972.

Smith, L. P. and E. R. Lacheman, "The Authorship of Zephaniah," *JNES* 9 (1950) 137–42.

Thomas, D. W. "A Pun on the Name Ashdod in Zephaniah ii.4," *ExpTim* 74 (1962) 63.

Williams, D. L., "The Date of Zephaniah," *JBL* 82 (1963) 77–88.

_____, *Zephaniah: A Re-Interpretation.* Durham, NC: Duke University, 1961.

The Book of
NAHUM

SUPERSCRIPTION (1:1)

1   *The burden of Nineveh.*
    The book of the vision
        of Nahum the Elkoshite.

Of the fifteen canonical prophetic books, eleven begin with an explicit indicator that their message is "the word of the Lord." Nahum is one of the
remaining four that make the same claim indirectly by referring to the
"vision" that was granted to them, or by speaking of the words that they
"saw." Yet Nahum is unique in that the entirety of his *book* is characterized
as a *vision* revealed by God. This prophetic material is not presented as the
product of an ecstatic dervish whose mind swirled with frenzied irrational-
ities. His *vision* could be laid out as an objective, rational piece of literature
with a unified theme embodying elaborate poetic structures.

The root meaning of the term translated *burden (maśśā')* as well as
the overwhelming majority of contexts in which it occurs favors a recognition of the "burdensomeness" associated with this message.[1] Anyone who in
real life has had to preach the solemn message of God's destruction of the
wicked will have no trouble agreeing with Nahum that this word is a burden
to bear.

---

1. For a treatment of the term favoring the meaning "burden," see P. A. H.
de Boer, "An Inquiry into the Meaning of the Term *maśśā'*," in *OTS* 5 (1948) 197–
214. De Boer notes that the term is often translated "utterance, oracle," in view of the
phrase *nāśā' qôl,* "to raise one's voice." But in examining the more than 60 times that
the word *maśśā'* occurs in the OT, he makes a rather convincing case in favor of the
meaning "burden." Exploring the earliest versions as well, he concludes: "The earliest exegesis does not support a distinction of two Hebrew words *maśśā'* with a different sense" (p. 209). For a recent treatment favoring the meaning "oracle," see the
comments of K. J. Cathcart, *Nahum in the Light of Northwest Semitic,* BibOr 26
(Rome: Pontifical Biblical Institute, 1973), pp. 36–37. Additional comments on this
term may be found under Hab. 1:1.

Who is this prophet *Nahum?* His name means "comforter," and in a certain sense his message comforts by announcing the destruction of Judah's most dread persecutor. But too little is known about him to conclude that his name was intended to reflect his message.

What is an *Elkoshite?* It is not likely that the term denotes Nahum's ancestry, since the normal pattern of speaking of a prophet's origins describes him as the "son of" someone. More probably the term refers to the place of Nahum's origin. Other biblical examples would include "Micah the Morashite" and "Jeremiah the Anathothite" (cf. Mic. 1:1; Jer. 29:27). As noted in the Introduction, the most ancient tradition, as recorded by Jerome in the 4th century A.D., identifies Elkosh as a little village in Galilee pointed out to him by a guide.[2]

It could be objected that the northern kingdom which would have included this "little village in Galilee" had been taken into captivity long before Nahum's day. Yet Scripture makes it plain that God continued to maintain his people in the territory of the northern kingdom, as seen in the incident of the reform instituted in the days of Josiah (cf. 2 K. 23:15–20). Furthermore, the prophet's allusion to the devastation specifically of Bashan, Carmel, and Lebanon supports a location for the prophet's origin in northern Palestine (see Nah. 1:4).

Although it cannot be affirmed with certainty, there is something fitting about the thought that Nahum, the prophet of Assyria's doom, had his origins in the northern kingdom. Even though God had brought Assyria as his instrument to scourge the nation of Israel, the brutal oppressor had gone far beyond the limits of propriety in its cruelty. Now a prophet representing the surviving remnant of the north would be called specifically to announce the inevitability of God's acts of retributive justice.

It is rather startling to note that one entire book of the Bible is devoted to the destruction of a single heathen city. It is true that the total thrust of Jonah also concerns itself with God's judgment on this same city of Nineveh. But the difference of approach between Nahum and Jonah only accentuates the remarkable character of the prophecy of Nahum. While the reluctant Jonah is literally driven by God to announce a message that leads to a wondrous manifestation of mercy to the wicked city, Nahum paints exclusively with the dark tones of judgment's inevitability. Each of his three chapters only advances this single theme of the certainty, the inevitability, of the awesome judgment of God. Even the slight message of hope addressed

---

2. *The Principal Works of St. Jerome,* tr. W. H. Fremantle, in *A Select Library of Nicene and Post-Nicene Fathers of the Christian Church,* 2nd series (New York: Charles Scribner's Sons, 1912), 6:501. Cf. Maier, p. 24.

to Judah as a point of reassurance (Nah. 2:1) can hardly lift the bleak cloud of negativism that provides the substructure for this prophetic word.

Indeed, the distinctiveness of this message of Nahum must be appreciated for its problematic character. The book is unquestionably about the "burden of Nineveh." Yet this unbroken note of judgment may provide a ministry today that is greatly needed by those who put their trust in the one true God. A recognition of the reality of divine vengeance provides a sobriety that ought always to characterize the relations of human beings and nations.

I. PUBLIC ANNOUNCEMENT OF NINEVEH'S JUDGMENT (1:2–14)

Nahum most likely prophesied in the latter days of Manasseh (ca. 687–642 B.C.), as proposed in the Introduction above. If so, his public proclamation of the utter devastation of Nineveh could not have been a very popular message. It hardly was the political thing to say, even in the days of Manasseh's reform. The northern territory of Israel was governed by Assyrian overlords, and the southern kingdom of Judah maintained an alliance with Assyria as a consequence of Manasseh's policy of syncretism. But this bold prophet of the Lord builds his case against Nineveh on the certainty of God's unchanging nature. Because of who he is, Nineveh shall experience firsthand the fierceness of his wrath. Indeed, this oppressive city shall feel it soon.

The poetic form of this chapter has generated extensive discussion. Primarily the question revolves about the possibility of an alphabetic acrostic imbedded in these verses. At least one edition of the Hebrew Bible has gone so far as to enlarge key letters of the verses in an effort to show the progression of the poem through the Hebrew alphabet.[1] But the poem as it presently stands is not a complete acrostic; not all the letters of the Hebrew alphabet follow one another in proper order. The Hebrew Bible that enlarges the supposed alphabetic succession of letters plainly displays elements missing and out of order.

If it is proposed that a more ancient acrostic poem has been disturbed and inserted into the text of Nahum, then convincing explanation must be given for the coherence as well as the poetic parallelism that manifests itself in the present form of material. The present structures simply do not give the impression of a disturbed composition. Be an adapter of literary materials

---

1. See the 3rd edition of R. Kittel's *Biblia Hebraica* (Stuttgart: Württembergische Bibelanstalt, 1937). In *BHS* the acrostic is indicated by letters in parentheses preceding the verses.

ever so clever, he seldom will succeed in disguising the traces of his trade with the creation of so fine a final product.

The identifications of the various words that supposedly follow an alphabetic order as proposed in the Kittel Bible are convincing only to a limited degree. The *beth* does not begin a word that starts a phrase; the *daleth* appears only as a consequence of conjectural emendation; the *waw* is simply the conjunction "and"; the *zayin* begins the second word of a Hebrew construct; and the *yod* follows a connective *waw*. When five of the eleven proposed instances of alphabetic succession manifest an irregularity, a certain self-restraint in assertions concerning the presence of an acrostic poem seems well-advised. Theories about the possible corruptions of an original acrostic have a great deal to overcome, particularly in view of the solid structures of parallelism within the text as it now stands.

The other poetic elements of parallelism and alliteration are much more impressive. By his extensive use of poetic devices, Nahum has intensified his capacity for communication and has led the people into an awesome confrontation with the God of Israel.

The opening verses display a variety of types of parallelism, including the following:

a-b-b-a	(vv. 2, 6)
a-b-a-b	(vv. 2–5)
a-b-c-c-b-a	(v. 6)
a-b-b-b	(v. 3)

In addition, the participle "one who takes vengeance" *(nôqēm)* occurs three times in the prophet's opening statement, along with the threefold use of the covenant name of God (v. 2). Particularly effective is the use of the identical verbal form at the beginning and end of one particular stanza ("is languishing"—v. 4).[2]

A. THE AWESOME TERROR OF GOD'S JUDGMENT (1:2–6)

1. His Person as Judge (1:2–3)

> 2 a   A God of jealousy
> b   and one who takes vengeance is Yahweh;

---

2. For a full discussion of poetic devices employed by Nahum, see O. T. Allis, "Nahum, Nineveh, Elkosh," *EvQ* 27 (1955) 67–80.

>   *b one who takes vengeance is Yahweh*
> *a and a master of wrath.*[1]

>   *a One who takes vengeance is Yahweh*
>   *b toward his adversaries;*
>   *a and he reserves (wrath)*[2]
>   *b for his enemies.*
> 3 *a Yahweh—*
>   *b longsuffering in anger*
>   *b and great in strength*
>   *b and by no means will he clear the guilty.*

> *Yahweh—*
>   *a in whirlwind and in storm*
>   *b (is) his way,*
>   *a and clouds*
>   *b (are) the dust of his feet.*

2 The impact of Nahum's poetic structure is felt immediately as the prophet opens with a picture of God's person as judge. He is *a God of jealousy, one who takes vengeance, a master of wrath* who *reserves (wrath) for his enemies.*

Generally *jealousy* conveys a negative image. The jealous man makes even his loved ones miserable. But God's jealousy must be seen in a different light. God is "jealous" or "zealous" that his own honor be maintained. A departure from wholehearted submission to God can only bring chaos into the world. Once a person creates in his mind another god, moral disorder follows inevitably. If covetousness idolizes the material creation, then the unending grasping for more will result in the horrors of war (cf. Jas. 4:1–3). If the intellect becomes a god to human beings, the consequences will be horrible, no matter how noble a person's ideas may appear. For deifying a platonic realm of ideas leads to an imbalanced neglect of material realities. Embracing a Kantian distinction between a scientific realm of the phenom-

---

1. Cathcart, *Nahum*, pp. 39–40, notes the chiasm which supports the repetition of "one who takes vengeance is Yahweh," and cites the Ugaritic parallel: "The wings of the eagles may Baᶜal break/May Baᶜal break the pinions of them."

2. Parentheses are used throughout the translation sections of this commentary to indicate words or phrases not specifically represented in the MT. Sometimes the added words may be implied by Hebrew language structure. At other times they are necessary to communicate in English the intent of the original text. Although modern translation theory might regard this use of parentheses as unnecessary, it has been employed as a device to allow the reader a larger opportunity to interact with the text of Scripture.

enal and a spiritual realm of the noumenal gives the illusion that it provides the correct key for the coexistence of science and religion for the modern person. But in the end, the separation of the noumenal from the phenomenal naturally will result in an ethic of the "categorical imperative," in which a person's inherent "ought" becomes the test of what is morally right. But as history has proved, that "ought" may promote the annihilation of a race as well as the loving of the neighbor.

Only whole-souled worship of the one true living God can assure a harmonious balance in the world so that all aspects of creation receive their proper due. God's "jealousy" clearly has the best interest of his creation in view. Just as a screeching mother mockingbird terrorizes any feline that comes near her nest, so the Lord zealously hovers over his own to avert any rival to his sovereignty and centrality.

Portions of v. 2 almost certainly represent a quotation from more than one earlier section of the OT. As the Lord initially solemnizes the provisions of the covenant with Israel, he declares: "For I, Yahweh your God, (am) a jealous God" (Exod. 20:5). When reinstituting the covenant after the incident of the golden calf, the Lord insists: "You shall worship no other God: for Yahweh, whose name is Jealous, is a jealous God" (Exod. 34:14). The very essence of God is associated with his "jealousy." By being the one and only true God, a zealousness for maintaining his unique role flows out of his very nature.

Contrary to modern latitudinarianism, tolerance toward holding to a multiplicity of gods is not commended in Scripture.[3] The effect of failing to respect the oneness of God's reality is clearly displayed in Israel's national experience. Because they provoked him to jealousy with other gods when they became fat with material prosperity, God withdrew his blessing from them. But by simultaneously bringing judgment on Israel and giving prosperity to the Gentile nations, God graciously intended to move Israel to their own experience of "jealousy" (cf. Deut. 32:16–21, esp. v. 21).

This interplay between God's jealousy and his response of provoking Israel to jealousy finds its consummate elaboration in Paul's explanation of the ways of God in the new covenant era. Paul magnifies his ministry among the non-Jewish community. Even though it was his heart's desire and prayer that Israel be saved (Rom. 10:1), he gloried in the extensive fruit of

---

3. Rudolph, p. 155, points out that the idea of the Lord's being a God of jealousy, vengeance, and wrath cannot be regarded as an underdeveloped religious idea, since all these characteristics are attributed to God in the NT: zeal in 2 Cor. 11:2; vengeance in Rom. 12:19; Heb. 10:30; and wrath in Rom. 1:18.

his preaching to the heathen nations. Why? Just to spite the rebellious nation? No! The apostle to the non-Jews hoped that by his ministry among Gentiles he might "provoke to jealousy" his own kinsmen according to the flesh (Rom. 11:13–14).

God's jealousy consumes, but it also redeems. Because he is jealous, he cares enough to redeem human beings out of their recalcitrant state. Because idolatry, covetousness, and brutality insult his honor, God shall destroy the wicked—*and* also shall save his rebellious people.

This twofold outworking of the jealousy of God explains the combination of contrasting attributes in God as depicted in the many passages that present his jealousy. He is jealous, full of wrath, and by no means will clear the guilty; yet simultaneously he is good, longsuffering, merciful and gracious, slow to anger, abundant in lovingkindness, and forgiving iniquity, transgression, and sin (Exod. 34:6, 14; cf. Nah. 1:2–3). This combination of elements inherently provides a framework for understanding such comprehensive doctrines as the love of God in providing atonement for sin, the sovereignty of God in working salvation, and the inevitability of the final destruction of sinners. If God "by no means will clear the guilty," then all human beings are condemned unless a real and effective atonement for sin is provided. If all stand under the wrath of God, the saving of some must have its root ultimately in the free and uncompelled love of God. If an effective atonement has not been made for all, then God's wrath must be poured out on those for whom there is no propitiation.

This twofold outworking of the jealousy of God in consuming the sinner in wrath and in propitiating for the sinner in mercy provides the ultimate explanation as to why the ministry of Jonah to Nineveh had a radically different consequence from the ministry of Nahum to the same city. In the one case, God manifested his propitiatory grace; in the other case he manifested his consuming wrath. Although eighth-century Nineveh repented and was saved, the same city found it impossible to repent one hundred years later.

But this passage emphasizes another aspect of God's reality more than his jealousy. Three times it is God as *one who takes vengeance* that capsules the thrust of these verses. If "jealousy" or "zealousness" characterizes God's attitude toward all rivals, then *vengeance* describes the action that emerges from that jealousy. This vengeance on the part of God might be defined as the measuring out of a just recompense. But it includes more. Not only does the Almighty, all-knowing, all-just God return to the sinner an appropriate repayment for every evil that he has done; he also renders this repayment in a context of righteous indignation, disgust, and wrath. The guilty sinner shall call for an avalanche of rocks to cover him not primarily as a way of escape from the pain inflicted on his body for his sin, but because of the awesome sense of rejection and repudiation emanating from the Presence before whom he must stand.

The difference between God's "jealousy" and his "vengeance" is clarified by noting that "zeal" for the Lord is reflected appropriately in the creature, but "vengeance" is an action reserved essentially for God himself. Repeatedly the Scriptures underscore the prohibition against man's taking vengeance into his own hands. God's people are not to take vengeance, but instead must love their neighbor as themselves (Lev. 19:18). Explicitly it is stated that vengeance belongs to the Lord (Deut. 32:35; Ps. 94:1). In suffering his repeated abuses from Saul, David declares: "May the Lord avenge the wrongs you have done to me, but my hand will not touch you" (1 Sam. 24:12). David does not deny the wrongs he has undergone at the hand of Saul. But he refuses to do anything that might approximate a just recompense. Only God may judge with righteousness and punish appropriately.

That God indeed shall repay the wicked for each one of their wicked deeds is seen in the emphasis on the "day of vengeance" which God has established (Isa. 61:1–2; 63:4; Jer. 46:10). A delay in God's administration of justice must not be misunderstood even for a moment as indicating an indulgent leniency on the part of the Almighty. With the full force of his righteous indignation, he shall consume the wicked from the face of the earth.

As a *master of wrath* and one who *reserves (wrath) for his enemies*, God displays a calculated control in his dispensing of vengeance. He never gives way to passions, he never exceeds propriety, he never compromises his ultimate goals because of a reactionary response to current provocations. His just judgments cannot be questioned, and ultimately can bear the most critical scrutiny of any and all because they always remain subject to his calm perfections as God.

From the perspective of the new covenant, God's "mastery" of his own just wrath is seen most clearly in the endurance by Father and Son in the hour of Christ's crucifixion. Despite the awful crime committed against the Son of God, despite the maltreatment inflicted by depraved sinners, the Father restrains his vengeance and heaps judgment vicariously on his Son instead. The Son could have called for legions of angels to consume his oppressors. But instead he cries, "Father, forgive them" (Luke 23:34).

Yet the day of the Lord's vengeance indeed will come. In that day he shall consume the wicked with the breath of his mouth. The utter destruction of the oppressive city of Nineveh demonstrates in history the reality of God's commitment to judge.

3   This verse continues the description of the nature of God as one who brings judgment on his enemies.[4]

When Nahum describes Yahweh as *longsuffering in anger* and one who *by no means will clear the guilty,* it is almost certain that he intends to echo a passage that played repeated significance in Israel's history. After God's judgment for Israel's apostasy related to the golden calf, God commanded Moses to duplicate the original tablets of stone. The Lord in his mercy would reestablish his covenant with Israel.

In this context of God's manifesting his nature before Moses, the covenant name of God is repeated twice, precisely as in Nahum. The Lord proceeds to declare himself as one who is "longsuffering in anger . . . and by no means will he clear the guilty" (Exod. 34:6–7). The wording is exactly the same as that which is found in Nah. 1:3, and it is repeated again in Num. 14:18. In the Numbers passage, Moses pleads: "Let it be according as you have spoken," apparently referring to the nature of God as it had been revealed to him after the incident of the golden calf.

But in the case of Nahum's appeal to the same text in Exodus, crucial omissions of particular phrases tell the tale. God is *longsuffering in anger,* which would explain the long delay in his bringing judgment on Nineveh. But Nahum mentions nothing of the fact that this same God is "merciful and gracious, abundant in lovingkindness and truth, keeping lovingkindness for thousands, and forgiving iniquity and transgression and sin," as is stated in both Exod. 34 and Num. 14. For Nahum wishes to stress the reality of judgment that must arise out of the nature of God. The Lord may be forgiving and merciful. But the point of no return has been passed by Nineveh, and the only thing left is waiting for the judgment that is sure to come.

Between his quotation of phrases from Exod. 34 Nahum introduces a new thought. Yahweh is *great in strength,* a concept which certainly places the emphasis on something other than the Lord's readiness to forgive. This phrase elsewhere refers to the mighty, the supernatural power of God which alone was sufficient to bring the universe into being and to redeem Israel (Deut. 4:37; Jer. 27:5; 32:17; 2 K. 17:36; etc.). It is this power that now shall be concentrated on the destruction of the national capital of the mighty empire of Assyria. Humanly speaking, it appeared impossible that any force

---

4. The poetic structure of this verse may be debated. "Yahweh" might belong at the beginning and end of a single phrase, but it seems more likely that two compound phrases are included in the verse, with "Yahweh" beginning each of the clauses. See the treatment of GKC, § 143a. A fuller discussion of this form of Hebrew construction may be found under the exposition of Hab. 2:4 below.

could retard their ever-expanding empire. But God the Creator, the Redeemer of Israel—he had the supernatural strength essential for just such an overthrow.

For God *by no means will clear the guilty.* This phrase creates no special problem of understanding in the context of Nahum's announcement of the coming destruction of Nineveh. The infinitive form followed by the negative indicates a total negation.[5] But in the original context of Exod. 34, the affirmation that God "by no means will clear the guilty" is balanced by the previous assertion that God is longsuffering and forgiving. The fullest appreciation of Nahum's words emerges only as they are set in this fuller biblical context.

Comparing the contexts of Exodus and Nahum, one realizes that the statement that God *by no means will clear the guilty* cannot be taken in the abstract. It is indeed an absolute of reality that is rooted in the unchanging nature of God. But this reality functions in a context in which absolution of guilt is a real possibility in the context of the covenant. So long as a person, city, or nation continues to bear the burden of its own guilt, it cannot be declared free and clear of liability to punishment. But if guilt is transferred to another party by way of substitution in accordance with the provisions of the covenant, then the Lord may manifest his forgiveness.[6]

The problem with Nineveh was that through their separation from the grace of the covenant, they bore their own guilt. At the preaching of Jonah the city had repented, called on the name of the Lord, and been spared. But that tenderhearted sorrow for sin had been replaced by an arrogant affirmation that they themselves were God (cf. Zeph. 2:15). Inevitably, such arrogance resulted in their own condemnation. Their guilt remained, and so judgment was inevitable.

The prophet does not stop merely with affirming these various aspects of the nature of God. He proceeds to present God in motion, God in action, God applying the realities inherent in his nature to everyday human situations.

The imagery of *whirlwind, storm, and cloud* serves the prophet well in his effort to convey this dimension of God's reality (v. 3b). Fitting indeed are these images, since they depict the activity of God in a realm between heaven and earth. As he descends from his lofty heights in heaven, the first

---

5. Rudolph, p. 151 n.3.

6. Calvin, p. 423, with his usual insightfulness, says that absolution comes only after righteous judgment, "for the faithful by repentance anticipate his judgment; and he searches their hearts, that he may clear them. For what is repentance but [self] condemnation, which yet turns out to be the means of salvation? . . . [God] absolves none except the condemned."

awesome stirrings of God's presence occur in wind and cloud. These natural intermediaries between the immortal and the mortal shuffle noisily above the heads of people who otherwise might remain engrossed in their sin-laden preoccupations.

The *whirlwind* or tempest *(sûpâ)* and the *storm (śeʿārâ)* appear totally arbitrary in their meanderings, striking first here and then there without rhyme or reason. But God is ordering them. Without confusion they follow the path of divine ordination (cf. Amos 4:7–8; Matt. 10:29–30).

One frequent visitor to Palestine recounts an incident which vivifies the suddenness, the devastation, and the fury of a storm in that part of the world:

> This plain of Ijon has lately been rendered famous by a most extraordinary storm . . . Some friends of mine . . . were coming down the hill . . . when one of them called their attention to tall columns of mist over the marsh of the Huleh. They came this way very rapidly, and soon broke upon them with awful fury. . . . Those who attempted to reach Khyam perished in the plain, although it is not more than two miles wide, and in full view of their houses. Thus ten men died in a few minutes from the mere chill of this wonderful wind. There was no snow, no frost, and not much rain; but the wind was perfectly awful, driving and upheaving everything before it. These cold winds draw out all animal heat with amazing rapidity. Not only were these men chilled to death almost instantly, but 85 head of cattle also perished before they could be brought to the village.[7]

The description of this winter sirocco sounds almost too fantastic to believe. But so also may have sounded the prophet's report of the coming devastations on the firmly fixed capital of Nineveh. Yet time and experience ultimately establish the awesome power of God both in nature and history.

When the prophet employs the imagery of *clouds* as *the dust of the feet* of God, he paints a picture of vigorous movement in haste. Not gay, puffy, white clouds, but ominous storm clouds depict the motions of the Almighty. God strides across the expanse of heaven, stirring up the commotion of thunder and lightning as his attributes of holiness and righteousness move into action (cf. Ps. 29:3–9).

When the NT depicts the Christ ascending in the clouds and promises his return in the same manner (Acts 1:9, 11), this picture of the prophet has reached its highest level of fulfillment. Every eye shall be drawn inevitably to him as he comes in glory, bringing destructive judgment on his enemies and blessing to his people.

7. W. M. Thomson, *The Land and the Book* (Hartford, 1910), pp. 200–201.

2. *His Action as Judge (1:4–5)*

4   *a*   *He rebukes the sea*
      b   *and dries it up,*[1]
      a   *and all the rivers*
      b   *he makes arid.*[2]

      a   *Bashan and Carmel*
      b   *are languishing,*
      a   *and the fruit of Lebanon*
      b   *is languishing.*

5   *a*   *Mountains*
      b   *quake at him,*
      a   *and hills*
      b   *melt.*

      a   *The earth heaves*
      b   *before him,*
      a   *the world*
      b   *and all its inhabitants.*

This great God depicted by Nahum is not just an abstract idea, a nebulous concept. He is a living person whose nature defines the meaning of personhood. He interacts powerfully with the world he has made, so that the attributes that Nahum has so vividly delineated have their telling effect on every element of creation. The sea, the rivers, the fruitful lands, mountains, hills, the earth, the world and all its inhabitants—these diverse segments feel the effect of God's jealousy, vengeance, wrath, anger, might, and justice.

4 As a master might rebuke a dilatory apprentice, so the Lord *rebukes the sea and dries it up.* Nahum recollects the great rebuke of the sea at the Exodus which resulted in the Lord's judgment on the host of Pharaoh (cf. Exod. 14:21; 15:1, 8; Ps. 106:9; 2 Sam. 22:16). Let haughty Assyria be warned of the fatal consequences of a nation that stands in the way of the Lord's redemptive plan. God has done it once, and he shall do it again.

Not only does the Lord "rebuke the sea"; *all the rivers he makes arid.* Since the ancient city of Nineveh depended on its natural water-barrier as a basic element of defense, these words vivify the city's hopeless state. For this

---

1. Keil, p. 10, notes: "the vowelless *y* of the third person" is "fused into one with the first radical sound." So the word appears as *wayyaḇᵉšēhû* rather than *wayᵉyaḇᵉšēhû.* Cf. GKC, §§ 68w, 70a.

2. Cathcart, *Nahum,* p. 49, notes several instances in Ugaritic material in which "sea" and "river" are set in parallelism.

feeble barrier of water cannot deter the Almighty when he moves into action. As a matter of fact, the streams about Nineveh ultimately became the way of their destruction.

Instead of specifically mentioning Egypt as the object of God's past judgment, the prophet recalls the more recent devastations on Palestine itself—devastations well remembered by Assyria, since it had been the agent perpetuating them. *Bashan, Carmel, and Lebanon* are joined at other places in the OT to describe the expanse of Israel's northern territories, particularly in terms of their fruitfulness (Deut. 1:4–7; 2 K. 19:23; Isa. 33:1; 35:2; Jer. 50:18–19). These locales are the most fertile, forest-clad, and well-watered areas of Palestine. Bashan stretches across the Transjordan area from Mt. Hermon in the north to the brook Jabbok in the south, including all the territory of Gilead. The whole realm became a type of fertility, and the cattle of Bashan were proverbial for their fatness (Ezek. 39:18; Amos 4:1; Mic. 7:14).

To the western extremity of northern Israel was Carmel, a fertile mountain jutting into the Mediterranean (cf. Isa. 33:9; 35:2; Jer. 50:19). In the days of Elijah, Carmel had experienced a great drought as a judgment for the baalism that had polluted the land (1 K. 18:19–20, 42). But Nahum envisions a far more severe circumstance. For the most prominent *fruit of Lebanon* would have to be its world-famous cedars. Nahum's declaration that these deep-rooted monuments to time are *languishing* indicates just how long the drought he conceives would continue.[3]

During its zenith of power, Assyria had threatened Lebanon. Sennacherib had said that he would cut down the tall cedars of Lebanon and its choice fir trees (2 K. 19:23). Now if the Lord would bring such scathing judgments on the naturally blessed areas of his own land, what reason does Nineveh have to expect that it would somehow be spared a similar devastation from the Lord? Judgment may begin with the house of God. But judgment unquestionably will fall on those outside the Lord's house. In the graciousness of God, Israel was promised that they would experience a return some day to the fruitfulness of Bashan, Carmel, and Lebanon (Isa. 33:9–10; 35:2; Jer. 50:18–19). But Nahum suggests no such promise for Assyria.

5 The terrors of the Lord in judgment cannot be restricted to one single area of the world. According to this verse, the very foundations of the world are disturbed by his wrath. *Mountains, hills, earth,* and *world quake, melt,* and *heave before him.* The imagery of a "melting" hill is particularly

---

3. The extent to which specialized commerce had developed is seen by the reference to the oars made from the oaks of Bashan employed by the ships of Tyre (Ezek. 27:6).

striking. Since the very elements of the universe are constantly held together by the mighty power of God, the withdrawal of that sustaining might would mean the disintegration of granite foundations, fertile valleys, and grass-covered peaks.

From a new covenant perspective, Peter speaks in climactic, cataclysmic terms of the final destruction of the earth as it is presently constituted. The heavens shall pass away with a great noise, and the "earth" shall "melt" with fervent heat. But according to his promise, we look for new heavens and a new earth in which righteousness dwells (2 Pet. 3:10–13).

3. Your Stance Before Him as Judge (1:6)

> 6 a   Before his indignation
>   b   who shall stand?
>   b   and who shall arise
> a   before the fierceness of his anger?
>
> a   His fury
>   b   is poured out
>   c   like fire;
>   c   and the boulders
>   b   are broken
> a   before him.

A rhetorical question demanding response now draws the listener directly into the pathway of the prophetic proclamation. The immediate rephrasing of the same query calls up short the inattentive.

Who shall stand before his indignation? Who shall rise up before the fierceness of his anger? Obviously no one. Not even Israel had been able to stand before him when he determined to mark their iniquities. Ironically, Assyria had been identified in an earlier day as the rod of the Lord's wrath (Isa. 10:5). But even then the prophet Isaiah had made it clear that after the Lord had finished with Jerusalem, he would punish the proud heart of the king of Assyria (Isa. 10:12).

As though intent on displaying the complete round of the Lord's wrath as it worked among the nations, other prophetic utterances identify Babylon as the nation to bring judgment on Assyria (Isa. 13:5), while noting that ultimately Babylon also would become the object of his indignation (Jer. 50:25). Again the question arises: Who shall stand? Who shall rise up? Israel? Judah? Assyria? Babylon? No. None of them. Each nation in its turn shall undergo the devastating judgments of the Lord. None is strong enough to resist the working of his power as the rising and falling tides of history display his wrath.

The latter portion of this verse makes it patently plain that the prophet is not speaking merely of a modest chastening of the wicked. The Lord shall not simply slap the naughty hand of the Assyrian. *Like fire* that totally consumes, his *fury is poured out.* This fire does not simply sting the flesh; it consumes utterly.

Furthermore, *boulders are broken before him.* Nothing is gained in attempting to reconstruct a shattered boulder. Never again will it possess the solidity of substance that once was inherent in its existence.

So what is your stance before the wrath of the Almighty? How do you respond to the prophet's rhetorical query? Shall you or your nation stand? The questions of Nahum demand appropriate self-examination.

B. THE SPECIFIC TARGET OF GOD'S JUDGMENT (1:7–11)

Having introduced the subject of God as judge, the prophet now moves to an identification of the specific target of divine judgment, which is the city of Nineveh. In zeroing in on this specific city as the point of God's wrath, the prophet sets the fierceness of divine wrath over against the tenderness with which he treats his own people.

1. Judgment in a Context of God's Care for His Own (1:7)

7　*Good is Yahweh,*
　　　a refuge[1] in the day of adversity.
　　　And he knows those who seek shelter in him.

The message of Nahum up to this point appears purely in negative terms. Almost nothing but judgment has been discussed. But now it becomes apparent that those who turn to the Lord have nothing to fear. He is *good,* and his people shall enjoy an abundant salvation. Actually the judgment on Nineveh must be viewed from the perspective of God's intent to show mercy to his people. He responds to their cry for relief from oppression by sending judgment on their enemies.

Indeed, it must be recognized that God's "own," his favored ones who

---

1. Cathcart, *Nahum,* p. 55, follows Dahood in treating the *l* prefix on *lᵉmāʿôz* as having a comparative force like *min.* In this case the meaning would be, "Better is Yahweh than a refuge." But the construction is not too common.

find him to be merciful, cannot be identified merely as "Israel" after the flesh. As a matter of fact, *precisely* the historical context of Nahum's declaration of the goodness of God to those whom he *knows* indicates that a simplistic or purely ethnic definition of "Israel" cannot apply. Earlier in God's dealing with the inhabitants of Nineveh through the ministry of the prophet Jonah, God indicated that he could be just as merciful to the heathen Ninevites as he had been to his own people. The fact that Nineveh in Nahum's day was targeted for devastation could not blot out the reality of the earlier mercy shown to the inhabitants of Nineveh in response to their faith and repentance. For Israel too would bear the brunt of devastations by the same Babylon that was to bring judgment on Assyria. The Lord is good—but only *to those who seek shelter in him.* This phrase suggests not merely faith, entrustment to the Lord. It recognizes an imminent danger from which the person who trusts must seek deliverance. The ultimate source of this danger is in the Lord himself as he manifests his righteous judgments. But the repentant sinner seeks for help in none other than him.

According to the prophet, God *knows* those who seek shelter in him. This "knowing" of the Lord must be understood in the full biblical sense of "loving" with the most intense care. When the prophet Amos declares that God has "known" Israel alone among all the nations of the earth, he cannot mean that God possesses cognitive information about only one nation in the world (cf. Amos 3:2). Instead, he means that this people alone as a nation has received the special love of God.

The Lord *knows those who seek shelter in him,* meaning that he loves them, cares for them, cherishes their well-being. This concept belongs precisely in this context because it provides a proper framework for understanding God's coming judgment that will devastate the earth. For the sake of his people, as a step toward the full realization of their salvation, God shall judge Nineveh and the Assyrians.

"Goodness" in God is most frequently associated with covenant fidelity (*ḥesed;* cf. 2 Chr. 5:13; 7:3; Ezra 3:11; Ps. 106:1; 136:1; etc.). Particularly in association with the glory of God manifested in his dwelling among his people it is declared that the Lord is good. Those who seek shelter in the temple of God will find out just how good and merciful he is.

2. Judgment Directed Specifically Against Seventh-Century B.C. Assyria (1:8–11)

8 *But with a cataclysmic flood*
he will make a complete end

> of her place;
> and his enemies
> he will pursue into the darkness.[1]
>
> 9 What do you think about Yahweh?
> He will make a complete end;
> adversity shall not arise a second time.
>
> 10   For as thorns twisted,
> and as (with) drink they are drunk;[2]
> so they shall be consumed
> as stubble fully dried.
>
> 11 From you
> he came forth,
> he who devises
> evil against Yahweh
> he who schemes
> ruthlessly.

This section is made particularly complex by the various alterations among subjects and objects. But such rapid interchanges are not uncommon in prophetic literature. Verse 8 says the Lord will make a complete end of *her* place, referring directly to the city of Nineveh. Verse 9 asks what *you* (masculine plural) think about Yahweh, apparently eliciting a faith-response from the people of Judah. Verse 10 announces that *they* shall be totally consumed, referring to the judgment which must fall on the inhabitants of Nineveh. Verse 11 returns to a feminine singular pronoun as in v. 8, indicating that from the city of Nineveh (feminine singular) had come forth one who had devised evil against the Lord. The reference to this last mysterious figure will receive special consideration later.

8 In an earlier day, the prophet Isaiah had used the imagery of a *cataclysmic flood* to describe the assault of Assyria against Israel. The king of Assyria would come like a river swollen over its banks, rising even to the neck, with its "wings" stretching to the breadth of the land (Isa. 8:7–8). But now Assyria shall be the one to experience submersion under a flood tide of invaders. *make a complete end of her place* suggests not only that the city itself would be destroyed, but that its site would become uninhabited and un-

1. The *maqqeph* argues against regarding "darkness" as the subject, as represented in the LXX and favored by some interpreters. Cf. Keil, p. 12.

2. BDB, p. 685, concludes that this verse "is prob. corrupt . . . and [the] sense obscure," and suggests that both these particular words should be deleted as dittographic. But in Hebrew the verse presents an excellent example of alliteration, which hardly could be due to a corruption.

occupied. Shortly after Nahum's prophecy, this extent of devastation became Nineveh's literal experience. The sites of cities such as Jerusalem, Damascus, and Hebron have been occupied continuously from patriarchal times until today. Yet a scant three hundred years after the fall of the colossal city of Nineveh, travelers hardly suspected that the area ever had been inhabited.[3]

Not only the site, but the people also shall experience the terrors of God's judgment. For *his enemies he will pursue into the darkness.* Just as the site of the city shall disappear, so its inhabitants will vanish into an oblivious, oppressive blackness.

Darkness in Scripture symbolizes distress, terror, mourning, perplexity, and dread.[4] A combination of all these experiences shall be the final fruition of Nineveh for all the years that she oppressed and brutalized other nations. Egypt once sat frozen while undergoing the plague of darkness; but Assyria shall have the added curse of being pursued into the darkness. Their terror shall be intensified as they stumble forward into an impenetrable blackness.

It may be difficult for modern people to identify with these terrors unless they have been victims of the horrors of modern war. But even those earthly agonies hardly compare with the outer darkness of eternal hell where the worm dies not and the fire is not quenched. The guilty conscience excited by the convicting powers of the word of God may do a more effective job than rational argumentations to convince the sinner of the reality of this inescapable judgment to come.

9 The phrase *He will make a complete end* is repeated here, but with the added emphasis that it is *he (hû')*—Yahweh—that shall annihilate Nineveh. The repeated phrase comes in response to the question, *What do you [masculine plural] think about Yahweh?* The verb employed *(ḥāšaḇ)* could mean either "think" or "devise." The decision between these two options hinges on the identification of the masculine plural *you* and whether the force of the preposition *('el)* should be taken as "about" or "against." If the *you* refers to the inhabitants of Israel, then the force of the question would be, "What do you Israelites think about Yahweh? Will he rise up against your enemies?" But if the *you* refers to the inhabitants of Nineveh, then the force

---

3. W. H. Green, review of *Nahum's Prophecy Concerning Nineveh Explained and Illustrated from Assyrian Monuments* by Otto Strauss, *Biblical Repertory* (1855), p. 127, notes that Xenophon led the retreat of the Greeks over the site of Nineveh less than 300 years after the words of Nahum had been spoken and hardly seems to have suspected that this great city ever had been there.

4. BDB, p. 365.

of the question would be, "What do you Ninevites (vainly) devise against Yahweh? Do you really think you can resist his power?"

The meaning of a similar phrase as it occurs two verses later is clear, but there other factors are present. The same verb *(ḥāšaḇ)* is used, but a different preposition *(ʿal)* connects the action to Yahweh. In addition, v. 11 specifically states that "evil" is the object of the "thinking" about Yahweh.

When this statement of v. 11 is compared to the question of v. 9, the differences tilt the decision in the direction of identifying the *you* of v. 9 with the inhabitants of Israel. Although a great variety of subjects, objects, and pronouns appears in the context, a certain consistency is maintained. In vv. 8 and 11, the city of Nineveh is represented by a feminine singular pronoun. In v. 10, the inhabitants of Nineveh are represented by "they," a third person masculine plural pronoun. This same people could be represented by a second person plural "you" in the immediately preceding verse (v. 9). But a reference to the inhabitants of Israel seems more appropriate, particularly in the light of the assurance offered to "those who seek shelter" in Yahweh as described in v. 7.

A further factor has to do with the change of prepositions between v. 9 and v. 11. "What do you think *concerning (ʾel)* Yahweh" (v. 9) compares to "He who thinks evil *against (ʿal)* Yahweh" (v. 11). While the preposition in v. 9 may mean "against" (cf. Gen. 4:8; 22:12; Exod. 14:5; Num. 32:14; etc.), its more predominant meaning is "about, concerning." Contrariwise, while the preposition of v. 11 may mean "about, concerning," it is frequently used "in a hostile sense . . . very often, after every kind of verb expressing or implying attack."[5]

As a consequence, the rhetorical question of v. 9 intends to stir up the faith of a downtrodden Israelite populace. "What do you think about Yahweh? Be assured that God will make a complete end of Assyria your oppressor." Israel needed this kind of statement to evoke their confidence. Yahweh whom they trusted would provide relief from their oppressor.

To reinforce the finality of the deliverance promised by the prophetic word of the Lord, Nahum adds: *Adversity shall not arise a second time* (v. 9c). Once this deliverance has been accomplished, the Assyrian shall be finished. A great message of hope indeed! Everyone is familiar—altogether too familiar—with those deliverances that last only a short time. But the prophet promises the end of this ceaseless round of troubles.

But of course, there are the Babylonians. The Assyrians may be wiped from the face of the earth, but demons seven times worse emerge in the form

---

5. BDB, p. 757.

of the Babylonian oppressors. This kind of problem in understanding prophetic promises necessitates an ultimate deliverance that shall break the
bonds of the OT teaching models. God's word is true, and all its fulness shall
be realized. But in the final analysis, this realization comes only on the occasion of the replacing of the old covenant forms with the new covenant
realities. So in the book of Revelation, Babylon appears as a figure of the last
great satanic force that opposes God and his people. This enemy, along with
Satan himself, shall be destroyed with utter finality. All tears shall be wiped
from the eyes of God's people, and they shall know oppression no more (cf.
Rev. 17–18).

10 The judgment of God shall come in a manner appropriate to the
stubbornness of the sinner. The phrase *as thorns twisted* figuratively describes the hardheaded, hard-hearted resistance characteristic of the Assyrian
to the authority of the one true living God. They have made taut their stubborn wills so that any and all approaches even from God will be met by prick-
ly resistance. *as (with) drink they are drunk* depicts the deadened stupor into
which they have sunk willingly.

This stubbornness is countered by the consuming fire of God's wrath:
they shall be consumed as stubble fully dried. Nothing burns more quickly
and with greater intensity than fully dried stubble. The tighter this tangle of
thorns, the more spontaneously it combusts. If the Assyrian abandons self-
control in drunkenness, then he has forfeited all control of self and shall be
turned into smoking vapors.

11 This stubborn rebellion against the will of God on the part of the
city of Nineveh has produced a leader, a prince who has turned passive resistance into active opposition. The feminine singular *you* refers to the city of
Nineveh, as did the "her" of v. 8 in this same section. The womb of wickedness which is Nineveh has produced a horrid monstrosity, a son of "Belial,"
as the text reads literally (here translated *he who schemes ruthlessly*).

The precise origin of this term *beliyaʿal* is difficult to determine. It
may have originated by the conjoining of two words: *belî,* meaning "without," and *yaʿal,* meaning "value" or "worth." A son of Belial would be a
"worthless one." The context in Scripture for the usage of the term points
consistently to a person who is depraved, despicable. A few examples may
serve to vivify its significance and to provide a framework for understanding
Nahum's use of the term.

The law code of Deuteronomy anticipates a situation in which "sons
of Belial" may lead astray the inhabitants of a city, luring them into the worship of another god (Deut. 13:14 [Eng. 13]). The use of the same phrase in
the book of Judges to describe the debased men who demanded the oppor-

tunity to abuse sexually the overnight guests of their neighbor probably intends to set the narrative in terms of the provisions of deuteronomic law about "sons of Belial" (cf. Judg. 19:22; 20:13). Other valid instances of the perverseness of the "sons of Belial" may be seen in Eli's sons, who were glutting themselves with the fattest portions of the sacrifices and fornicating with the women who served the tabernacle (1 Sam. 2:12ff.); in Nabal, the wealthy fool who refused to aid David (1 Sam. 15:17); in Sheba, the arrogant rebel who instigated a revolt against David (2 Sam. 20:1); in the two scoundrels who were bribed by Jezebel to testify falsely against Naboth (1 K. 21:10, 13); and in those who resisted the rule of Solomon's son when he was young and indecisive (2 Chr. 13:7). A climactic prophetic designation of a man to whom a "thing of Belial" clings is found in the Psalter. The psalmist describes the close friend in whom he had trusted, who had betrayed him by lifting up his heel against him (Ps. 41:9–10 [Eng. 8–9]; cf. Matt. 26:23).

Nahum alone of the prophets uses the term *b^{e}liya'al*, and he employs it twice (1:11; 2:1 [Eng. 1:15]). This "counselor of Belial" is evidently the king, the leader of this wicked people. He conspires against the Lord himself, and not merely against his nation. In terms of a specific individual, Nahum could be referring to Sennacherib, who is described elsewhere in Scripture as one who set himself not merely against Israel, but "against Yahweh" (2 K. 18:32b–35). But although Sennacherib at the time of his invasion of Palestine in 701 B.C. fits the bill of this "counselor of Belial" who has come forth out of Nineveh, the phrase is best understood as having a more general application. Not only Sennacherib, but all those wicked kings and leaders of the enemies of God's people who have come forth from Assyria manifest the characteristics of that brutal figure described by Nahum.

The term *b^{e}liya'al* at first had a broad application to designate men generally possessing a set of scoundrelish characteristics. Subsequently the term narrowed so that it became a designation of Satan himself, the archenemy of God. It is so used in the Testament of the Twelve Patriarchs, the Ascension of Isaiah, the book of Jubilees, and the Sibylline Oracles.[6] This intertestamental application of the term helps to explain its only appearance in the NT, found in 2 Cor. 6:15. As the middle member of a fivefold contrast, Paul sets "Christ" and "Belial" over against one another. Righteousness and wickedness have nothing to do with one another; light and darkness cannot fellowship; believer and unbeliever cannot merge; the temple of God and the temple of idols have no agreement with one another; and Christ and Belial represent rulers of two diametrically opposed kingdoms. Paul's contrast rep-

6. Maier, p. 200.

resents the climax of the conflict represented in Nahum. An ominous figure stands behind the ruler from Nineveh, prodding him on in his wicked determinations. But one stands against him, the divine counterpart to his position of power. It is "the Christ," the anointed king who rules for the Lord throughout the ages. These two persons and the kingdoms they represent remain in conflict with one another until their struggle is finally resolved.

So the judgment directed specifically against seventh-century Assyria represents a critical moment in the divine program for persevering in the redemption of his people. The Lord displays through the destruction of Assyria that the most powerful of nations cannot succeed in their opposition to the purposes of the Lord.

C. THE IMMINENT CHARACTER OF GOD'S JUDGMENT (1:12–14)

A theme repeatedly associated with God's judgment of the wicked in Scripture has to do with the imminence of that judgment. It is hopeless for the wicked to think that somehow eventually they may become fortified against the coming devastations. When everyone says "peace and safety," then sudden destruction will come on them. Nahum underscores this principle in the present section.

1. Judgment Now Despite Assyrian Strength (1:12a)

12a *Thus says Yahweh:*
> *Though they be complete*
> *and also numerous,*
> *yet they shall be mowed down*
> *and he shall pass over.*

For the first and only time Nahum employs the customary *Thus says Yahweh* that introduces a "word from the Lord." The intent of the phrase in this context is not to remove all doubt that this indeed is a word from God in contrast with Nahum's previous utterances. Instead, Nahum wishes to underscore the certainty of Nineveh's fall, all appearances to the contrary.

Imminence is underscored by the fact that judgment shall come even though the Assyrians *be complete and also numerous.* God will not wait until the enemy degenerates into a weakened state before initiating calamity. Even while they are undiminished in strength, full of arrogant self-confidence, God shall level them to the ground.

Israel knew firsthand the massive human resources which the Assyrian empire possessed. According to 2 K. 19:35, the casualties of Sennacherib totaled 185,000 after a single encounter with the Lord outside the gates of Jerusalem. Nineveh was known to be a great city, "of three days' journey" (Jon. 3:3). Yet this numerous populace would be *mowed down* like so many blades of grass. Once a mowing operation has begun, thousands of blades of grass disappear in an instant.

The abrupt switch from "*they* shall be mowed down" to "*he* shall pass over (away)" causes difficulty. Is it the king of Assyria who shall pass away? Or could it be that the singular form "is used with special emphasis, the numerous army being all embraced in the unity of one man"?[1] More likely God is *he,* the one who shall *pass over.* In the very way in which he "passed over" in the land of Egypt, so now again he through his agent the death angel shall smite Assyria. The next phrase supports this interpretation by its declaration of grace to God's people. Although he has *afflicted* them in the past (just as he had done in Egypt), he shall not do so again.

2. Judgment Now as Relief from Judah's Suffering (1:12b–13)

12b *Though I have afflicted you,*
    I will never afflict you again.
 13 *And now*
        a *I will break*
        b *his yoke from upon you,*
        b *and your bonds*
        a *I will burst.*

God never is insensitive to the sufferings of his people, although they may think he has forgotten them. The faith of the psalmist enabled him to acknowledge that it was good for him to be afflicted, because before he was afflicted he went astray (Ps. 119:67, 71). Even the length of time that God's people remain under trial is determined by the good purposes of God for them. But at the right time the Lord acts to deliver his people. God afflicts, and God relieves from affliction.

12b The categorical statement of Nahum that God *will never afflict you again* finds a challenge in the facts of history. For although Assyria was set aside once and for all, Babylon and its persecution of Judah soon followed.

It might be suggested that Nahum had reference to affliction only as

---

1. Keil, p. 15.

it would come at the hand of the Assyrian. But Nahum's message of comfort implies more. Possibly the prophet views Nineveh as a typical representation of Israel's archenemy, and her destruction as symbolic of God's final act of judgment. Whoever might prove to be the archenemy of God's people in the future generations could be sure from Nineveh's experience that God would destroy them and deliver his people. God remains vitally concerned for his people in all their afflictions. When the right time comes for their deliverance, he shall break them free from all oppression.

13 *And now* reinforces the imminence of God's judgment on Nineveh. Because in the mysterious counsels of God the time had come for his people to be delivered from affliction, the judgment of their oppressors had to occur at the present moment. This *now* would not necessarily imply judgment at the precise instant of Nahum's pronouncing the words. But more broadly in the general circumstance of the day, judgment was imminent.

I will break his yoke and the *your bonds I will burst* suggest relief from foreign domination. Rather than being deprived of the freedom to enjoy the fruit of their own hands and lands, Judah shall participate in all the bounties of God's grace. The heavy weight of slaving long hours with excessive burdens will give way to the glorious liberty of the children of God, each person living in freedom to pursue his own labors to the glory of God.

3. Judgment Now as the Lord Has Decreed (1:14)

14 *Yahweh has given command concerning you:*
None shall be sown
bearing your name again.
From the house of your gods[1]
I shall cut off graven and molten image;
I shall dig your grave;
for you have no significance.

The clinching indicator of the imminence of God's judgment on Assyria is found in the establishment of the divine decree. God has *given command.* Once that decree has gone forth, it cannot be recalled. Assyria may appear impregnable. But the publication of the divine decree seals their fate.

The masculine singular object *(you)* of this threefold judgment would appear to refer to the king of Assyria himself. Ashurbanipal (669–627 B.C.),

---

1. Rudolph, p. 159 n.14d, may be correct in proposing that the reference to the place of worship should be plural: "from the houses of your gods." He suggests that a pluralizing occurs because of the construct state. Cf. GKC, § 124r.

the last great king of Assyria, prays that the son who follows him would honor and preserve his name on the building inscriptions he had carved as his own memorial.[2] But the decree of God declares that no one shall survive to maintain his name. *None shall be sown,* apparently indicating that his descendants would perish.

Ashurbanipal warns in this same inscription that anyone who dares to remove his name shall be judged by Ashur, Sin, Shamash, Adad, Bel, Nabu, Ishtar of Nineveh, the queen of Kidmuri, Ishtar of Arbela, Urta, Nergal, and Nusku.[3] These most important deities of Assyria certainly should prove adequate to guarantee the perpetuity of the king of Assyria's name. But the one true living God, Yahweh of Israel, has determined something contrary. The Assyrian king's *name* shall not *be sown.* His descendants shall not carry on his tradition.

Furthermore, the *graven and molten image* of the gods of Assyria shall be *cut off.* Like the idols of Dagon who fell on their faces in humiliation before the ark of the Lord (1 Sam. 5:2–4), so the mighty gods of Assyria shall come to naught.

As a final blow to the royal ego, God declares to the king of Assyria, *I shall dig your grave.* The end of his illustrious career shall display the vanity of his power. As the terminal humiliation of a crowned head, his enemy shall bury him.[4] So shall it be with all that set themselves against the Lord and his people.

Why shall these repeated blows fall against the king of Assyria? Contrary to the modern emphasis on self-esteem, this Scripture declares that the king of Assyria has *no significance,* that he is worthless. Instead of being worthy of restoration, he is empty, hollow, trifling. His worthlessness before God assures the deliverance promised for Judah which shall be accomplished by his destruction.

So now the prophet Nahum has laid his life on the line. From two perspectives he has opened himself to the threat of death.

The powers that be would not be pleased with his message of the devastation of Assyria and its kings. A monarch is not generally happy over a subordinate who declares the curse of death on him. Subordinate officers in a puppet kingdom are generally more than happy to ingratiate themselves to their lord by eliminating any source of criticism that might arise. Nahum could well expect the worst.

2. D. D. Luckenbill, *Ancient Records of Assyria and Babylonia* (New York: Greenwood, 1927), 2:323, no. 838.
3. Ibid., no. 839.
4. Cf. Rudolph, p. 162.

In addition, Nahum has exposed himself to the possibility of death at the hands of his own people by venturing this bold prophecy. For the law of Moses had warned that the prophet who presumed to predict the future must die if his words should not come to pass (cf. Deut. 18:20–22). But now the public announcement has gone forth. That word of God which possesses in itself the power to enact what it decrees now has been unleashed upon the world. Even though spoken by the trembling lips of a mortal man, these words shake the sure foundations of empires.

Since God remains the same, the words of Nahum continue to have significance for all individuals, powers, and nations that oppress God's people and live in wickedness. God will by no means clear the guilty (Nah. 1:3). Through destroying the wicked, he will provide deliverance for his people.

II. DRAMATIC DEPICTION OF NINEVEH'S JUDGMENT (2:1–14 [ENG. 1:15–2:13])

Nahum had been called of God to stand against the powers that be. But he did not discharge his duty of prophetic proclamation in a perfunctory manner. Instead, he summoned the full force of his fertile imagination to communicate the fact that the mighty oppressor, still hovering over its cowed victims, would crumble into dust.

To vivify his message, the prophet plunges his reader into the midst of the struggle between Nineveh and its prophesied assailants. You chill at the shock of the first warning alert. You jar at the pulsating rumble of approaching war chariots. You panic in flight from the warriors who have broken through the city's last defenses. You watch through doleful eyes as the gleeful, sweaty victors sweep down to gather their spoils.

This divine judgment is flesh-and-blood reality. Far worse than the pain, the panic, and the havoc created by a marauding band of soldiers will be the punishments inflicted in the fury of God's wrath. Terrible to behold will be God's enforcement of the vengeance of the covenant.

Nahum has done all mankind a noble service through his vivid depiction of the outpouring of the wrath of God on the city of Nineveh. By this very concrete, physical portrayal of the event, he has come closest to that consummate description of divine judgment reserved for the lips of Our Lord alone (Matt. 13:40–42, 48–49). A world so accustomed to gratifying the desires of the flesh should take heed to this most vivid of warnings before it is too late!

The chapter naturally falls into three sections, following the progress of the siege and plundering of the city. The first verse of the chapter sets this lifelike description of conquest in the context of redemption for God's own people.

INTRODUCTION: THE ANNOUNCEMENT OF ACCOMPLISHED JUDGMENT MEANS JOYFUL NEWS FOR JUDAH (2:1 [ENG. 1:15])

2:1 (1:15) *Behold! On the mountains!*
> *The feet of*
>> *the one who brings glad tidings,*
>> *the one who publishes peace.*
> *Celebrate your festivals,*
>> *O Judah!*
> *Fulfill your vows!*

> *For never again will Belial*
>> *pass through you;*
> *he is altogether cut off.*

Look! Take note! The messenger who brings the word of salvation and deliverance has appeared! See him on the ridge of the nearby mountains? He has run a long distance bringing the glad tidings!

The *mountains* which provide the exalted platform for this herald of good news most probably are the mountains of Judah, for Judah is the one who is expected to respond by celebration. This messenger has witnessed the fall of Nineveh and rushes to proclaim the joyful word. No longer will Judah's oppressor torment them.

A focus on the *feet* of the messenger possibly alludes to the haste with which he bears the message. The public proclamation of *peace* must be taken in term of the full implications of the Hebraic *šālôm*. Good health and fulness of blessing in the whole of life is the implication of this peace.

This first phrase of the verse is essentially a verbatim quotation of Isa. 52:7, the only difference being that Isaiah reads "*How beautiful* are the feet . . ." rather than "*Behold* the feet. . . ." Perhaps Nahum's setting of a messenger rushing from the gore of battle restrained him from alluding to the "beauty" of these feet.[1]

---

1. Surprisingly, Rudolph, p. 163, denies a dependence of Nahum on Isaiah, or vice versa. Yet the phraseology is so strikingly similar that it is difficult to imagine the two prophets independently arriving at the same mode of expression.

Is it, after all, appropriate to take joy in the devastation of enemies? Can it be that the crushing defeat of Nineveh with all its greatness would be an appropriate cause for celebrating among the people of God? A sentimental blindness to the realities of history might stumble over this kind of academic question. But hear just a selection of the annals of Ashurnasirpal II, dating to the 9th century B.C. Note the items of accomplishment (showing some imagination) which this ruler of Nineveh felt worthy of being engraven in stone:

> I built a pillar over against his city-gate, and I flayed all the chief men who had revolted, and I covered the pillar with their skins; some I walled up within the pillar, and some upon the pillar on stakes I impaled, and others I fixed to stakes round about the pillar; many within the border of my own land I flayed, and I spread their skins upon the walls; and I cut off the limbs of the high officers, of the high royal officers who had rebelled. (lines 89ff.)
>
> Many captives from among them I burned with fire, and many I captured alive. From some I cut off their hands and their fingers, and from others I cut off their noses and their ears . . . and the eyes of many men I put out. I made one heap of the living, and another of the heads, and I bound their heads to vines round about the city. Their young men and maidens I burned in the fire. (lines 116ff.)[2]

These kinds of international atrocities the kings of Assyria had committed over the centuries. God had responded with amazing grace by commissioning Jonah to preach to this same great city. For a while repentance had characterized their response to the announcement of judgment. But by the time of Nahum, they had hardened their hearts against the pleas of God and man once more. No wonder, then, that God's people would be summoned by a vision sent from God to rejoice in the defeat of this recalcitrant enemy of humanity as well as of God.

Specifically by a quotation of these very words, the new covenant believer also is summoned to enter this celebration of salvation (Rom. 10:14–15). It is true that Paul uses Isaiah's *"How beautiful are* the feet . . ." rather than Nahum's *"Behold* the feet. . . ." But the substance of the quotation is the same, one prophet giving expression to the positive side of deliverance, and one emphasizing the negative side. This balance of perspectives is vital for a proper appreciation of the ministry of the prophets, since the salvation of God's people is announced regularly in association with the destruction of God's enemies.

2. As cited in Roux, *Ancient Iraq,* pp. 263–64.

A closer look at the NT usage of this announcement that summons to celebration makes it apparent that Paul intends to stress the significance of God's sending a messenger to bear this report: "How can they believe in the one of whom they have not heard? And how can they hear without someone preaching to them? And how can they preach unless they are sent? As it is written, 'How beautiful are the feet of those who bring good news!' " (Rom. 10:14–15). God's people are not charged with the responsibility of accomplishing their own deliverance. Instead, they are informed they must *believe* what has been reported to them as an act of God on their behalf.

Only if Israel should trust the hand of God's grace to deliver them from the chastening bondage which they themselves deserved might they expect the continuing freedom granted by the Lord. The dramatic, sudden deliverance from Assyria as a fulfillment of this gracious prophecy should convince the people that God's hand alone could be the source of their deliverance.

So this message of Nahum is a glorious one! Deliverance shall come from the oppressor of God's people by the sovereign intervention of God, even though the sin of God's people had brought them into their calamitous state. How glorious will be that coming deliverance.

Because of the broader redemptive-historical structures of Scripture, this deliverance from Assyria's oppression may be perceived as a microcosmic depiction of deliverance from all the oppression that comes as a consequence of sin, Satan, and death. In an OT context, this oppression finds its fullest manifestation in the empires that arise in opposition to the kingdom of God. Daniel's vision of the successive empires that ultimately crumble because of the force of the "stone made without hands" (Dan. 2) begins with Babylon. But Assyria, which historically was Babylon's immediate predecessor, fits within the same redemptive-historical pattern.

Some discussion has developed over the subject of how the message of Nahum relates to a new covenant context. This discussion gravitates naturally to these particular verses, with their reference to the *feet of the one who brings glad tidings.* Martin Luther's wrestling with this issue is reflected in his interpretation of this passage from Nahum in relation to Christ: "There is no other passage in this prophet which we can take as related to Christ except this one."[3]

More fulsome in his treatment of the place of Nahum's message in relation to the gospel of the new covenant is William Henry Green, one of

---

3. *Luther's Works,* ed. Hilton C. Oswald (St. Louis: Concordia, 1975), 18:295. Cf. further comments in Maier, p. 219 n. 2.

the older Princeton theologians. Green notes the connection of Nah. 2:1 (Eng. 1:15) with Isa. 52:7, where deliverance from the Babylonian captivity is more immediately connected with God's work of redemption for Israel. He calls attention to the distinctive methodology of the writers of Scripture, "by which terms and expressions primarily descriptive of the fall of one hostile power are applied interchangeably to that of others."[4] He concludes that Nahum applies Isaiah's precise words about deliverance from Babylon to Assyria's defeat as a way of "calling attention to the connection which really subsists between the two events, as in essence really one."[5] Green notes that Paul repeats this same language in Rom. 10:17, and so intimates "an innate oneness between the message which announced the fall of those great persecuting powers, and the erection of that Kingdom which was finally to supplant them."[6]

This broader perspective on the message of Nahum in relation to the ongoing redemptive-historical purposes of God provides a much broader framework for a transferral of the values of these words into an NT context. As Green summarizes: "Thus Nahum's predictions have a meaning for all time to come, so long as there remains aught in which the spirit of Nineveh survives—aught which has inherited its criminality and its hostility to God's people. The doom of Nineveh shall attach in substance, if not in form, to all its successors. Not until the last foe of God and of human salvation shall be finally destroyed, shall it in its full import be accomplished."[7]

The glorious announcement of Nineveh's fall and the consequent liberation of Judah leads the prophet to summon God's people to *celebration* and *consecration*. The admonition is addressed specifically to Judah as that portion of God's people living under the yoke of Assyrian oppression. Individually and as a nation they must observe a year-round pattern of celebration.

But this irruption of national holiday must not be perceived in a secularistic fashion. It is the *festivals* and *vows* ordained by divine direction that provide the structured framework for long-term jubilant living. Not like the meaningless mad-hatted horn-tooters' hailing of another midwinter's "Happy New Year" shall God's people celebrate. Instead, they shall respond

---

4. Green, review of *Nahum's Prophecy Concerning Nineveh Explained and Illustrated from Assyrian Monuments* by Otto Strauss, *Biblical Repertory* 27 (1955) 131.

5. Ibid.

6. Ibid., p. 132.

7. Ibid.

to redemption by renewed consecration to the Lord. This celebration shall have no hangovers or sober regrets.

Perhaps a certain element of duty is involved in the summons to celebration. It is an obligation of God's people to render a full round of thanksgiving for their rescue from misery.

In concrete terms, Israel's three annual festivals and their new covenant counterparts might be considered as the natural vehicles by which God's people may give expression to their continuing joy in salvation. The Passover meal, which finds its NT counterpart in the celebration of the Lord's Supper, reminds that the Death Angel has "passed over" because of the substitutionary blood of the Lamb. All the power of the ultimate enemy has been destroyed. The festival of Pentecost, which corresponds to the new covenant reality of the outpouring of the Holy Spirit, celebrates the newness and fulness of life freely given to the redeemed. The fruit of the Spirit in a person's daily experience provides continual cause for celebration.

The harvest festival of Booths reminds of the abundance of provision that God makes for his people, even as they continue along their pilgrim pathway. A plentiful harvest in a context of humble tent dwelling combines images that define the contrasting sides of current reality. If they will accept both these facts of redemptive life, God's people by faith shall be enabled to celebrate continually the goodness of the Lord despite numerous constraints.

From an old covenant perspective, *vows* might involve the covenantal commitments of the nation, or the voluntary vows made out of a sense of personal blessedness, obligation, or need. But once a vow had been taken, it had to be honored. Jacob vowed to pay a tithe to the Lord (Gen. 28:22), and Jephthah vowed to consecrate his daughter to the Lord's service (Judg. 11:30–31). Once those commitments had been made, it would have been sin to turn back. But because of a continuing awareness of deliverance from such massive oppressions as those inflicted by the Assyrians, the carrying out of these commitments should become a joyful way of life, rather than a burdensome duty to fulfill.

The ultimate reason for a celebration that can be sustained over the years is contained in the last phrase of the verse. Never again shall *Belial* pass through their land, for he is totally *cut off*. The tyrannical tool of Satan situated on Assyria's throne never shall be seen again. His overthrow is absolutely permanent.

No deliverance can be much of a cause for rejoicing if it has not this element of permanence. If Judah must expect the Assyrian dictator to return next year in the season "that kings go out to war" (2 Sam. 11:1), their celebration could hardly be very enthusiastic. But because of the permanence of this deliverance, they can rejoice without restraint.

The Christian gospel provides the fullest possible framework for permanent celebration of victory. Death has lost its sting. The believer has died to sin. The loss of all material possessions can be only temporary, and soon will be replaced with the permanence of the new heavens and the new earth. Celebration by keeping the vows of the Christian life is always in order.

A. THE CITY IS TAKEN (2:2–8 [ENG. 1–7])

The prophet continues with his unbroken message of the fall of Nineveh. But now he moves on to a detailed description of the siege of the city. If the reader is tempted to question the edifying value of such an imaginative depiction of the destruction of an ancient city, John Calvin has provided a ready answer: "Now this accumulation of words was by no means in vain; for it was necessary to confirm, by many words, the faith of the Israelites and of the Jews respecting the near approach of the destruction of the city Nineveh, which would have been otherwise incredible."[1]

It should be remembered that this detailed report of Nineveh's siege and fall was written some decades before the event itself took place. The form of the writing was just the kind of material which might have functioned well in stirring up the faith of an oppressed people.

1. Announcement of the Coming Siege (2:2–3 [Eng. 1–2])

2 (1)   *One who scatters has come up against you.*
      Guard the fortress!
      Watch the way!
      Strengthen your loins!
      Muster together all your might!
3 (2)   *For Yahweh has returned the eminence of Jacob*
         as the (ancient) eminence of Israel;
         for the emptiers (once) emptied them;
            evacuators evacuated,
         and they destroyed every one of their tender sprouts.

2 (1)   All through the previous decades the Assyrians had been the great dispersers of peoples and nations. Now suddenly they stand face to face with an adversary who intends to do with them as they have done with others. This

1. Calvin, pp. 463–64.

one who scatters could refer to God himself as Nineveh's adversary. But it is more likely that the reference is to a ruthless ruler who would match the Assyrian kings in their brutality.

The four rapid-fire imperatives *(Guard! Watch! Strengthen! Muster!)* challenge the Ninevites to be alert and throw all their strength into their defense. Satan's method may be to subvert by striking at the heel. But the seed of the woman, raised up by God, strikes the deathblow at the head.

The reason for this divinely engineered devastation is found in Assyria's previous devastation of Israel. Nineveh had *emptied* or *evacuated* Israel of every remnant of glory.[1] They had left nothing, not a *tender sprout* that might have signaled the possible return of glory for God's people. So Nineveh shall experience a similar fate. Divine retribution, repaying with perfect justice, shall fall on the brutal inhabitants of Nineveh.

3 (2)   In the case of his own people, the Lord does the impossible. The eminence that once belonged to Israel in the hour of highest glory shall return in all its fulness. The contrast between the *eminence* or glory of *Jacob* and that of *Israel* is not a contrast between the relative majesty of the northern and southern kingdoms. Instead, the contrast is between the time of Israel's glory under the united monarchy and the time of the nation's humiliation as it passed through God's judgments, leaving Judah alone intact. Nahum envisions a day in which the same kind of transformation worked in the patriarch Jacob shall characterize the nation as a whole. The devious, Jacobean side of the people led to their devastation. But they shall experience fulness of restoration, and shall revel in the kingdom's being raised again to all its glory.

2. Approach of the Assaulters (2:4–5 [Eng. 3–4])

4 (3) a *The shields of his mighty men*
   b *(are) red;*
  a *men of strength*
   b *(are) scarlet-clad.*

  a *Flashing with metal*
   b *(is) the chariot*
    c *in his day of readiness;*
  a *they brandish*
   b *cypress spears.*

---

1. The Hebrew word meaning "to empty" *(bāqaq)* may reflect by its pronunciation the meaning of the term. The enunciation of the related noun *(baqbuq,* "flask") approximates the gurgling sound made by a vessel being emptied. Cf. BDB, p. 132.

5(4) *a* *In the streets*
     b *the chariots race madly;*
     b *they rush*
   a *in the broad places.*

   a *Their appearance*[1]
     b *(is) like torches;*
     b *like lightning*
   a *they run about.*

"Total domination of the terrain" may be a phrase that captures the impact of this description of the approach of Nineveh's assaulters. They do not draw near the city as a disorganized mass incapable of coordination. Instead, they display total utilization of the most modern, most sophisticated strategies of warfare.

4 (3) The reference to the *red shields* may be interpreted in a variety of ways. They could be reddened by the blood of victims of past conflicts, or by the reflection of the sun on a copper shield, or by the use of a decorative dye. But the context of determined assault by a most powerful adversary suggests that this redness comes from the blood of the resistance offered by Nineveh. The fact that the assaulting army has not yet broken into the city proper would not preclude preliminary skirmishes as the territory about the city came into dispute. In any case, these reddened shields serve as awesome forebodings of the sentence now to be executed on all Nineveh's inhabitants.

A brighter red, a flaming *scarlet* characterizes the uniforms of these *mighty men.* Their brilliance of dress proclaims an emboldened confidence that no power can stand before them.

Fuller concentration is placed on the fearsome *chariot* of the invader. *Flashing with metal*[2] possibly refers to a covering of metal, which would make the chariot almost impenetrable. These awesome vehicles are manned by soldiers bearing *cypress spears,* whose length, strength, and suppleness made them almost impossible to repulse.

his day of readiness refers to God's day. His longsuffering with the

---

1. The feminine plural suffix "their" is particularly problematic, since it almost certainly refers to the "chariot(s)," a term which elsewhere is masculine (as in the next phrase: "*they* [masculine plural] run about"). Possibly the suffix may be taken as though it were neuter, and might refer to the chariots and everything on them (Keil, p. 21). Maier, p. 245, notes that "chariot" is collective, and that many collectives are regarded as abstracts and thus feminines.

2. Literally, "in fire of metal." The phrase might refer to decorative or protective metal plating as it flashed in the sunlight. For the numerous other proposals concerning this phrase, most of them involving textual emendation, see Maier, p. 240.

brutality of the Ninevites has come to an end. Now he has readied his instrument of vengeance so that they are armed to the teeth. Nothing shall deter their assault.

5 (4) But where is it that these vehicles of devastation are rushing about like flashes of lightning? The breach of the wall has not yet occurred, so they are not careening about inside the city. Most likely the imagery intends to depict the intermediate step of the approach of the assault force. Having been dreaded at a distance when the approaching hoard's brilliant uniforms first came into view, they can now be observed more closely. They have laid claim to all the territory immediately outside the city walls. Suburban roadways and intersections crisscrossing on the way to the various gates of the city are fully under occupation now. The last resistance has retreated behind the safety of the city's walls, and the fearful chariotry of the enemy rushes about securing every possible escape route.

So all the enemies of God may be considered as enclosed to await the judgment of the great Day. No escape from the sword of the vengeance of the covenant is possible.

3. Resistance of the Inhabitants (2:6 [Eng. 5])

6 (5) *He remembers*
>   *his noble ones!*
> *They stumble*
>   *in their going;*
> *they hasten*
>   *to her wall;*
>   *but the (siege) covering*
>   *is prepared.*

Up to this point, the description has concentrated on the approaching adversary. But now an image of the panicked Ninevites is provided in a quick flash. The king of the city (*he* who *remembers his noble ones*) calls for his brave defenders, charging them to confront the foe.[1] With a double stroke of irony, Nahum depicts this mighty monarch who stares blankly at the progressing assault on his city and suddenly *remembers* he has these fine, *noble* soldiers to defend him.[2]

---

1. Rudolph, pp. 167–68, notes that the subject of v. 6 cannot be the aggressor of vv. 4–5, since the image of v. 6 is one of troops who arrive too late. He concludes that the subject of v. 6 is the king of Assyria.
2. Ibid.

But the defenders are hardly adequate to the challenge. *They stumble* to their places of defense at the wall of the city. Then they discover that they are too late to repel those erecting the siege equipment. Already the *(siege) covering* is in place, and the incessant pounding of the walls of the city begins.

How shall people protect themselves against the Almighty when he rises up against them? Even his temporal judgments are irresistible. A bow drawn at a venture in the heat of battle invariably finds its target when divine providence sets the aim (see 1 K. 22:34). How much more sure is the fact that God has appointed a Day in which he shall judge people by Jesus Christ the resurrected One? No one shall escape the divine scrutiny associated with that Day.

4. Entry Is Gained (2:7 [Eng. 6])

7 (6) *a The gates of the rivers*
        b are opened,
     a and the temple
        b is melted.

The gates of the rivers are opened has been variously interpreted. It could refer to access easily gained through the defenses of the city that naturally would be the most difficult to assault. If this interpretation is correct, then those particular gates opening to the moat about portions of the city somehow would become the very route by which this invading army would breach the wall. The point of strongest defense would become the place of greatest weakness.

More likely the *gates of the rivers* refer to the sluices which first would have been closed by the invaders and then opened so as to flood the wall of the city, breaking it through. This interpretation corresponds essentially with the testimony of Diodorus Siculus, an ancient Greek historian, who indicates that in the fall of Nineveh a series of heavy rains swelled the Euphrates (an error for Tigris), flooded parts of the city, and overthrew the wall for a length of about two miles (twenty stadia).[1]

This analysis of the events associated with Nineveh's fall also coincides with the next statement that *the temple is melted.* Even though this expression apparently must be taken figuratively because of the impossibility of flooding the palace area of Nineveh, the language would be appropriate as an allusion to a flooding episode.

---

1. Diodorus Siculus, *Bibliotheca Historica,* 2.26. Cf. Cathcart, *Nahum,* p. 96; Laetsch, pp. 298–99.

Concentration by Nahum on the fall of the temple or palace of the city is fitting. Those brutal Assyrian monarchs who had dominated so many human lives for hundreds of years would have no more place of residence on the face of the earth.

5. The City Falls (2:8 [Eng. 7])

8 (7) *It is settled!*
   She is stripped!
   She is carried away!
   And her handmaids—
      moaning as the voice of doves,
      smiting on their breasts.

Not a few versions and commentators have proposed that the first phrase of this verse is to be taken as referring by name to "Huzzab," a queen of Nineveh.[1] But the context in no way prepares for the mention of an otherwise unknown Assyrian queen.

The first word of the verse *(huṣṣaḇ)* is a passive perfect form from a root meaning "set," "establish," or "determine." The destruction of Nineveh is *settled* by the Almighty, and so can be announced with the imaginative gusto displayed by this appointed prophet. So it is. And so it shall ever be with all God's enemies.

Now stripped and carried away into exile by an international policy which Assyria itself made famous, nothing is left of the hustle and bustle of the once-great city. Nothing, that is, except the *moaning* of a small remnant of her female servants. As an expression of deepest agony and heartfelt emotion, they *smite on their breasts* at the hopelessness of their once glorious habitation.

So this great conglomerate of corruption comes to its appointed end. God's people had suffered much at the hands of the kingdom of Assyria because of their own sin. But finally the messenger of the Lord is released to tell the good news. The destruction of the wicked city is so certain that the prophet may use all the powers of his descriptive imagination to depict the certainty of the city's fall.

---

1. Rudolph, p. 168, has called the first words of this verse "eine crux interpretum erster Klasse." Maier, pp. 259–61, lists twelve different options for understanding the first term. The simplest solution is to take the word as being derived from the root *nṣb.* Maier objects to the RV translation "it is decreed"; and yet he cites Deut. 32:8 and Ps. 74:17 where the same word seems clearly to mean "to set, to decree."

C. THE CITY IS PLUNDERED (2:9–11 [ENG. 8–10])

9 (8) *Nineveh (has been) as a pool of water*
 from her (ancient) days.
Yet they are fleeing!
 "Stand! Stand!"
 But none even turns to look.
10 (9) *a Plunder*
 b   the silver!
a Plunder
 b   the gold!
 For there is no end
 of the treasure,
 rich
 with every vessel of desire.
11 (10) *Destruction, devastation, decimation!*
 a And the heart
 b   melts;
 b   totter
 a   the knees.

 a Convulsion
 b   in all the loins;
 b   and all their faces
 a have gathered paleness.

The prophet continues his vivid depiction of the coming destruction of
Nineveh. The besiegers have been seen from afar. They have advanced to the
wall, where the terrified inhabitants have mustered a pitiful resistance. The
wall has been broken through, and the city has been claimed.

 Now the scene moves into the confines of the city itself. Every inhabitant, wide-eyed with terror, ashen-faced with anxiety, flees for his life.
The assaulters bury themselves in the gold and silver of their spoils. The
wealthiest of all the cities of the world is quickly left empty, void, and waste,
with all its greatness decimated.

 9 (8) The comparison of Nineveh to a *pool of water* may be interpreted in a variety of ways.[1] The imagery could suggest a flourishing pool,

---

 1. For a discussion of the problems associated with this verse, see Carl E.
Armerding, "Nahum," *The Expositor's Bible Commentary* (Grand Rapids: Zonder-
van, 1985), 7:477–78. Despite his objection to the obscurity of the MT, it appears to
provide the best alternative.

a leaking pool, or a flooding pool. The rather unusual phrase, *from her (ancient) days,* suggests a recalling of the city's former glory.

A proposed emendation of this phrase on the basis of a supposed dittography results in a rather inane statement: "Nineveh is a pool from her waters."[2] The suggestion that the pronoun "she" or "her" *(hî')* should be read as a rare noun meaning "lamentation" *(hî)* as in Ezek. 2:10 appears to be a rather strained grasping for meaning.[3]

The imagery of an ancient flourishing pool fits well the circumstance of the city of Nineveh. Throughout the ages it had made full use of its natural habitat, which makes its disappearance from the face of the earth even more remarkable.

Now that the wall has been broken through, the inhabitants panic. Those who had made a career of gleefully pursuing others suddenly discover the terrors of being hunted down themselves. *Stand!* Wait! someone shouts after them. But they dare not lose even the split second it might cost them to cast a glance over their shoulder.

The rout is total. Justice prevails. Those who had made themselves wealthy by terrifying others now find themselves impoverished and in terror.

10 (9)   The kings of Assyria boasted repeatedly in their annals of the massive treasures they had collected in their robbing of other nations. For two hundred years, from the time of Ashurnasirpal II (884–824 B.C.) to the time of Sennacherib (705–681 B.C.), the stone-engraven inventories of treasures taken from all the nations continue endlessly. Not only through the spoils confiscated at the time a new nation was conquered, but through annual tributes the wealth of Nineveh increased beyond all measurable proportions.[4] Carved in stone, the annals of Assyria's sovereigns mention:

> chariots supplied with the equipment for men and horses;
> numerous talents of silver, gold, lead, copper, iron;
> brightly colored garments of every fabric;
> golden bowls, golden beakers, golden goblets, golden pitchers;
> camels, oxen, elephants, monkeys, apes;
> ivory couches inlaid and bejeweled;
> elephants' hides, lambs, birds, horses, mules, cattle, sheep, camels.

2. Cf. Maier, p. 265. Rudolph, p. 169, proposes the emendation *mimmennâ,* (a pool) "from which" the water escapes.

3. Contra Maier, p. 266.

4. See Maier, pp. 267–70, for a sampling of the booty lists of the various kings of Assyria.

The mention of every *vessel of desire* anticipates subsequent prophetic reference to the day in which the "desire of all nations" would flow to the Lord himself (Hag. 2:7). The treasures of the world may change hands from conqueror to conqueror. But ultimately they all shall flow to him alone. All the glory of all the wealth of all the nations shall be consecrated to him.

11 (10) The play on words is obvious in the original language, and effectively conveys the pounding rhythm of devastation accomplished by the invasion. The first two words are noun forms of *bûq* or *bāqaq*, meaning "to empty out." The third word is a noun formed from the Pual participle of *bālaq*, meaning "to destroy." Each successive word is slightly longer than the former, so that a rhythmic buildup reinforces the message. The first two terms occur only here in the OT, and the third appears elsewhere only in Isa. 24:1, where it is connected again with the verb *bāqaq*.

The human reaction to all this devastation is predictable. In spirit and in body, the fearsomeness of the events paralyzes the Ninevites. The *heart melts, knees totter,* and the *loins convulse.* Calvin has summarized well the effect of the crumbling of Assyria's defenses: "There is in men no courage, except as far as God supplies them with vigour. As soon then as He withdraws His Spirit, those who were before the most valiant become faint-hearted, and those who breathed great ferocity are made soft and effeminate."[5]

The last phrase of this verse is especially difficult. Obviously the intent is to describe the effect of terror on the faces of the Ninevites. The *heart,* the *knees,* and the *loins* all have been described in terms familiar to mankind's common experience. Hearts *melt,* knees *totter,* loins *convulse.*

And *faces* . . . well, they *have gathered* something. But what is it that they *have gathered?* The phrase occurs in virtually identical form in Joel 2:6, and the context is similar. But the meaning remains obscure. The significance of the radicals *(p'r)* relates to the idea of "beauty" or "glory." But obviously the faces in this context do not become radiant with "glory." Probably the idea is that the faces become "pale," luminescently colorless with fright. Their absence of coloring presents an image of radiating paleness. This pallid look does not belong to the natural shading of the human face, but has been *gathered* or developed as a consequence of viewing the devastated environment about them.[6]

---

5. Calvin, p. 471.
6. The suggestion that the phrase means "gather blackness" on the basis of a reference to a pot *(pārûr)* that has been "blackened" stretches the imagination a bit. Cf. Laetsch, p. 305; Maier, pp. 275–76.

In any case, the picture pulsates with the reality of the situation. Terror reigns on every side. They who for generations have made a way of life out of striking fear in the hearts of others now know firsthand the horrors of divine judgment.

D. THE CITY IS HUMBLED (2:12–14 [ENG. 11–13])

1. A Mockery Song of the City (2:12 [Eng. 11])

12 (11)   *O where now (is)*
  a   the lair
   b   of the lions,
  a   and that which was the feeding place
   b   of the young lions?
  a   That place where
   b   the lion and the lioness strode—
   b   the lion's whelp
    c   and none could make afraid?

Having completed this vivid depiction of the siege and fall of Nineveh, the prophet now mocks the hollow strength of the city (v. 12 [Eng. 11]), recalls the brutal rapacity which has sealed its fate (v. 13 [Eng. 12]), and lets the Lord himself speak the final word of doom (v. 14 [Eng. 13]). All of this material is presented under the imagery of a lair of ferocious lions.

The lion's den obviously is the unifying imagery of the verse. The pronouns (*hû'* and *'ašer*), as well as the adverb *(šām)* all refer back to the *lair of the lions*. Nineveh once had been the inviolable sanctuary of conquering kings, proud queens, and offspring of nobility.

But the honors associated with past nobility are no more. The sting of the mockery song cannot be missed. *Where now* is this once-great place, this sanctuary of kings? Its place is no more.

Extremely appropriate is the imagery of a den of lions for the royalty of Nineveh. The royally commissioned reliefs carved in stone depict repeatedly a number of lions. The kings of Nineveh often presented themselves in their annals in terms reflecting the behavior of the lion.[1] In addi-

---

1. Both Adadnirari II and Ashurnasirpal declare: "I am lion-brave." Sennacherib says: "Like a lion I raged." For the text, see D. D. Luckenbill, *Ancient Records of Assyria and Babylonia* (New York: Greenwood, 1927), 1:110, no. 358; 1:140, no. 438; 2:126, no. 253.

tion, the Assyrians' cruel tearing of their enemies suits well the crushing assaults advanced by lions.

The prophet employs a variety of terms for different kinds of lions: the full-grown male lion (ʾaryēh), the Asiatic lion or possibly lioness (lāḇîʾ), the young lion large enough to seek his own prey (kᵉpîr), and the lion's whelp (gûr ʾaryēh).[2] The whole species manifests the same kind of brute force in the devouring of its prey. Kings, queens, and princes of Nineveh manifest these beastly traits.

Even a ferocious beast like a lion treasures its moments of calm and safety. It too likes to relax in its den, to stride about oblivious to dangers. But now his lair has been cleared out, and the lion has no place where he can relax safely. The particular phrase *and none could make afraid* is used frequently to summarize the blessings of the covenant which God made with his people (cf. Lev. 26:6; Deut. 28:26; Mic. 4:4). God, who alone brings judgment for sin, has the capability of restoring peace among man and beast.

But such a blessing never again can be Nineveh's possession. The mocking *Oh where now . . .* indicates the end of an era.

2. The Brutality of the City (2:13 [Eng. 12])

13 (12) *The lion*

        a was tearing enough
         b for his whelps,
        a and was strangling
         b for his lionesses.
        So he filled
             a with shreds
              b his caves,
              b and his lairs
             a with strips.

Two elements of the lion's behavior stand out in this verse: the brutality of his predatory ways and his instinct to provide for his clan. Without concern for the feelings of his victims, the lion strips and shreds and tears flesh from his prey, whether living or dead. Totally oblivious to the shrieks of agony coming from its victim, the predator plunges his bloody muzzle again and again into the warm and cringing flesh. Having satisfied his immediate cravings, the beast drags the carcass to his lair where all his bloodthirsty brood may join in the feast.

2. Note the discussion in *TDOT*, 1:374–77; cf. BDB, pp. 71, 158, 498, 522.

Human sensitivities recoil at the sight of such brutality among the beasts of the forest. But what is to be said when the same kind of behavior characterizes man made in the image of God? How could a human being, made to reflect the compassion of the Creator, sink to such levels of bestiality? Yet it is not merely a dramatic figure of speech that the prophet employs in his depiction of the Assyrian monarchs as stalking, prey-hungry lions. The kings of Nineveh themselves chose to memorialize their greatest feats in terms fitting only of the wild beasts of the earth: "They suspended their corpses from poles, tore their skin off, and affixed it to the city walls. . . . I let dogs, swine, wolves, vultures, the birds of the heavens, and the sweet-water fish devour their cut-off limbs. . . . The people who lived in the city and had not come out and had not acknowledged my rule, I slew. I chopped off their heads and cut off their lips. . . . I bored through his jaw with my cutting dagger (?), pulled a rope through his cheek and the sides of his face (?), and attached a dog chain to him, and let him guard the cage at the east gate of Nineveh."[1]

These samples of brutality, taken from the annals of only one of the kings of Nineveh, could be multiplied easily. Torture and inhumanity of the worst sort were a major characteristic of royal life. For two hundred years they ravaged the various peoples of the ancient Near East, just as lions prowl daily for their prey.

But Nineveh has one adversary that it cannot so easily manhandle. One more mighty than all the kings of the earth has set himself against this ungodly community. He shall bring this tyrant down to the lowest place on the earth.

3. The Lord Speaks Against the City (2:14 [Eng. 13])

14 (13)   *"Behold Me! I am against you!"*
> *is the pronouncement of Yahweh of hosts.*

a   *"So I will burn up*
   b   *in smoke*
      c   *her chariots.*
a   *So the sword shall devour*
      c   *your young lions.*
a   *So I will cut off*
   b   *from the earth*
      c   *your prey;*
         and never shall be heard again
         the voice of your messengers."

---

1. Selections from the annals of Ashurbanipal, as cited in Maier, p. 282. Cf. *ANET*, pp. 295, 298, 300.

God himself stands against the tyrant. The full weight of this divine antipathy must be appreciated: *I am against you.* Up to this point, the prophet has served as spokesman for the Lord. But now the Lord himself steps forward to reinforce his own determination. The Lord's word comes as the voice of a committed aggressor.

The outcome of this confrontation between Yahweh of hosts and the king of Nineveh already is determined by the simple allusion to the fact that Yahweh stands at the head of the heavenly *hosts.* A single representative of his mighty servants could utterly devastate all the armies and chariots that the king of Assyria might muster. But the Almighty stands so appalled at the atrocities committed by the kings of Nineveh that he declares that he himself shall war against them.

The mixture of images that speak of the *burning* of *chariots,* the *devouring* of the *young lions,* and the *cutting off* of the *prey* is altogether appropriate. The *young lions* would represent the princes of the militant hosts of Assyria, and would tie in with the extended imagery of the previous verses. The destruction of Assyria's chariotry represents the wiping away of those instruments of oppression by which they have tormented the nations.

The silencing of the *voice* of Nineveh's *messengers* echoes the opening statement of this chapter. The messengers of peace declare on the mountains the word of the destruction of Judah's oppressor (Nah. 2:1–2 [Eng. 1:15–2:1]). These bearers of glad tidings have replaced altogether the emissaries of Assyria that had tormented Israel with their arrogant words of defiance.

Remember how Rabshakeh, sent by Sennacherib, mocked Jerusalem with his taunts in the days of Hezekiah (cf. 2 K. 18:17ff.)? Never again shall these messengers speak their oppressive, boastful words. Instead, the beautiful feet of the messengers sent from God shall declare peace, prosperity, and safety for the Lord's people. All of these blessings shall come in conjunction with the destruction of God's enemies.

The final declaration in Scripture announcing Babylon's consummate judgment may apply equally to Nineveh and all the oppressive power it represents:

> Give back to her as she has given;
>   pay her back double for what she has done.
> Mix her a double portion from her own cup.
> Give her as much torture and grief
>   as the glory and luxury she gave herself.
> In her heart she boasts,
>   "I sit as queen; I am not a widow, and I will never mourn."

Therefore in one day her plagues will overtake her:
    death, mourning and famine.
She will be consumed by fire,
    for mighty is the Lord God who judges her. (Rev. 18:6–8)

III. THE SURETY OF NINEVEH'S JUDGMENT (3:1–19)

For his final word, the prophet Nahum underscores the surety of the judgment he has pronounced. A rhetorical question enforces the certainty of what is to come in each of the three major sections of the chapter:

"From whom will I seek comforters for you?" (v. 7)
"Are you better than No-Amon?" (v. 8)
"On whom has not your wickedness passed continually?" (v. 19)

By adopting this distinctive form, the prophet requires the Ninevites themselves to interact with the surety of their coming judgment. Rather than merely asserting one more time the inevitability of Nineveh's fate, the word of God now demands that they respond to their threatening circumstance.

The surety of Nineveh's judgment is established on three bases: because of their sin (3:1–7); just as No-Amon (3:8–13); despite their strength (3:14–19).

A. SURE BECAUSE OF THEIR SIN (3:1–7)

Similar to the previous chapter, this section contains a vivid imaginative depiction of the assault of Nineveh (vv. 2–3). But going beyond ch. 2, it also rehearses the sins of the city—sins that seal the certainty of this coming destruction (vv. 1, 4). The Lord's expressed determination to bring vengeance on the city places the matter of Nineveh's fate beyond any mere human prognostications (vv. 5–7).

In this section consider first the sins of the city (vv. 1, 4), then the assault of the city (vv. 2, 3).

1. The Sins of the City (3:1, 4)

1 *Ahh! Bloodthirsty city!*
    a   The whole thing
        b   (lives) a lie;
        b   profiteering

99

a   is incessant.
     Victimizing will never be eliminated.
. . . .

4 *Because of the repeated acts*
    of the whoredoms of the whore—
      "Charming madame—"
      Mistress of witchcrafts!
      a   who barters
        b   over nations
          c   by her whoredoms,
        b   over families
          c   by her witchcrafts.

Shedding blood, lying, profiteering, and victimizing constitute the first list of specifications against the city of Nineveh. In the case of each of these sins, repeated persistence in the violation is emphasized. It is not merely that the city has slipped occasionally into these abuses. Instead, the poisonous vapors diffusing from every heart pollute the total atmosphere of the community.

1 The exclamation *Ahh! (hôy)* does not precisely communicate a curse, a woe. Instead, it gives expression to an agony, a pain at an offense being witnessed. It hurts to watch people being slowly crushed by a system calculated to squeeze the last breath from the defenseless.

The *bloodthirsty city* (lit., "city of bloods") aptly describes the life-style of a metropolitan community devoted to the glory of man rather than to the glory of God. E. B. Pusey appropriately recalls the contrast found in Augustine's *City of God:* "Two sorts of love have made two sorts of cities; the earthly love of self even to contempt of God; the heavenly love of God even to contempt of self. The one glorieth in itself, the other in the Lord."[1]

The first mention of a city in the Bible notes that Cain named his settlement after his son (Gen. 4:17). That seemingly simple act actually represented a consecration of his handiwork to man rather than to God, a dedication of man's highest cultural and communal efforts to the sinful egocentric self. Other early civilizations in Scripture include Nimrod's Nineveh (Gen. 10:11–12) and the city of Babel (11:4). The avowed intent of the designers of the latter was to resist with all their might the will of God that man should scatter over the face of the earth (1:28; cf. 11:4).

In the light of the rebelliousness associated with man's earliest cities, the blessing of Israel in term of their inheritance of cities that they themselves had not built takes on even greater significance. The awful product of man's

1. Pusey, 2:148.

machinations is redeemable after all. Ultimately Jerusalem the holy city stands in contrast with the *bloodthirsty city* of a depraved humanity.

The plural form ("city of bloods") suggests the multiple violence associated with the shedding of innocent blood. The voice of Abel's "bloods" cried out for vengeance (Gen. 4:10). Ezekiel speaks of the "city of bloods" in his day (Ezek. 22:3).

Bloodthirsty indeed was the ancient city of Nineveh. On one of the sculptured reliefs found in Ashurbanipal's palace is a scene featuring the king and queen celebrating victory over the Elamites. Depicted near the banqueting table is a fruit tree with the severed head of the king of Elam dangling from one of the branches.[2] Bloodthirsty indeed. Let all generations remember the atmosphere for banqueting created by this specter situated about the table of the Assyrians. Carved in stone by their own hands and so representing how they themselves chose to be remembered—so be it.

This bloodthirsty mind-set displays itself by never-ending *lying, profiteering,* and *victimizing.* No sin can exist by itself. Always the viper's nest in the sinner's heart is named "legion."

Because Satan is the father of lies, his offspring cannot help but lie. But Nineveh has carried the matter of lying to the extreme limit. *The whole thing (lives) a lie.* Every time each citizen opens his mouth, beneath his most convincing, straightforward statement is a twist, a hidden intent, a conscious ambiguity. In order to flatter, to cover up, to detract from actual intent, the citizen of Assyria dissimulates, equivocates, veils the true purpose of his heart by the cautious form of the words he utters. By the prearranged pointing of the foot, by the wink of the eye, he and his secret accomplices victimize even the most cautious.

The term used for the *lie (kaḥaš)* derives from a root which also can mean "fail" or "grow lean."[3] The fact that the product of the olive tree has "failed" (Hab. 3:17) suggests that the expectation created by full foliage is sadly disappointed when an examination is made for fruit. So the city of Nineveh promises prosperity and every advantage to those who will barter with it. But beware! "All of it is a lie," as the text reads literally.

The phrase recalls the honey-coated words of Rabshakeh, emissary

---

2. Laetsch, pp. 307–8. For a selection of the self-inscribed record of Assyria's brutalities, see Maier, pp. 291–92. Fiendish activities such as gouging out eyes, cutting off noses, and gradually removing the skin of a living man's body are all too common. "With their blood I dyed the mountain red like wool" represents a proud boast of this heathen, bloodthirsty monarchy.

3. BDB, p. 471.

of Sennacherib, as he insists on speaking Hebrew before the populace rather than negotiating honorably with the appointed representatives of King Hezekiah. He uses every guise to turn the people against Hezekiah: "Do not listen to Hezekiah. This is what the king of Assyria says: Make peace with me and come out to me. Then every one of you will eat from his own vine and fig tree and drink water from his own cistern, until I come and take you to a land like your own, a land of grain and new wine, a land of bread and vineyards, a land of olive trees and honey. Choose life and not death!" (2 K. 18:31–32).

Ahaz of Judah had the same experience when he petitioned Tiglath-pileser III of Assyria to aid him in resisting the Syro-Ephraimite coalition. According to the Chronicler, "Tiglath-pileser king of Assyria came to him, but he gave him trouble instead of help" (2 Chr. 28:20).

Profiteering and *victimizing* also are a steady trait of the Assyrian. Both terms suggest a forced ripping of person or possessions *(pereq* and *ṭerep)*. Like a wild beast shredding its prey, so the Assyrian devours his defenseless victim.

4 The prophet becomes bluntly abusive in his language. Nineveh is a "whore of the whores." With the poisoned dart of satire, Nahum mocks this *charming madame* who actually is a devilish *mistress of witchcrafts.* No modern diplomat would address a rival political entity as a "whore of whores." The modern reader might regard this coarse way of speaking as an interesting curio of a less sophisticated culture of bygone days.

Yet there is more than mere cultural crudeness behind these blunt words. As Calvin aptly says: "it is necessary that those who are too self-indulgent and delicate should be roughly handled."[4] People of authority such as ministers or other dignitaries tend to mask their grossest behavior by a pretended air of astonishment that anyone should dare to question their morality.

By coarse, insulting language the Holy Spirit through the prophet tears away these pretenses and lays bare the moral degradation of the inner recesses of the heart. "Look at the soul of this harlot," says Nahum. Dressed in the finery of love, this common street-whore gratifies her own lust for manipulation, then wipes her mouth and says, "I have done nothing wrong."

What makes Nineveh as well as all others like her so lethal is that outwardly she appears as a *charming madam (ṭôḇaṭ ḥēn,* lit., "fair of grace"). As the bathing Bathsheba appeared "exceptionally beautiful to look upon" (2 Sam. 11:2: *ṭôḇaṭ marʾeh mᵉʾôḏ),* so that David was ready to throw away

4. Calvin, pp. 483–84.

everything of worth in terms of position and potential for service to God, in the same manner the admirers of Nineveh were enchanted by the shapely beauty and endless charm of the city's treasure store of pleasures.

But the city was actually like a lovely wife bedecked in all the extravagant gifts of her husband, while using them to allure others into repeated acts of degrading immorality. Behind all the external charm, she is a *mistress of witchcrafts,* casting an evil spell over each of her successive victims. She uses her bodily endowments to allure her victims, and then destroys them.[5] By appealing to the sinful heart to get intimate and hold back nothing, she encourages the lustful man to cast off all restraint. So the sinner quickly is absorbed in his own passionate desires for sensual pleasure. Like Esau, he sells his soul for a bowl of porridge that stimulates the senses.

Although Babylon rather than Nineveh is the subject of the Bible's final exposé of the sensual human heart, the description of its destruction no less fits the point of Nahum's condemnation: "The merchants of the earth will weep and mourn over her because no one buys their cargoes any more—cargoes of gold, silver, precious stones and pearls; fine linen, purple, silk and scarlet cloth; every sort of citron wood, and articles of every kind made of ivory, costly wood, bronze, iron and marble; cargoes of cinnamon and spice, of incense, myrrh and frankincense, of wine and olive oil, of fine flour and wheat; cattle and sheep; horses and carriages; and bodies and souls of men" (Rev. 18:11–13).

It is these things that people worship in the place of God. They glorify the sensual pleasures of the moment, and will sell their soul for the titillation of an instant's sensation. Nineveh knows this weakness of the human flesh, and organizes a massive machine to capitalize on man's proneness to fall. But "woe to the one that makes even a single one of these little ones to fall" (Matt. 18:6; Mark 9:42).

Behind all her perfumed pretenses, charming Nineveh actually is a *mistress of witchcrafts,* who *sells off nations and families.* The city is no amateur in the art of sorcery. She is a master at black magic. Rather than doing what is right and leaving the future to God, this entire community sets to itself the task of determining the course of the future so that it will result in its own benefit. Employing every means—even resorting to the trade of the wizard—the inhabitants of Nineveh deny the sovereignty of God over the affairs of men.

---

5. It is somewhat amusing to discover in the middle of a scholarly German commentary's analysis of Nineveh's allurements a parenthetical reference to "das, was man heute *sexy* heisst" (Rudolph, p. 177; emphasis added).

Recent archeology has uncovered literally thousands of tablets from Nineveh attesting to their intense concentration on sorcery.[6] Use of the magical arts functioned as a veritable way of life. Demons and evil spirits plagued their victims as a consequence of malicious incantations.

Generally it is thought that only uneducated people go for the practices of the sorcerer. But perhaps the most superstitious are the so-called scientific. Out of a misplaced confidence in their own theories and hypotheses they somehow convince themselves that they control the future. Economists and political scientists set themselves to determine and declare the future. They call for faith in their predictions, even though they are proven to be wrong over and over.

The victims of these acts of whoredom and witchcraft are *nations* and *families.* Not just an isolated individual here and there, but entire populaces are wholesaled. The most basic God-ordained societal unit—the family—is decimated. No one remains in the family to provide a way of deliverance, since the entire unit is destroyed. Children as well as fathers and mothers are sold into slavery.

It is because of the sins of the city that Nineveh's devastation is sure. The iniquity of the people is full. For approximately two hundred years they have been the tormentors of all their neighbors near and far. In this context, it is no wonder that the prophet includes such a vivid description of the actual assault soon to be launched against the city.

2. The Assault on the City (3:2–3)

2   a   *Crack*
      b   *of whip*
      a   *and rumble*
      b   *of wheel;*[1]
      a   *steed*
      b   *rearing*[2]
      a   *and chariot*
      b   *lurching;*[3]
3   a   *horseman*
      b   *charging*

---

6. Maier, pp. 302–3.

1. Literally, "voice" *(qôl)* of whip and "voice" *(qôl)* of chariot.

2. The term translated "rearing" *(dōhēr)* occurs only here and in Judg. 5:22. It has the meaning of "to rush, dash"; or in the case of horses, "to gallop, charge."

3. The term used to describe the activity of the approaching chariots *(mᵉraqqēdâ)* suggests a dancing, leaping, or bounding movement.

> c with flash[4]
>   d of sword
> c and glitter[5]
>   d of spear;
>
> a countless
>   b casualties,
> a heaps
>   b of carcasses,
> a endless
>   b corpses,
> a so that they stumble
>   b over their corpses.

Progression may been seen in this vivid description of assault. First only the sharp crack of the whip and the distant rumble of the chariot wheels is heard. Then sight joins with sound as the rearing steed and lurching chariot appear. Finally the shape of the individual horseman charging with flashing sword and glittering spear come into focus.

2 The curt language spurs the reader's imagination so that sight and sound join in electrifying the moment of the charge against the city. The "almost photographic vision" in a "staccato style"[6] is reinforced in its vividness by the onomatopoeic "shhoot, shhoot" (Heb. *šôṭ*) of the lashing whip. The distant rumbling of the war chariot's wheel must have been an awesomely terrifying sound to a populace scurrying about on foot. The infectious panic of the masses must have spread instantly throughout Nineveh. These people frequently had gloated over the terror they struck in the hearts of others. But until now they had no experience of sensing that terror in themselves.

But this vividness of language—what was the prophet's purpose? Was it merely to capture the "existential moment" of terror experienced in the siege of a city? No. By enlivening the imagination of his readers, the prophet intends to encourage surety in the faith and hope of the suffering Israelites. As Calvin aptly puts it: "All these things were intended for the purpose of fully convincing the Israelites that Nineveh, however much it was supplied with wealth and power, was yet approaching its ruin, for its enemies would prevail against it."[7]

---

4. The term for "flash" *(lahab)* depicts a blade of a sword moving through the air with the swiftness of a leaping flame.

5. The term for "glitter" *(bᵉraq)* suggests the swiftness of a lightning flash.

6. Maier, p. 295.

7. Calvin, p. 482.

When the word of God comes with such preciseness of detail in describing the destruction of the enemies of God's people, then the Holy Spirit can use that description to rekindle the faith of the most discouraged of his people. When Satan and his emissaries succeed over and over again in promoting deceit, untruth, and lies, when they are successful in discrediting the righteous, when they repeatedly wield the sword of power and popular support to devastate the godly, then even the strongest in faith begin to weaken and to doubt that God ever will vindicate the cause of truth and righteousness.

But doubting saints need only turn their enlivened imaginations to the descriptions of Nahum and apply them to their own struggles with Satan's forces. With *crack of whip* and *rumble of wheel,* with *steed rearing* and *chariot lurching,* the God-appointed avenger shall soon and suddenly appear. The contemporary enemy of truth and righteousness shall not stand any more than did ancient Nineveh.

Take heart! Lift up your downcast eyes! For even today *your* redemption draws near.

3 Only one who himself has trodden over a bloody field of battle a few days after the conflict can fully imagine the repulsive horror of maimed, bloated, decaying corpses. Without excessiveness of detail, the prophet Nahum underscores the extensiveness of the divine devastation: *countless casualties, heaps of carcasses, endless corpses, so that they stumble over their corpses.* Pusey speaks of the "vast field of carnage."[8] As far as the eye can see, bodies lie facedown and still. No more alarm is sounded; the stillness of death prevails.

By the use of three different terms for dead bodies, the prophet forces the reader to a fuller comprehension of the scene. The word translated *casualties (ḥālāl)* refers to a person fatally pierced or wounded. A *carcass (peger)* describes someone who has collapsed from exhaustion. The word translated *corpse (gᵉwîyâ)* derives from the root which refers to a person's "back" *(gaw),* perhaps viewing a body lying facedown.

If these OT Scriptures seem excessively gory, the context of this word of judgment must be remembered. Jonah had been commissioned decades earlier to bring the message of salvation to Nineveh despite their previous history of unending cruelty. But now the people had reverted to their evil ways. God had warned the Assyrians by his devastation of Sennacherib's army at the gate of Jerusalem when 185,000 men died overnight. The people arose the next morning to look out at the countless dead bodies (2 K. 19:35).

Isaiah concludes his prophecy with an awesome reminder of the divine destruction of the wicked which anticipates both the words of Nahum and the

8. Pusey, p. 149.

words of Jesus: "And they will go out and look upon the dead bodies of those who rebelled against me; their worm will not die, nor will their fire be quenched, and they will be loathsome to all mankind" (Isa. 66:24; cf. Mark 9:47–48). Although human sentimentality might wish to deny it, the word of God is consistent in its picture of the destruction of the wicked. Part of the great work of the conquering priestly Messiah will be the crushing of kings in the day of his wrath, filling the place of battle with dead bodies (Ps. 110:5–6).

3. The Lord Against the City (3:5–7)

5 Note it well!

> I am against you,
>> declares Yahweh of hosts,
> a and I will uncover
> b your skirts
> c before your face;
> a and I will let stare
> b nations
> c (at) your nakedness,
> b and kingdoms
> c (at) your shame.

6 So I will pelt you

> (with) detestable things;
> and I will mock you like a fool,
> and I will display you
> as a spectacle.[1]

7 So be it!

> Everyone who sees you
>> will flee from you,
>> and will say:

>> "Devastated
>> is Nineveh.
>> Who will grieve
>> for her?"
>> Where can I find comforters
>> for you?

1. Ronald J. Williams, *Hebrew Syntax: An Outline*, 2nd ed. (Toronto: University of Toronto Press, 1976), § 261, treats the *k* of *kᵉrō'î* as a *Kaph veritatis:* "I will make you a veritable gazing-stock." Cf. GKC, § 118x. In every respect, Nineveh shall be like a gazingstock. No corner for the slightest semblance of self-dignity will remain. Rudolph, p. 175, supports the sense of "spectacle" for this word despite some contextual support for the late Hebrew meaning of "mud" as promoted by Rashi.

Now an oracle from Yahweh changes the perspective on this announcement concerning the surety of Nineveh's judgment. God declares that he himself personally will bring devastation on Nineveh. Seven times over in these three verses the Lord speaks in the first person, declaring that he himself will exercise judgment against the city.

5 *Note it well!* is literally "Behold me!" I Yahweh—the Creator of all—*I am against you.* I will not send an angel to devastate you; even I myself will come to bring judgment against you. He who takes on the Lord of worlds—he shall end up in shame before the whole of the world. God will set him as an example before his entire universe. Ezekiel, prophet of Israel's exile, frequently uses this phrase "I am against you." According to Ezekiel, the consequences of this direct opposition from the Lord are quite shocking:

> the false prophets shall not be listed in the records of the house of Israel (13:8–9)
>
> no foot of man or beast will pass through the whole of Egypt (29:10–11)
>
> both of Pharaoh's arms shall be broken and his sword shall fall from his hand (30:22)
>
> God shall hold the false shepherds accountable, and remove the sheep from their hands (34:10)
>
> God will make Mt. Seir a desolate waste, and will turn its town into ruins (35:3–4)
>
> God will put flesh hooks in the jaws of Gog (38:3–4)
>
> God will send ravenous birds and beasts to devour his enemy (39:1, 4)

The consequences of God's setting himself against a people are awesome indeed. For "who shall stand when he appeareth?" (Mal. 3:2, AV). In this case of God's being against Nineveh, the consequences of divine opposition are strikingly different from the kinds of consequences described in the various passages in Ezekiel. Instead of calamitous devastations wrought by armies and wild beasts, the Lord declares in five different ways his determination to make an open exposure of all the gross depravity of this sinful city.

First, God will uncover Nineveh's skirts before her own face (v. 5). Like an alluring harlot, Nineveh had flaunted her gypsy skirts, tantalizing with the enticing slips underneath. Flowered, free-flowing, colorful skirts vibrating with movement and life. But the shameful use of all that appeal is exactly like the wife "dressed like a prostitute" whose "feet never stay at home" (Prov. 7:10–11). She aggressively seizes her next victim, boldly kisses him, arouses his senses by describing a perfumed bed covered with colored linens, and whispers that her husband has gone on a long journey so that they can drink deep of love until morning (Prov. 7:11–19).

But God will expose the harlot for what she really is. Her game is up. Before the public eye, but also *before her own face* so that she cannot hide from the disgrace of it all, her lewd conduct shall be exposed.[2]

Second, God will let nations and kingdoms stare at Nineveh's nakedness and shame. Even as the brutal armies of Nineveh had marched across the borders of numerous nations, so now the shame of her name will reach a universal scope. All the dirty facts of her undercover deals will be fully known. Just like a politician or businessman caught in a criminal act whose name and face is exposed on the front page of every newspaper in the nation, so Nineveh's true character will be visible before all. Just as the man's name became a symbol of ignominy in the phrase "Your name is Mudd," so Nineveh will forever be remembered as the city shamed by the Lord.

6a   Third, God will pelt Nineveh with detestable things. Marked outwardly with the inner filth of the heart! God shall bring an end to those deceitful pretenses of the hypocritical Ninevites. Splotched and spattered with outward filth, they will no longer be able to pretend piety. Those abominations declared to be "unclean" (Lev. 7:21; 11:10ff.) shall be openly smeared on the skirts of the harlot.

The LXX term for *detestable things* (Gk. *bdelygmón;* Heb. *šiqquṣîm*) is also used to describe the "abomination of desolation" in the temple of God which marks the consummate defilement of the ages (Matt. 24:15). But when the Lord finally sets things right, those abominations which might be esteemed highly among men (Luke 16:15) shall be denied any corner in the city of God (Rev. 21:27). Babylon, the archetype of Nineveh, the mother of harlots, shall herself drink the putrefication of her own abominations from the pretentious golden cup she holds in her hand (Rev. 17:4–5).

6b   Fourth, God will mock Nineveh like a fool. There comes a time when a person is confirmed in his chosen ways of folly and ungodliness. At that point, God will treat them precisely as their confirmed character deserves. So the time has come for God to mock Nineveh like a fool. He shall treat them contemptuously, lightly esteeming their worth. The fool shall be answered according to his folly (cf. Prov. 26:4–5).

6c   Fifth, God shall present Nineveh as a spectacle. The kings of As-

---

2. D. R. Hillers, *Treaty-Curses and the Old Testament Prophets,* BibOr 16 (Rome: Pontifical Biblical Institute, 1964), p. 59, notes the apparent parallel in the curses of a treaty text, but acknowledges that his reading and translation of the text "can only be regarded as a plausible conjecture."

syria often found crude delight in exposing their captives to public ridicule. Ashurbanipal boasts in one of his inscriptions: "I put him *[Daite]* into a kennel with jackels and dogs. I tied him up and made him guard the gate in Nineveh."[3] Such inhuman treatment of one person by another deserves like punishment. So the Lord declares that just as Nineveh has abused its captives, exposing them to public ridicule, so he shall make Nineveh a spectacle of shame that the nations will never forget. Everyone shall come and stare at Nineveh the gazingstock. International shame and disgrace shall replace pomp and pride.

All five of the actions described above are attributed to the Lord himself, not some chosen servant. By his own immediate involvement, the Lord shall humble Nineveh before all the nations of the earth, and before all the ages of time.

7 The consequences of this public exposure and humiliation are described in the last verse of this section. The specter of Nineveh devastated so startles the nations that they gasp with horror, cup their hands over their faces, and turn to flee. Michaelangelo's portrait of himself in hell as painted on the Sistine ceiling captures the facial expression of stunned horror that the spectacle of Nineveh must have inspired.

Although all nations are stunned at the sight, they cannot find one among themselves to grieve over Nineveh's calamity. *Who will grieve for her?* say the nations as they confer with one another.

There is in the person who has suffered violence something that cries out for justice. Not so often in those dwelling in unruffled security, but common in those who have been stripped and humiliated, there arises a sense of the need for someone to intervene, to expose the guilty, and to bring the haughty oppressor down from his position of power.

Justice must be done even from a new covenant perspective, the Scripture asserts. "Vengeance is mine, I *will repay,* says the Lord" (Rom. 12:19; cf. Deut. 32:35–36; Heb. 10:30). Indeed, Christ on the cross cried "Father, forgive them" (Luke 23:34). But it must not be forgotten that it was Christ *on the cross* who made this cry. Only in the context of being himself the propitiatory sacrifice for sin would he assume a foundation had been laid for God to forgive. As the sinless Son of God, he alone could make this sacrifice; and apart from faith in his blood, there is no forgiveness of sins.

In Nineveh's case, all nations had suffered from its incessant brutality. The battered and bruised bodies and souls of people from all nations looked at the horrors of Nineveh's demise, but they could not find it in themselves

3. Cited in Maier, p. 310. Cf. *ANET,* pp. 298, 300.

to weep. So universal had been this city's policy of oppression that no one could be found to grieve for her.

Not even the Lord himself (the *I* of the last phrase of v. 7) knows where to find comforters for the wicked city. Nineveh must languish alone in its doleful state of devastation.

So shall it be in every age. The plague of darkness at the time of the Exodus set every Egyptian alone, fearful of moving from his seat (Exod. 10:23). In the day that everyone looks on the One they have pierced, every family shall mourn by itself alone (Zech. 12:10–14). Part of the judgment of hell shall be the isolation of people altogether from one another in a darkness that separates from all possible comforters.

So Nineveh's judgment is sure because of their sin. Their endless oppression of others sets a seal on their fate. All nations agree that their judgment is long overdue.

B. SURE JUST AS NO-AMON (THEBES) (3:8–13)

Now the prophet offers a second ground for the certainty of Nineveh's coming judgment. Let the city consider what happened to their major rival, the metropolis of No-Amon (Thebes, the capital of Egypt).

It is not so much that Nahum is attempting to convince the inhabitants of Assyria that God's judgment is coming on them so that they may turn in repentance. Instead, this mounting case against the sinful city is intended to spur the faith of true believers concerning the certainty of the coming judgment of God which shall deliver them from years of oppression.

In this new section the prophet first indicates that Thebes (No-Amon) has been devastated despite her many natural advantages (3:8–13).

1. Thebes Devastated Despite Her Many Advantages (3:8–10)

8 *Are you better*[1]
  than No-Amon,
  the one dwelling
    in the midst of the rivers
    (with) the sea surrounding her;
      a whose rampart

---

1. The word for "Are you better" combines elements of a Qal (*tîṭ^eḇî*) and a Hiphil (*têṭîḇî*) stem. Cf. GKC, § 70c. Rudolph, p. 181, concludes in favor of the Hiphil, since the context is not speaking of a developed moral quality ("to do good"— Qal) but of an appointed state ("to have been made good"—Hiphil).

> b *(was) the sea;*
> b *from the sea*
> a *(was) her wall?*
> 9 *Cush*
> *her strength,*
> *—and Egypt;*
> *and there was no end . . .*
> *Put and Lubim*
> *were your helpers.*
> 10 a *Even she (ended)*
> b *in exile;*
> a *she went*
> b *into captivity.*
> a *Even her young children*
> b *were dashed into pieces*
> c *at the head of all the streets.*
> a *For her honored men*
> b *they cast the lot,*
> a *and all her great men*
> b *were bound in chains.*

Having ended the previous section with a rhetorical question addressed to Nineveh itself, the prophet now begins this section with the identical form. In both cases, the answer which the question intends to elicit is quite obvious. Where are comforters for Nineveh to be found? *Nowhere.* Is Nineveh better than devastated Thebes? *By no means.*

Although it is quite clear that Nahum expects a negative answer to his question concerning the superiority of Nineveh to Thebes, the point of the comparison is not immediately clear. Does he mean that Nineveh is no better than Thebes with respect to moral or religious virtues? Or does he intend to suggest that Nineveh is no better than Thebes with respect to the fate that ultimately shall befall the two cities?

The subject of the next two verses seems quite clearly to indicate that the comparison has to do with the many natural, geographical advantages that relate to Thebes in comparison to Nineveh. The wall of water that surrounded Thebes provided a year-round buffer difficult for any invader to overcome (v. 8). The coterie of kindred nations that encompassed the capital city of Thebes added military and political difficulties for any potential enemy (v. 9).

This understanding of the comparison has been vigorously resisted, principally on the basis that Nineveh had as a matter of fact previously defeated Thebes within the memory of contemporaries of Nahum. How then could it be supposed that Ninevites of Nahum's day would readily concede that Thebes was better situated than they?[2]

Although this objection has merit, its very basis provides the strongest counterpoint. The militia of Nineveh had seen the strength of Thebes first-hand. Nahum's decision to compare the capital of Assyria with the capital of Egypt appears to be based on Nineveh's personal knowledge of Thebes' natural advantages. Even though Thebes had fallen to the superior powers of Nineveh, the Assyrian invaders could not but have been impressed by the formidable bulwarks that surrounded its Egyptian rival. Four hundred miles down from the Nile Delta an invading army from the north had to march. To the right and to the left they had to expose their flank to retaliatory assault from kindred nations friendly to Thebes. Having finally arrived before the massive city, twenty-seven miles in circumference, the heated glare of a horizontal wall of water blinded them everywhere they looked. Surrounded by rivers, streams, canals, and lakes formed by the Nile as it distributed over the broadened delta, any invader would have to be overwhelmed by the sight that greeted their eyes. A field of massive statues, memorials, temples, and great halls with no equal in the world stood before them. On both sides of the Nile they observed structures made of stones almost 300 tons in weight, and colossi weighing up to 900 tons apiece. If they had been fully informed, they would have known of the tunneled "valley of the kings and queens" beyond the many carvings in the western cliffs.

They faced the ancient locale of the sun-god Amon, known to the Greeks as Diospolis, the city of the chief god of Egypt. For at least a thousand years, pharaohs of Egypt had ruled their part of the world with the full blessing of this supreme deity. Renowned today as the ruins of Luxor and Karnak, the city was identified as the town with one hundred gates.[3] The locale was not important in the 3rd millennium B.C., but beginning about 2000 B.C. the 11th and 12th Dynasties restored the unity and prosperity of Egypt from this center at Thebes. The powerful 18th Dynasty expelled the foreign Hyksos rulers about 1550, restoring Thebes as the capital where it remained through the 20th Dynasty (ca. 1085).[4]

Would these audacious invaders from the distant East actually be able to overthrow the capital of Egypt? Even if they did succeed, they would have to be impressed with the natural advantages of this famed metropolis of the world, this first of the great monument-cities of mankind.

2. Cf. Rudolph, p. 184.
3. Cf. Homer, *Iliad* 9.381.
4. Cf. K. A. Kitchen, "Thebes," in *ZPEB*, 5:714.

8 Could Nineveh actually boast that it was *better than No-Amon* with respect to its situation? Although the Euphrates was there, it did not supply the natural defense that the Nile gave to Thebes.[5] And as for neighboring supporters, what could Nineveh boast that would compare to Cush, Egypt, Put, and Lubim? No neighbors loved and supported Nineveh out of a natural bond such as these nations felt toward Thebes. Even though Nineveh had eventually prevailed over Thebes, it could hardly fail to imagine some young, energetic nation one day marching up to its gates just as they had marched to Thebes. But then Nineveh would not be able to boast of the kinds of natural fortifications so obvious at Thebes.

Was not the conclusion inevitable? One day Nineveh would fall, just as did Thebes. Nothing could withstand the inevitable march of time as one great and ambitious nation replaced another.

The identification of Nahum's *No-Amon* with Egyptian Thebes as presumed to this point finds its base in Egyptian texts which refer to Thebes simply as *nȋwt,* "the City," or *nȋwt ʾImn,* "the city of Amon."[6] Jeremiah 46:25 as well as Ezek. 30:14–16 refer to the city as Amon of No. The AV "populous No" is based on the medieval Jewish interpretation of "Amon" in the light of the Hebrew term *hāmôn,* which means "multitude."[7] Earlier identifications of "No-Amon" with Alexandria are not well-founded.[8]

Thebes appropriately is characterized as *the one dwelling in the midst of the rivers, (with) the sea surrounding her.* The reference would be to the channels into which the Nile divides at Thebes. Elsewhere the Nile and other great rivers are designated as a "sea" (for the Nile, cf. Isa. 18:2; 19:5; Job 41:23 [Eng. 31]; for the Euphrates, cf. Isa. 27:1; Jer. 51:36). It has been indicated that when the Nile floods, it is two or more miles wide at Thebes. The result is that the various cities appear like islands of the Aegean.[9] This unique setting of the city provided a natural wall of defense. As a consequence, the encompassing water served as a *rampart* and a *wall* to protect the populace (v. 8c).

The multiple blessings provided by the Nile became a source of contention between the living God and the Egyptians. Their pride led them to claim: "The river is mine: I made it" (cf. Ezek. 29:2–3, 9–10). By boasting so arrogantly, they forgot what God had done to the river at the time of Israel's Exodus.

---

5. Cf. the description by D. J. Wiseman in "Nineveh," *The Illustrated Bible Dictionary,* 3 vols., ed. J. D. Douglas et al. (Leicester: Inter-Varsity, 1980), 2:1089–91.

6. T. O. Lambdin, "Thebes," in *IDB,* 4:615; cf. BDB, p. 609.

7. S. R. Driver, 2:39 n.2.

8. Cf. Calvin, p. 490.

9. Pusey, p. 155 n.9.

Assyria was guilty of the same kind of folly. They boasted that they had dried up rivers of besieged places simply by trampling through the land (2 K. 19:24; Isa. 37:25–27). So they forgot that God was the one who determined that they should lay waste fortified cities. Of all people, they should not forget that the rampart and the wall of water surrounding No-Amon could protect them only so long as God had ordered it so.

9 In addition to the strengths of Thebes' locale was the support that could be expected from the warlike nations flanking the city. *Cush, Egypt,* and *Put* all represent nations with natural connections with Thebes (cf. Gen. 10:6). *Cush* was the nation located in the southern Nile valley. Earlier Cush had come out to oppose Sennacherib of Assyria during one of his excursions into Palestine (2 K. 19:9). So the Assyrians would have known firsthand of the strength of this enemy. The nation of *Put* is generally included in lists with other African nations (Jer. 46:9; Ezek. 30:5), and apparently refers to Libya. The *Lubim* are the Libyans of North Africa, located west of Egypt (cf. 2 Chr. 12:3; 16:8).

In any case, Thebes was surrounded by allies and blood-relatives who would be willing to intervene if ever the capital city of Egypt should be threatened. These forces are described in relation to Thebes as *her strength* (v. 9a) and *your* (i.e., Thebes') *helpers* (v. 9c). The alteration between the second and third person pronouns is typical of the oracles of the Hebrew prophets.[10]

Indeed, it is extremely tempting to count strength and help in terms of support that can be enlisted from other human sources. Once an alliance has been achieved, a nation may breathe a sigh of relief that those forces have been intertwined with their cause. From that human perspective, Thebes was certainly in a favorable position. Their allies were strategically placed and vast in numbers. The incompleted phrase *and there was no end* . . . (v. 9b) apparently refers to the endless number of troops available to Thebes.

Of course, from the divine perspective those measurements of relative strength had little significance. To those that have no might (*ʿoṣmâ*) God increases strength *(kōaḥ)* (Isa. 40:29). Isaiah had specifically warned of the futility of resorting to Egypt, as did Jeremiah (Isa. 31:1; Jer. 37:7).

But in comparing these resources among the arena of nations, Thebes

---

10. With regard to the sudden change of persons, M. Dahood, *Psalms,* 3 vols., AB (Garden City, NY: Doubleday, 1965), 1:35, notes that this practice "is analogous to the unexpected change from the second to the third person sometimes encountered in Northwest Semitic curses." Cf. S. Gevirtz, "West-Semitic curses and the problem of the origins of Hebrew law," *VT* 11 (1961) 147n.4; Cathcart, *Nahum,* p. 132.

obviously had every advantage over Nineveh. The army that dared march 400 miles into the interior of Africa between the pinchers of the allies of Thebes was exposing itself to awesome possibilities of retaliation.

10 Yet *Even she (ended) in exile.* Despite her own strength, her natural fortifications, and the support of "the majority," Thebes fell. But it was more than that. She did not merely experience defeat. Occupation by foreign troops would have been bad enough. But most awesome was the exile and captivity that Egypt experienced. Just as the armies of Assyria had marched around the perimeter of the Fertile Crescent and then down 400 miles into the interior of Africa, so now the populace of Thebes must retrace those same steps, bearing the burdens and humiliations of a defeated nation.

What ancestries must have been traceable among the inhabitants of Thebes! For the past fourteen hundred years the city and its inhabitants had remained intact. But now they had been uprooted and driven across two continents where they must live as strangers in a strange land. Defeated, humiliated, bound, and dragged away, they hardly looked like the ancient proud people that had ruled the world.

The prophet specifies both the young and the old as having been devastated by the fall of Thebes. In each case, the consequence of defeat was tragic indeed.

First he depicts the fate that befell prospective generations. The *young children were dashed into pieces at the head of all the streets.* Who can imagine such brutality? Yet in Thebes this maltreatment of young children (ʿôlēl) became a public commonplace at every street corner. Their inhumane conqueror determined on a course of genocide as a way of assuring perpetual submission by an enemy that had been conquered only at great cost.

In a similar way, the aged and honored of the populace of Thebes were treated as the lowest commoners. No effort was made to determine any particular personal ability of one individual over another. The chance casting of the lot determined the fate of the most valuable citizens of Thebes. As the most talented "zeks" of Aleksandr Solzhenitsyn's *First Circle* were separated from family, incarcerated for no crime, and milked of every skill without any consideration of proper remuneration, so these ancient peoples of Thebes were forced to live with perpetual maltreatment as a consequence of their being sold into slavery.

In synonymous parallelism with the *honored men* of Thebes are the *great men* who were *bound in chains.* Now the prophet indicated that *all* of the prominent men of the city experienced this fate. Whether their greatness was achieved through heredity, wealth, skill, or wisdom, they were equally subjected to enslavement.

116

So the fate of Thebes is recalled with vividness. Since Assyria itself had been the conqueror, it could hardly deny the truthfulness of the terrible picture the prophet presented. With relentless determination, Ashurbanipal (ca. 668–627) had taken up the banner of his father Esarhaddon (ca. 680–669) and marched into the south of Egypt. On the way, he had forced the enlistment of 22 kings in his support, including Manasseh of Judah (ca. 687–642): "I [Ashurbanipal] . . . took the shortest road to Egypt and Nubia. During my march 22 kings . . . [including] Manasseh king of Judah . . . brought heavy gifts to me and kissed my feet. I made these kings accompany my army over the land—as well as over the sea-route with their armed forces and their ships."[11] Thirteen hundred miles on foot away from home, Ashurbanipal had overrun Thebes. The mightiest of cities had fallen to him. And that was just the point. The mightiest of cities had fallen to him, and Nineveh should expect the same.

2. Nineveh May Expect the Same (3:11–13)

11 *Even you (Nineveh)*
   shall (stagger like a) drunk;
You shall be
   hidden away,
Even you
   shall seek shelter from the enemy.
12 *All your strongholds*
   (are like) fig trees with firstripe figs;
      If they are shaken,
      Then they fall into the mouth of the eater.
13 *Behold!*
   Your people
      are women in your midst!
   to your enemies
      the gates of your land
         shall be flung open;
      fire shall devour
         your bars.

All this talk about the fall of Thebes (No-Amon)—what is the point? The point is that Nineveh may expect the same. Just as surely as Thebes fell, so Nineveh shall fall. With the same kinds of horrible circumstances that accompanied the devastation of Thebes, Nineveh also shall be devastated. The retributive justice of God shall see to it that just those horrors that Nineveh

11. *ANET*, p. 294.

has inflicted on others shall be inflicted on them. Since Nineveh's own warriors had been the ones to ruin Thebes, they could know firsthand the things to which the prophet was referring.

The "turning of the screw" at the beginning of v. 11 is made more apparent in the original text of Scripture. The same kind of emphatic conviction that begins v. 10 also begins and ends v. 11:

> v. 10 (of Thebes): "Even *she (gam-hî")* (ended) in exile"
> v. 11 (of Nineveh): "Even *you (gam-'at)* shall be drunk"
> "Even *you (gam-'at)* shall seek shelter."

As was the fate of Thebes, so also shall be the fate of Nineveh.

The prophet then uses five different images to vivify the helplessness of the city that by unrighteousness and brutality has made itself God's enemy. Nineveh is described as a nation that has become:

> like a staggering drunk
> like a panicked fugitive
> like a trembling fig tree
> like a feeble woman
> like a city with gates thrown open.

Consider the boldness of this prophet. He dares to address an internationally renowned overlord with the directness and forcefulness of these figures. Each one ridicules the proud people of Assyria.

11 First, Nineveh *shall stagger like a drunk.* Reeling helplessly from the blows of divine wrath, the city will have no hope of defending itself against its enemies. As a consequence, it shall be *hidden away* like a drunk who has collapsed under the table. In a way the fate of Thebes was not quite as bad as that of Nineveh. At least the ruins of Thebes still stand as witness to its greatness in the distant past. But for centuries even the site of Nineveh was "hidden" in obscurity.

Second, Nineveh shall flee like a panicked refugee (v. 11b). Like a bully in retreat, this brute of a nation shall cower and cringe as it searches for some hole for hiding. In reality, the disintegration of the kingdom of Assyria shows the nation cowering and cringing as one blow after another destroys its shrinking remnant. First the ancient capital of Asshur fell in 614 B.C. Then the combined forces of the Medes and the Babylonians assaulted Nineveh in 612 B.C. The city collapsed and was burned after a three-month siege. Retreating toward the west, a remnant of loyal Assyrians established a new king and capital in Harran, approximately 250 miles toward the west. Two years later in 610 B.C., the remaining Assyrian forces were defeated again by Babylon. Although a combined Egyptian and Assyrian force retained some presence in the area for a while, the decisive battle of Carchemish in 605 B.C. eliminated the last vestiges of Assyrian presence in the Fertile Crescent. Just as Nahum had predicted, they sought refuge like a retreating fugitive. But they found none.

12 Third, Nineveh's strongest fortifications are compared to fig trees with ripened figs. The slightest jar sends the plump fruit plummeting into the mouth of a ravenous eater. The *strongholds,* the most fortified places of the city, will be no more effective in their defense against assault than over-ripened fruit poised to be plucked. According to Nahum, this characterization applies to *all* Nineveh's fortifications. No effective defense shall remain.

This imagery of falling fruit has such a vividness about it that it naturally was picked up in the book of Revelation to describe the cataclysms associated with the end of the present age. The Apostle John sees the day in which the stars of the sky shall fall to the earth "as a fig tree casts its unripe figs" (Rev. 6:13). Like Nahum, John depicts kings of the earth, great men, rich and strong, hiding themselves in the caves of the mountains, pleading for the rocks to fall on them so that they can be hid from the wrath of the Lamb (Rev. 6:15–17). The readiness for judgment which ripened for Nineveh in Nahum's day soon shall characterize the whole of the earth. The same Lamb of God that showed compassion for sinners by exposing himself to the consuming wrath of God shall appear in wrath to bring judgment on all who have denied him.

13 Fourth, Nineveh's inhabitants are compared to feeble women. Although the modern feminist movement may deny it, generally speaking women are weaker physically than men. Particularly when speaking of the hand-to-hand combat of battle, men retain predominance.[1]

The prophet also may refer to a person's dreading of combat. As John Calvin says, ". . . the hearts of men are so in the hand of God that he melts whatever courage there may be in them whenever he pleases."[2] Sometimes God may leave men with courageous hearts so that they will run into ruin. But in either case, when the time of God's judgment has arrived, escape from judgment will prove impossible.

Fifth, Nineveh shall be like a besieged city whose gates have been flung wide open (v. 13b). Like the foolish Canaanites who rushed out of their

---

1. D. R. Hillers, *Treaty-Curses and the Old Testament Prophets,* BibOr 16 (Rome: Pontifical Biblical Institute, 1964), pp. 66–67, compares this phrase to the Ashurnirari treaty: "May his nations become women." He notes also the Hittite soldier's oath: "Let them change his troops into women."
2. Calvin, p. 496.

city leaving the gates wide open (Josh. 8:17), so Nineveh's gates shall be flung open to give their enemies free access to their city. Total exposure to the ravages of alien forces shall characterize the entire nation. For it is not merely the city gates, but the gate of the *land* that shall be opened (v. 13). The last remnants of defense in terms of the heavy *bars* that seal the gates shall be consumed with *fire.*

So Nineveh may have gloated earlier when Thebes fell before their own relentless assaults. They may have experienced a twisted glee as they publicly smashed Egyptian children, those supposed sons of the god Amon. Yet having sowed the wind, they shall reap the whirlwind. Because Thebes fell, they too may expect to fall.

It is a twist of divine inspiration. The prophetic voice informs the sinner that his triumphs confirm his fate. His victories must be viewed as the harbingers of his own final defeat.

So where then may the sinner stand? Nowhere—except with Nineveh. Awaiting the inevitable destruction assigned by the Almighty. Crying out for the rocks to cover him.

C. SURE DESPITE THEIR STRENGTH (3:14–19)

It is most likely that this little-known figure named Nahum prophesied at the precise time when Nineveh achieved its zenith of glory under Ashurbanipal (669–627 B.C.). Entering Thebes a second time after a brief revolt by the Egyptians, the Assyrians carried away "booty heavy and beyond counting."[1] Tyre was strangled from the mainland and forced to surrender. To the east, Babylon was subdued, and Susa the capital of Elam was plundered in about 639. As Roux has appropriately noted: "Never had the Assyrian empire looked so strong, the Assyrian might so invincible."[2]

Now comes the word of the Lord by Nahum. Now God makes it plain that the destruction of the wicked is sure despite all their strength.

1. The Utter Futility of Human Resources (3:14–18)

14 *Waters for the siege*
    draw for yourself.

    a Strengthen
    b   your fortifications;

---

1. Roux, *Ancient Iraq*, p. 300, apparently quoting the Assyrian inscriptions.
2. Ibid., p. 304.

    a immerse yourself
      b in the clay, and
    a tread out
      b the mortar;
    a hold firmly
      the brick-mold.

15   *Just at that point*
          a fire
            b shall devour you,
          a sword
            b shall cut you down.
          It shall consume you
            like the young locust.

    a Multiply yourself
      b like the young locust,
    a multiply yourself
      b like the aged locust.

16   *You have made your merchants more numerous*
      than the stars of heaven;
        (but) the young locust
          strips
          and flies away.

17   *a Your crowned ones*
      b are as the aged locust;
    a and your captains
      b as the hordes of grasshoppers
      that encamp in the hedges on a cold day.
      The sun rises
        and they flee away;
        and their place is not known.
        Where are they?

18   *a Your shepherds*
      b slumber,
        O King of Assyria;
    a your nobles
      b lie down;
    a your people
      b are scattered on the mountains,
      b and no one gathers them.

In this section the prophet spurs the Assyrian to contemplate the futility of every human effort to evade the inevitable judgment of God that is coming.

Preparations will do no good (vv. 14–15a); numbers will do no good (vv. 15b–16); officialdom will do no good (vv. 17–18).

14–15a Preparations will do no good. Now it is as though God were mocking Assyrian resistance by echoing the encounter between himself and the forces of Assyria that had occurred a century earlier. At that time Sennacherib's deputy offered horses to Judah for its own defense if only they could provide riders (cf. 2 K. 18:23). Now as God's prophet, in his imagination, has approached the very gate of Nineveh, he shouts the commands that might be emitted from within the walls of a city bracing itself for a coming siege. In rapid-fire succession, five distinct commands are given to activate a program of preparation:

(1) *Waters for the siege draw for yourself.* Water naturally symbolizes refreshment, joy, life, and peace (cf. Isa. 12:3; 32:2; Ps. 23:2; Zech. 14:8). But *waters for the siege* ring an ominous note. They speak of rationing, of deprivation, of a dreaded struggle for the most basic elements of life. Only extensive preparation and stringent self-discipline may provide any hope for survival.

But the Lord has no intention of giving hope to the Ninevites. Instead, he mocks them by urging them to consider the most extreme measures they might take to avoid the coming calamities. All their efforts will prove to be utterly futile. Their diligence, discipline, and self-denial will be of no use. Calvin has captured the precise flavor of this urging: "Thy frugality, exertion and care, not only will avail thee nothing, but will also turn out to thy ruin; for the Lord pronounces accursed the arrogance of men, when they trust in their own resources."[1]

Sennacherib earlier had boasted that before he made his improvements at Nineveh, its fields were in ruin through lack of water. People had to turn their eyes heavenward for showers of rain. But he had built an aqueduct system and dug eighteen canals to bring water to the city and alleviate the problem.[2] Yet in the day of God's judgment, this elaborate system would be of no avail. All too easily an aggressive adversary would cut off those sources, leaving the city desperate for water.

(2) *Strengthen your fortifications.* Nineveh already possessed fortresses that had given it a sense of security for a hundred years. But now their strength must be increased. Every bit of energy must be poured into these frenzied acts of preparation and self-protection. Those untiring, last-minute efforts may make the difference.

---

1. Calvin, p. 499.
2. Luckenbill, *Ancient Records,* 2:149, no. 332.

(3) *immerse yourself in the clay* (lit., "go [or 'come'; Heb. *bō ʾî*] into the clay"). The literal meaning of the phrase suggests total absorption in a project or circumstance. Joseph's soul "came [Heb. *bā ʾâ*] into" iron (Ps. 105:18), meaning that his life was absorbed in this new condition of imprisonment. "Coming into" old age meant that a person's life was characterized by that circumstance from that point on (Gen. 24:1; Josh. 13:1; 23:1). If a city "came into" siege (2 K. 24:10), then all the activities of the community had to be adjusted for the sake of this new reality. In the modern slang, a person may be said to be "into" art, or "into" computers, meaning that the person is totally absorbed in the one particular interest.

Nahum's admonition to Nineveh is "*Go into* the clay." Immerse yourself in this particular project. Get up to your elbows in mud. Make a superhuman effort in your defense preparations. And all of it will be to no avail.

By this mockery Nahum is not saying that all human effort is pointless. His message is much more specific. He is saying that all human effort to avoid or escape the coming judgment of God is futile. People often get the wrong impression, thinking that in their lives they strive only with human forces or natural circumstances. So they conclude that a little more effort may enable them to evade the threatening calamity.

But the sinner is in error. He fails to reckon with the living God. Although he is a Spirit, and invisible to human perceptions, it is he with whom we have to do. It is for that reason that all human efforts at defense against the Almighty are futile. Let the Ninevites immerse themselves in raising their fortifications to the highest heavens. Apart from God's blessing, they will be to no avail.

(4) *tread out the mortar.* Trampling involves extensive exertion. Whether performing the work oneself, or urging slave labor to the task, intense effort must be made to mix mortar for brick under the burning sun of the ancient Near East.

Yet the stringent effort must be made. If Assyria for the past century has brutally tormented many nations with regular rituals of cruelty such as skinning people alive, how can they expect anything less for themselves? So they must shake off their dull lethargy and stir themselves to the toils involved in self-defense. So a person reaps what he sows, and so his inflictions on others become inflictions on himself.

(5) *hold firmly the brick-mold.* Since the Assyrians apparently used both fired and unfired brick,[3] the term associated with brick formation (*malbēn*) could refer to a brick kiln or to a mold for shaping unfired clay. This

3. Cf. Keil, p. 37.

particular admonition to *hold firmly* or "make strong" the instrument suits a reference to the brick-mold which must be held firmly to enforce its shape on the heavy moist clay mixture. The admonition is all the more fitting in the light of the hours of tedious exertion necessary to produce adequate brick for reinforcing, enlarging, or heightening a wall the size of Nineveh's. Muscle fatigue would set in long hours before the end of the day's toil.

These five admonitions of irony addressed to the Assyrians sound like a call to shackles of self-enslavement. The tiring tasks necessary for erecting crude military defense formations must have taken on the air of frantic measures doomed to failure. Normally such work would be committed only to slaves, but now all Nineveh's citizens must undergo these rigors.

The "vanity of vanities" that characterizes all human efforts without faith in the one true living God is enforced in v. 15a. The emphatic "There!" that begins the verse (translated *Just at that point*) points to the most recently constructed defenses as the very place that shall be leveled. Precisely where man in revolt against God makes his grandest effort, there he is subject to the severest divine blow.

Yet it is not merely these frail defenses so recently constructed that shall be consumed. The whole of the city is the object of each of these three verbs, as indicated by the feminine singular pronouns. Fire shall devour, the sword cut down, and the locust consume the entirety of the city.

15b–17 The identity of the various kinds of locusts mentioned in these verses is not easy to determine. In the book of Joel, four different kinds of "locust" or swarming pest are mentioned. In the AV they are designated as the "palmerworm" (*gāzām*), the "locust" (*'arbeh*), the "cankerworm" (*yeleq*), and the "caterpillar" (*ḥāsîl*) (cf. Joel 1:4). It is very difficult to determine whether these terms refer to different kinds of locust or to different phases of development of the same insect. But the variety of terminology indicates the greater awarenss of this phenomenon in the Near East than in Western cultures.

The devouring of an entire metropolitan area by a small creature like the locust underscores the futility of man's grandiose plans. The most obscure and seemingly defenseless of God's creatures brings to their knees the most powerful of God's adversaries.

15b–16 Numbers will do no good. The picture of the locust swarm is complicated further by vv. 15b–17. The imagery of the innumerable locust horde is used to describe both the inhabitants of Nineveh and the enemy devouring Nineveh. That much is evident. But it is not clear which sections of these verses apply the locust imagery to Nineveh itself and which apply the same imagery to the enemies of Nineveh.

The natural reaction of a self-sufficient military machine to a threat by hordes just might be: "Well, we shall multiply ourselves so that we shall be just as numerous as you." So the prophet proposes: "Go ahead. Multiply yourself like a locust swarm. It will do you absolutely no good" (v. 15b). The combination of a masculine and feminine form for *multiply yourself (hiṯkab-bēḏ, hiṯkabbᵉḏî)* indicates the greatest possible fulness, or the totality of the nation in all its aspects.[4]

16   Already the Assyrians have made their *merchants more numerous than the stars of heaven.* Their insatiable desire for more stirred them on to dominate the trade of the world. Located just at the point where East and West met, Nineveh was ideally situated to multiply its wealth. As Maier indicates: "Under Ashurbanipal, for the first time in 800 years, western Asia was dominated by a single political rule. With the vast territory of the empire under one central government, commerce could flourish throughout this area as never before."[5]

But although the number of Nineveh's merchants was *like the stars* ("astronomical" in a literal sense), it would do them no good. The nationalizing of Esau's passion for the satisfaction of sensual desire could only mean the loss of an entire nation's birthright and blessing. To worship and serve the creature more than the Creator meant in this case not merely that God would "give them up" (cf. Rom. 1:25–26), but that God would multiply their enemies beyond them. As the last portion of v. 16 indicates, by the shear strength of numbers *the young locust strips and flies away,* leaving nothing to identify what they had devoured. Not a leaf of foliage, not a thread of cloth, not a dietary delicacy shall be left. In the eyes of the God of hosts, multiplication by men means absolutely nothing.

In a day in which "church growth" has become the passing fad, Nahum's prophecy has something directly to say. The Lord is not impressed by numbers. David's sin of numbering the troops brought plague on the whole of the nation of Israel (2 Sam. 24:1, 10ff.). "These sheep, what have they done?" was a plaint of the shepherd's heart that came too late (2 Sam. 24:17).

The action of *stripping* and *flying away* underscores the thoroughness of the destruction by the locust and the emptiness of what is left when God's instruments of judgment are done. Left bare and exposed to the elements, nothing remains of the long labors of the merchants of Nineveh.

17–18   The effectiveness of the Assyrian war machine indicates that it must have been under good leadership. Certainly the Assyrians must have

4. Cf. GKC, § 110k.
5. Maier, p. 348.

respected their officials. The prophet Nahum provides a different picture. Their leaders may be vast in number, but they are inept, ineffective, and essentially looking after their own interests.

The first term for an official in v. 17 *(minn^{e}zār)* could refer to a *crowned* person, alluding to the diadem worn by a king or other official; or it could refer to a "separated" or "consecrated" person, also denoting someone in a leadership role; or the term could be understood as a Hebraized form of a native Assyrian title, as seems more clearly to be the case with the next term *(ṭipsār,* from the Assyrian *dupsarru),* here translated *captains.* In any case, the reference is to those persons in roles of leadership or authority within the Assyrian empire.

Because the number of the Assyrian populace is so great, the leadership is also virtually without number. They are as the *aged locust ('arbeh)* and as the *hordes of grasshoppers (gôb gōbāy).* The repetition of the same word in this last phrase has been interpreted by some as a sign of a copyist's error. But the construction may be better understood as expressing the idea of the superlative.[6] Their leaders are so many in number that they compare not only to the grasshopper, but to the hordes of grasshoppers.

But this multiplicity of leadership will do them no good. The prophet appeals to a phenomenon common to the Near East. Huddled en masse, grasshoppers coat leaves and branches along a hedge on a cloudy, cold day. But the moment the sun warms their cold-blooded shells, *they flee away; and their place is not known!* They leave not a trace of their previous presence.

So it is with human leadership. Now fallen from their kingly position of domination over the whole earth, even the leaders among men have no more kingly bearing than the lowliest of earth's swarming creatures. Frozen, immobile—perhaps cowardly and indecisive—Nineveh futilely places its hope in human resources.

Nahum's term for the departure of the locust horde *(nôḏaḏ)* elsewhere describes the flight of people from war (Isa. 33:3), of men from battle (Isa. 21:15), of rulers and kings of armies (Isa. 22:3; Ps. 68:13 [Eng. 12]). So the crowned and the captains of Assyria disappear in the heat of battle. They leave no trace of their existence. Consequently their followers experience merciless mutilation by the enemy.

Where are they? asks Nahum with a note of stinging satire. When the battle really begins to rage, where are those impressive princes of Assyria? They are nowhere to be counted.

18 In a climactic word about Nineveh's leadership, the prophet ad-

---

6. Cf. GKC, § 133i.

dresses the king himself. It is this bold move that has led some to the conclusion that Nahum's message must not have been spoken to his contemporaries, but only written and disbursed in a secretive fashion. Such a suggestion at least displays an awareness of the radicalness of what the prophet is doing. Although his words may be regarded as diplomatically framed, they are nonetheless cutting in their directness.

O King of Assyria, he says. Pay attention to me! Mine may be the voice of an unknown citizen in the least of your vassal states. But my words are truth, and therefore of more significance than all the missives sealed by dignitaries of state.

What is the message of the prophet to the mighty king of Assyria?

First, he declares the doom of the king's leaders: *Your shepherds slumber . . . your nobles lie down.* The reference could be to the "sleep" of death (cf. Ps. 13:4 [Eng. 3]; 76:6 [Eng. 5]; Job 3:13; 14:12; Jer. 51:39, 57; Dan. 12:2). But the immediately previous context describing leaders that *flee away* like a locust horde suggests that Nahum critiques the indolence, the negligence, the slovenliness of Assyrian leadership. The parallelism of *sleep* with *lie down* supports this conclusion, since the latter term is seldom used of death, particularly without specifying that a person lies down in "death" or "the grave," as in Isa. 26:19.

The king of Assyria may be oblivious to what is happening across his kingdom, but he shall learn of the effects of negligence and dissipation on the part of his leadership soon enough. Already his people *are scattered on the mountains, and no one gathers them* (v. 18b). A contingency of clever subordinates may keep the king in the dark about the true state of his empire, but the truth will out. The inevitable result of the leaders' neglect must be the collapse of the kingdom.

The term *shepherd (rô'eh)* indicates a role of responsibility in caring for those needing direction for their lives. *noble ('addîr)* characterizes various objects, including ships, trees, and the waters of the sea (cf. Isa. 33:21; Ezek. 17:23; Exod. 15:10). It speaks of the majestic expanse of a lofty object. But the leadership of Assyria has been neither majestic nor caring. As a consequence, the citizens all across this far-flung empire have been forced to flee to the mountains.

The imagery of a disseminated people scattered like sheep without a shepherd is found repeatedly in Scripture. Moses prays for a successor to himself "who shall go out before them and come in before them, and who shall lead them out and bring them in; that the congregation of the Lord may not be as sheep which have no shepherd" (Num. 27:17). Micaiah the prophet anticipates the death of Ahab, and sees "all Israel scattered upon the mountains, as sheep that have no shepherd" (1 K. 22:17). Scattered across the mountains, the remnant of a once great nation cowers in caves without hope of restoration apart from a caring leadership.

Of course, the king of Assyria himself must bear the brunt of the responsibility for this dissolution of his people. He first set the example of a ruthless monarch who claimed everything for his own selfish ends. No surprise, therefore, that his underlings, his appointees, manifest the same rapacious behavior. By use of the masculine form of the pronoun throughout v. 18 in contrast with the feminine pronouns in the earlier verses of this section, Nahum indicates that these negligent nobles are the servants of the king.

Like his contemporaries Habakkuk and Zephaniah, Nahum presents little or nothing in terms of explicit messianic expectation. He does not speak of a coming shepherd-king who shall give hope to the devastated that would contrast with the unfeeling actions of the king of Assyria. But his contemporary Jeremiah does (Jer. 23:4–6). The prophet Ezekiel also proclaims his expectation of a revived Davidic shepherd who shall contrast with the selfish shepherds of Israel (cf. Ezek. 34:22–24).

Standing in historic contrast with the unfeeling king of Assyria is the Son of David as presented in the good news of Matthew. Observing the state of the multitudes, Jesus was moved with compassion "because they were distressed and downcast like sheep without a shepherd" (Matt. 9:36, NASB). He then commanded his disciples to pray that the Lord of the harvest would send forth people who would *work (ergátas)* (Matt. 9:38). He had no place in his kingdom for the sluggards, the indolent, the drones, the polishers of the brass. Jesus then took decisive action. He commissioned the twelve and commanded them to "go to the lost sheep of the house of Israel" announcing that the *kingdom* of heaven had come (Matt. 10:1, 6–7).

The people of the king of Assyria had been scattered on the mountains and not one of his appointees had an inclination to gather them. Much less had the king himself any inclination to gather the sheep. What a contrast with the King of Kings and Lord of Lords, the Son of God who as the good shepherd laid down his life for the sheep (John 10:11).

2. The Final Tragedy of Persistent Sin (3:19)

19 *There can be no lessening*
of your blow;
your plague
is fatal.

All who hear your story

> *will clap their hands over you.*[1]
> *For upon whom*
>   *has not your cruelty been inflicted*
>   *continually?*

Having declared the utter futility of all human resources that Nineveh might muster in their self-defense, the prophet now comes to his final word. For the third time in this chapter he addresses a rhetorical question to the Assyrians themselves, now forcing them to acknowledge the tragic proportions of their collapse as an empire.

The person to whom this final query is addressed is different from the two previous cases. In both other instances, the question was addressed in a feminine singular form (vv. 7–8). But now the question apparently comes in a masculine singular form (v. 19). The feminine singular pronouns in the first two instances almost certainly would refer to the city of Nineveh. The masculine singular of v. 19 appears to refer to the king of Nineveh, following as it does the specific word addressed to him in v. 18.

So the *blow* and the *plague* describe the striking of the mighty monarch, the king of Assyria. Historically, the king on the throne in Nahum's day probably was Ashurbanipal, one of the cruelest and most despotic of the Assyrian rulers. But Nahum's reference might be more general, referring to the succession of rulers in Nineveh.

Why can there be no *lessening* of his punishment? Because although the wheels of God's justice may grind slowly, they grind exceedingly fine. The time comes when the longsuffering of God will endure no more. Then he shall bring swift vengeance on his enemies. Such a message applies to every oppressor. At a certain point, the time comes when the Lord will endure no more. For a while he may suffer the tyrant to live in luxury bought by the blood of his martyrs. But a complete reckoning shall be required.

Perhaps the most tragic dimension of the demise of the king of Assyria is Nahum's note that all people everywhere will rejoice in his end. *All who hear your story will clap their hands over you.* Universally the response shall be the same. Without newspapers, television, radio, or satellite, the word will spread overnight. When an oppressive monarch like Ashurbanipal falls, the reverberations are heard to the ends of the earth.

A vigorous, jubilant, uninhibited applause shall break out spon-

---

1. The AV reads "all that hear the bruit of thee"; *bruit* was a common term in the 16th century meaning "report," borrowed from the French *bruit,* meaning "noise." Cf. Driver, p. 46.

taneously at the death of Nineveh's king. Even as the allies hailed the fall of Nazi Germany and the apparent death of Adolf Hitler, so all nations were to greet the news of the demise of Assyria's king. Like infamous King Jehoiakim of Judah who had the burial of an ass (Jer. 22:19), so Assyria's monarch shall end in infamy.

The reason for this response among the nations is plain to see. The prophet poses his final question in unavoidable terms: *upon whom has not your cruelty been inflicted?* To the mighty monarch he says, What can you expect? No person and no nation has been spared your brutality. Three continents have reeled for decades from the irrational extremes of your passion. Shall those whose eyes you have gouged out shed tears at your death? Shall those whose ears and noses you have cut off lament now? Shall the tongues you have chopped off recite your praises?

With his very last word the prophet heightens the horrors of the Assyrian monarch: *continually (tāmîd).* Continually and continuously the king has brought havoc on the nations. Rather than softening at the moans and sighs of the multitudes, the tyrant has relentlessly tormented his subjects.

In radical contrast, the God of Israel has shown himself to be *continually* patient and longsuffering. The showbread of the tabernacle was to represent his beneficence *continually* (Exod. 25:30). The cloud of God's glory covered the Israelites *continually* (Num. 9:16). The eyes of the Lord observed the land *continually* (Deut. 11:12).

The continuous patience of the Lord with the king of Assyria should have led him to repentance. His experience of the goodness of God ought to have turned his head toward mercy and grace in his dealing with others.

The ultimate tragedy of persistent sin is vividly displayed in the final word about the king of Assyria. God will destroy him along with his nation, and people universally will break out in shouts of jubilation, clapping their hands at the destruction of their tormentor.

Could Nahum actually have uttered these words in the teeth of the king of Assyria and survived? It has been suggested that the peculiar reference to the *book* of the prophecy of Nahum in the heading indicates that he wrote but did not proclaim his words.[2] Granted that Nahum's freedom and his life would be at stake for the utterance of such a message. Tens of thousands had been brutally maltreated by the king of Assyria for no crime other than belonging to the multitudes of his conquered peoples. Would he tolerate the open condemnation found in Nahum's words? Perhaps not. Perhaps Nahum did not survive to see the fulfillment of his word from the

2. Rudolph, p. 188.

Lord. Perhaps he should be listed among those of whom the world was not worthy.

But in any case the pattern of prophetic preachers of the word of God does not suggest that Nahum might have distributed his message unsigned and unspoken because of a fear of the consequences of public proclamation. A significant portion of the book is addressed directly to the inhabitants of Nineveh and to their king. In accord with the pattern of history among Israel's prophets, a street-corner declaration of the truth could be expected, whatever the consequences.

It must not be forgotten that Jonah also had been commissioned one hundred years earlier with a word of judgment addressed specifically to Nineveh. In his case, Jonah had been commanded to deliver his message within the public squares of Nineveh itself.

One further point of comparison between Jonah and Nahum is worthy of note. A question ends only two books of the Bible's sixty-six: Jonah and Nahum. Both books are found among the twelve Minor Prophets; both are about the same length; both concern the fate of Nineveh; both end with a question.[3]

Nahum's question proclaims justice. *For upon whom has not your cruelty been inflicted continually?* explains why God's vengeance at last must fall on the unrepentant city. Jonah's question proclaims mercy. "Should not I have compassion on Nineveh . . .?" (Jon. 4:11, NASB) explains why the longsuffering of God means salvation even for those who have done great wickedness.

T. F. Glasson has suggested that the ending of Jonah "is perhaps consciously designed to refute the implication of Nahum's final question."[4] On the basis of this proposition, it is concluded that Jonah must have been written after Nahum. But a conclusion about the relative dating of the two books on this kind of theological analysis nullifies the whole message of the book of Nahum and ignores the uniform testimony of the Scriptures that a time comes in which the offer of mercy must be superseded by divine judgment. The reality of retribution on the wicked does not appear suddenly at the end of Nahum's prophecy in the form of a final rhetorical question. Instead, the entire substance of the prophecy guarantees that the right answer shall be given to Nahum's question.

How glorious is the wisdom of God in dealing with sinners!

---

3. Cf. T. F. Glasson, "The Final Question—in Nahum and Jonah," *ExpTim* 81 (1969–70) 54–55.
4. Ibid.

In the 8th century B.C., Jonah was commissioned to proclaim a message that would eventuate in the salvation of the city of Nineveh, including its king, despite their great sin. Coming approximately one hundred years after Jonah, the message of Nahum in the mid-seventh century provides a framework of integrity for God's offer of mercy. The unrepentant ultimately shall be judged. The utter destruction of the city of Nineveh in 612 confirms the validity of Nahum's words. He was indeed a prophet of God according to the criterion established by Moses (cf. Deut. 18:21–22).

The truthfulness of his prophecy means that in principle each successive world kingdom, its king, its officials, and its citizens must take heed. For the message of the judgment of Nineveh applies: "to all the kingdoms of the world which have risen up against God since the destruction of Asshur, and which will still continue to do so to the end of the world."[5]

5. Keil, p. 48.

The Book of
HABAKKUK

SUPERSCRIPTION (1:1)

1 *The burden which Habakkuk the prophet saw.*

Habakkuk's prophecy possesses a burdensome dimension from start to finish. The book begins with a plaintive cry, "How long . . .?" It ends with the prophet's resolve to endure the severe judgment of God that is sure to come. This message is appropriately designated *the burden* of Habakkuk.[1]

Only the gift of the inspiring Spirit of prophecy could make it possible for a person to declare with faithfulness the utter destruction of his own people and land. That solemn office and calling belonged to Habakkuk. Although his call to office is not recorded, he is designated as *the prophet.* Thus he spoke as the appointed mouthpiece of God.

Various conjectures and myths have arisen to fill out the picture of the life of this servant of the Lord.[2] But neither the Scriptures nor outside sources provide any solid information concerning the life of Habakkuk. Like

---

1. It is quite clear that the term *maśśāʾ* may apply to a literal "burden" that must be borne (cf. Exod. 23:5; 2 K. 5:17; 8:9). It is not so clear that the term also may mean simply "utterance," despite the opinion of most modern and some ancient interpreters. The term introduces a message of judgment or doom in almost every case in which it precedes a prophetic pronouncement. Particularly in the case of Habakkuk's message, it seems appropriate to translate the term as "burden" rather than merely as "utterance." For further discussion and reference to relevant literature, see the commentary above on Nah. 1:1.

2. Jerome and Luther trace the root of the prophet's name to a term meaning "to embrace." More recently it has been related to an Akkadian name of a plant. Habakkuk is mentioned in the Greek addition to the book of Daniel as one who appeared to Daniel in the den of lions (Bel and the Dragon, 33–39). On the basis of the reference in Hab. 3:19 to "my *neginoth*," it has been concluded that Habakkuk was levitical in origin and participated in the temple worship at Jerusalem. But this suggestion assumes that only Levites could compose poems or make use of musical instruments. For comments on these various conjectures regarding Habakkuk, see Rudolph, p. 199.

Elijah as well as John the Baptist, that prophet par excellence of the new covenant, Habakkuk appeared as a "voice" and nothing more. He must be heard because he was the bearer of God's message, not because of what he was in himself.

The fact that Habakkuk *saw* his message probably stresses more the revelational character of the vision than the mode by which it was communicated. Rather than originating from the prophet's own subconscious, this word came directly from God himself.

The message of Habakkuk is distinctive in both its form and its substance. In addition to the parallelism which might be expected in a prophetic book, Habakkuk's message introduces other significant forms. Most striking is the dialogue form of ch. 1. But the five woes of ch. 2 as well as the full-fledged psalm in ch. 3, completely readied for celebration, also deserve notice.

Despite this diversity in form, the prophet's message has a distinctive unity. The underlying theme of the book may be summarized as follows: *A matured faith trusts humbly but persistently in God's design for establishing righteousness in the earth.*

Remarkably, the reader is allowed the unique privilege of witnessing the progress of the prophet himself in submitting to a new concept of the Lord's purposes among Israel and the nations. The idea of growth or maturing in faith is essential to appreciating the genius of this prophecy. Trust in the purposes of the Lord despite confusing perceptions of precisely what he is doing lies at the center of the thought of Habakkuk. Broader intentions of the Lord come to the fore as the prophet wrestles with progressive disclosures.

I. THE DIALOGUE OF PROTEST (1:2–17)

The form of direct dialogue with God is distinctive in itself as a mode of prophetic revelation. But careful observation of the particulars of this form as found in Habakkuk discloses other noteworthy elements.

The prophet speaks as an individual addressing God. But the Lord returns answer to a plurality of people rather than to the prophet himself. This divergence of addressees is appropriate to the perspective of both God and the prophet. Habakkuk suffers with a sense of aloneness as a consequence of the estrangement created by the violence God's people have experienced at the hands of one another. He addresses God as an isolated voice, although he speaks on behalf of others in his position as prophetic mediator. So the Lord returns answer, not in a way that bypasses his agonizing prophet, but only by including him among those others scattered throughout Israel that remain steadfast in faith despite their perplexity.

Even the mode employed by the prophet in recording the divine response deserves notice. Clearly a change of speakers occurs in 1:5. In response to a single individual addressing God ("How long, O Yahweh, shall *I* cry for help," v. 2), the Lord himself addresses all his people ("Look [*ye*] among the nations and see," v. 5). Yet the prophet employs none of the standard formulae for introducing a divine oracle, so that the reader is left to his own devices to determine who happens to be the speaker at any given point in the dialogue. Not until 2:2 is a speaker specifically identified.

This particular literary mode heightens the drama of dialogue. The critical nature of the situation demands directness of address, and the book of Habakkuk provides God's word in a form adequate to the situation. God speaks directly to his people, rather than addressing first the prophet as an individual.

A. THE PROPHETIC SPOKESMAN COMPLAINS AGAINST UNANSWERED PRAYER FOR RELIEF FROM INJUSTICE (1:2–4)

2 *a How long, O Yahweh, shall I cry for help?*
   b But no! You will not hear.
   a I cry out to you, "Violence!"
   b But no! You will not save.
3 *a Why do you make me look*
   b   on trouble?
   b At suffering
   a you force me to stare.

Plundering and violence confront me;
there is strife, and contention arises.
4 *Therefore*
   a God's law
   b is numbed;
   a justice
   b is not carried out to its proper end.

For the wicked surround the righteous;
therefore justice goes forth perverted.

2–3 Two expressions introduce the complaint of the prophet: *How long* and *Why.* The first implies that the prophet had spent some time already in petition to God out of his deep concern for the prevailing circumstances of his day. Many times over he had returned with heart broken to pray over the awful situation. Finally he has come to the point of utter puzzlement over the silence of God. He cannot understand how the Almighty can allow the situation to continue any longer.

2   Perhaps it might have been some consolation to the prophet if he had recalled that the Lord himself was the first to cry "How long?" Long before Habakkuk had begun his struggle with the problem of the prevalence of evil, oppression, and injustice, the Righteous One had asked "How long?" The God of grace had asked "How long?" when Israel ignored the goodness involved in his granting a double portion of manna on the day before the sabbath (Exod. 16:28). When the people showed their unbelief by accepting the report of the skeptical spies, the Lord had asked "How long?" (Num. 14:11). Without doubt the Lord entered sympathetically into the agonies of his prophet. Although his own longsuffering explains his delay in the establishment of justice, he nonetheless agonizes with his people in their grief.

This perspective may provide a proper context for answering the question concerning whether the prophet remained within the bounds of propriety in asking these questions. Since prayer is provided specifically as the framework in which all the burdens of God's people may be poured out before the Lord, prayers expressing perplexity are appropriate so long as they are offered in a context of trust. So long as the mystery of iniquity is at work, God's people shall long earnestly for relief from its pain. Even saints in perfection are depicted as longing for the righteous retribution that must fall on the wicked, crying with a loud voice, "How long!" (Rev. 6:10). If a deficiency of his disciples' faith to work miracles provokes the Mediator of the new covenant to ask "how long" he should be patient, it should not be surprising to find a prophet of the old covenant asking "how long" the Lord would tolerate the gross injustices of his contemporaries (cf. Matt. 17:17).

The substance of the prophet's complaint centers on unanswered prayer. He has cried for relief from injustice; he has not been answered. A previous historical situation explains in part the perplexities of this circumstance. At the time of Israel's insistence on the establishment of the monarchy, the Lord warned them through his servant: "You will cry out for relief from the king you have chosen, and the Lord *will not answer you* in that day" (1 Sam. 8:18). The consummate consequence of their rejecting God as king is that a wicked monarchy would bring them into a state of oppression. Then the Lord would not hear their cry for relief. The prophet cries, but the Lord does not hear. The wickedness brought in by Manasseh and his predecessors has sealed Israel's fate. Left to themselves, they suffer endless abuses.

Most often the references to God's people crying in distress are balanced by the affirmation that God has heard their cry (Exod. 2:23; Judg. 3:9; Ps. 22:6, 25 [Eng. 5, 24]; 30:3 [Eng. 2]; 72:12; Jon. 2:3 [Eng. 2]; Isa. 58:9). But hints also appear that the sin of God's people may lead the Lord not to respond with deliverance immediately when they cry. In the days of the judges, the Lord forced the people to remember their sin before he even hinted at deliverance (Judg. 6:7). The psalmist implies that a prolonged period of prayer preceded his own deliverance (Ps. 22:7 [Eng. 6]). Particularly Job as a wisdom figure puzzles over God's failure to answer his cry. His language strikingly parallels that found in Habakkuk:

Job 19:7   *ʾeṣʿaq ḥāmās*
                       wᵉlōʾ ʾēʿāneh

            I cry out, "Violence!"
                       and you do not answer.

Hab. 1:2   *ʾezʿaq ʾēleykā ḥāmās*
                       wᵉlōʾ tôšîaʿ

            I cry out to you, "Violence!"
                       and you do not hear.

Indeed, only the wisdom of God can answer this admittedly perplexing question of prayer for deliverance that remains unheard and unanswered.

Unwittingly, the prophet may have anticipated a major aspect of the answer to his own query by the very form of this question. When he announces his distress over *violence (ḥāmās)* in the land, he echoes the description of the prevailing circumstances in the days of the flood. At that time also, the earth was filled with "violence" (cf. Gen. 6:11, 13). But now the unique situation prevails in which those set apart to be God's own people are instigating violence among themselves.[1] For that reason, judgment will have to begin with the house of God. Because they have violated the stipulations of the covenant, they must undergo the curses promised in the covenant made hundreds of years previously: "Day after day you will be oppressed and robbed, with no one to rescue you" (Deut. 28:29).

A further complication in this case is seen in the fact that Habakkuk stands among the innocent rather than as a propagator of violence. As pro-

---

1. The ones propagating violence cannot be the Chaldeans, for they are to be God's instrument of judgment (v. 6). They cannot be the Assyrians, for they could not be characterized very convincingly as "more righteous" than the Chaldeans (v. 13). The abuse of *torah* points to God's own people oppressing one another.

phetic mediator, his petition is offered in behalf of the whole of the faithful remnant. Why should not this prayer be answered?

It is out of this context that the prophet registers his protest with the Lord. In view of the Lord's intention to maintain a people for himself, how can he refuse to provide deliverance in such desperate circumstances?

3 The specifics of Habakkuk's complaint are spelled out more fully in three couplets: *trouble and suffering, plundering and violence, strife and contention.*[2] Earlier, Balaam had reflected on the blessing of God's people by noting that he could find no "trouble" (*'āwen*) and "suffering" (*'āmāl*) in Israel (Num. 23:21). But now the entire nation is plagued by these griefs. Both sin and its consequences prevail throughout the country.

4 In this situation, possessing the law does Israel absolutely no good. *God's law is numbed.* Its sensitivity to the cause of right has been stifled. The best law in the world profits nothing if its statutes are not maintained. The *wicked* outnumber the righteous, *surround* them, and enforce their own will on the people. *Justice* is not carried out, but is *perverted* instead. The worst thing a righteous person could do would be to appeal to the courts of the land for the adjudication of his case. For it is certain that the decision would be rendered against him.[3]

---

2. The precise understanding of these terms in this context is difficult. *'āwen* and *'āmāl* may describe either the consequences that come from sin (trouble, sorrow; toil, suffering, as in Gen. 35:18; Ps. 7:15 [Eng. 14]; 10:14; Jer. 20:18), or the sin that brings these circumstances (troublesomeness, perverseness; mischief, evil, as in Job 34:36; Isa. 1:13; Ps. 7:17 [Eng. 16]). *šōd* may describe "devastation" in general or "plundering" as a particular manner in which devastation occurs. *rîb* may communicate the general idea of "strife," or may refer more specifically to a "lawsuit" as a formal manner of instigating strife.

3. The commentary on Habakkuk from the Dead Sea Scrolls (1QpHab) interprets "the righteous" (singular in form) as referring to *môreh haṣṣedeq,* "the teacher of righteousness." W. H. Brownlee, *The Midrash Pesher of Habakkuk,* SBL Monograph 24 (Missoula: Scholars Press, 1979), p. 46, conjectures that the missing portion of the commentary on this verse interpreted "the wicked" (also singular in form) as referring to the wicked priest. Thus the scroll would have introduced at this early point the two major antagonists. Brownlee regards this analysis as appropriate, since "the text itself indicates a persecuted righteous one who is the object of injustice on the part of the wicked man."

While 1QpHab is intriguing for the insight it provides into the historical situation of the Qumran community, it does not seem likely that Habakkuk intends to refer to a singular righteous sufferer who is the victim of a single adversary. Instead, the contemporizing hermeneutic of the Dead Sea community has enforced its historical circumstance on the prophetic words of Habakkuk.

So the prophet offers his complaint. It is indeed a strong one. He can find no justice among God's own people. Instead, a brutal perversion of God's law prevails throughout the land. The righteous people of the Lord suffer endless abuse. Prayers of the devout go unheard. How does the Lord explain this terrible circumstance, and his own lack of response to the cry of the prophetic mediator?

B. THE LORD UNVEILS HIS AWESOME INSTRUMENT OF RETRIBUTION (1:5–11)

Now comes the divine response. The Lord had listened patiently to the complaint of the prophet. Since the divine response is addressed to a plurality of persons, it may be assumed that Habakkuk was viewed as speaking for a group of people rather than simply for himself.

Awesome is the answer of the Lord to the complaint of the prophet. Interestingly, in no way does the Lord dispute the analysis of Habakkuk concerning the circumstances prevailing in the nation. The Lord agrees with the prophetic indictment against the behavior of the covenant people. Violence prevails. Strife, contention, plundering, and perversion of justice permeate the nation.

Agreement from the Lord on all these counts must have disarmed the prophet to a certain degree. He can no longer object that the Lord does not see the corruption of the land. Habakkuk may not yet be completely disarmed. But the process has begun.

The total absence of rebuke to the complainer also should be appreciated for its disarming effect. The Lord himself is fully in sympathy with the prophet's agony over the suffering righteous ones. Although having larger concerns as well, the Lord knows and sympathizes with these who have been surrounded by the wicked.

The stunning character of the Lord's revelation relates to the awesomeness of the divine response that hovers on the horizon of history. When this coming reality is appreciated, it becomes plain that the Lord perceives the problem even more deeply than does the prophet. His resolution of the problem therefore appears overwhelming.

Preparatory to unveiling his resolution to this injustice, the Lord warns with ominous words of the awesomeness of that which prophet and people shall see (v. 5). Then he identifies specifically the instrument he has prepared to bring judgment (v. 6a). Finally he characterizes with as many as twenty details the coming force for retribution (vv. 6b–11).

1. Preparation for the Unveiling of God's Instrument of Retribution (1:5)

> 5 *Look among the nations*
> *and see!*
> *Be astonished!*
> *Wonder!*
>
> *For I[1] am working a work in your days;*
> *You would not believe*
> *even if it were told.*

God is no alarmist. Yet he assembles no less than four words of alert to awaken the recipients of this message: *Look! See! Be astonished! Wonder!* The prophet had presented a perplexing problem. The divine response is of such an overwhelming nature that even this kind of alarm is not excessive in preparing the people for its reception.

The announcement of impending judgment that must fall receives additional vigor in that it occurs without introduction. No formula such as "the Lord replied to me saying . . ." occurs. Yet it is clear that a change of speakers has occurred, and that God now addresses the people and their prophet. The calls to alertness in v. 5 are in the plural; and in v. 6 the speaker declares that he is raising up a foreign nation to judge Israel. Such a sovereign action could be accomplished only by the Almighty himself.

Who are the people addressed by these admonitions? Does the Lord speak to the Israelite nation as a whole? Does he seek to alert more particularly the faithful remnant for whom Habakkuk serves as spokesman? Or do these terrible words of judgment address more directly the wicked among the nation who shall receive in themselves the brunt of God's astounding work of devastation? The answer to this question hinges largely on the reading adopted as the original text of the oracle.

Two textual options must be considered:

(1) "Look among the nations" *(rᵉʾû baggôyim),* (2) "Look, you who deal treacherously" *(rᵉʾû bōgᵉḏîm).* The first possibility is supported by the

---

1. GKC, § 116s, expresses uncertainty about the possibility of a first person pronoun serving as the understood subject of a participle in Hebrew. In view of this consideration, Rudolph, p. 203 n.5(c) suggests a passive pointing (Paʿul rather than Poʿel; a work "is being done"). Brownlee, *Midrash,* p. 54, favors "he is working." Yet the understood first person subject is not excluded by GKC. The LXX reads *egṓ ergázomai;* and the next verse of Habakkuk indicates that God actually is the subject ("Behold *me* raising up" the Chaldeans—*exegeírō).*

MT and some Greek manuscripts, while the second reading is supported by the LXX, by 1QpHab, and by the NT text (Acts 13:41). A choice between these two options is difficult to make. The full weight of the surviving Hebrew texts as represented in the Massoretic tradition must be recognized. At the same time, the joint testimony of the LXX, 1QpHab, and the NT must be appreciated.

In evaluating the evidence supportive of a reading other than that which is represented in the surviving Hebrew text of Habakkuk, several factors must be noted.[2] With respect to the LXX rendering, one must first recognize that the Greek term chosen actually means "ye scornful" or "ye who think lightly" *(kataphronētaí)*, which is not exactly the same as "you who act treacherously" *(bōg^edîm)*. It is not surprising, then, to find that of the approximately 50 times in which the Hebrew term *bāgad* is found in the MT, the LXX translators chose to use *kataphronéō* only about five times, or ten percent of the total.

However, since the same plural participle *bōg^edîm* in Hab. 1:13 is rendered by the LXX as *kataphronéō* and the singular participle *bôgēd* in 2:5 is rendered in the LXX as *kataphronētḗs,* the greater likelihood is that the LXX supports a reading of *bāgad* in Hab. 1:5 as well.

A second consideration has some bearing on the evaluation of the LXX's testimony. The words "and perish" *(kai aphanísthēte)* are introduced by the LXX translators, apparently having no basis in the Hebrew text. The introduction of these words may indicate that the Greek translators had sensed an incompleteness in the thought of the passage as they had rendered it apart from this addition. If the MT is followed, the admonition to "look among the nations" is completed quite naturally by the reference in the next verse to that particular "nation" (the Chaldeans) whom the Lord would raise up. But if the LXX is followed, nothing in the succeeding verses satisfactorily completes the thought begun by an address to "scoffers" that they "behold . . . and look." What is to be the consequence for them specifically when God raises up the Chaldeans? Although it could be concluded that the implication is that they would "perish," the LXX sensed a need to fill out the thought by adding this comment. This factor offers some support in favor of the genuineness of the MT. For it has the advantage of representing a complete thought in context.

Some comment also must be made with respect to the testimony of 1QpHab. This particular document is quite amazing in that approximately

---

2. It ought to be underscored at this point that the reading *baggôyim* is the only extant representation of the text in Hebrew. 1QpHab reads *bwgdym* in its interpretative remarks, but the text itself is missing at this point.

eighty percent of the text of the first two chapters of Habakkuk has been preserved from about the 2nd century B.C. This representation of the text is interspersed among interpretative comments.

However, the text of the crucial portion of this verse in Habakkuk has not been preserved. Only on the basis of a conjecture from the interpretative comments that follow may the reading be reconstructed. Since a reference is made to the *bōgᵉḏîm* in the interpretative remark that follows the space where the text of Hab. 1:5 had originally stood, a good case may be made for assuming the text would have read in the same way.

Yet the matter cannot be concluded with full certainty. For it is fairly clear that in their zeal to contemporize the message of Habakkuk, the Qumran scribes often departed rather radically from the text of the prophecy in their interpretations. In the next verse, their representation of the biblical *text* clearly reads *kaśdîm*, identifying the "Chaldeans" as the nation that is to arise, in full agreement with the MT. But in their *commentary*, the scribes read *kittîm*, referring apparently in a cryptic manner to the contemporary Romans.

In opposing the Massoretic "Look among the nations," it has been argued that no reference is made to "nations" in the subsequent verses of Habakkuk.[3] But this argument is based on a false premise. For the very next verse refers to the Chaldeans as "the nation" (Hab. 1:6). Certainly the identification of a single "nation" as the instrument of God's judgment is appropriate as a development of the admonition to "Look among the nations."

A problem of some substance arises with the context of Habakkuk if the reading supported by the LXX and 1QpHab is adopted. If those addressed are to be identified as the "traitorous ones" *(bōgᵉḏîm)*, then Habakkuk the prophet is excluded from those to whom the divine response is directed. He had posed the question on behalf of the remnant in Israel. But God's response would not address him specifically, for he would not be included among the "traitorous ones" to whom the vocative would refer.

When all these various considerations are weighed, the MT after all should be preferred.[4] The prophet is awed by the violence being experienced by the people of Judah. But God tells him to look on the international horizon.

---

3. Brownlee, *Midrash,* p. 54.

4. The NT may be regarded as a witness to the OT text only in a secondary manner. A quotation from the LXX by the NT does not involve intentional endorsement of the Greek text as representing the more faithful witness. For further comments on this matter, see O. Palmer Robertson, "Genesis 15:6: New Covenant Expositions of an Old Covenant Text," *WTJ* 40/2 (1980) 279–80.

The prophet must expand his perspective on the divine purposes. He must appreciate the Lord's intent among the heathen as well as for Israel.[5]

So the Lord's admonition to *see! Be astonished!* and *Wonder!* is directed to the covenant nation. The whole of his people should stand amazed at the awesome judgment that is coming. For no less than the whole of the nation shall be struck by this judgment. The covenant people of God are told to watch the storm arising, to observe it closely as it advances, and to wonder at the force with which it finally breaks on Israel itself.

Not only the fourfold character of the admonition, but also the distinctive combination of words underscores the intensity with which Judah is to marvel at the revelation now coming.[6] The psalmist of Israel had taught the nation how to dramatize the Lord's deliverances of Jerusalem in their worship:

> When the kings joined forces,
>   when they advanced together,
> they saw, they wondered [*hēmmâ rā''û kēn tāmāhû*]
>   they fled in terror. (Ps. 48:5–6 [Eng. 4–5])

But now the word of the Lord reverses this phenomenon completely. Israel is to look at the nations, to see and to wonder (*rᵉ'û . . . tᵉmāhû*). For a terrible judgment is coming on the covenant people themselves.

But had not Israel been warned? Had not the nation heard regularly at the reading of the law that the Lord would smite Israel with madness, blindness, and "astonishment of heart" (*bᵉṯimhôn lēḇāḇ*—Deut. 28:28, AV)?

The particular event for which Israel was to be astonished had to be viewed ultimately not as an example of human brutality but of the awesome work of God. The Lord himself affirms his initiative in bringing forth the Chaldeans as his instrument for judgment when he says, "I am doing a work. . . . Behold me . . . as I bring forth my awful instrument of judgment."

Part of the amazing character of this work of God is that it is to be accomplished in the days of the hearers of this prophecy. *in your days* this event shall occur, says the word of the Lord.

---

5. Others supporting the MT over against the LXX include M. Burrows, *The Dead Sea Scrolls* (New York: Viking, 1955), p. 265; G. Vermes, *Dead Sea Scrolls in English* (Baltimore: Penguin, 1963), p. 276; L. K. Silberman, "Unriddling the Riddle. A Study in the Structure and Language of the Habakkuk Pesher," *RevQ* 3/2 (1961) 335–36.

6. The forms *hittammᵉhû tᵉmāhû* combine a Hithpael and Qal imperative of the same root to underscore the astonishment with which his vision of the coming judgment of God is to be greeted. Note the similar combination of forms with the same root in Isa. 29:9.

Swiftness in the execution of judgment is characteristic of the Lord's activity throughout the ages. Although extremely patient and forbearing with rebellious sinners, the Lord is not slow to act once he has determined that the iniquity of the people is full, and the time for judgment has arrived.

This same suddenness in executing a decree of retribution also characterizes the activity of God under the provisions of the new covenant. All the signs anticipating the consummating judgment were to be fulfilled in Jesus' own generation (Matt. 24:34). Yet the suddenness of his appearing assures that people shall remain unprepared even up to the day of his coming (Matt. 24:36–44). Unbelievable! The wonder which God is about to announce to the people is simply beyond belief. The mystery of God's way of working shall so permeate this particular deed that people will not be able to accept its reality.

Apparently these words intend to describe the unbelievable character of this event even though it should be compared to God's saving events of the past. The Israelites customarily recalled wondrous works of God's previous acts of salvation (Judg. 6:13; Ps. 44:2 [Eng. 1]; 75:2 [Eng. 1]; 78:3). But even if this event which now is being prophesied were to be presented as an act of God's power, it would not be believed.[7] The calling from Ur of the Chaldees, the mighty works associated with the Exodus and conquest could be accepted as true. But a devastating judgment such as now is to be described would not be believed.

What precisely makes this divine work so incredible? Many facets could be noted, including the rapidity of the rise of power of God's instrument for judgment, the intensity of the judgment that is to come, and the fact that God himself is to be involved in this action.[8] But most incredible is the fact that God's own people could be cast off, and at the hands of Gentiles more wicked than they. Such deep mystery veils this aspect of the design of God that it cannot be permeated by the human mind. The prophet Habakkuk had prayed, hoping for some form of purging of the wicked element of the nation. But the divine response speaks of such an utter devastation that even greater puzzlement will grip the mind of the pious prophet.

It is most instructive to note that this very statement concerning the unbelievable character of the coming judgment of God was employed by Paul to forewarn the Jews that they were hardening themselves against his proclamation of the saving acts of God found in the death and resurrection

---

7. The LXX has correctly interpreted the Hebrew imperfects by the use of Greek subjunctives (*pisteúsēte . . . ekdiēgétai*).

8. Rudolph, p. 207.

of Jesus the Messiah (see Acts 13:3ff.). Far from simply taking up a mode of expression found in Habakkuk, Paul captures the heartthrob of the prophet's message and applies its awesome insights into the ways of God with people in his own day.

If the principle of contextual quotation has validity, Paul's application of Habakkuk's words at this point implies several things. First, it implies a unity of the message of the book of Habakkuk. Structurally, the book clearly manifests this unity. But Paul's quote further implies that the message of ch. 1 about a coming judgment on Israel may be understood properly only when it is seen as supportive of the message concerning justification by faith found in ch. 2. By the devastation of those who thought themselves to be righteous by their deeds, the foundation is laid for the message of justification by faith alone.

Second, Paul's quotation indicated that at the heart of justification is the forgiveness of sins. Habakkuk certainly establishes this fact. For in the full context of his prophecy, none can stand righteous in his deeds. Only faith in the promises of God can open the way to forgiveness, which is essential to right-standing with God for any and all transgressors.

Third, Paul's direct application of Habakkuk's words to his contemporaries reveals his concept of the history of redemption. Paul is not appealing to a moralistic truism when he warns his hearers about the possibility that what the prophet has said might come on them.[9] Instead, he is seeing Israel's experience of judgment as anticipating the judgment that should come in the context of the eschatological proclamation of the gospel. This awesome potential for God's turning from the Jews finds its fulfillment on the next sabbath. The Jews of the city reject Paul's proclamation, and Paul indicates that he now would turn from them to the Gentiles (Acts 13:44–46).

This analysis of the thrust of Paul's quotation accords precisely with the purposes of God in the history of redemption as developed by Paul in passages such as Rom. 11 and Eph. 2. By judgment on Israel, the way of salvation is opened for Gentiles.

Fourth, the form of the quotation itself indicates that the apostles did not concern themselves with establishing precisely the original text of an OT passage before "quoting" it. This citation of Habakkuk includes the additional phrase "and perish" *(kai aphanísthēte)*, which has no representation in any

---

9. The manuscript evidence more strongly supports the reading "See that it not come" rather than "See that it not come *on you.*" But it would be pushing the context to suggest that Paul intended to imply that no fulfillment of the prophecy would already have occurred.

extant Hebrew text. Its origin may be explained best as an elaboration of the implications of the text arising from the reading "ye traitors."[10] Those who have betrayed the Lord of the covenant are not only to "wonder" at what is coming; they are to "perish" by what is coming.

In his quotation, Paul has been true to the central thrust of Habakkuk, even to the point of indicating an awareness of the thematic unity of the book. He has brought the prophecy into the framework of its eschatological significance. The complaint against "violence" practiced by brother against brother (Hab. 1:2) now finds its strongest ground in the deliverance of Jesus to Pilate for execution, although no reason for such an action had been found (Acts 13:28). But God's raising him from the dead indicates the uniqueness of Jesus Christ in the ongoing program of redemption.

2. Identification of God's Specific Instrument of Retribution (1:6a)

6a *For behold me raising up the Chaldeans*[1]

The term translated *Chaldeans (kaśdîm)* is used regularly in the OT for the Neo-Babylonian empire founded by Nabopolassar (ca. 626–605) and reaching its zenith of power under Nebuchadrezzar (605–562).[2] They are especially of central concern in the prophecy of Jeremiah, since they were eventually the nation which took Israel into captivity.[3] It is rather remarkable to note the rapid ascendancy to power of this nation, the extent of their domain, and their equally rapid decline in prominence. This whole international escapade underscores the prominence of the divine hand in *raising them up* and also bringing them down. Who would believe that a virtually nonexistent entity could conquer the old capital of Assyria in 614, Nineveh in 612, Harran

10. The inclusion of the additional "and perish" in the NT quotation indicates why the appearance of "ye traitors" rather than "among the nations" in the NT cannot provide the conclusive word on the question concerning the original reading of the Hebrew text.

1. Bernhard Duhm's replacement of *kaśdîm* with *kittîm* and application of the term to the Greeks of Alexander's time is vigorously opposed by Rudolph, p. 206. He regards this interpretation as contradicting all healthy exegetical methods.

Interestingly, 1QpHab reads *kaśdîm* in support of the MT, but interprets the term to refer to the Kittim, apparently alluding either to the Greeks or the more contemporary Romans. This interpretation accords with their intent to denounce contemporary Judaism for its alliance with the Romans.

2. Cf. 2 K. 24:2; 25:4–5, 10, 13, 26; Isa. 13:19; 43:14; 48:14, 20; Ezek. 23:14, 23; 2 Chr. 36:17.

3. Jer. 21:4, 9; 22:25; 32:4–5, 24–25, 28–29, 43; 35:11; 37:9–10; 39:5.

in 610, and rout the armies of Pharaoh Neco at Carchemish in 605? They became the world rulers over Babylonia, Assyria, Syria, Palestine, and Egypt, when twenty years previously they hardly were known to exist. Yet their energy dissipated almost as rapidly, so that they were easily overcome by Cyrus king of Persia in 539, just in time to fulfill the prophecy of Jeremiah concerning Israel's return in seventy years (Jer. 29:10). Astounding indeed are the ways of God among the nations. "Not by their own instinct, but by the hidden impulse of God" do the nations rise and fall.[4]

It is indeed remarkable to note the explicitness of the announcement concerning the designated instrument of God's judgment. The Lord's control of the nations is so great that he orders their rise and fall according to his own plans and purposes. He may choose to disperse his people among the heathen as a way of claiming for himself a populace from all the nations. Yet this dispersion will occur in perfect coordination with the time in which his own people are ripe for judgment because of their persistence in rebellion over the centuries.

3. Characterization of God's Instrument of Judgment (1:6b–11)

After preparing the people for the unveiling of this awesome instrument of judgment and identifying the instrument more specifically, the Lord characterizes the nation that shall judge his people. As many as twenty different features are noted, a number of them coming in couplets.

> 6b *That bitter and impetuous nation*
> *which covers the breadth of the earth*
> *to take possession of territories not rightly*
> *belonging to it.*
> 7 *Fearsome and terrible is it;*
> *from itself shall come forth its (own) justice and honor.*
> 8 *Its horses*
> *a are swifter*
> *b than leopards,*
> *a and are keener*
> *b than wolves of the evening.*
>
> *Its horsemen*
> *gallop (furiously);*
> *Yes, its horsemen*
> *a shall come*
> *b from afar;*

4. John Calvin, p. 27.

a   *they shall fly*
   b   *as a vulture rushes for food.*
9 *Every one of them shall come*
    for violence;
the assembling of their faces
   is forward.
And they shall gather like sand
   captives.
10 *So he*[1]

   at kings will mock;
   and sovereigns are a joke
to him.

He

   at every fortification
    will laugh;
   for he will heap up dust,
    and will take it.
11 *Then*

   his spirit changes,
   and he becomes angry,
   and sins.

This

   his strength
   is his god.

6b *bitter and impetuous.* Not just a few isolated individuals, but this whole *nation* may be characterized as irritated and ill-tempered. Like a bear robbed of its cubs, this mighty nation strikes out irrationally in every direction (see 2 Sam. 17:8). Because of a spirit of bitterness over life, its inhabitants act with irrational cruelty and disruptiveness. The nation also acts precipitously. Because they are not willing to take time to sort out the facts, all the people they conquer suffer great injustices.

covers the breadth of the earth. A fearful and uncertain army advances slowly, cautiously, and by that very procedure provides opportunity for many to escape the miseries they might inflict. But this proud people, confident of victory, does not hesitate to expose its flanks to the enemy. Not a portion of the world escapes its brutal tyranny. Many modern leaders such as

---

1. The masculine pronoun "he" *(hû')* is used in this verse to refer to the nation rather than the more customary "she." *hû'* also appears in v. 7, but the English "it" seems to fit that context better.

Napoleon and Hitler have destroyed their armies by exposing a limited troop to too broad a territory. But this nation has gathered such strength that it has no fears.

Interestingly, Rev. 20:9 echoes precisely the LXX rendering of this phrase. Satan goes out to deceive the nations. His troops are like the sand of the seashore in number. Their vastness mimics the promise of an innumerable seed made to Abraham. This awesome army "marched across the breadth of the earth." Their target is the camp of God's people, the city he loves (Rev. 20:9). But in accord with the experience of God's prophet Elijah, fire comes down from heaven and devours this apocalyptic host.

Habakkuk in his vision has not yet arrived at the point of the destruction of Satan's forces. The army which he confronts still possesses the strength and boldness to take on the world.

to take possession of dwelling places not rightly belonging to it. This characteristic of the instrument of God's judgment on his people sounds strangely similar to the promise made to Israel at the time of their conquest of the land. They were to possess wells they had not dug, vineyards they had not planted, homes and cities they had not built (Deut. 6:10–11). Could it be that these barbaric Babylonians now were to step into the role once occupied by God's people? Did the possession of the holy land imply for them the inheritance of the promises? A subsequent word of the Lord to his prophet will indicate that judgment also shall come for the Babylonians (Hab. 2:6–20). But now the word of prophecy concentrates on the role of this Gentile nation as executor of divine judgment.

So now it is the displacement of Israel that receives attention. In a very real sense, Israel is being placed in the role once occupied by the Canaanites before them. As those people once were driven away from their possessions because their iniquity was full, so now Israel must be driven away from its possessions because its iniquity is full. Their place of comfort, enjoyment, pleasure, relaxation, security, and refreshment shall be taken from them.

The rapacious behavior of the Chaldeans thus shall serve the Lord's purposes. He shall make the wrath of man to praise him. Their oppressive ways shall be fitting judgment for the oppressive.

7 *Fearsome and terrible is he.* The term *Fearsome (ʾāyōm)* occurs as an adjective only here and in Cant. 6:4, 10, where it refers to the awe-inspiring character of an army with banners. But as a noun *(ʾēmâ)* it appears frequently, describing the terror instilled by the bared teeth of a crocodile (Job 41:6 [Eng. 14]), the snort of a warhorse (Job 39:20), or the presence of God (Gen. 15:12: Exod. 15:16; Deut. 32:25). So this fast-approaching enemy shall not come tenderly to reap judgment on Israel.

The second term *(nôrā')* may be translated "awesome," "fearsome," "terrible," or "dreadful." In any case, it describes a response of troublesome terror which might be inspired by a wilderness filled with serpents, scorpions, and drought (Deut. 1:19; 8:15), by hostile nations (Zeph. 2:11), by Yahweh's mighty deeds (Exod. 34:10; cf. 15:11), or by direct confrontation with the Lord himself (Gen. 28:17). But now the recoil of terror shall be fostered by the invading enemy. The terrified ones shall be those of the covenant community.

from itself shall come forth its (own) justice and honor. "Autonomous" summarizes this characteristic of the instrument which God shall employ for judgment. Paradoxical indeed is this circumstance. The Almighty God, who is jealous that he alone be acknowledged as God, shall raise up a nation whose stated policy builds on the premise that it is totally self-determining. This nation shall not look to God for a criterion for righteousness; it shall determine its own standard of truth. Even its own *honor* (lit., "its lifting up") it shall accord to itself. No glory for its accomplishments shall go up to God. Only its own name shall be its concern. Like Nietzsche's *Übermensch,* G. B. Shaw's *Superman,* Goethe's *Prometheus,* and W. W. Henley's *Invictus,* this great memorial to self shall declare boldly its lack of indebtedness to anyone but itself.[2]

Yet clearly it is God who has raised up this nation for his own purposes. He alone is its source of power. Despite all its will for self-determination, the King of Kings shall mete out the tasks of this nation.

8 *Its horses are swifter than leopards, and are keener than wolves of the evening.* No doubt the Israelites might comfort themselves in the fact that they had lived at such a distance from this threatening enemy. Certainly the Assyrians would serve as a buffer, and they had learned how to survive with them through the occasional payment of tribute. In addition, Egypt would be sure to protect its vested interests in the realm of Palestine against any proposed incursions from Babylonia.

But this instrument of divine judgment would shrink long distances to nothing of consequence by the speed of its *horses.* Flight from this avenger would be futile, for with the agility of a *leopard* leaping upon its prey this Chaldean nation would rush after Israel.

Raw hunger for power and for spoils would drive the nation in stalking its prey. As a ravenous appetite drives the *wolves of the evening,* making their senses even keener as the night wears on, so this barbarous nation would search out every fugitive from its powers of consumption.

Its horsemen gallop (furiously); yes, its horsemen shall come from

2. Cf. Laetsch, p. 322.

afar. The horse and chariot of old would be roughly equivalent to today's tanks, submarines, and jets. In attacking, they would overwhelm any opposition placed in their path. Though the distance was great, the Babylonian nation would arrive in Palestine with a full contingency and mounted troops. No weapons would be able to stand against them.

they shall fly as a vulture rushes for food. As the curses of the covenant had declared, God would bring a nation from the ends of the earth, "like an eagle swooping down" (Deut. 28:49).[3] With all the speed belonging to a swooping bird of prey, this instrument will leap on the nation of covenant breakers before they can find shelter. Like a *vulture,* its oppressive body shall grasp and tear the flesh of its exposed victims. In accord with the curses of the covenant, no one shall bury the carcasses (cf. Gen. 15:11; Jer. 34:20). This same graphic curse finds echo in the description of the final judgment which the Lord shall bring on all his adversaries (cf. Rev. 19:17–18). Awesome indeed is the divine purpose of retribution.

9 *Every one of them shall come for violence.* The divine standard of justice is terrible in its consequences. Habakkuk had complained against his own community because violence characterized their relations to one another (1:2b). So now as a just recompense these sinners shall experience *violence* at the hands of a brutal invader.

the assembling of their faces is forward. This particular phrase is the most difficult in this list of characteristics of the instrument of judgment being raised up by the Lord. The precise meaning of the three Hebrew words is in doubt, and a variety of meanings is possible as they are combined in different ways.

The term translated *assembling (mᵉgammaṭ)* is a Piel participle in construct with the word which follows. It occurs only here in the OT, which makes the determination of its meaning quite difficult.[4] But since the other two words in this phrase are more common, it may be best to delay the interpretation of this first term until the other elements in the expression have been explored.

The second term, *pᵉnêhem* (lit., "their faces"), probably refers to the front ranks of the advancing troops of the Chaldeans. This meaning is supported by a parallel passage in Joel 2:20, in which the "front" *(pānāyw)* of a troop is contrasted with its "rear" *(sōp̄ô).*

---

3. Other references to this same figure of judgment may be found in Jer. 4:13; 48:40; 49:22; Lam. 4:19; Hos. 8:1.

4. Its authenticity is attested by 1QpHab. The LXX translates *anthestēkótas,* "resisting," which is not helpful.

The "front" of this troop is directed *forward* or "eastward" *(qādîmâ).*[5] An easterly direction for the front ranks of this advancing horde would be conceivable in this context only if it be assumed that the army has made its way to the edge of the Mediterranean, and is now turning eastward for its assault on Jerusalem. This route would be the normal path for an army invading Palestine.

However, the progression of thought in the passage has not arrived at this point. "Kings" and "princes" still must be subdued (v. 10). So the more likely significance of this word is *forward.* The front line of the troop moves forward.

The precise nuance to be given to the forward movement of the front ranks depends finally on the meaning of the difficult word which stands first in this clause, *m^egammat.* It could mean "eagerness," hence "the *eagerness* of their front rank is to move forward."[6] But the more likely reference is to the *assembling* or "collection" of their front rank.[7] Irresistibly, inevitably, uninterruptedly, this horde of warriors moves toward the land of God's covenant people. Relentlessly they move on, and certainly they shall arrive one day to bring total judgment and devastation.

And they shall gather like sand captives. Abraham had been promised that his seed would be as the sand of the seashore. But must their multiplication end in this tragic condition? Must they be gathered in heaps and carried into captivity?

According to the laws of God's covenant, transgressors must end up in this condition. For according to the deuteronomic law code, Israel would beget sons and daughters, but they would be taken into captivity if the nation fell into sin (cf. Deut. 28:41). Once more, the prophetic word concretizes in history the original stipulations of the covenant.

This instrument appointed for judgment shall possess little or no sympathy for human suffering. A vast number of human souls shall mean no more than the innumerable grains of sand along the seashore.

10 *So he at kings will mock; and sovereigns are a joke to him.* Is-

---

5. The reading *qāḏîm,* omitting the final *h,* is supported by 1QpHab and makes possible a reference to the "east wind." Cf. the supportive renderings of Symmachus, Theodotion, and the Vulgate. Rashi interprets: "The exhalation of their face is like the East Wind, the strongest of winds." Cf. Brownlee, *Midrash,* p. 70.

6. BDB, pp. 169–70, questions a possible derivation from *gāmā',* "to swallow."

7. Probably derived from *gāmam,* "to become abundant." Cf. BDB, pp. 169–70. For other possibilities, see Brownlee, *Midrash,* p. 69, who favors "the mutterings of their faces are the east wind."

rael always previously had been able to count on buffer nations to absorb the lethal blows of invaders. But this adversary makes fun of the most powerful figures of the earth. How then may the remnant of Judah expect to resist successfully the invasion of this enemy?

He at every fortification will laugh; for he will heap up dust, and will take it. When Israel was about to take possession of the land of promise, spies were sent to determine whether the inhabitants lived in tents or in fortifications (Num. 13:19). The results of such an evaluation would have a very definite effect on their approach to the land. For a fortified city not only represented a greater obstacle to be overcome by an invader. It also represented a positive threat. For the armed inhabitants of a well-stocked and well-fortified city would work havoc on an invader, while exposing themselves to little danger. An army must count carefully the cost of entering the territory of a fortified city.

But this invading nation shall mock at the resistance implied in all such fortifications. He shall not fear the danger the sieging of a city might mean to his men. With little effort he shall break down all opposition and claim the spoils of the city for himself.

11   *Then his spirit changes, and he becomes angry and sins.* Too abrupt a change of direction in the flow of the argument would be involved to support the idea that these words indicate an intervention on God's part in entering into judgment with the Babylonian because he had passed over the bounds of propriety in bringing judgment on Israel ("he passes over").[8] Instead, the verse contrasts the mild-mannered mockery of fortifications (v. 10b) with the deadly serious attention he turns to his task of murderous mutilation when *his spirit changes, he becomes angry and sins* in his brutal tormenting of his victims.

This his strength is his god. Unbelievable as it may seem, this instrument of the Almighty for judgment on his own people now exalts itself to the level of deity. But this insight into the Babylonian self-image provides a framework for understanding their brutality in the treatment of Israel. Having deified their own brute force, they regard themselves as being incapable of doing wrong with that force.

So the Lord characterizes for his prophet this instrument by which he shall establish some semblance of justice in the earth. The wicked in Israel shall not by any means escape judgment. As a matter of fact, they shall be devastated by the awesome tool raised up by the Almighty.

8. Calvin, p. 35.

C. THE PROPHETIC SPOKESMAN CHALLENGES THE LORD'S PROGRAM FOR PUNISHMENT (1:12–17)

This portion of Scripture does not represent the first time in which a person's faith received greater challenge even as he was granted fuller insight into the plans and purposes of God. Habakkuk had asked "How long?" and the Lord had promptly answered, "Very suddenly and very soon." Habakkuk had asked, "Why is not justice upheld?" and the Lord had answered, "My impartial justice shall bring awesome vengeance even on my own people."

Although the answers of the Lord dealt precisely with the issues raised by his prophet, they ended up troubling him more than his original questions. In fact, Habakkuk becomes exceedingly bold. He actually challenges the Lord over his intention to punish the wickedness of Judah. Although approaching his subject cautiously by expressing confidence in the nature and purpose of God (v. 12), he ends up by questioning God and his program (vv. 13–17).

1. Confidence in God (1:12)

> 12 Are not you from eternity,
>   Yahweh, my God, my Holy One?
>   We shall not die.
>
> a Yahweh
> b for justice
>   c you have set him;
> a and O Rock
> b for rebuke
>   c you have established him.

This intensive probing of the purposes of God by the prophet should not be analyzed as a manifestation of weak faith.[1] Both the nature and purpose of God elicit from the prophet expressions of confidence. Not a weak faith but a perplexed faith torments Habakkuk. If the Chaldean conqueror is ordered by God to treat Israel with the same ruthlessness with which it shall manhandle other nations, then what will have happened to the distinctive role of Israel as God's covenant people? The utter annihilation of the northern tribes was altogether too fresh in the minds of the thinking populace of Judah. If

---

1. Contra Laetsch, p. 325, who supports Luther in his analysis of Habakkuk's questioning as indicating weakness of faith.

Jerusalem should suffer the same fate as Samaria, what then would remain of the special role of Israel?

The prophet bolsters his confidence by reminding the Lord of the everlasting character of his own nature: *Are you not from eternity?* Intentionally or otherwise, the prophet echoes the reassuring words spoken by Isaiah to the faltering faith of King Hezekiah when Sennacherib of Assyria had threatened Jerusalem earlier (2 K. 19:25; Isa. 37:26). God was from eternity, and from eternity he had settled on a purpose. History provided the framework in which the Sovereign Lord would bring to pass his everlasting intentions.

Since the choice of Israel originated in the eternity of God's own nature, how could he now speak in tones threatening annihilation? Corrective justice indeed the prophet desired for Israel. But utter devastation at the hands of the Chaldeans seemed to be far too much.

The seriousness of the problem faced by Habakkuk may be seen in the prophet Micah's earlier use of similar language to express his anticipation of Israel's future. A "ruler" would arise from Bethlehem of Judah. His "goings forth" had been "from eternity" *(miqqeḏem),* stretching throughout all the days of the past *(mîmê ʿôlām,* Mic. 5:1 [Eng. 2]). If these saving purposes of God "from eternity" hinged on the Davidic ruler who would arise from Bethlehem, how then could the entire kingdom be subjected to the ravages of a deportation like that which had recently been experienced by the kingdom of the north?

We shall not die, the prophetic faith affirms.[2] Linking himself with the eternity of God which he had just developed, the prophetic mediator conjoins the covenant people with himself. Yahweh is their God. Therefore it is impossible that they could perish. Instead of serving as an instrument of annihilation, the enemy being raised up by God against Israel must function as the divine tool *for justice* and *for rebuke.* Set in poetic parallelism, the

---

2. Laetsch, p. 323, takes the phrase as a question, and suggests the prophet is harassed by grave doubts. Ancient recognition of the problem created by the abrupt switch to the first person plural ("we shall not die") is found in the notes of the Massora. According to Keil, p. 64, this phrase contains one of the eighteen *tiqqune sopherim* (scribal corrections) of the Massora. Rather than witnessing to textual variants, these notations propose to explain what the original author intended to write. In this case, the supposition is that the original author *intended* to write "not shall *you* [i.e., God] die," thereby developing his assertion, "You are from eternity." But because this statement would not have maintained the proper lines of decorum in speaking of God in this manner, the author wrote instead, "not shall *we* die." This notation of the rabbis has some value as an item of curiosity, but it does not provide a proper solution to the exegetical problem.

prophet's affirmation underscores the nature of God as a *Rock* who administers *justice*. The prophet is confident that the God of all the earth shall do right. His certainty arises from the ancient revelation of God's nature in the covenant.

Further echoing of covenantal provisions is found in the assertion that God has *established* the Chaldean as his instrument *for rebuke (lᵉhôkîaḥ)*. This same term is employed to describe the response that God promised to disobedient descendants of David at the time of the establishment of the eternal covenant. God would "rebuke him" *(hōkaḥtîw)* with the rod of men (2 Sam. 7:14). Israel had grown accustomed to having God rebuke the nations on their behalf (Ps. 105:14), and understood their role as the source from which the rebuke of God would go forth against the nations (Isa. 2:2–4). But they were prone to forget that inherent in the provisions of the Davidic covenant was a conditional clause promising a most severe chastening for the Davidic descendant that dared to violate the *torah*.

So the prophet expresses his confidence in God. His nature is unchanging, and his eternal purpose finds faithful reflection in the events of history now being unfolded to him. But still he must proceed in all honesty to offer his questions before God.

2. Questioning God (1:13–17)

Having grounded his confidence in the nature and the purpose of God, the prophet now moves into his questioning of God. First he deals with the source of the problem (v. 13). Then he points to two factors which intensify the problem (vv. 14–17).

a. Source of the problem (1:13)

13 *a* *(You are of) purer eyes*
    b *than to see evil;*
    b *and to look on perverseness*
 a *you are not able.*

Why
    a *do you look*
       b *on those dealing treacherously,*
    a *and you are silent*
       b *while the wicked swallow up those more righteous than they?*

Habakkuk's questioning of God does not arise out of the Lord's announcing punishment for Israel. For he himself had initiated this dialogue with the Almighty out of a sense of the necessity of judgmental intervention to correct the injustices committed by God's own people. Instead, the prophet's concern centers on the problem (from his perspective) of God's using the obviously depraved Chaldeans to carry out judgment on his own chosen people. He also expresses a stunned horror at the awesome prospect facing Israel.

Many patterns of the ceremonial law of Israel enforced the concept of God's *purity*. Only pure gold could be used in his holy tabernacle (Exod. 25:11ff.). The priesthood must be clothed in pure garments if they were to approach the holy God of Israel (Exod. 25:2ff.). What now would be the worth of all such didactic ritual if the Holy Lord himself should tolerate the grossest of immoralities? How could he favor the depraved Chaldeans over the well-being of his own beloved people?

Habakkuk eases into this problem by first affirming what he knows must be true despite his own perceptions. His God is *of purer eyes than to see evil.* Obviously God does in some sense "see" evil. His omniscience extends to all the affairs of his creation. But he never looks to *condone* or *tolerate* evil. As the organ of perception, the eye represents the organ of sense that most often first contacts an object. Long before the hand touches, the eye sees. Even a momentary glance toward iniquity while it still remains at the farthest distance is not possible for God. His holiness cannot abide iniquity.

Particularly when sin is committed against his own people, the Lord is stirred to definitive action. Possibly Habakkuk reflects the older prophecy of Balaam concerning the impossibility of cursing Israel. Balaam declares:

> He has seen
> no misfortune
> in Jacob;
> and he has perceived
> no trouble
> in Israel. (Num. 23:21)[1]

God will perpetuate no wrong against his own people. He is *not able* to look on perverseness because it contradicts his very essence. This certain reality, grounded in the very nature of God, only heightens the puzzlement that must be felt in the prophet's plaintive *Why?* God's tolerance of the treacherously

---

1. The possibility of an allusion by Habakkuk to Balaam's prophecy would hold even though the combination of terms in Numbers (ʿāmāl, ʾāwen) referred to "misfortune" and those in Habakkuk (rāʿ, ʿāmāl) referred to "moral wrong." In either case, God's protection of his people would be the subject at hand.

wicked baffles the prophet even more because the object of their abuses are *more righteous than they.*

A facile explanation of the prophet's perplexity must not be advanced too quickly. Habakkuk was no lightweight in wrestling through the deep things of God. He poses no infantile questions about judgment and the world to come. It is not enough to suggest that Habakkuk's question could have been answered readily by an appeal to the multiplied guilt of Israel resulting from the abuse of their favored position before the Lord. His puzzlement represents one of the most basic questions that must arise if God is to effect redemption among a fallen humanity. Finding its precursor in the constant query of the psalmists of Israel (Ps. 22:3 [Eng. 2]; 44:25–26 [Eng. 24–25]; 74:1, 11), this question reaches its apex of perplexity in the "Why?" of Christ from the cross (Matt. 27:46). How can the favored of God suffer such devastations?

Chastenings? Yes, they must be taken with a sober humility. The prophet Habakkuk himself had called on God Almighty for just such a treatment of his own contemporaries. But a destruction that resembles an utter devastation? How could it be? A deportation that reverses the total direction of God's electing mercies? Certainly in some sense Israel must be seen as *more righteous* than those Chaldeans who had never been called out of Ur.[2]

The prophet's problem is intensified by the fact that the Lord in his dealing with Israel appears to be contradicting those principles which he himself had laid down for his own people. God will not look on perverseness *(wᵉhabbîṭ ʾel-ʿāmāl lōʾ ṯûkāl,* v. 13a); yet he makes his prophet look on perverseness *(wᵉʿāmāl tabbîṭ,* v. 3). The Lord had declared it wrong for a witness to keep silence when a matter was brought before the public (Lev. 5:1); yet the Lord himself remains silent while the wicked swallow up those more righteous than they (Hab. 1:13b).

The descriptive imagery of the wicked "swallowing up" the righteous portrays an utter annihilation. In the past God had acted on Israel's behalf in "swallowing up" the wicked. The earth had swallowed up Egypt at the Red Sea (Exod. 15:12), and Dothan and Abiram in their rebellion (Num. 16:30, 32, 34; Ps. 106:17). But now God's own people face the prospect of being

---

2. Laetsch, p. 325, is certainly right when he states that the prophet may be thinking of "the small remnant of such as are righteous by faith in the promised Redeemer," and notes that "they must suffer together with the mass of unbelieving Jews." Yet this perspective does not answer the entire question. It might be observed that this insight represents a part of the divine answer (Hab. 2:4), and therefore it is not likely that it provides the perspective from which the prophet asks his question.

"swallowed up" by their enemies, an awesome prospect which actually came to pass in the Exile (Jer. 51:34; Lam. 2:2, 5, 16).

So the puzzlement of Habakkuk arises out of the seeming injustice of the judgment which the Lord has shown him, and the utter devastation which the coming of the Chaldeans forces him to envision.

b. Intensification of the problem (1:14–17)

14 *For you have made man*
> *as the fish of the sea;*
> *as a swarm not having a ruler over him.*

15 *Each of them*
> *a with a hook*
>> *b he has led out.*
>> *b He will drag each*
> *a with his net,*
>> *b and he will gather each*
> *a with his dragnet.*
>>> *Therefore he will rejoice and be gleeful.*

16 *Therefore*
> *a he will sacrifice*
>> *b to his net,*
> *a and burn incense*
>> *b to his dragnet.*

For with these
> *a he has made fat*
>> *b his portion;*
>> *b and his food*
> *a is luscious.*

17 *So is it to be*
> *that he will empty his net*
> *in slaughtering nations perpetually?*
> *Never will he show pity.*

Now the prophetic spokesman challenges the Lord's program for punishment with greater intensity. He rehearses before the Lord the infamous manner in which the Chaldeans have treated people in the past. He furthermore points directly at God himself as the ultimate source of these international atrocities.

14 Habakkuk begins these remarks by addressing God: *you have made man as the fish of the sea*. This statement probably represents the prophet's most pointed accusation against the Almighty. In recognizing the sovereignty of God among the nations, he must conclude that God himself is ultimately behind this massive maltreatment of humanity.

When he states that God has made *man as the fish of the sea,* he apparently is envisioning the effect of the Chaldean aggression on the various segments of mankind brought under their oppressions. His concern extends beyond the calamities threatening Israel itself to include all mankind as those made in the image of the Almighty with responsibility to "rule . . . over the fish of the sea and over every living thing that swarms on the earth" *(reₑdû bidgaṯ hayyām . . . ûḇeₑkol-ḥayyâ hārōmeśeṯ ʿal-hāʾāreṣ,* Gen. 1:28; cf. Ps. 8:9 [Eng. 8]). Contrary to the creational order in which man was to have dominion over the totality of the world, he is now brought low, treated as the nondescript mass of the ocean's bounties, having no ruler to protect or to guide. In the days of Israel's splendor, King Solomon had displayed his authoritative position over the "fish of the sea . . . and swarming things" *(weₑal-hāremeś weₑal-huddāḡîm)* by capturing the essence of their significance in his many proverbs (1 K. 5:13 [Eng. 4:33]). To what depths of degradation has Israel now sunk that they should be treated with the disregard that someone might display toward these swarming creatures!

No interruption of "man's inhumanity to man" has occurred since the time of the prophet. Power-hungry oppressors devastate whole populaces, treating them as less in significance than the dust of the earth rather than as God's own vicegerents. In such a context, the hope represented in the man par excellence shines forth in more glorious light. Although we do not yet see all things brought into subjection to humanity, we do see Jesus, made a little lower than the angels for the suffering of death, now crowned with glory and honor (Ps. 8:6 [Eng. 5]; cf. Heb. 2:7).

Not only does God's direct involvement in this event of dehumanization create deep concern for the prophet (v. 14). The depth of the wickedness of the Babylonians also intensifies his problem. Brutality (v. 15), sensuality (v. 16), and relentlessness (v. 17) combine to stir the depths of the prophet's complaint.

15 What could epitomize more dramatically the cruelty of the Chaldeans than the historical witness of their own monuments?[1] Not just figuratively but literally they carried on the Assyrian tradition of driving a hook through the sensitive lower lip of their captives and stringing them single file. In such a diabolical method they enforced docility. At least the

1. Cf. the sources cited in Rudolph, p. 211.

Chaldeans showed impartiality in their cruelty. Every single one of their captives was to be favored with a hook, according to Habakkuk.

By a second and related figure, the prophet enforces his depiction of the brutality of the Babylonians. If not led with a hook, the faceless captives are dragged in a net.[2] Again the inscriptions of Babylon enforce the soberness of the prophet's description. In one relief, the major Babylonian deities Ningirsu, Shamash, Enlil, and Marduk drag a net in which their captured enemies squirm.[3]

Perhaps the most repulsive element of the entire picture is the fiendish gloating of the Chaldeans. They gleefully inflict these humiliating brutalities on their victims.

How can it be, says the prophet? Is this procedure actually the righteous way for the Lord to deal with his own people? Must the sting of cruel mockery be added to the horrors of an oppressive judgment?

16   Further perplexity to the whole matter is introduced by the sensuality of the instrument which God has chosen for the punishment of his own people. That which is dearest to the heart of the Babylonians is the booty of their rapacious aggressions, as seen in their worship practices. Their instruments of human torture and cruelty they worship, because these instruments have given to them an abundance of temporal pleasures. In their twisted imaginations, they somehow have found a way to claim righteousness in their brutal deeds, and so can memorialize them by sacrifice in their solemn hours of worship.

Perhaps Habakkuk by this vivid imagery intends to provoke the God of Israel to jealousy. How can he tolerate such perversity? The Chaldeans are clearly worshiping and serving the creature more than the Creator. Certainly God's wrath must be upon them. He had carefully taught his people to count the Lord himself as their portion above all other material possessions (cf. Num. 18:20; Deut. 10:9; Ps. 16:5; 73:26). But these barbarians make a god of sensual pleasure.

17   Habakkuk's problem with the maltreatment of his people is intensified not only by the brutality and sensuality of the instrument of divine judgment. The relentlessness of the oppressor also causes him to tremble. Is it to be that this invader will empty his net perpetually? He turns his net up-

---

2. The term used to describe the dragging of a net (*yegōrēhû*) has an onomatopoetic significance. It is used to describe the munching of a cud (Lev. 11:7), the grinding of a saw (1 K. 7:9), and the roaring of a whirlwind (Jer. 30:23).

3. Cf. Laetsch, p. 326.

side down, dumps out the maimed humanity he has captured, and then without interruption goes forth to collect more victims. Is this determination to execute unending atrocities to continue without interruption forever?

He never shows pity in the slaughtering of nations. The dimensions of this brutality can hardly be grasped. The prophet envisions a holocaust that cannot be comprehended. The victims of this oppressor are not merely individuals. Whole nations fall prey to his brutalities.[4] Such wholesale slaughter must have as its ultimate source only Satan himself. If Cain killed his brother "because he was of the evil one" (1 John 3:12), certainly the merciless slaughter by the Babylonians must be inspired of the archenemy of the Lord himself.

How then can it be that this process goes on continually? Shall it roll over God's own people and pass on to an endless line of defenseless victims? Does the God of compassion still reign? The lack of mercy on the part of the enemy clearly shows that he operates contrary to the nature of the Lord himself. Is his activity then to be allowed to continue perpetually?

So the prophet Habakkuk questions God and his revealed intention for resolving the problem that he himself had raised. Admittedly Israel needed some form of corrective chastening. Their own exercise of brutality deserved a proper reprimand from the Lord. But Habakkuk could not understand the breadth of the oppression that the Lord now revealed to him. His heart and mind were wounded from such awesome prospects. He dared to question the Almighty—and then had to await a response.

God's people are repeatedly compelled to struggle with the depth of the suffering that falls upon God's own. If it were possible for the feeble human mind to grasp in some small way the reality of the sufferings of the Son of God, it would no doubt reel in stunned awe. For both the depth of God's righteousness and the depth of his love are incomprehensible.

On behalf of the Lord's people through the ages, the prophet wrestles with the depths of the riches and wisdom of God. For his ways are unsearchable, past finding out. Yet the truth has been made known to the people of the Lord. It is right therefore to search out that revelation in all its profundity. So long as the harness of faith restrains the energies of the Lord's own people, they may be edified as they join Habakkuk in his efforts to search out the depth of the mysteries of the Almighty.

---

4. This description of the victim of the oppressor as including a multitude of nations suggests that it was not merely an internal oppressor that the prophet was describing; but neither does it exclude the possibility that the first oppressors mentioned by Habakkuk in his dialogue with the Lord (1:2–4) came from Judah itself. See the Introduction above, § IV.C. .

II. THE RESOLUTION OF WISDOM (2:1–20)

Using the boldest possible mode of expression, Habakkuk has challenged the intentions of the Lord as they have been revealed to him. How is it possible that the Almighty could treat human beings as though they were fish of the sea (Hab. 1:14)? Is the brutality of the invading oppressor to go on forever? Is he to keep on emptying his net, destroying nations without mercy (Hab. 1:17)?

The "dialogue of protest" initiated in ch. 1 must find some resolution. Such a bold challenge to the integrity of God himself must be given appropriate answer. So ch. 2 of Habakkuk provides the resolution of divine wisdom. The prophet braces himself for the rebuke he is sure will come (2:1). But the Lord responds gently by disclosing his purpose for the ages (2:2–20).

A. THE PROPHET DILIGENTLY WATCHES FOR THE REBUKE TO HIS FOLLY (2:1)

1   *a*   *On my watchtower*
      b *I shall stand,*
      b *and I shall situate myself*
   a *on (my) siege tower.*
    And I shall watch to see
    what
       he will say to me,
    and what
       I shall answer
          to my rebuke.

Habakkuk is quite aware of the audacity of his most recent remarks. He has challenged the propriety of the purpose of the Lord himself. It is understandable therefore that he braces himself for a straightforward rebuke from the Lord.

The prophet is right in the position he takes with respect to his own role in the resolution of this perplexing issue. He will not attempt to reconcile in his own mind the apparent contradiction between the election of Israel by God as the object of his special love and the devastation of Israel at the hands of the rapacious Chaldeans as ordered by the Lord himself. He will not resort to the resources of human wisdom. Instead, he will watch for an answer that can come only from the Lord. Habakkuk knows that, in accordance with the nature of the prophetic office in Israel, revelation from God alone can answer his perplexity.

Both the humility and the hope of the prophet provide appropriate direction for the Church through the ages. God's ways are higher than man's ways. Only by revelation can the genuine perplexities of God's dealings with human beings be comprehended.

On my watchtower I shall stand. Three earlier instances of prophets who had to "stand in waiting" as did Habakkuk for God's self-revelation may be noted: *Moses* hid in the cleft of the rock and "stood in waiting" to see God's glory pass before him (Exod. 33:21–23). *Balaam* went aside to "stand in waiting" for the revelation that God might bring to him (Num. 23:3). *Elijah* was commanded to go to the mountain and "stand in waiting" for the revelation of God that would come (1 K. 19:11). In similar fashion, Habakkuk situates himself on a watchtower to "stand in waiting" for the revelation that shall come from God. Although a solitary figure, he represents the people of God as their prophetic mediator at this critical juncture of their history.

I shall watch to see what he will say to me. Habakkuk himself is intently involved in this entire procedure, but he looks for a message that concerns all God's people. The responses of the Lord underscore the fact that it is not for the prophet alone that this interchange progresses.

The prophetic role of being a "watchman," looking out for God's word, had been depicted in an earlier day when the Lord commanded Isaiah to post a "lookout" (Isa. 21:6). This prophetic lookout stood on his "watchtower" day after day, remaining at his post through the night (Isa. 21:8). Finally the divine revelation came.

The "watchman" who waits for God's word stands in vivid contrast with those who resort to their own imaginations. The egotistic, humanistic alternative to passive dependence on the divine word merits the pointed rebuke provided by Calvin: "All . . . who indulge themselves in their own counsels deserve to be forsaken by God, and to be left by him to be driven up and down, and here and there, by Satan; for the only unfailing security for the faithful is to acquiesce in God's word."[1]

and what I shall answer to my rebuke. Although Habakkuk clearly accepts the stance of the prophet watching for the word of God, he introduces a distinctive perspective concerning his own anticipations. He shall watch, but simultaneously he shall be preparing an answer to the rebuke he expects from the Lord. Habakkuk had dared to question the earlier revelation of the Lord which had come in response to his complaint. He did not understand how the Lord could tolerate the destruction of his own people at the hands of ruthless barbarians. Now as he looks for the Lord's response to his further

1. John Calvin, p. 62.

166

complaint, he could hardly anticipate anything other than rebuke for himself. Though placing himself submissively beneath the divine revelation that was sure to come, he nonetheless presumed that he would be required to respond to this further word from the Lord by additional disputation.

Some translations have offered a different rendering which relieves something of the audacity implied in Habakkuk's words.[2] Admittedly, it is rather difficult to imagine the prophet actually planning in advance to answer a rebuke from the Almighty. Yet the radicalness of the problem with which Habakkuk wrestles, as well as the nature of the interchange with the Almighty up to this point, naturally leads to just such an expectation.

In his continuing dialogue with God in terms of *rebuke* and *answer,* Habakkuk adopts a pattern reflecting a recognized procedure in the quest for wisdom in Israel. In seeking to understand God's way with him, Job longs to "dispute" *(hôkēaḥ)* his case with God (Job 13:3). He urges his friends to hear his rebuke *(tôkaḥtî)* and the controversies *(ribôt)* of his lips (v. 6). He longs to find God so that he can fill his mouth with arguments *(tôkāḥôt)* (23:4). By this bold manner of entering into dispute with God, the wise of Israel hoped to receive divine clarification of their perplexities.

Similarly, in the book of Proverbs the Lord appears as the one who instructs by reproof. Wisdom will teach a person to turn at the rebuke of the Almighty (Prov. 1:23). Great calamity will fall on the foolish who will not listen to his reproofs (1:25, 30). The role of the divine rebuke in imparting wisdom is a theme that appears in numerous other proverbs (cf. 6:23; 10:17; 12:1; 13:18; 15:5, 10, 31–32; 27:5; 29:1, 15).

In accord with this tradition, Habakkuk braces himself for the rebuke of the Lord. He has presumed to breach the silence enshrouding the relation of his people to their God. Now having entered this dialogue, he must prepare to respond to the reproof that is sure to come.

B. THE LORD GENTLY DISCLOSES HIS PURPOSE FOR THE AGES (2:2–20)

Surprisingly, the Lord's response to the prophet's challenge comes in the form of a vision of hope that the prophet must write for future generations. God does not rail against the prophet for his accusations, contrary to Habakkuk's expectations. First, he gives him a vision which contrasts the righteous

---

2. The RSV reads "my complaint," and the NIV reads "this complaint." Calvin, p. 62, interprets the phrase as referring to the "reproofs" that might come from Satan or self, not from God.

by faith with the resolutely proud (2:2–5). Then he offers five proverbial bywords which ridicule the haughty (2:6–20).

1. The Righteous by Faith and the Resolutely Proud (2:2–5)

The Lord's gracious condescension is seen in the significance, the character, and the substance of this vision.

a. Instructions indicating the significance of this vision (2:2)

2   *And Yahweh answered me and said:*
    a *Inscribe*
     b   *the vision*
    a *and make it plain*
     b   *on the tablets,*
       c *so that he who proclaims it may run.*

The response of the Lord comes in the form of a *vision*. This fact immediately takes this word out of the realm of a personal response directed only to the prophet himself. Although it is conceivable that the Lord might have granted to his prophet a message directed to him personally through a vision, the repeated pattern of OT prophetic revelation suggests that God communicates vision to his prophet in his role as mediator of a divine message.

The specific instructions to *Inscribe the vision and make it plain on the tablets* underscore its significance not only for the crucial hour in which Habakkuk lived, but also for the generations to come. The context suggests an intentional allusion to the inscribing of the original "ten words" of the book of the covenant (Exod. 31:18; 32:15–16; Deut. 9:10). Originally Israel also had been directed to "inscribe" on whitewashed stones all the words of the law, and to "make very plain" *(baʾēr hêṭēḇ)* this inscription (Deut. 27:8). Now Habakkuk is directed to *make it plain [bāʾēr] on the tablets* the vision being given to him. Reflecting the long-established pattern of inscribing a fresh copy of covenant law as an essential step in covenant renewal, Habakkuk's instructions include inscribing his vision on *the tablets*.[1]

Isaiah had been instructed to write his revelation on a "scroll" and a "tablet," while Jeremiah was told to write in a "book" (Isa. 8:1; 30:8; Jer.

---

1. Cf. Deut. 1:1; 27:2–3; Josh. 8:32; 24:25–26. G. E. Mendenhall, *Law and Covenant in Israel and the Ancient Near East* (Pittsburgh: Biblical Colloquium, 1955), p. 41, notes that it was the customary practice to "draw up a new covenant" with the heir to the vassal's throne, bringing the historical prologue and the stipulations up to date.

30:2). But Habakkuk must write on *the tablets*. The use of the article as well as the pluralization of *tablets* are distinctive. Habakkuk's "vision," apparently contained in vv. 4 and 5 of this chapter, would not appear by its length to justify the need for a plurality of tablets, and there would seem to be no particular reason in the immediate context for specifying *the* tablets on which Habakkuk is to write.

These features apparently intend to recall "the tablets" of the covenant made at Sinai (Exod. 24:12; 31:18; 32:15; 34:1, 28; Deut. 9:9–11; 10:2, 4; 2 Chr. 5:10). This vision now revealed to Habakkuk compares in significance with the original giving of the law to Moses. Perhaps with good reason Jewish tradition declared that the 613 laws of the Pentateuch had been reduced to one by Habakkuk.[2]

As though these factors were not enough, the significance of this vision finds further emphasis by the reason given for its clear inscription. Habakkuk is to make it plain on the tablets *so that he who proclaims it may run.* Rather than envisioning a placarded statement so large that a person running by might read it, the context of a prophetic vision inscribed on tablets for the ages to come suggests the "running" of a messenger to "proclaim" the vision.[3]

Prophets frequently are presented in Scripture as "running" with their announcement. In clear poetic parallelism, the Lord through Jeremiah protests the activity of the false prophets:

I have not sent these prophets,
  yet they ran;
I have not spoken to them,
  yet they prophesied. (Jer. 23:21)

In this utterance of Jeremiah, it is quite clear that "running" (with a message) is equivalent to "prophesying." In similar fashion, Gehazi must "run" for Elisha (2 K. 4:26), and Zechariah hears the Lord command his messenger to "run" and deliver his announcement (Zech. 2:4).

Although it would be legitimate to interpret the task of this running messenger to be the "reading" *(qr᾿)* of the vision, more likely the text is indicating that he has the responsibility to "proclaim" it *(qôrē᾿ bô)*. The term employed regularly means "to proclaim" as well as "to read." But particularly

---

2. H. L. Strack and P. Billerbeck, *Kommentar zum Neuen Testament aus Talmud und Midrasch,* 5 vols. (Munich: Beck'sche, 1926–1961), 1:907; 3:542–43.
3. Cf. John Marshall Holt, "So He May Run Who Reads It," *JBL* 83 (1964) 298–302; W. H. Brownlee, "The Placarded Revelation of Habakkuk," *JBL* 82 (1963) 319–25.

striking in comparison with this text in Habakkuk is the "proclaiming" (qrˀ) of the name of the Lord associated with the deliverance of the two tablets to Moses (Exod. 34:4–5). The Lord passed before Moses and "proclaimed" (wayyiqrāˀ) his name (Exod. 34:6).

Habakkuk must inscribe his vision plainly *so that he who proclaims it may run.* The abiding inscription of the vision suggests that the bearer of this message shall not be a single individual. Instead, many through the ages to come shall rush to declare this divine word.

Once Abraham the first father of God's people had to be weaned from expecting too sudden a solution to the tension of his childlessness despite God's promises. His experience forced him by faith to look beyond the current experience of his day to the distant future. Now Habakkuk struggles with an identical tension. How can God fulfill his promises to his people when he is about to devastate them? The divine answer to his perplexity must be inscribed on tablets, and many proclaimers in the ages to come must run with the message that resolves this problem. The very delay that Habakkuk must accept provides a further indicator of the broader significance of the vision. It is not merely for the present generation. It is for the ages to come.

b. Statement concerning the character of the vision (2:3)

3   *For yet the vision*
> *(is) for the appointed time,*
> *and it yearns for the end;*
>> *it cannot lie.*

If it tarry,
> *wait for it;*
> *for it is sure to come,*
>> *nor will it delay.*

Not only does this vision have a significance that makes it comparable with the revelation to Moses at Sinai. This vision is also noteworthy for its basic character: it is eschatological and it is certain. Its realization awaits events that are yet future, which helps the prophet understand why the vision must be written.

Abraham had to believe that even though his wife had passed the age of childbearing, nothing could be too hard for God. The messenger that appeared to the patriarch made it quite clear that the fulfillment of the promise concerning the birth of Sarah's long-awaited seed would be "at the appointed time" (Gen. 18:14). Not according to man's anxiously conceived timetable, but according to the unshakable divine decree the promise would come to pass. As previously noted, Habakkuk's problem essentially was the same as Abraham's. How could God be true to his promise if the people of God experienced extermination?

So Habakkuk in his day had to face the stark reality of the devastation of God's people by exile. Yet he must believe that nothing would be too hard for God. For his vision would find its fulfillment at the *appointed time* (cf. Dan. 10:14; 11:27, 35).

This vision *yearns* or "pants" *(pûaḥ)* for the end. Although this term on occasion may mean simply "speak," the context suggests its more vivid significance. "True prophecy is inspired. . . . by an impulse to fulfill itself."[1] Not only the prophet, but God himself as author of this vision has a longing to see the vindication of his own word of prophecy.

The *appointed time* and the goal toward which this vision yearned was the *end*. Only at the "end" would the hope of Habakkuk be fulfilled. What could be meant by this reference to the *end?* It hardly seems likely that the word simply means "later on," or "after the circumstances that now prevail," or even "after the anticipated judgment has fallen." The *end* quite consistently refers to a termination point (cf. Gen. 4:3; 8:6; 41:1; Exod. 12:41; Ezek. 35:5). In this case no specific framework is provided which might aid in defining the precise "end" in view. Yet the reference to the *appointed time* of fulfillment that shall come after many messengers have run with the vision suggests that this *end* refers to the final stage in God's outworking of a purpose of redemption for his people.

By the time of Daniel, the "appointed time" and the "end" clearly possessed eschatological significance (cf. Dan. 8:17, 19; 11:35, 40; 12:9). But even in Habakkuk's day a vision of the end was quite appropriate, particularly in view of the cataclysmic event of the Exile which the nation faced. In the context of the coming exile, it is quite legitimate to see eschatological significance in Habakkuk's reference. After the devastations of the judgment coming from the Babylonians, the "end" would appear imminent.

So the questions raised by Habakkuk merit an answer with eschatological dimensions. His perplexity and his probings were well directed. The coming devastation of God's own people at the hands of the Chaldeans was a matter of most solemn consequence. The final resolution of this problem would come to pass only at the eschaton.

Not only did this vision now being given to Habakkuk have an eschatological character. By the very nature of the case, it was certain and true despite all appearances to the contrary. This vision is for the appointed time,

---

1. Hitzig, as quoted in Keil, p. 71.

it yearns for the end, and *it cannot lie.* The divine asseveration that this vision *cannot lie* implies that appearances would contradict the message contained in the vision. Just as Abraham's observable experience contradicted the divine promise concerning a seed, so Habakkuk's experience would contradict the message given him. Even God might appear to be a liar. But God cannot lie. As had been asserted so pointedly in an earlier prophetic context: "God is not a man that he should lie" (Num. 23:19).

The prophet is admonished: *If it tarry, wait for it.* The fulfillment of the vision almost certainly will be delayed, yet delay is placed in a conditional setting. *If* the vision should tarry, you must wait for it. This manner of describing the future prospect forces the prophet always to wait hopefully, and stresses the imminence of the divine action to fulfill his word. At any moment, the Lord may initiate those events which will bring about the eschatological fulfillment of this promise.

The certainty of the fulfillment of this vision, despite all appearances to the contrary, finds reinforcement in the final phrases of this verse: *for it is sure to come, nor will it delay.* By combining verbal forms communicating infinity and finitude built on the same root, the Hebrew language effectively underscores the certainty of an anticipated event.[2] The vision granted Habakkuk must come to pass.

nor will it delay. The bald statement that this vision will not delay appears to contradict the opening clause of this sentence, which grants the possibility that the vision might *tarry.* A resolution of this difficulty by appeal to distinctive shades of meaning between the two Hebrew words for *tarry* and *delay* falters for lack of clear evidence that an adequate distinction exists between the two words. More probable is the line of resolution proposed by John Calvin, who suggests that from the human perspective the vision may appear to tarry in its fulfillment because of the long period involved in its realization. But from God's perspective, the certainty of its fulfillment precisely according to the divine plan cannot be questioned.[3]

At first it appears that the LXX translation of this verse has modified the thrust of Habakkuk's prophecy by focusing the vision on the coming of a person. If a reference to the "vision" had been intended by the Greek translators, the corresponding feminine pronoun *(autén)* would have been used. But instead of reading "If (the vision) should tarry, wait for it" (lit., "her"), the LXX reads "If he tarry, wait for him *[autón]."*

2. Cf. GKC, § 113n. In English, this effect of infinitive absolute is achieved often by a corresponding adverb: "You shall *surely* die."
3. Calvin, p. 65.

The Hebrew text could certainly be read just as it is found in the LXX. Further support for this rendering may be seen in the dependence of Hab. 2:3–4 on Gen. 15:6. Abraham's belief in God had a very specific focus in that ancient context. He believed God respecting the promise of a seed (Gen. 15:4–5), and so his faith was reckoned as righteousness. This blessing of a seed finds its full meaning only in term of a salvation for God's people accomplished by a singular saving hero (cf. Gen. 3:15).

So the personification of the hope of salvation by the LXX translators should not be viewed as a strange perversion of the words of Habakkuk, even though the Hebrew text does not appear to specify so pointedly a reference to a "person" who will bring about the fulfillment of the prophecy. This personification of Habakkuk's prophetic expectation finds support in the subsequent messianic interpretation given to these same verses by several rabbis in Jewish tradition.[4]

Presumably following the tradition of the LXX, the writer to the Hebrews underscores this explicitly messianic perspective by rendering the next phrase in Habakkuk with the definite article. The righteous by faith must wait for "the one who comes" (*ho erchómenos,* Heb. 10:37). Very likely the writer to the Hebrews turned to this passage because of its stress on the necessity for patience in possessing the substance of the promises of God. God had told Habakkuk that if the vision should tarry, he must wait patiently. Now in a new covenant context, the same admonition applies to those who suffer, not seeing the promise of God realized immediately for them. They too have need of patience (Heb. 10:36).[5] By viewing Habakkuk's prophecy from this personal perspective, the writer to the Hebrews has not interjected an element foreign to the prophecy, even though he does make personal that which originally was stated in an impersonal way.

c. Revelation of the substance of this vision (2:4–5)

4 *Behold!*
    a   *The proud—*

---

4. T.B. Sanhedrin 97b. Cf. the discussion of C. Spicq, *L'Epître aux Hébreux,* Etudes Bibliques (Paris: Gabalda, 1952), 2:332.

5. The writer to the Hebrews employs a phrase from Isa. 26:20 which stresses the shortness of the time before the Lord's coming in judgment to introduce the quotation from Habakkuk: "In just a very little while," he who is coming will come (Heb. 10:37). The further emphasis on the coming of the Lord himself in the LXX rendering of Hab. 2:3 had captured the personal dimension that the writer to the Hebrews wished to stress. The people shall confront the Lord himself. He is the one for whom they must wait.

b his soul is not upright in him;
a but the justified—
   b by his steadfast trust he shall live.
5 *However,*
   wine deceives him—
a mighty man who boasts and will not rest,
   who
      multiplies
         as Sheol
            his soul;
and he (is)
      as death,
         and will not be satisfied.

a So he gathers
b to himself
   c all nations,
a and he collects
b to himself
   c all peoples.

Although the matter has been disputed, it seems fairly clear that the "vision" promised in the previous verses now is being reported.[1] The fivefold "woe" concluding the chapter may be regarded as an expansion of one aspect of Habakkuk's vision, although not constituting the substance of the vision itself.

Three elements stand out in these verses: (1) the proud cannot be upright (v. 4a); (2) the justified (by faith) shall live by his steadfast trust (v. 4b); (3) yet the wicked continue in their boastful ways (vv. 4c–5).

4a The proud cannot be upright. *Behold!* The term introduces the substance of the vision itself. In considering the circumstance over which he had puzzled so greatly—even to the point of challenging God—Habakkuk must note with care God's analysis of *the proud*. Descriptive of their very essence is the term employed to designate them. They are "puffed up," "bloated," or even "tumorous" (*ʿuppᵉlâ*).[2]

This condition of self-exaltation and personal esteem brings with it certain consequences. Such an individual cannot be upright in himself. His own pride of person condemns him. This position of pride and self-reliance

---

1. W. Rudolph, p. 216.
2. The term is used elsewhere in Scripture to refer to a mound or a tumor. Cf. 1 Sam. 5:6, 9, 12.

also excludes from the proud the possibility of finding a righteousness out-side himself. For he has presumed to define himself as the source of his own goodness. The consequence of such self-exaltation is seen concretely at another point in the case of Israel's "acting presumptuously" (ʿpl—Num. 14:44; cf. Deut. 1:43). They were beaten mercilessly by their enemies be-cause they presumed that in themselves they possessed adequate resources for victory.

So by these words of Habakkuk Scripture makes it plain that the proud cannot be upright. As a consequence, neither can they live. They must expe-rience condemnation and judgment. To Habakkuk it may seem that the boisterous, boastful Chaldeans shall continue to prosper. Yet the fact that their soul *is not upright* in them should be an adequate indicator of their ultimate judgment.

4b *but the justified—by his steadfast trust he shall live.* Now the complementary aspect of Habakkuk's vision is presented. The watershed character of this revelation is underscored by the significance that must be recognized in each word in the phrase.

but the justified (weṣaddîq). The concept of righteousness (Heb. ṣedāqâ) in the OT develops a distinctive flavor in that it is bound insepara-bly to the idea of judicial standing. John Skinner has summed up this perspec-tive in noting that in the OT the forensic element everywhere predominates: "What is meant is that questions of right and wrong were habitually regarded from a legal point of view as matters to be settled by a judge, and that this point of view is emphasized in the words derived from ṣdq. This, indeed, is characteristic of the Hebrew conception of righteousness in all its develop-ments: whether it be a moral quality or a religious status, it is apt to be looked on as in itself controvertible and incomplete until it has been confirmed by what is equivalent to a judicial sentence."[3]

Considering the legal bond lying at the foundation of Israel's cove-nant relation to God, how could it be otherwise? The nation was profoundly conscious of the fact that it was a covenant people, bound by solemn oath with life-and-death consequences centering on the law solemnly dictated by the Lord of the covenant. Everything hinged on the legal decision of the God of the covenant. It was the duty of the earthly judge to see that his rendering corresponded to the decision already made by the Lord of heaven and earth.

Therefore, in its OT context righteousness should be regarded first of all as a religious rather than an ethical term, which "takes its origin in the

---

3. J. Skinner, "Righteousness in OT," in *A Dictionary of the Bible,* ed. James Hastings (New York: Charles Scribner's Sons, 1902), 4:273.

forensic sphere, and makes its home in the law of God."[4] The legal context of the idea appears repeatedly in Scripture. God solemnly pronounces "woe" over the ones who "make righteous the wicked" for a bribe and turn aside the "righteousness of the righteous" from him (Isa. 5:23). In the first instance, it cannot be that the bribed judge actually affects the moral character of his subjects when he "makes righteous" the wicked. Nor can it be that he corrupts the upright when he turns aside the "righteousness of the righteous." In both cases, it is the legal standing of the individual that is affected. While the judge ought to confirm God's judgment, he has perverted justice.

The same situation is evident in the judicial framework of interchanges between God and Job. The patriarchal figure has set in order his cause and is confident that he will be declared righteous (Job 13:18). Ultimately the Lord responds to Job's insistence that a divine judicial decision be rendered to uphold his cause: "Will you disannul my judgment? Will you declare me wicked so that you can be declared righteous?" (Job 40:8). Job is not represented as attempting to pollute God's personal morality. The entire framework for the interchange centers on contrasting judicial standing.

At other points in Scripture God warns about falsehood against the innocent and "righteous" (in a judicial context), for he will not "justify" the wicked (Exod. 23:7). Jehu exonerates the people from guilt associated with the slaughter of Ahab's sons by the rulers of Samaria by announcing, "You are righteous" (2 K. 10:9). Isaiah proclaims that as "their righteousness," God's people shall refute every accusatory tongue (Isa. 54:17), meaning that they will be able to stand the scrutiny of public judgment. As has been well said: "God's righteousness or His judicial reign means that in covenant faithfulness to His people he *vindicates* and saves them."[5]

In Hab. 2:4b, the term for *the justified* or "the righteous," *ṣaddîq,* contrasts with the reference to the soul of the proud, which is not "upright" (*yāšᵉrâ*), in the immediately preceding phrase. The soul of the proud is not *morally upright (yāšᵉrâ)* in him; but the one who is *legally righteous (ṣaddîq)* shall live.

But the question then arises, "How does a person come to be declared righteous?" Does a human being actually exist who can stand before the scrutiny of God's judgment seat and be found absolutely guiltless? The immediately following phrase *(by his steadfast trust)* might be interpreted as

---

4. Cf. L. Morris, *The Apostolic Preaching of the Cross* (Grand Rapids: Eerdmans, 1956), p. 235.

5. Gottlob Schrenk, "*díkē, díkaios, dikaiosýnē,* etc." in *TDNT,* 2:195. Emphasis added.

explaining directly the way of justification. But grammatically this phrase more naturally connects with the statement *he shall live,* as indicated by the Massoretic accents. Instead of stating explicitly that the justified-by-faith shall live, the phrase asserts that the justified shall live-by-faith.

This analysis is confirmed by the common pattern of the compound sentence in Hebrew.[6] In this structure, a subject first appears, preceding the verbal clause (in contrast to the normal pattern in Hebrew). The subject is then followed by an independent clause which often includes a retrospective suffix (i.e., one referring back to the initial noun). Examples of this structure are common: "The Lord—in the storm (is) *his* way" (Nah. 1:3); "God—perfect (is) *his* way" (Ps. 18:32 [Eng. 31]); "My son Shechem—*his* soul longs for your daughter" (Gen. 34:8); "And I [as for me]—this (is) *my* covenant with them" (Isa. 59:21). Following this pattern, the text at hand reads: "But the justified—by *his* steadfast trust he shall live" (Hab. 2:4). Because of this structure, *by his steadfast trust* must be taken in construction with *shall live* rather than with *but the justified.* The phrase explains the way by which the gift of life continues to be received rather than the way by which a sinner is declared righteous.

The LXX text does not conform completely to this construction of the sentence, although it follows its main outline. It reads: "the just by *my* [i.e., God's] faith (or faithfulness) shall live." This representation breaks the pattern of the retrospective suffix commonly found in the Hebrew compound sentence, although otherwise following the basic structure of the words.

The parallelism of the two clauses in Hab. 2:4 offers additional support to this reading of the Hebrew text. The construction of the verse may be represented as follows:

   a The proud—
      b not upright (is) *his* soul
        c in him;
   a but the righteous—
        c by *his* faith
      b he shall live.

The first half of this verse follows the same pattern of the compound sentence in Hebrew. First the subject occurs ("the proud"), followed by an independent clause including a pronoun suffix which refers back to the initial subject ("*his* soul is not upright in him"). The parallelism of construction

---

6. See the discussion and illustrations of the structure of the compound sentence in GKC, §§ 140d, 143.

between these two portions of the verse supports the connection of *by his steadfast trust* with *he shall live* rather than with *the justified*.

The emphases resulting from this structure are noteworthy. *the justified* receives a stress it could not realize in the simple sentence structure of verb followed by subject. *by his steadfast trust* is also emphasized due to the inversion of the expected word order in the predicate, and is further underscored by the variation of order of the elements in contrast with the order of the first half of the verse. While the parallelism is maintained, the inversion of word order stresses *by his steadfast trust*.

The message that a person shall "live by faith" underscores the fact that life is a gift, received gratefully from the Lord's hand. Standing in sharpest contradiction to the "proud" who are "not upright" in themselves and therefore must die, the one who trusts God's grace for his existence every moment shall live. He shall survive the devastations of God's judgment.

Understanding *by his steadfast trust* to connect grammatically with *he shall live* rather than with *the justified* may appear to leave open the question of *how* a person becomes righteous. But the resulting emphasis only reinforces the fact that the source of true righteousness always remains outside the person. If continuing life is a gift received by faith, then the righteousness that is the basis of life must have the same source.

This understanding of the way of judicial right standing for the sinner is underscored by what appears to be a deliberate echo of Gen. 15:6. Related terms for the root concepts of faith and legal right standing *(heʾĕmin, ʾĕmûnâ; sedāqâ, saddîq)* occur in both passages. In the context of Habakkuk, a test of faith similar to that experienced by Abraham due to the nonfulfillment of divine promises is evident. Under such circumstances, a divine judgment confirming the existence of a righteousness that assures the fulfillment of God's promises is essential.

The judicially righteous of Hab. 2:4b therefore are those justified precisely as was Abraham. He *believed* God, and it was *reckoned* to him as righteousness.[7] The *justified* of Hab. 2:4b therefore are the "justified by faith." Although the phrase *by his steadfast trust* relates to the gift of life rather than to the way of justification, the echo of Gen. 15:6 in Hab. 2:4 indicates that justification *is* by faith for Habakkuk even as it was for Abraham.

With this perspective in mind, it is possible to look more closely at the next crucial word of Habakkuk: *by his steadfast trust (beʾĕmûnātô)*. Al-

---

7. Cf. the fuller treatment of the concept of imputed righteousness as it comes to expression in Gen. 15:6 in O. Palmer Robertson, "Genesis 15:6: New Covenant Expositions of an Old Covenant Text," *WTJ* 42 (1980) 265–66.

ready it has been indicated that this phrase describes the way in which a person shall continue to live rather than the way in which he is to be justified. The positioning of the phrase before the verb that it modifies emphasizes the importance of this idea.

How then is a person to experience life? By his "steadfast deeds"? To be sure, "steadfastness" is the root meaning of the term. Is that the meaning of the term used by Habakkuk? Particularly as the concept is applied to God, his "steadfastness" is a virtue constantly praised in Scripture. He is characterized as a "God of steadfastness" (Deut. 32:4). All his works are done in steadfastness or faithfulness (Ps. 33:4). He has established repeatedly his faithfulness (Ps. 89:2–3, 6, 9, 25, 34, 50 [Eng. 1–2, 5, 8, 24, 33, 49]). His steadfastness guarantees the pattern of his works and provides the basis of trust.

So now is it to be concluded that once the sinner has been justified by faith, life comes by works? Such a suggestion would contradict directly the point just established by Habakkuk. For as the proud man by the nature of the case cannot be upright within (Hab. 2:4a), so the sinner claiming life before God because of his steadfast works must be proud.

The root meaning of the term *ʾᵉmûnâ* is "steadfastness," and Habakkuk promotes "steadfastness" as the way of receiving the gift of life. But by the very nature of his argument it cannot be by (steadfast) *works*. The principle of the sinner's ongoing life is identical with the principle of the sinner's righteousness. Steadfastness in *faith* is the way of receiving the gift of life. Continuation in trust alone can assure continued possession of the gift of life.

While steadfastness in deeds may be connected inevitably with the term used by Habakkuk, the framework in which the prophet's statement must be understood, as has been indicated, is found in the affirmation that Abraham "believed in Yahweh," and "he reckoned *it* to him for righteousness" (Gen. 15:6). The striking appearance of the feminine pronoun ("he reckoned *it*") that has no explicit referent in the Genesis passage must be considered carefully.

What is to be understood by the "it" of this phrase? The feminine singular pronoun refers back to the verb "he believed" *(heʾᵉmin)*, and therefore presumably would allude to the corresponding noun—"belief" *(ʾᵉmûnâ!)*. Precisely this word describes the way to life in Hab. 2:4: "The justified shall live *beʾᵉmûnāṭô.*" The noun here, like the corresponding verb of Gen. 15:6, affirms that *steadfast trust* is the way of receiving the gracious gift of life.

As strange as it may seem, the Hebrew language does not abound in nouns that might be regarded as equivalent to the English term *faith*. As a matter of fact, *ʾᵉmûnâ* would have been the most natural candidate if "faith" were the idea that Habakkuk was intending to convey. Too quickly, it seems, have exegetes been ready to identify the meaning of this term *('ĕmûnâ)* exclusively with "faithfulness."[8] But a careful consideration of the OT contexts in which the term occurs indicates that "trust" or "faith" may well explain its usage at several points.

A number of passages contrast the way of "falsehood" with the way of *'ĕmûnâ* in a judicial context. In this circumstance the one who "trusts" will tell the truth, thereby indicating his faith that God shall defend his cause. In contrast, the person of falsehood counts on his own ingenuity and deceit to maintain his interests. So Ps. 119:29–30 could be rendered:

> The way of falsehood
> turn aside from me. . . .
> The way of *steadfast trust*
> I have chosen;
> In your just judgments
> I have set my heart.

Proverbs 12:17 offers a similar contrast:

> The one who speaks (in) *steadfast trust*
> will make known righteousness;
> But a false witness
> will bring forth lies.[9]

Other passages where "faith" or "trust" may be the appropriate rendering of *'ĕmûnâ* include Prov. 28:20; Ps. 31:24 (Eng. 23); 37:3. With respect to this last passage, Alfred Jepsen characterizes *'ĕmûnâ* as "that inner attitude which is prerequisite to a genuine life."[10] Suffice it to say that in several cases in the OT the leading aspect of the term *'ĕmûnâ* appears to reside in this inner

---

8. In his insightful article on faith, B. B. Warfield is probably correct in seeing Hab. 2:4 as the only OT passage where the context *demands* that the Hebrew noun be rendered as "faith." But other passages certainly appear to have this possibility. Cf. B. B. Warfield, "Faith," in *Biblical and Theological Studies* (Philadelphia: Presbyterian and Reformed, 1952), p. 431.

9. Similar contrasts may be found in Prov. 12:22; 14:5.

10. Alfred Jepsen, "'āman, etc.," in *TDOT*, 1:318. Jepsen also states that *'ĕmûnâ* in contrast with *'ĕmet* "seems more to emphasize one's own inner attitude and the conduct it produces" (p. 317). At another point, he defines *'ĕmûnâ* as "a way of acting which grows out of inner stability" (p. 317). Jepsen's treatment of the essence of the biblical use of the term as meaning "conscientiousness" moves the central thrust of the term too far into an abstract moral quality that is foreign to the biblical contexts. "Steadfastness" in relation to Yahweh lies at the heart of the concept.

attitude of entrustment. Habakkuk 2:4 is distinctive but perhaps not unique in this usage of the term.

John Calvin has aptly described the grace which Habakkuk commends. It is "that faith which strips us of all arrogance, and leads us naked and needy to God, that we may seek salvation from him alone, which would otherwise be far removed from us."[11] He notes that the teaching of Rome allows that sinners are justified by faith, but will not tolerate the idea that they are justified by faith *alone.*

But "steadfastness" in faith is a grace that produces good works and must not be confused with the works it produces. In the context of Habakkuk, when considered in the light of Gen. 15:6, it is "steadfast trust" in God that is the way the gift of life must be received. This way contrasts with all arrogance and boastfulness.[12]

The distinctive rendering of this phrase by the LXX may have arisen out of a sense of tension between righteousness by faith and life by faithful works on the part of the sinner. Instead of reading "the just by his faith shall live," the LXX reads, "the just by *my* (i.e., God's) faithfulness shall live." Yet it is also possible that "by (the) faith of me" in the LXX actually means "by faith *in* me." A parallel expression may be found in a passage such as Mark 11:22: "If you have (the) faith of God *(pístin theoú)* . . .," clearly meaning "If you have faith *in* God. . . ."[13]

The NT treatment of the text corresponds appropriately to the central message of Habakkuk. Particularly Paul displays a magnificent grasp of the prophet's message when he adopts this single phrase as a basis for constructing the entire letter to the Romans. Not merely as a keynote sounded to introduce his treatise, but as a well-balanced theme that structures the entirety of his message, this verse from Habakkuk permeates the whole of the epistle.

In setting forth his theme in Romans, Paul declares that a righ-

11. Calvin, p. 74.

12. C. von Orelli, p. 248, is quite correct in his remarks on the term *steadfastness* as it appears here. It is "in keeping with the contrast, a loyal attitude to God, and as such, according to Gen. xv.6 (the noun here corresponds to the *h'myn* there) is to be regarded as humble trust, therefore *pístis,* faith, believing fidelity." However, he violates every point he has established when he proceeds to assert that faith saves from death "because it is the fundamental element in righteousness."

13. The simplest explanation for the reading of the LXX may be "on the basis of the well-known confusion in Hebrew scribal orthography between *y* and *w*" (P. J. M. Southwell, "A Note on Habakkuk ii.4," *JTS* 19 [1968] 615). While it is possible that the LXX represents the original reading of the text, the role of the retrospective pronoun in the Hebrew compound sentence as discussed above, as well as the parallelism with the first half of the verse, supports the correctness of the MT.

teousness of God has been revealed *from* faith *to* faith (Rom. 1:17). Faith serves as the origin of righteousness in justification, and as the framework for the continuation of righteousness in sanctification. The apostle then develops this twofold role of faith as originally presented in Hab. 2:4, dealing with the faith that receives the gift of justification in Rom. 1–5, and the faith that receives the gift of sanctification in Rom. 6–8. Thus Paul offers a well-balanced gospel in his development of his theme that "the justified (by faith) shall live by his steadfast trust."

When Paul first introduces his quotation from Habakkuk, he attaches "faith" with "justification" rather than with the "life" of the sinner. But how may it be explained that while Habakkuk apparently relates the "by faith" phraseology to the way of *life*, Paul has no compunction in relating "by faith" to the way of righteousness instead? Is he exercising a liberty with the inspired text that goes beyond its original intention?

If the earlier exegesis of Hab. 2:4b was correct, this problem is imagined rather than real. The "just" of Habakkuk are none other than the "justified," and in accordance with the parallel to Abraham, their justification is "by faith" even as was Abraham's. Although Paul omits the pronoun altogether from his quotation, he interprets the "faith" of Habakkuk to refer to the trust exercised by the sinner, in contrast with any works he might do (cf. Rom. 3:22, 25–28, 31; 4:3, 5, 9, 11–14, 16–20, 24; 5:1–2). Although the "faithfulness" of God obviously is essential for the salvation of sinners, in all these references Paul is treating Habakkuk's "faith" as that trust in God required of sinners for salvation. As Paul proceeds in Rom. 6–8, he then stresses continually the possession of the gift of "life" as it had been mentioned in Hab. 2:4 (Rom. 6:4–5, 8, 10–11, 13, 22–23; 7:4, 6; 8:2, 6, 10–11, 13). "Resurrection" and the "Spirit" in these chapters relate directly to this "life" promised by Habakkuk to the one who believes. So Paul simply is emphasizing the heart and core of the proclamation of Habakkuk. This great message of justification and life by faith alone is eschatological in nature and shall be true to the end of the age.

The writer to the Hebrews cites Hab. 2:4 in Heb. 10:37–38, but for a different purpose. His concern is to stress the importance of persevering in faith. He wishes to stir his readers to claim the gift of *life* by faith, despite many obstacles. The positioning of the "my" in Hebrews corresponds to its location in some LXX manuscripts ("*my* righteous one"—*ho dè díkaiòs mou*, instead of "by *my* faithfulness"—*ek písteōs mou*). As a consequence, the writer to the Hebrews avoids giving the misimpression that he is understanding Habakkuk to affirm simply that it is by God's faithfulness that the righteous shall live. Although such a statement is true in itself, it was not the precise truth that the suffering believers of the 1st century needed at this point. Instead, they needed to be reminded that God has his righteous ones, and they indeed shall live by faith!

The catalogue of the faithful in Heb. 11 which immediately follows this citation from Habakkuk does not make faith itself a work, thereby cancelling out the heart of Habakkuk's message. Instead it is "*by* faith" that all these works have been performed throughout the ages.

So two diverse authors of the NT quote the same OT Scripture with a different emphasis to make significantly different points. Yet each author remains true to the essence of the OT Scripture as recorded by Habakkuk. Paul stresses that *by faith* a person is justified, and the writer to the Hebrews stresses that *by faith* a person who has been justified shall live. As has been noted, Paul also develops the idea of *life* by faith in Rom. 6–8.

The locating of the channel to life in a person's steadfast trust occurs repeatedly in the OT Scriptures. Israel is admonished to hearken to the Lord's voice and to cling to him, "for he is your life" (Deut. 30:20). Only by oneness with God, the source of life, may Israel expect to live. Only by a steadfast entrustment that inevitably produces obedience may this life-giving relation to God be maintained.

The problem that Habakkuk faced was the prospect of the devastation of Israel, signifying the end of life for God's own nation. The prophet's frustration in grasping the divine message of judgment is epitomized in his spontaneous interjection, "We shall not die!" (Hab. 1:12). Yet the revelation of God to him seemed to be that Israel indeed would die. But the Lord gives this vision of the eschaton: "... *shall live!*" (Heb. 2:4). The justified (by faith) shall live by his steadfast trust.

In a very real sense, the problem faced by Habakkuk was identical with the problem Paul later confronted in Rom. 11. Had God cast off his people? The devastation of Israel was obvious to the first-century Christian. The richest blessings of God's ancient covenant now had become the possession of all nations, while Israel had been "cut off" by the very words of Christ himself. The kingdom had been taken from them and given to another nation bearing its proper fruit (Matt. 21:23). Paul responds to this confusing picture by the same perspective as that found in Habakkuk. For as Israel turns from its unbelief, it shall be grafted in (Rom. 11:23). Even today a believing remnant remains according to the election of grace (Rom. 11:5).

So the justified by faith continue to live by faith. Despite the just judgments of God, a remnant shall survive. By steadfast trust through the darkest hours, they shall live.

5 Yet the wicked will continue in their rapacious ways. The perplexing queries of Habakkuk about the forthcoming destruction of Israel brought about the eschatological vision of God, which established that the proud cannot be upright and the justified (by faith) shall live by his steadfast trust.

These points of reassurance offered some comfort to the perplexed prophet. Yet they seemed to be contradicted directly by the imminent circumstances he faced. The third point made in the Lord's vision to Habakkuk confirms the reality of this tension with which the prophet must live. The wicked will continue on their brutal way in apparent prosperity, despite the truth of God's work of salvation for the righteous by faith, and his declaration of the certainty of the ultimate destruction of the wicked.

This verse begins with a contrasting *However.* Because of the deceiving powers of *wine,* the one who is puffed up is blinded to his true state. He lives in a deluded condition intensified by wine.

The "handwriting on the wall" for the Babylonian kingdom, it may be remembered, came in the midst of Belshazzar's feast. The book of Daniel pointedly notes that while the king was drinking his wine, he sent for the gold and silver goblets which Nebuchadrezzar had taken from the temple of Jerusalem. As he, his nobles, wives, and concubines drank and praised their gods of gold and silver, the hand appeared, writing a sentence of doom on the wall (Dan. 5:1ff.). In the midst of their prideful celebration, the divine decree of destruction was revealed.

It should not be supposed that Habakkuk's vision is singling out the sin of drunkenness as the chief transgression. But neither should the introduction of this specific sin be seen as inappropriate. Strong drink does not in itself engender the pride that is so obnoxious to God. But it serves as an agent by which latent human pride comes forth in all its ugliness. Strong drink evokes expressions of bloated self-esteem inherent in the sinful mind and heart.

As a consequence, the proud person *boasts and will not rest.* Nothing can satisfy him. His lust for possession expands like the insatiable appetite of *Sheol,* the grave, which continues over the ages to swallow up everyone. As Habakkuk himself had observed earlier in his complaint, the Babylonian finds contentment only in swallowing up all nations for himself (Hab. 1:15–17).

So the Lord's response to Habakkuk's complaint offers hope, but not apart from a grim prospect for the future as well. Those who have believed shall continue to live in their faith. But the wicked also shall have their day, devouring nations by their brutality.

This vision is truly eschatological in its significance. It appropriately characterizes the present age until the time of the final consummation. "The justified (by faith) shall live by his steadfast trust" summarizes the essence of the Christian gospel, while the pride of the unbeliever explains his unending brutality against the people of the Lord.

2. The Ridicule of the Haughty (2:6–20)

Having unveiled the essence of his resolution of Habakkuk's problem, the Lord now turns to elaborate on the certain fate of the haughty, who stand in contrast with the humble who believe. Receiving nothing more (and nothing less) than they deserve, the boastful Chaldeans are made the subjects of wise sayings calculated to humble them. A series of five mocking statements expresses the righteous recompense that is sure to come.

Introduction: A proverb and a byword—riddles against him (2:6a)

6a *Will not all of them*
    hold out against him
 a proverb and a byword—
    riddles against him?[1]

Israel itself had been warned that if it did not keep the commandments of God, it would become the object of taunts among all the nations of the earth (Deut. 28:37; 1 K. 9:7). Now the Lord declares that the day shall come when all those nations whom the Chaldeans have bullied shall mock their conqueror.

Nothing stings more permanently than being made the brunt of an obscure taunt. The enigmatic character of the jibe establishes the permanence of the hurt.

It might appear beneath the dignity of God to embarrass the proud before the watching world. But a part of his reality as the God of history includes his public vindication of the righteous and his public shaming of the wicked. His glory before all his creation is magnified by the establishment of honor for the humble and disgrace for the arrogant. In this case, the shame of Babylon shall be as extensive as its conquests. *all of them,* all those nations conquered by Babylon, shall join the mockery. Even the tiniest of the nations shall rehearse these sayings without fear of reprisal.

1. Three separate terms describe the mockery which is to fall on the Babylonians. *māšāl* is used frequently in Scripture and may refer to a proverbial saying, a figurative discourse, or a mocking byword. *mᵉlîṣâ* derives from the root *lîṣ,* meaning to scorn, to deride, or to mock. *ḥîḏôṯ* connotes the idea of a riddle or an elusive saying. The third term, plural in form, describes the frequently puzzling effect of the first two words.

a. Ha! the pillager pillaged! (2:6b–8)

6b *And he shall say,*
> *Ha!*
>> *The one who multiplies*
>>> *that which is not his—*
>>>> *O, how long (will it be)?*

>> *And makes himself glorious*
>>> *by pledges—*
7 >>>> *will it not be suddenly?*
>>>>> *Your creditors*
>>>>>> *will form an uprising,*
>>>>> *and your disturbers*
>>>>>> *will awake;*
>>>>> *you will be*
>>>>>> *plunder for them.*
8 *Because you have pillaged*
>> *many nations,*
>>> *all that remains of the people*
> *shall pillage you.*
>>>> *For the bloody gorings of men,*
>>>> *and the violence done to the land,*
>>>> *the city and all its inhabitants.*

This particular pronouncement of judgment combines a number of devices for constructing a wise saying that will be remembered, one that will rise up and haunt the Babylonians in their arrogance for years to come. As a matter of fact, the number of devices employed in these verses is quite remarkable. Most of them are lost in the process of translation. But the following may be noted in particular:

(1) Assonance and alliteration. *Ha! The one who multiplies that which is not his* (v. 6b). The last words of this phrase are pronounced the same in Hebrew. Like "lo" and "low" in English, the same sound conveys a different meaning.

For the bloody gorings of men (v. 8b) is *midd^emê ʾāḏām* in Hebrew. While this device may not appear particularly noteworthy to the English reader, the larger role of this kind of assonance in Hebrew underscores its significance. The similarity of sound enhances the memorableness of the phrase.

(2) Double meaning in words. A standard hermeneutical principle asserts that a single word can have only one meaning in a given context. Yet a deliberate departure from this rule in human communication has the effect of multiplying the impact of a particular word.

186

Your creditors (nōšᵉkeykā) regularly means "to bite." The root is used appropriately to refer to a creditor, for figuratively speaking that is exactly what he does. He bites his chunk from the possessions of the person to whom he lends money. So Babylon's *biters/creditors* will rise up against them suddenly. The double meaning of the word underscores the judgment to come on the oppressive nation.[1]

Another possible instance of double entendre in this first proverb is found in the word translated *pledges* (ʿaḇṭîṭ, v. 6b). Yet the term may also be viewed simultaneously as a compound word meaning "heap of mud." The Babylonian has made himself *glorious by pledges/heaps of mud.*[2]

(3) Appeal to proverbial truth. Every civilization and language inevitably develops its capsuled gems of insight into life. As Habakkuk lances the Chaldean with his verbal barbs, he feathers his shafts with proverbial truths to assure that they strike their mark. In describing the futility of Babylon's *multiplying* to itself ill-gotten gain, Habakkuk echoes recognized proverbial truth:

"He that *multiplies* his substance by excessive interest rates *(bᵉnešek)* . . . shall gather it for the man who pities the poor" (Prov. 28:8).

"He who oppresses the poor to *multiply* for himself . . . surely shall lack necessities" (Prov. 22:16).

"Wealth which comes by questionable ways will shrink to nothing; but he who gathers by his own hard work will *multiply*" (Prov. 13:11).

1. Further discussion of this term may be found in n. 5 below.

2. The term ʿaḇṭîṭ, a *hapax legomenon,* most likely is an intensified form from ʿāḇaṭ, "to pledge," created by a doubling of the third radical (cf. Rudolph, p. 219; GKC, §§ 84b, m). Yet the term also could derive from two words: ʿb, meaning "cloud" or "mass"; and ṭyṭ, meaning "mud" or "dirt." The latter possibility finds support in some Hebrew mss. which divide the word, as well as in the Syriac and Vulgate. It seems to have been known by 1QpHab, which refers to "every kind of defiling impurity" (8:13).

Very possibly this choice of words by Habakkuk would represent a case of double entendre, so that from one perspective the ill-gotten gain of the Chaldean would be viewed as wealth derived from oppressive pledges, and from another perspective as a "hunk of mud" which the Chaldean has heaped on himself. Calvin's remarks are particularly insightful in terms of the application of this message. He notes that all the wealth of this world is nothing more than a heap of clay (p. 95). The more the greedy heap together, the more they become a burden laid on themselves. Almost without fail the covetous person makes a burden out of his own wealth. As he becomes older, he is fearful of losing what he has gained, and in his greedy grasping he cannot spend what he possesses.

The judgment that will come *suddenly (peṭaʿ)* on the Babylonian also finds its reinforcement in Israel's proverbs:

"In an instant shall disaster come (to the wicked); *suddenly* he will be destroyed, without hope of healing" (Prov. 6:15).
"The man who stiffens his neck against many warnings shall be broken *suddenly,* without hope of healing" (Prov. 29:1).

(4) Retribution as a theme emphasized by phraseology and content. As harsh as the principle of "an eye for an eye" may appear in a modern context, it represents the law of justice in which a willful oppressor receives from the hand of God what he deserves. So Habakkuk underscores by form and substance the certainty of God's orderly rewarding of the ruthless: *Because you have pillaged many nations, all that remains of the people shall pillage you (kî ʾattâ šallôṯā gôyim rabbîm yᵉsāllûḵā kol-yeṯer ʿammîm).*

(5) Rhyming of phrases. It is generally denied that the rhyming of words plays any role in Hebrew literature. Yet it must be recognized that the use of rhyme as a device for reinforcing a statement certainly was a possible device that could have been employed. That rhyme does occur in the present prophetic proverb cannot be denied. No less than three instances are quite clear:

yāqûmû nōšᵉḵeykā
wᵉyiqṣû mᵉzaʿzᵉʿeykā (v. 7)

kî ʾattâ šallôṯā
  gôyim rabbîm
yᵉšāllûḵā
  kol-yeṯer ʿammîm (v. 8a)

qiryâ
wᵉḵol-yōšᵉḇê ḇāh (v. 8c)

It is somewhat more difficult to determine whether the rhyming of these words was intentional. In this case, the presence of three instances in such a short scope, together with the avowed intention of composing a proverb that would not be forgotten, suggests that these rhymes were not accidental. Although the matter has not been explored in studies on Hebrew poetic device very extensively, the presence of similar kinds of apparent rhymes in other biblical proverbs ought to be noted (cf. Prov. 11:2, 7, 10; 13:3; 18:17; 22:10).

In any case, this first judgmental byword on Babylon is replete with examples of literary devices proved effective in the construction of a proverbial saying. It will be difficult indeed for the oppressor to escape these phrases once they have been hung about his neck.

6b   The contrast between *all of them* (v. 6) and *he* who speaks the proverbial bywords has been handled variously.³ Most likely the change represents the common alteration in Hebrew between a group corporately considered and a single member of the group who speaks for the whole.

The *Ha!* (Heb. *hôy*) that marks off the five separate proverbial sayings in this section (vv. 6b, 9, 12, 15, 19) is an onomatopoeic word that does not mean precisely "woe," although it is used frequently to introduce a statement of judgment. It connotes instead the broader idea embodied in an exclamatory "Ahah!" or simply "Ah!" In the present context it takes on something of the tone of mockery inherent in these taunt words. The closest thing to Habakkuk's stringing together of five such consecutive statements introduced by this word is found in Isa. 5, where the term occurs six times in succession.

Poetic justice or reciprocity is the main point of this first byword. Has the Babylonian unjustly multiplied that which is not his (v. 6b)? He will become booty to his awakened destroyers (v. 7b). Has he made himself glorious through goods taken by (defaulted) pledges (v. 6b)?⁴ Then those who turn out to be his creditors will mercilessly exact payment from him (v. 7).⁵ Has he rifled a multitude of nations, driving through his armies and leaving a trail of looting and burning behind (v. 8)? Then those scattered survivors from many nations shall rise up one day to devastate all of Babylon's holdings (v. 8).

---

3. The LXX translates *kaì eroúsin,* "and they shall say." The Vulgate renders the Hebrew impersonally: *et dicetur,* "and it shall be said." Calvin, p. 91, simply notes the change in number, observing that it does not obscure the sense. Keil, p. 77, does not comment on this particular point, but observes that "all these" could refer only to believers among all the nations. Others have identified the "he" who speaks as the "justified" of Hab. 2:4, or as God himself. Rudolph, p. 219, says the subject is indefinite. He characterizes the plural forms in 1QpHab and the LXX as obvious corrections.

4. The idea of a defaulted pledge might arise from a conquered nation's disregarding the stipulations of a suzerainty treaty imposed by the Babylonian conqueror.

5. The term *nōš^eḵeyḵā,* "your creditors," would appear at first to make more sense if it were rendered "your debtors." For it seems more appropriate to consider the nations conquered by Babylon as its *debtors* rather than its creditors. But further consideration leads in the opposite direction, and supports the more natural meaning of the word. The prophet now is talking about the point at which justice finally shall be exacted on the Babylonians. At that time, it is not the oppressed nations that are debtors to Babylon, but Babylon who is their debtor. By oppressive brutality, it has robbed the nations of their personal wealth. But the day will dawn in which these oppressed nations will be in a position to demand of Babylon repatriation for all the damage done to them. In that day the little, defenseless nations of the earth will become the demanding creditors of a humbled Babylon.

If this weighted emphasis on reciprocation in judgment seems distinctively "Old Testament" in orientation, two passages from the New Testament may serve to indicate the continuing validity of this message. Christ himself climaxes his parable of the unforgiving servant who confines his fellow servant to a lifetime in debtor's prison for a few pennies with a lesson on reciprocation. This man will be sentenced to hell until he has paid the last penny of his own million-dollar debt (Matt. 18:21–35). According to Paul, God is just and will pay back trouble *(thlípsin)* to those who trouble Christian believers *(toís thlíbousin)* (2 Thess. 1:6). The God of all the earth shall do right, and part of his rightness will be expressed in the just punishment of all who oppress others.

Injected into the treatment of the reciprocal nature of God's judgment are questions concerning the timing of that judgment. Particularly for Habakkuk this question had relevance. *how long (will it be)* before justice shall be manifested in all its self-convincing uprightness (v. 6b)? The prophet had begun his complaint in view of the rampant cruelty among his own countrymen. He then expressed astonishment at the horrors of the Babylonian invasion. But how many years would it be before oppression would be no more? When would the scales of justice cease swinging from one imbalanced extreme to another?

7 The answer of this divine saying is *suddenly!* This answer should not be perceived as polite evasion to the prophet's direct query by answering in terms of "how" rather than "when." For the answer of divine judgment in terms of the "suddenness" provides more information than the question asked. It reveals in a balanced way both God's desire to be merciful to hardened sinners and his determination to establish justice in the earth. For some considerable length of time God will show his long-suffering toward those committing repeated acts of cruelty. But such people never may presume that God's mercies will continue any longer than the present moment. Divine retribution is sure to come, and it may come without additional prior warning.

8 The final reason for this coming divine judgment is the cruel violence done to the whole of creation. Human and nonhuman elements of the world are a concern to the Almighty. *Men* and their *lands, the city and all its inhabitants,* have suffered untold *violence.* For this combined reason, the haughty conquerors shall suffer appropriate retribution.

The message of reciprocal judgment should sober up the sentimental outlook of modern civilizations. If each person exacting excessive interest of debtors would consider that in the dispensations of God he shall receive precisely the same treatment he inflicts, he might be led to repentance. If politicians and commanders of military forces accustomed to functioning in brutal, ruthless fashion would understand that they and their people shall one day receive the same treatment at the hands of those they oppress, a genuine crying to God for mercy in a context of repentance might become more frequent. While the mills of God may grind slowly, they grind exceedingly fine.

This divine proverb, set in its memorable form, makes it quite plain that the Almighty is vitally concerned with these "nonreligious" issues of man's inhumanity to man. Not just in some distant, nebulous eternity, but within the present lifetime, God's hand of justice shall make returns to people according to their works. Although the final balancing of the scales of justice must await eternity, time now will show a greater equity than might at first be imagined.

b. Ha! the fortified dismantled! (2:9–11)

9 *Ha!*

> *The one who covets wickedly*[1]
>   *for his house,*
> *to set on high*
>   *his nest,*
> *to deliver from the hand of evil!*
10   *You have counseled shame against your house*
>   *by cutting off*[2] *many peoples,*
>   *and sinning against your own soul.*[3]

---

1. The grammatical function of the term for "evil" *(rāʿ)* here is difficult. Keil, p. 100, takes it as adjectival: "an evil covetousness." Rudolph, p. 220, views it as a noun: "for the *misfortune* of your house," which requires that he interpret this phrase as a parenthetical anticipation of the consequences of covetousness that are explained only in the following verses. The above translation, being more "dynamic" than "literal" in nature, has rendered the sense as adverbial, although the syntax strictly speaking would favor the adjectival function.

2. The "cutting off" *(qᵉṣôt)* of many peoples in v. 10 is an infinitive construct in form from the verb *qāṣâ*. The reading of 1QpHab 9:14 is another matter: it reads *qᵉṣāwôt*, although the *pesher* in 10:2 reads *qᵉṣāwît*. The text and its interpretation refer to the "confines" or extremities of the place of punishment of the "wicked priest." According to Brownlee, *Midrash,* p. 159, the word *qᵉṣāwôt* would be "the plural of the theoretical absolute singular feminine noun *qᵉṣāt,*" meaning boundary limit. 1QpHab combines this word with a modification of *ḥôṭēʾ* ("sinners") into *ḥûṭê* ("bonds"), to support its interpretation that the phrase refers to a "confinement" in hades of the wicked. Rudolph, p. 220, notes that according to the versions it would be pointed as a finite verb: *qaṣṣôtā* from *qāṣaṣ.* The meaning is not affected materially by these variations.

3. "Forfeiting your own life" (NIV) is a possible rendering, particularly in the light of Prov. 20:2. But "sinning against your own soul" captures more of the idea

11   *a For the stone*
      b   from the wall
      c   will cry out,
a and the beam
      b   from the timber[4]
      c   will answer it.

This second proverbial byword contains some of the same devices for insuring its memorable character as were found in the first taunt. Alliteration is created by the repetition in verbal and nominal form of the same root (*bōṣēaˁ beṣaˁ*, v. 9). Intentional play within the multiple meaning of a single word is evident in the use of the term *house,* which may denote either "dynasty" or "dwelling place." Although it must be acknowledged that the phenomenon could be incidental to the author's purpose, rhyming of end-words in phrases occurs again:

> *bōṣēaˁ beṣaˁ raˁ*
>   *leḇêtô*
> *lāśûm bammārôm*
>   *qinnô*

The consequences of covetousness for a household is spelled out in a form that appears to echo earlier proverbs in Israel's wisdom thought:

He troubles his house who is greedy of gain [*bōṣēaˁ beṣaˁ*],
but he who despises gifts shall live. (Prov. 15:27)

They ambush their own blood,
They lurk in hiding for their own lives,
So are the ways of all who are greedy of gain [*bōṣēaˁ baṣaˁ*].
                                                                (Prov. 1:18–19)

By use of these various modes of expression, the prophet has made this second byword against the Babylonian equally as memorable as the first.

9 The *house* about which the Chaldean is concerned refers primarily to his dynasty, although it may apply to the commoner's family line as

---

of a long-term retribution against the covetous. In time he shall see the dissolution of his entire person.

4. The term *kāpîs* is a *hapax legomenon.* The significance of the word is not completely clear. The best possibility seems to be a reference to a central beam that binds the walls of a building together, as supported by Jerome, by some of the Greek versions, and by the Aramaic word *kpt,* "to bind." For the references, see Rudolph, p. 220.

well. He wishes to place his descendants above the reach of all enemies, real or imagined. He trusts that somehow accumulated wealth will assure that they will be unassailable.

The vice of covetousness naturally connects with a person's concern for those of his household, his posterity. As a bird achieves security for his young by building *his nest* (v. 9) on the peak of a rocky crag, so the covetous person, possibly the king of Babylon, strives by illegal as well as legal means to establish his dynasty as unassailable (for this same imagery cf. Num. 24:21; Obad. 4; Jer. 49:16).

According to one of his own inscriptions Nebuchadrezzar said that one of the chief purposes for his strengthening the walls of Babylon was to make an everlasting name for his reign. He also prays to his god Marduk: "Life for many generations, an abundant posterity, a secure throne, and a long reign, grant as thy gift."[5]

But the consequences of covetousness are just the opposite of what the greedy desire. His schemes only guarantee shame for his house. Just as Achan's sin of covetousness led to the disgrace and damnation of his whole family (Josh. 7:24–26), so this sin of illegally amassing wealth will inevitably destroy an entire clan.

10   The covetous have only *counseled shame* against their own house. A dramatic outworking of such tragic circumstances may be seen in the life of Ahithophel, counselor to David (2 Sam. 15–17). This one whose counsel was like the oracle of God turned from David to advise Absalom, apparently for personal gain. When Ahithophel learned that his counsel would be spurned, he went to his own hometown, set his house in order, and hanged himself. So he brought shame on his entire family (2 Sam. 17:23).

In similar fashion, the king of Babylon has *counseled shame* for himself and his own household. Little did the king understand that by his covetous ways he was *sinning against his own soul*. He had thought that he was assuring the preservation of himself and his own house. But ironically he was only laying a foundation for their destruction along with his own.

11   The last phrases of the proverb return to the imagery of the "house" and its destruction. The agonizing process of self-destruction continues as one element of the structure moans in agony only to be answered by another. The *stone from the wall will cry out* and *the beam from the timber will answer it*. The king's dynasty crumbles despite all the efforts to secure the throne by amassing unlimited wealth.

5. Cf. Laetsch, p. 336, for the references.

c. Ha! the civilized demoralized! (2:12–14)

12 *Ha!*
    a He who builds
        b a city
            c with bloodshed,[1]
    a and establishes
        b a town
            c with violence!
13 *Behold, is it not from Yahweh of hosts*
    a that they will labor
        b the nations—
            c for the sake of fire;
        b and the peoples
            c for the sake of vanity
    a will become weary?
14 *For the earth shall be filled*
with the knowledge of the glory of Yahweh
as the waters cover the sea.

This third in the series of proverbial bywords uttered against Babylon also contains distinctive devices to assure that posterity will remember this judgmental denouncement of the oppressor. Prominent in these verses is the employment of Hebrew parallelism. Although this mode of expression is present in the first two proverbs, it is particularly worthy of note at this point.

The first instance of parallelism in this proverb is structured on an *a-b-c, a-b-c* pattern:

    a He builds (Qal participle)
      b a city
        c with [*b^e*] blood(s);
    a he establishes (Qal participle)
      b a town
        c with [*b^e*] violence.

It may be noted that both grammatical and lexical considerations contribute to the impact of the parallelism.

The second instance varies the structure, following an *a-b-c, b-c-a* pattern:

    a They will labor (Qal imperfect)
      b the nations

---

1. The Hebrew reads lit. "bloods."

    c for the sake of [*beḏê*] fire;
 b the peoples
    c for the sake of [*beḏê] vanity*
a they will become weary (Qal imperfect).

Again, both grammatical and lexical parallels enhance the effectiveness of the poetic structure.

Especially noteworthy in the present section is the introduction of a device calculated to cause this denunciatory proverb to be remembered. Habakkuk now cites more ancient sayings than his own, incorporating them into his utterance and thereby contemporizing their message.

The principal instance of a quotation from an earlier saying is the reference to the earth being filled with the knowledge of the glory of God as the waters cover the sea (Hab. 2:14). This statement in Habakkuk gives every evidence of being an intentional conflation of two different older sources. The precise wording may be compared as follows:

Num. 14:21	Shall be filled [*yimmālē*']	all the earth
Isa. 11:9	Shall be full [*māle*'*â*]	the earth
Hab. 2:14	Shall be filled [*timmālē*']	the earth

Num. 14:21	(with) the glory of Yahweh
Isa. 11:9	(with) the knowledge of Yahweh
Hab. 2:14	(with) the knowledge of the glory of Yahweh

Num. 14:21	(no references to the waters covering the sea)
Isa. 11:9	as the waters for the sea make a covering
Hab. 2:14	as the waters cover over the sea.

Each of the three instances depicts the spread of the knowledge of God to universal boundaries. Isaiah introduces the simile of the waters covering the sea. Habakkuk appears intentionally to combine the reference to the filling of the earth with the *glory* of God and the universalism of the *knowledge* of God. So far as precise phraseology is concerned, Habakkuk maintains his own independence at almost every point. But the net effect of this conflating of older sources, apparently well-known to Habakkuk's contemporaries, certainly makes this judgmental utterance more memorable.

A similar kind of allusion may be intended by the reference to the Babylonian king's building a city by bloodshed and violence (Hab. 2:12), even though a precise quotation of words is not involved. For perhaps the most ancient of the proverbial sayings of Scripture has to do with Nimrod, founder of the most ancient Babylon. Because of his prowess as a "mighty hunter in the earth," an ancient saying developed: "Like Nimrod, the mighty hunter before the Lord" (Gen. 10:9–10). First named in Scripture as a powerful city builder, Nimrod's description as a "mighty hunter" may refer to the hunting, the oppressing of people who were brought under his dominion and enslaved to his ambitions.[2] It may be remembered that Habakkuk already had alluded to the moral problem raised in his mind by the prospect of the Babylonians' dragging people in fishing nets, a practice illustrated by contemporary inscriptions of the Babylonians themselves (Hab. 1:14–17).

Nothing in the precise wording of these verses indicates a specific quotation from the earlier proverb concerning the first king of Babylon. Yet the concept of excessive violence inflicted by the current Babylonian king for the purpose of building a city as described in 2:12 may have been intended to recall to his readers this primal instance of brutality for the sake of establishing a civilization.

This particular proverbial byword of Habakkuk apparently is quoted in turn by another prophet in Israel. In one of his most extensive denunciations of Babylon, Jeremiah quotes the word of Habakkuk:

a And they shall labor
  b the nations—
    c for the sake of vanity,
  b and the peoples
    c for the sake of fire;
a and they shall become weary. (Jer. 51:58)

Although maintaining his independence by several modifications of expression, Jeremiah appears to quote Habakkuk.[3]

Habakkuk has succeeded in his goal of pronouncing a memorable saying, a proverbial byword over the mighty Babylon. His seemingly perishable words have proved to outlast the mighty resources of this once-great empire.

12 A city represents the final fruition of mankind's efforts to "subdue the earth." This responsibility was originally given to man as the only being created in the image of God (cf. Gen. 1:26). The city solidifies into a single whole the resources of intelligence and skill provided by a number of diverse individuals. In accord with the purposes of God in creation and

---

2. The commentaries generally understand the phrase to refer to a literal hunting of animals as a display of the potentate's prowess.

3. Jeremiah reverses Habakkuk's order of "fire" and "vanity," and reads $w^e yig^e \hat{u}$ instead of $w^e yig^{e^c} \hat{u}$. He also adds a connecting *waw* before the last verb, which has the effect of making the last line an independent clause.

redemption, the populace of a city should work together to form a culture and a community which performs all its functions to the glory of God.

The early history of cities in Scripture indicates that hardly any semblance existed between the divine intention for human civilization and the concrete development of the city. Cain built the first city, and dedicated it to the glory of his own son (Gen. 4:17). Nimrod was an empire builder, apparently on the basis of his strength and prowess in enslaving others (10:8–12). Man's arrogance led to the debacle at Babel (11:4). The obscenities committed in the plushest of Canaan's valleys brought about the consuming fire of God's judgment on Sodom (13:10; 19:24–25). The treasure cities of Egypt became the occasion for the enslavement of God's own people (Exod. 1:11).

But God has uttered a memorable saying. He has spoken in unforgettable fashion against anyone who *builds a city with bloodshed and establishes a town with violence.*

13 The entire massive endeavor will do the oppressor no good. Labor and weariness in erecting an entire city for the sake of self will prove to be pointless. Although endless self-justifications may be offered in terms of the cultural and defensive advantages for the inhabitants of the community, the whole project shall end in shame.

The end, according to Habakkuk, had to be *fire* and *vanity.* Although directed specifically to Babylon, this text includes *nations* and *peoples* of all generations. Fire from the Lord consumed the debauched luxury of the cities of the plain (Gen. 19:14). God went before Israel as a consuming fire, destroying all its enemies (Deut. 9:3). Even the nation privileged to be called by God's own name in its turn had its cities burned in the fire for persisting in disobedience (Isa. 1:7; Amos 2:5). So the Lord shall come with fire at the last judgment, utterly destroying all his enemies (Isa. 66:15; cf. 2 Pet. 3:10).

Every human culture in its turn prides itself in its achievements won by discipline, devotion, and hard labor. But in the end the rotten core of violence done against other human beings—ironically, for the sake of achieving humanistic goals—shall be exposed and the whole of the corrupted metropolis destroyed.

14 The certitude of the vanity, the pointlessness of people's oppressive ways that build seemingly stable and worthwhile communities rests on the unchanging word of God that Habakkuk now quotes. Their consumption in the fire of God's judgment is not guaranteed simply by the rise and fall of many previous civilizations. Instead, it is the oath of Yahweh himself that *the earth shall be filled with the knowledge of the glory of Yahweh* that guarantees the vanity and futility of all efforts to the contrary. Beauty in song, in dance, in literature, in architecture—all to the glory of God—shall fill the earth *as the waters cover the sea.*

This beautiful statement at first appears so unrelated to the consuming fires of God's judgment that it has been regarded as ungenuine among the original utterances of Habakkuk.[4] Yet its previous contexts in both Numbers and Isaiah contain significant elements reflecting on human depravity that must be dealt with as a way of preparation for the inbreaking of the glory of God. The Lord swears to Moses that the earth shall be filled with his glory, because those who have tempted him in the wilderness "these ten times" shall not enter the land of promise (Num. 14:21–23). Isaiah prophesies that the earth shall be filled with the knowledge of God when the descendant of Jesse slays the wicked with the breath of his lips (Isa. 11:4, 9).

The dialogue of Habakkuk began with puzzlement over the prosperity of the wicked among the people of God. Confusion deepened when God indicated that a nation more wicked than Israel would serve as his chosen instrument for punishment. Despite all the surrounding turmoil, the just by faith would live.

But shall the wicked continue to contradict the expressed laws of God without ever receiving some kind of final correction? How can it be said that the glory of God fills the earth so long as such practices continue?

Only when the problem of the wicked is resolved will the glory of God fill the earth. Only when righteous judgment rewards the wicked according to their deservings will true knowledge of God's holiness shine forth in all its splendor. The imagery of *waters covering the sea* for this universal spread of the knowledge of God's glory inspires optimism. To the farthest corners of the globe the proclamation, the explanation, of God's glory shall be carried.

Distinctive to Habakkuk is this combination of *knowledge* with *glory* covering the earth. Man in the totality of his rational facilities is distinctive for his capacity to appreciate God's creation.

Elsewhere in the old covenant Scriptures a filling with God's glory is associated particularly with the tabernacle or temple as the place of God's dwelling on earth (Exod. 40:34–35; 1 K. 8:10–11; Ezek. 10:3; cf. Hag. 2:7). But now the splendors emanating from the presence of God shall fill the entirety of creation.

Obviously it cannot be said that this great prophetic expectation found its fulfillment at the point of Babylon's destruction in 539 B.C. God's uprightness certainly was manifested at that time. People through all the ages have

---

4. Cf. Rudolph, p. 223.

been reminded of the dramatic "handwriting on the wall" that declared the end of this most oppressive regime (Dan. 5). But Habakkuk's word expects more.

Paul, apostle of the new covenant, captures something of this same vision in his description of the new temple of God constituted by a universal fellowship in which the glory of God is manifested throughout creation. He prays that those united to Messiah "may have power . . . to grasp how wide and long and high and deep is the love of Christ, and to know this love that surpasses knowledge," that they "may be filled to the measure of all the fullness of God" (Eph. 3:18–19, NIV). As Habakkuk's announcement that the just shall live by faith travels among the nations, the earth shall be filled with the knowledge of the glory of God as the waters cover the sea.

The words of Habakkuk must await the consummation for their final fulfillment. Yet the events contemporary with Habakkuk's day must not be discounted. Babylon's destruction gave great relief to a troubled world, just as God's continual exercise of his righteous judgments serves to advance his glory.

d. Ha! the shameless defamed (2:15–17)

15 *Ha!*
>   *the one who makes his neighbor drink,*
>>   *mixing in your wrath—*
>>   *even[1] making (them) drunk*
>>>   *so you can gaze on their nudity.*

16 *You are satiated*
>>   *with shame rather than glory!*
>>   *You do some drinking!*
>>   *Expose yourself as uncircumcised.*
>   *The cup of the right hand of Yahweh*
>>   *shall rotate around to you,*
>>>   *and putrid shame (shall be) all over your glory.*

17 *For the violence done to Lebanon*
>>   *shall overwhelm you,*
>   *and the devastation to beasts*
>>   *(by which) you terrified them;[2]*

---

1. ʾap serves as a particle of intensification. Cf. GKC, § 153.

2. yᵉḥîṭan has been explained variously. As the form now stands in the MT, it may be regarded as a modified Hiphil form derived from ḥtt, "terrify," with a feminine plural suffix referring to the animals terrified. The pointing would be modified by the addition of the suffix, causing yᵉḥîṭēn to be read instead of yāḥēṭ. As Keil suggests, the long î would take the place of the first t of the doubled letter, and the final short a would substitute for the long e of the last syllable because of the pause

> *because of human bloodshed*
> *and violence (done)*
> *to the land,*
> *the city,*
> *and all its inhabitants.*

Now the baseness of Babylon's sin surfaces. Drunkenness, bullying, coarseness, and perversion characterize their king.

It is somewhat difficult to choose between understanding this description of a coarse bully as depicting personal behavior or as describing a nation's brutalities in the process of conquests.[3] It may be that the prophet intends to describe the actual behavior of the king of Babylon and his court as a backdrop for depicting the larger atrocities associated with Babylon's treatment of the nations it invades.

The bully that forces others into debauchery exudes pride, cruelty, and brutality. Previously Israel itself had attempted to silence the prophetic witness of the Nazirite by forcing him to drink, contrary to his lifetime vow of abstinence (Amos 2:12). David the king had abused the power of his office by forcing Uriah to drink (2 Sam. 11:13). Now the king of Babylon uses his authority to humiliate those around him.[4]

But this depraved brute does not have as his ultimate goal simply the mocking of his acquaintances. He manifests a deep-felt hatred, a psychotic rancor toward his neighbor. He *mixes* an irrational *wrath* with the *wine* he pours.

(athnach). However, several earlier versions (LXX, Syriac, Targum) substitute a final *kā* for *n*, reading *yᵉḥitteḵā* or *yᵉḥiteḵâ*, "will terrify (shatter) you," as noted by Rudolph, p. 222. The LXX has "will dismay you" *(ptoései se)*. 1QpHab reads *yaḥteh*, which, as Brownlee *(Midrash*, p. 197) notes, has been emended by some to read *yᵉḥitteḵâ*. Brownlee *(Midrash*, p. 196) translates "will snatch away."

It is true that the suffix "you" would fit the parallelism of the verse better (will overwhelm you/will terrify you). Yet the frequent interchange of suffixes in Hebrew supports the more awkward "them."

3. Calvin, pp. 110–11, has some rather harsh things to say about anyone who understands the passage as presenting the king of Babylon as compelling participation in the vices of debauchery. Such interpreters are "contriving what is fabulous," concluding "this or that without any discrimination or shame." He says the passage must be interpreted as a metaphor.

4. Calvin, p. 113, understands the reference to drunkenness as an expanded figure of a nation drunk on avarice: "for there is no intoxication that stultifies men more than that eager appetite by which they devour both lands and seas." The Babylonian nation, by its covetousness, inspires other nations to the same attitude.

15   The phrase rendered *mixing in your wrath* could be understood in a number of ways. The word translated *mixing (mᵉsappēaḥ)* may mean "to join, to attach to" (1 Sam. 2:36; Isa. 14:1); or in noun form, an "outpouring" (Job 14:19; cf. the similar *šāpak*). The term translated *your wrath (ḥᵃmātᵉkā)* could be taken in at least three principal ways. It could mean "anger, fury," which occurs as many as eighty times in Scripture (cf. 2 K. 22:13; Deut. 9:19). Or it could mean "poison" (as in Deut. 32:24; Ps. 58:5 [Eng. 4]). But if the consonants are read as *ḥmt* instead of *ḥmh*, it could mean "skin," "skin bottle" (cf. Gen. 21:14–15, 19). Interpreters and translators have offered various alternatives and combinations in explaining this phrase.[5] The advantages of the rendering "joining" or "mixing in your wrath" are that it fills out the imagery of the rancorous brute of the text, and provides an easy transition to the expanded description of the conquest depicted in the next verse.

Part of the depravity inherent in sin is its insistence on involving others in its debauchery. The Babylonian king is not satisfied with making himself drunk; he can rest contentedly only when he has forced his degradation on others. He delights with a twisted glee to see others indulging in the same sins (cf. Rom. 1:32). He must forever add more subjects to his own darkened kingdom with the consequence of excluding people from God's kingdom. For no drunkard can have any part in the kingdom of God (cf. 1 Cor. 6:10). Instead of anointing with a spirit of holiness, he saturates people with the "spirits" by which they become drunk with wine (cf. Eph. 5:18). Instead of encouraging people to be subject to one another as the fruit of a spirit submitted to God, he fosters that determined arrogance which would have all others groveling at one's own feet.

It is almost a universal principle that the sin of drunkenness is associated with sexual impurity and the degradation of the body. Lot's daughters made him drunk so that they could commit their shameful act of incest (Gen. 19:32–35). Noah became drunk, which led to the exposure of his nakedness before his son (Gen. 9:21).

The case of Noah is particularly significant for the present context in Habakkuk. Noah's son Ham "saw . . . the nakedness of his father" *(wayyarʾ . . . ʾēt ʿerwat ʾābîw)*. This identical phrase elsewhere describes a sin in which a man "takes" his sister and "sees her nakedness" *(rāʾâ ʾet-ʿerwātāh*—Lev. 20:17). In the immediate context of Leviticus a man is forbidden to "uncover the nakedness" *(gillâ ʾet-ʿerwātāh)* of a menstruating woman (v. 18). While the

---

5. The suggestion of BDB, p. 706, that the text ought to be emended to read "from the goblet of your fury" *(missap ḥᵃmātᵉkā)*, supposing a copyist mistakenly wrote the *ḥ* twice, is not necessary in view of other viable options.

two phrases in these verses are not identical, the context suggests that in each case the phrase serves as a circumlocution for a sexual sin grosser than simply viewing a naked person. In the first case, a man "takes" his (half-) sister and "looks" on her nakedness, suggesting that he had sexual relations with her. This understanding would also provide some fuller rationale for the severity of Noah's curse as a consequence of Ham's "looking on his nakedness."

So the Babylonian makes his neighbor drunk with a view to looking on his nakedness (*l^ema^can habbîṭ ʿal-m^{eʿ}ôrêhem*). But his interests are not merely in humiliating his neighbor by leading him into an act of indecent exposure. His heart is more depraved than that. Very possibly the reference is to a homosexual act. In his perversity the Babylonian is worse than the cursed Ham, who at least was not guilty of initiating the drunkenness of his father.

16 No wonder the prophet exclaims: *You are satiated with shame rather than glory!* The Babylonian's actions bring his own shame. He is saturated with shame because of the perverseness of his sin.

In the description of the judgment that must come on Babylon, the retributive character of the punishment becomes very apparent. As Babylon has treated others, so God shall treat them. If they have made others drunk, they shall be made drunk. If they have brought shame and dishonor on others by depraved sexual activity, God shall shame them before all the nations.

You do some drinking, says the Lord. You have compelled others. Now the Lord shall compel you.

Instead of reading *Expose yourself as uncircumcised (hēʿārēl)* as in the MT, 1QpHab 9:9 reads, "You stagger!" *(hērāʿēl)*. But then curiously in its own commentary on this phrase, the document speaks of the wicked priest who "did not circumcise the foreskin of his heart" (1QpHab 11:13).[6] This interpretative reference to circumcision supports the MT rather than the scroll's own reading. The LXX (in some mss.) appears to support the text of Habakkuk in 1QpHab rather than its commentary: "Shake, O Heart!" *(kardía saleúthēti)*. These readings may represent ancient efforts to tone down what may have been regarded as a crude admonition. But if the phrase intends to represent a reciprocal punishment for the sin of "looking on the nakedness" of others, God's demand that the Babylonian show himself to be uncircumcised seems quite appropriate.

This attaching of significance to the uncircumcised character of a heathen king presupposes the appropriateness of the universal reign of the God of Israel. Shame attaches to uncircumcision only because it represents a lack of submission to the God of all the earth.

6. Brownlee, *Midrash*, p. 190.

Special attention must be paid to the *cup of the right hand of Yahweh* from which the Babylonian must drink. In a distinctive phrase, Habakkuk depicts the cup of the Lord rotating around among the nations of the earth. Babylon has been God's instrument of distributing the judgmental wine of the Lord among the nations. Subsequently, Jeremiah spoke of the Babylonians as a "golden cup" in the hand of the Lord (Jer. 51:7).[7]

In one particularly vivid passage, Jeremiah says Jerusalem itself would drink the cup of the fury of God's hand. But all other nations also must share in its dregs (Jer. 25:15–29). If the city called by God's own name would experience this evil, should not all other nations deserving his judgment also undergo this punishment for sin?

The argument of Jeremiah is similar to the message brought out by the book of Habakkuk. The Babylonian may be the instrument of God's hand, the cup of the fury of the Lord poured out on Jerusalem. But their service in this fashion did not by any means indicate that they would escape the judgment of God.

When Christ under the new covenant speaks of the cup which the Father has given him, he echoes this awesome figure (Matt. 20:22; 26:42). The wrath of the Father against the shameful sin of mankind finds a consummate manifestation in the outpouring of God's judgment on his own son. As repulsive as "wrath" in God may appear to the sophistications of the modern mind, it is a scriptural reality that found awesome expression as the Son of God suffered in the sinner's place, drinking the cup of the fury of God.

This repeated use in Scripture of the image of a cup of fury in the hand of God may aid in the interpretation of the difficult phrase previously discussed in v. 15. *mixing in your wrath (mᵉsappēaḥ ḥᵃmāṯᵉḵā)* may refer to the personal fury the Babylonian has added to the wine of God's anger which his victims must drink.

The pouring of wrath into the cup finds consummate expression in the book of Revelation, where "Babylon" emerges as a symbol of the epitome of wickedness among the nations. Babylon has made all nations drink of the maddening wine of her adulteries (Rev. 14:8). But anyone who has shared in these perversions must drink of the wine of God's fury, which has been poured into the cup of his wrath (Rev. 17:4).

---

7. It is understandable that John Calvin insisted that this entire section be interpreted as a figure of speech. The "cup" from which the Babylonians have made the nations to drink represents the judgment inflicted by the chastening hand of God. Elsewhere in Scripture the judgment of God on the nations is described in terms of a cup which they must drink (Ps. 75:9 [Eng. 8]; Isa. 51:17, 22; Jer. 49:12; Ezek. 23:30–35).

From yet another perspective the tasting of the bitter cup may not necessarily await the final destruction of the wicked. Because a righteous substitute has drunk its dregs, it becomes a cup of blessing that is offered sincerely to participants in the intimacies of the new covenant, although the unworthy partaker may drink damnation to himself (1 Cor. 11:29).

So Babylon has made the nations drink of the cup of the fury of Yahweh. Babylon has been the instrument of God's righteous judgments in the earth. Even God's own people have drunk this bitter cup at the hands of the Babylonians. But now it is the *Babylonians'* turn. They have been simply the instrument of judgment for the Lord. Ultimately it is the right hand of the Lord himself that administers this cup.

The consequence of this divine judgment is that *putrid shame (shall be) all over your glory* (v. 16c). The term translated *putrid shame (qîqālôn)* occurs only here in the OT, and apparently is a compound word constructed by Habakkuk to intensify the concept of disgrace to be experienced by the Chaldeans.[8] It may be regarded as a proverbial device similar to the term that may be viewed as a compound word found in 2:6 (*'abṭîṭ*). The first syllable of this word (*qî*) may be an abbreviation of *qî'*, meaning "to spew, to vomit" (Lev. 18:28; 20:22; Jer. 25:27; the noun form designates "vomit," as in Isa. 19:14; 28:8; Jer. 48:26). The latter portion of the word (*qālôn*) reinforces the occurrence of this word in the first half of this same verse and means "shame, disgrace" (cf. Prov. 11:2; 12:16; etc.).

So the Chaldean lies drunk and naked in his own vomit. "Putrid shame" covers his glory. All those features of his kingdom which once were the source of pride and boasting now are covered with the repulsive vomiting of the drunkard.

The exchange of *shame* for *glory* (*qālôn* in place of *kābôd*) finds proverbial expression elsewhere in the wisdom literature of the OT (see Prov. 3:35). Shame particularly falls on the person guilty of sexual sins, as was the Babylonian (Prov. 6:33). Habakkuk once more may be appealing to established truisms of Israel's wisdom literature as a means of making memorable his byword about Babylon.

17 The devastating humiliation of Babylon must come because of the *violence done to Lebanon.* But why Lebanon? Why not for the violence done to Jerusalem? Very likely the oracle of the Lord specifies Lebanon because of its proverbial beauty, which contrasts so drastically with its appearance after the destruction wrought by the Babylonian invaders. In offer-

---

8. Cf. Keil, p. 88. In any case, the word seems to have the meaning "shame, disgrace." Cf. BDB, p. 887; KB, p. 838.

ing his final plea for the privilege of entering the land of promise, Moses had specified Lebanon as that "good land" which he longed to see (Deut. 3:25). So proverbial for their majesty were the cedars of Lebanon that Solomon gave them special place in his wise sayings (1 K. 4:33).

Notoriety was attained in the eyes of the Lord himself by the king of Assyria for his boast that he would come with the multitude of his chariots and cut down the tall cedars and the choice fir trees of Lebanon (2 K. 19:23). For these great giants were the trees planted by God himself (Ps. 104:16). The cedars of Lebanon were regarded as the most majestic of all God's plantings on the earth, just as the giant sequoias and redwoods of America might be today.

The *devastation to beasts (by which) you terrified them* also is cited as a cause for the utter destruction done to the Chaldeans. Righteousness in the wisdom traditions of Israel was associated directly with a person's attitude toward his beasts. A righteous person had genuine concern for the welfare of his animals in contrast with the wicked, whose mercies proved to be cruel (Prov. 12:10).

The gentle downturn of the last phrase of the book of Jonah has memorialized forever the compassions of the Lord for the entirety of his creation. Should not Jonah have compassion on Nineveh, a city with numerous people, "and also much cattle" (Jon. 4:11)? God takes note when his lowliest creatures are terrified by the brutalities of insensitive human beings. He hears the groanings of his entire creation, and will see that the whole created universe joins in the final redemption of mankind (Rom. 8:19–21).

But the brutal Babylonians in their lust for conquest have done violence to plants and animals, not to speak of the devastation of *the land, the city, and all its inhabitants.* For this reason, their violence shall return upon their own heads. The violence done to Lebanon shall *overwhelm* them. The term employed literally indicates that their own violence shall "cover" *(kāsâ)* them.

Is the prophet imagining one of those towering cedars crashing down on the heads of those who had presumed to chop them down? Shall the oppressors of the forest be smothered under the trunks of its great trees? Possibly Habakkuk intends to project this very image. In any case, this fourth proverbial byword of Habakkuk is memorable for its mode of expression. It echoes earlier proverbs in Israel. It makes use of wordplays and creates new compound words to enhance vividness of expression.

But most strikingly, this particular byword enforces the idea of reciprocity in judgment:

If the Babylonian makes others drink . . . he shall be made drunk

If the Babylonian indulges in sexual perversity . . . he shall be
  exposed
If the Babylonian advances his own glory . . . he shall be shamed
If the Babylonian lives by senseless violence . . . he shall die by
  righteous violence.

This concept of the execution of reciprocal justice does not appeal to
humanity. But it is God's way. By this way he proves himself to be impartial
and righteous as judge. By this way he finally establishes himself as just and
yet also the justifier of the ungodly who believe. For Jesus the Christ drank
the cup of God's fury to the dregs, and so became the Savior of all who would
renounce their own pride and violence, looking to him alone for salvation.

Habakkuk clearly has succeeded once more in establishing a byword
about Babylon that would stick, as clearly proved through its quotation by
Jeremiah in his denunciation of the heathen. Although Babylon is a "golden
cup" in the hand of the Lord, God will ultimately make Babylon also drink
(Jer. 51:7, 39, 57). It was not long before the righteous ways of the Lord were
made manifest to this mighty nation. As the king of Babylon drank with his
companions from the golden cups of his conquests, the handwriting of God
that sealed his fate appeared on the wall (Dan. 5:1–31).

e. Ha! the idolatrous powerless (2:18–20)

18 *How can a carved idol profit?*
     For his designer carved it (himself);
   and a poured image—
     a teacher of lies.
       For he who designs his (own) design trusts in it,
       making speechless nothings.
19 *Ha!*
     a He who says to the tree,
     b Awake!
     b Arise!
     a to the silent stone.

          a He
          b will teach?[1]

1. Rudolph, p. 222, argues that the phrase "He shall teach" should be
eliminated as secondary because it crowds the line. While it is true that the phrase
tends to stand out, its similarity in form and emphasis with the next phrase suggests
that its distinctive role is intentional ("*He* shall teach; behold *he* is covered over . . ."").
Keil, p. 91, suggests the phrase communicates "astonishment at such a delusion."

        a *Behold, he*
            b *is covered over*
                c *with gold and silver,*
            b *and no spirit at all*
                c *is in him.*
 20 *But Yahweh*
        is in his holy temple.
        Hush before him,
        all the earth.

This fifth and final proverbial byword against the Babylonians assumes a distinctive form. It begins with denunciation before reciting the customary *Ha!* that has introduced the previous four sayings.

Why this alteration of form? Is it to be supposed that this break of pattern indicates the nongenuineness of v. 18? Rudolph rejects this suggestion, and proposes that Habakkuk may have been intent on establishing that his condemnations of the king of Babylon up to this point were wholly justified in view of his religious deficiencies.[2] Nebuchadrezzar may have been a very religious person. In a future day he may even come to be known as God's "servant" (Jer. 25:9; 27:6; 43:10). Yet all heathen piety must be viewed as totally worthless, since it gives honor to a human fabrication, which can never substitute for moral failings.

This explanation of the alteration of form in the final byword against the Babylonian has some credibility. Yet Habakkuk offers no hint that he had a need to anticipate criticism of his condemnations. As a matter of fact, it appears rather unlikely that Israelites themselves would have complained against the condemnation of the destroyer of their own nation. More likely Habakkuk alters the order of the oracle simply as a literary device to provide variety and climax in his expression. He certainly has shown himself capable of employing any number of literary features to lend weight to his argumentation.

Furthermore, the idolatry of the Babylonian may have been viewed as the source of all the other atrocities previously mentioned. Because their religious orientation was wrong, their moral standards had to be perverted. As the creators of gods who could not speak, they had to make up their own standards for a way of life. In this light, it is quite understandable that the condemnation of idolatry would be reserved for last, and that this message would be emphasized by a departure from the previously established form of the proverbial byword.

    2. Rudolph, p. 229.

Habakkuk also makes use of poetic parallelism and alliteration to enforce his point. The final verse suitably concludes this entire section, while simultaneously serving as a meaningful transition to the final prayer of Habakkuk in ch. 3.

By now four solemn sayings have been hung as ill omens about the neck of the Babylonian. Each one has threatened severe judgment. The pillager shall be pillaged (vv. 6–8), the fortified dismantled (vv. 9–11), the civilized demoralized (vv. 12–14), and the shameless defamed (vv. 15–17).

Now in this last byword the Babylonian receives the message of absolute certainty concerning the outworking of God's righteous purposes. No gods, no powers in heaven or earth can stand against the reality of the one true living God.

18 The heathen rivals to the God who speaks to Habakkuk appear in the form of dumb idols. They are impressive, even awesome in their external appearance. But *How can a carved idol profit?* Their very origin as well as their constitution testify to their uselessness. The divine description of them mocks their very existence. They are hardly worthy of the attention given by the threefold pun which memorializes their impotence. The idol is:

a *carving of its carver (pᵉsālô yōṣᵉrô)*
a *design of its designer (massēkâ ûmôreh)*
a *speechless nothing (ᵃᵉlîlîm ᵓillᵉmîm).*

Each of these phrases displays the folly inherent in anyone's looking for aid that is greater than his own resources in anything which he himself has designed. The *carved idol (pesel)* refers to anything shaped or carved by an instrument, whether of wood or of stone. The *poured image (massēkâ)* describes the metal image shaped by melted materials such as silver or gold.[3] Israel was categorically forbidden to make such forms of any created or imagined thing (Exod. 20:4). At the renewal of the covenant, the assembled nation had to utter its own curse over any person who made an idol carving or a molten image, for such an object would be an abomination to the Lord (Deut. 27:15).

Not only did idol-making assure the curse of God. It also had the effect of deluding even the maker himself. Although the image could not speak, it communicated a falsehood by giving the appearance that it had the power of a supernatural being. It thereby encouraged its viewers to put some trust in its striking form, to plead to this image for help in time of need, or to attribute unexpected prosperity to special intervention by this man-made shape.

3. Cf. KB, p. 770; BDB, p. 651.

But the ridiculousness of the whole scheme! The person trusts in a speechless, immobile nonentity that he himself has created. How can he be so foolish as to expect that this carving, this poured design, shall intervene on his behalf? The idol seems to have a mystical power to hypnotize, an uncanny ability to make an obvious lie believable. It is designated appropriately *a teacher of lies*.

Modern people in their sophistications may regard themselves as free from the obvious folly of idolatry. What educated, self-respecting person would be deluded into expecting special powers to emanate from the form of an antiquated idol? Yet the new covenant Scriptures make it plain that covetousness *is* idolatry (Eph. 5:5). Whenever a person's desire looks to the creature rather than the Creator, he is guilty of the same kind of foolishness. An insatiable desire for things not rightly possessed assumes that things can satisfy rather than God himself. Whenever a person sets his priorities on the things made rather than on the Maker of things, he is guilty of idolatry.

speechless nothings. The pungence of Habakkuk's mockery has been captured somewhat in the translation that describes the idol as a "dumb dummy."[4] The first word of the phrase (*'ĕlîlîm*) looks and sounds very much like the Hebrew term for God (*'ĕlōhîm*) and is frequently used in Scripture in a way that places the *nothingness* (*'ĕlîlîm*) of the gods of the nations over against the reality of Israel's deity (cf. Lev. 19:4; 26:1; Isa. 2:8, 18, 20; 10:10; Ps. 31:7 [Eng. 6]; 96:5; 97:7). But Habakkuk alone positions this term for *nothingness* or "worthlessness" back to back with the similar word meaning "to be tongue-tied, to be dumb" (*'illᵉmîm*). What could be more profitless than *speechless nothings?* Yet that is the essence of the heathen idol.

The unprofitableness of the idol, due particularly to its inability to speak, may be contrasted with the speaking God of Israel. These gods cannot see, hear, eat, or smell (Deut. 4:28; Isa. 44:9–10). But the Lord God of Israel is distinctive as the God who has declared the end from the beginning (Isa. 41:21–29; 42:9; 43:8–13). Because he is the living God, he can both speak and do. For this reason, every word that he says continues to have profit through all the ages, in contrast with the profitlessness of the idols (cf. 2 Tim. 3:16). His people will hear the word of their God behind them saying, "This is the way, walk in it" (Isa. 30:21–22).

In addition to degrading the glory of God, the creating of imaginary gods has the inevitable effect of debasing human behavior in other areas, as

---

4. Brownlee, *Midrash*, p. 211.

Israel's experience with the golden calf had clearly shown (cf. Exod. 32:4, 8). It is therefore not surprising that the new covenant documents indicate that no idolater shall inherit the kingdom of God (1 Cor. 6:9–10; Eph. 5:5; Rev. 21:8; 22:15).

19 This proverbial byword continues by mocking those who would look to the idol for relief and help, calling on it in time of trouble. How foolish it is for someone to attempt to stir up a tree, to awaken a stone.

Perhaps a *tree* symbolized to its worshiper the source of life, since numerous blessings are derived from this largest specimen of plant life. The tree provides fruit and shade, lumber for building, and fuel for fire. Possibly the *stone* symbolized stability for a creature always undergoing change. However fortunes varied, the expression carved on the face of a stone remained ever the same. Yet in response to a cry for help from its devotees, the tree and the stone remain forever silent, mocking anyone looking for aid. The priests of Baal long ago had found that it was impossible to arouse their sleeping god (1 K. 18:26–28).

Is the *stone* god really to be expected to *teach?* Shall he instruct people in the way they should go so that prosperity will be assured? The *silent stone* stands in starkest contrast with the God of revelation found in the Scriptures. God made it plain to Moses that as the One who made man's mouth, he also could make even the dumb to speak (Exod. 4:12). Because the people could not endure hearing the voice of God himself, he provided instruments of revelation to *teach* his people the way they should go (cf. Exod. 24:12; Lev. 10:11; 1 Sam. 12:23; Ps. 27:11).

In contrast, the gods of the heathen are *covered over with gold and silver,* having not the slightest breath of life in them. The glitter of the idol cannot conceal its lifelessness.[5] Its spectacular outer coatings may exude a shimmering illusion of liveliness. But the very coverings themselves attest to their deadness. As the mode of expression chosen by Habakkuk emphasizes, there is no breath at all in the idol *(wᵉkol-rûaḥ 'ên bᵉqirbô).*

But more to be desired than gold with all its glamour are the precepts of the Lord (Isa. 19:10). His commandments are better than unlimited treasures of material wealth (Ps. 119:72, 127).

So the point is made plain. The gods of the Babylonians can offer no help.

20 *But Yahweh is in his holy temple.* Although a specifically adversative conjunction is lacking, this last verse contrasts the vitality of the one true God with the deadness and silence of the idols. The temple, from

5. Rudolph, p. 229.

the time of its dedication by Solomon, was established as the source from which divine instruction and help would go forth. Even if God should have to chasten a disobedient people, the consecrated temple would remain as the place where God would hear, forgive, and teach his people the good way (1 K. 8:36).

According to Isaiah's vision, the mountain of the Lord's house would be established on the top of the mountains, and from this place he would teach many peoples his ways. For out of Zion, from its temple, the law would go forth (Isa. 2:3–4). Significantly for the context of Hab. 2, Isaiah's vision depicts a day in which God would judge many nations from Zion, and would rebuke many peoples (*hôkîaḥ;* cf. Hab. 2:1). Like their gods, the nations of the earth would stand silenced before Yahweh.

The *temple* stood in the midst of Israel as the place of his presence and his lordship among his people. The term for *temple (hêkal)* seldom describes the palace of an earthly king in Scripture. But it appears in a succession of narratives as the place from which God would rule in Israel, including the tabernacle in Shiloh (1 Sam. 1:9; 3:3), Solomon's temple (1 K. 6:1–2; etc.), Ezekiel's temple (Ezek. 41:1, 4, 15); and the temple constructed after the restoration from exile (Zech. 8:9; Hag. 2:15, 18). From a new covenant perspective, the equivalent concept is applied to the body of Jesus Christ (John 2:19), the body of the individual Christian (1 Cor. 3:16–17), and the corporate community of the Christian church (Eph. 2:21).

The essence of the idea of the Lord's temple may be seen in the declaration in the book of Revelation concerning the absence of the temple in the new heavens and the new earth. The Lord God Almighty and the Lamb will be the temple of the new Jerusalem (Rev. 21:22). The presence of God and of Christ shall so permeate the final city that no need shall exist for a temple building.

Appropriately then, *all the earth* is told to *Hush before* the Lord (Hab. 2:20b). This same command appears in both Zephaniah and Zechariah in a context of expectant judgment (Zeph. 1:7; Zech. 2:17 [Eng. 13]). Both cases may offer further support to the significance of Habakkuk's prophecy.

Habakkuk had begun his dialogue in an effort to understand the mysterious ways of a holy God with sinful people. Now he stands in the presence of the Lord's holy temple, hushed in reverential awe. He may not have grasped fully all the implications of the divine answer to his query. Yet he stands assured of the abiding lordship of his God, of his justice in prosecuting all violators of his holy law, and of his infinite mercy in granting life to all who will trust in him and in the provisions he has promised for the sinner.

211

III. A PSALM OF SUBMISSION (3:1–19)

Now at last the struggles of Habakkuk come round for a final resolution. As often happens when finite human beings venture to dialogue with infinite God, the solution to Habakkuk's problem does not come in the manner in which he might have expected. Instead of God's announcing a controlled and modest chastening of the disobedient in Israel, Habakkuk had heard with alarm the word of utter devastation. Instead of stern rebuke for his personal audacity in complaint, Habakkuk had received a word of comfort, consolation, and reassurance.

So the prophet has been forced to readjust radically what he might expect from the Lord. It is not that the God of the covenant has proven himself capricious or inconsistent. But the prophet must alter his perspective on the ways of God with mankind.

Some commentators have insisted that Hab. 3 could not be an original part of this prophecy.[1] Nowhere else do the words of an Israelite prophet take the form of a poem composed for celebration in the context of the worshiping community. More particularly, the idea that the fig tree would not bloom and no cattle would be in the stall (v. 17) appears to point to calamities associated with drought rather than the chaos created by an invading army.

These various suggestions are sufficient to cause one to pause and consider carefully the questions being raised. But the reasons suggested hardly are sufficient to dislodge Hab. 3 from its present position in the book. The day has passed when it might be assumed that prophet stood categorically over against priest and had nothing to do with temple and sacrifice. The prophet in Israel did not function wholly apart from the cult of the temple. It may be that no other example of extant prophetic material compares to this psalm of Habakkuk, framed as it is with the formalities of liturgical direction. Yet with all their denunciations of the empty procedures of priests and sacrifices in Israel, the prophets also participated in the worship of the community.

With respect to the absence of a reference to this chapter in 1QpHab, it ought to be noted immediately that this chapter is found in the LXX, which may be regarded as a roughly contemporary document. It could be that the Qumran manuscript never was finished, particularly in the light of some significant evidence that the last three verses of ch. 2 were completed by a second hand.[2] Possibly the omission represents the result of a selection of

---

1. See the discussion in section V of the Introduction above.
2. Brownlee, *Midrash Pesher of Habakkuk*, p. 218.

materials by the community of Qumran on which to comment. In this case, the distinctive form of Hab. 3 could explain its omission.[3]

The objective testimony of the various Hebrew manuscripts cannot be ignored. Habakkuk 3 has always appeared along with the rest of the book.

But the substance of the material in ch. 3 itself provides the strongest evidence for its connection with the first two chapters. Chapter 2 closes with the proclamation that the Lord is in his holy temple, summoning all people to keep silence before him (2:20). This announcement naturally prepares for the celebration of Habakkuk's third chapter in the context of Israel's worship.[4] Habakkuk's "hearing" the "report" of Yahweh which begins in 3:1 echoes precisely the posture assumed by the prophet after his previous interchange, in which he situated himself to wait and see what the Lord would say to him (2:2).[5] The emphasis on the coming of the Lord for the salvation of his people and for the destruction of his enemies (3:3–15) connects naturally with the emphasis on these same two elements of the Lord's visitation as described in chs. 1–2. The final acceptance by the prophet of the program determined by the Lord (3:17–19) provides the necessary resolution of the contention between God and Habakkuk found in the earlier chapters. The prophet concludes by the use of the first person, in accord with the form of the earlier portion of the book. In sum, the substance of ch. 3 naturally rounds out the themes introduced in chs. 1 and 2.

The form of this poem is characterized by a variety of patterns of parallelism in expression. Noteworthy is the establishment of a regularity of cadence at the point of the climax of the prophet's reconciling himself to the divine revelation concerning the course of the future (vv. 17–19). No fewer than five stanzas in these three verses follow the *a-b-b-a* pattern formed by the inversion of the order of subject and verb.

The inclusion of a superscription and subscription together with a threefold use of the term *selah* (vv. 3, 9, 13) should be noted.[6] These notations indicate that the poem was designed for use in the worship of Israel.

Such an incorporation of a prophetic utterance into the regular worship celebrations of the corporate community of Israel underscores the fact

---

3. Ibid.

4. Weiser, *The Old Testament: Its Formation and Development,* tr. Dorothea M. Barton (New York: Association Press, 1961), p. 260.

5. Cf. Rudolph, p. 240, who says the connection of Hab. 3 with chs. 1 and 2 is unmistakable.

6. H.-J. Kraus, *Psalms 1–59,* tr. Hilton C. Oswald (Minneapolis: Augsburg, 1988), pp. 27–29, indicates that the liturgical significance of the term *selah* may be safely assumed, although the precise meaning remains uncertain.

that the prophet, although dialoguing with the Lord in the first person singular, was actually spokesman for the whole of the community. His role reflected the function of the prophet in Israel as covenantal mediator.

The presentation of this poem in a form appropriate for a continual corporate celebration in the worshiping community of Israel also provides an early indicator of the significance of this word to Habakkuk. As indicated earlier, the message that "the justified (by faith) shall live by his steadfast trust" (2:4) was a prophetic word as significant as the Ten Commandments. It was to be inscribed on "the tablets," and would have eschatological consequences. By presenting his message in a form readied for rehearsal in the worshiping community, Habakkuk has prepared a way for the generations following him to enter into this same life of faith despite awesome calamities.

The overarching theme of this chapter may be seen as a poetic elaboration of 2:4. Despite all the cataclysmic calamities and judgments that shall come from the hand of God himself, "the justified (by faith) shall live by his steadfast trust." This permeating theme of the book now finds explicit elaboration in terms of the necessity of God's intervention for faith to be victorious. *Faith triumphs in life by the intervening power of God* may serve as a theme of this chapter.

SUPERSCRIPTION (3:1)

1 *A prayer of Habakkuk the prophet. On shigionoth.*

It is impossible to determine with finality the source of this superscription, or the other notes related to the celebration of this psalm in the context of Israel's public worship. These directions could have been introduced by Habakkuk himself, or by some other dignitary responsible for ordering the worship of the congregation. In any case, the notations suggest that this chapter circulated independently of the other two chapters, even though it apparently belonged to the original form of the book itself.

The term *a prayer* is found in the heading of five psalms (Pss. 17, 86, 90, 102, and 142). The centrality of the temple in the prayers of God's people is underscored in the dedicatory prayer of Solomon. He urges the Lord that he hear and answer when Israel's enemies have defeated them and they turn to pray "in this house" (1 K. 8:33). Habakkuk is anticipating just such a situation. Having recognized that the Lord is *in his holy temple* (Hab. 2:20), he now offers his prayer to that temple with the expectation that the Lord will hear and answer.

This prayer indicates that the prophet now has no further case to make. He has pleaded his cause, he has concluded his dialogue with the Almighty. Now he leads God's people to an acceptance of the just and merciful orderings which the Lord has revealed to him. He reflects the wisdom that has arisen out of confrontation with the will of God.

Specifically, this prayer is said to be offered by Habakkuk *the prophet.* The prophet in Israel served as covenantal mediator. As such, he had the responsibility of offering intercession on behalf of the people (cf. Gen. 20:7; Exod. 32:11–14; Isa. 63:15; Jer. 14:7–9). In the critical situation which Habakkuk faced, only the intervening and preserving grace of the Lord could sustain prophet and people.

The precise meaning of *shigionoth* is difficult to determine. Some of the early Greek translators (Aquila and Symmachus) apparently understood it to refer to errors committed in ignorance *(epì agnoēmatón).* But in the title of Ps. 7 the term appears as a musical directive. Possibly it could refer to a kind of performance that would reflect the excitement that should accompany the celebration of a psalm with such a disturbing topic.[1]

A. THE PROPHET PRAYS FOR THE SUSTAINING OF LIFE FOR THE BELIEVER (3:2)

2 *a Yahweh,*
  b I have heard
     c your report;
  b I have feared,
a Yahweh,
  c your work.

     a In (the) midst
       b of (the) years
         c make him live;[1]
     a in (the) midst
       b of (the) years
         c make (him) understand;
     a in (the time of) trembling
         c remember mercy.

Now the prophet begins his song, a song to be rehearsed in the congregation

---

1. Keil, p. 93; cf. BDB, p. 993.
1. Keil, p. 94, identifies the pronoun of "make it/him live" with the "work" of Hab. 1:5. But it seems highly unnatural to imagine Habakkuk praying that this awesome "work" of judgment shall "live."

of Israel throughout the dark years which Israel must soon begin to experience. The song comes as a response to the revelation given the prophet concerning the coming days.

In adopting this form for his word of acceptance concerning the future prospect, the prophet echoes a tradition as old as Moses. As the Lord anticipated the unfaithfulness of Israel after they had entered the land, he instructed Moses to write a song and place it in the mouths of the Israelites as a vehicle for instructing future generations (Deut. 31:19). It would be a song that could not be forgotten by the children to come (Deut. 31:21). So now as Habakkuk looks down the corridors of time, he too composes a song. He has heard the *report* about the Lord,[2] and fear has come into his heart.

Several instances in the law book of Deuteronomy indicate the naturalness with which "hearing and fearing" may be regarded as the expected reaction (Deut. 13:12; 17:13; 19:20; 21:21). Is Habakkuk to be blamed for trembling at the revelation he had received? Clearly not. If fear is a natural reaction on the occasion of personal tragedy, how much more is it understandable that the prophet should react with a sense of awe and fear when he is informed that the favored nation of the Lord shall be utterly devastated? Even though he is assured that the righteous by faith shall live, he cannot but be awestruck at the judgment to come. As a matter of fact, the prophet's response of fear at hearing of the Lord's activity indicates that he accepts as true the message that he has received. In this case, fear is a significant indicator of the faith of the prophet.

Most translators and interpreters take the reference to *your work* in direct grammatical connection with the second half of the verse.[3] But the poetic parallelism of the section as well as the pronoun attached to the verb in the second section of the verse ("make *him* live") suggest that *your work* should be taken in conjunction with the first half of the verse. The prophet has *heard* the *report* about the Lord, and has *feared* his *work*. Under this construction, it is quite natural to see the reference to the *work (pō'al)* of the Lord as referring to the announcement given earlier to Habakkuk: "I am working

2. The "report" could refer to the words communicated from the Lord to Habakkuk. But the prevailing usage of the term refers to a report *about* someone (cf. Gen. 29:13; Exod. 23:1; Num. 14:15; Deut. 2:25; Isa. 66:19).
3. Sample renderings of the versions read as follows: AV and NASB: "O Lord, revive thy work in the midst of the years"; NIV: "Renew them [i.e., the works, plural] in our day." None of these versions actually translates the pronoun attached to the verb ("make *him* live"), although they do translate the pronoun attached to the noun (*your* work). The LXX favors dividing the verse as I have, although it adds its own features in the process of translation.

a work *[pō ʿal pō ʿēl]* in your days which you would not believe if told" (Hab. 1:5). Now the prophet has come to understand just how awesome is that *work* which the Lord shall perform, and he fears.

In the second half of the verse, the prophet formally enters his petition, a petition that must have been repeated many times over by the community of Israel as they celebrated this psalm of Habakkuk. No doubt the fervency of this rehearsal must have intensified as the day drew nearer when the Babylonians would overrun the land of Palestine and even Jerusalem itself.

The prophet sets his petition *in (the) midst of (the) years.* Twice he repeats this peculiar phrase, which occurs only here in the OT; then he parallels it with a second expression *(in [the time of] trembling remember mercy).*

Scholars have offered various explanations of this phrase *in (the) midst of (the) years.* It does not likely refer to the boundary line between the OT and NT aeons. Calvin's suggestion that it alludes to the midpoint of history between Abraham and Christ is more plausible, since this understanding would have greater meaning to Habakkuk as an old covenant prophet.

The quaint rendering of the LXX, "between the two beasts," has provided the inspiration for numerous nativity scenes.[4] This picture was filled out by Origen, who concluded on the basis of Isa. 1:3 that the two animals must have been an ox and an ass.[5]

Most likely the *midst of (the) years* refers to the time between the two acts of judgment revealed to Habakkuk in the process of his earlier dialogue. In the time between the purging judgment that must fall on the house of God itself and the consuming judgment that must avenge God's elect—in that crucial period before the destruction of God's enemies—may the Lord be sure to preserve life.

Habakkuk's prayer that the Lord would *make him live* may represent a deliberate reflection on the vision for the eschaton which he had received earlier. The proud will not stand; but the just—he shall *live!* (Hab. 2:4). In other words, Habakkuk provides a prime example of one who is pleading the promises. Having received the word of reassurance that the justified (by faith) shall *live* by his steadfast trust, the prophet now makes this promise the focal

---

4. While this translation appears altogether unrelated to the customary English rendering, the Hebrew for this reading actually would not be very different from the MT. Rudolph, p. 233, has suggested that the translation "(between) the two beasts" presupposes the reading *šᵉnê(m) ḥayyîm* instead of the Massoretic *šānîm ḥayyêhû.*

5. Rudolph, p. 242. Other explanations based on the LXX reading *(en mésī dýo zṓōn)* include Christ between the two thieves, Christ between death and resurrection, and Christ between the two aeons.

point of his petition. By this form he encourages Israel continually to plead for life through all the dark years of judgment to come.

On a broader scale, the pattern of Habakkuk's prayer provides the framework for understanding the present era. According to Peter, judgment must begin with the house of God (1 Pet. 4:17). This present era represents the time in which God continues to purify his own by many chastening judgments. In these circumstances, the believer must plead the promise that the Lord shall preserve the life of his own despite temporal calamities. Between the time of God's chastening of his own and his bringing final judgment on his enemies, the cry must go up for the Lord to uphold his word and to sustain life for the believing. *make him live,* the prophet pleads. While the pronoun *him* attached to the verb could be taken to refer more abstractly to Israel as the one that God would preserve in life, the connection with the earlier monumental saying of Hab. 2:4 suggests that it is the just by faith whom the Lord shall preserve in life. Make him, the one who believes, to live.

The prophet also prays, *make (him) understand.* Standing in parallel construction with *make him live,* this verb has the same object, although it must be implied by the context. By this petition, the prophet asks that the Lord will make known to the believing the program and plan that he has designed. Even as Habakkuk had agonized in coming to an understanding of the mysterious ways of God and finally had rested his case in the light of the revelation provided him, so he intercedes on the behalf of others that the Lord will make plain to them the understanding necessary for survival in the midst of calamity.

Finally, the prophet pleads, *in (the time of) trembling remember mercy.* The term translated *trembling (rōgez)* does not mean essentially "wrath" as it is rendered customarily ("In wrath remember mercy"—AV, NASB, NIV). Instead, the word indicates a condition of agitation, excitement, or disturbance. The term is prominent throughout this poem, occurring no less than four times (vv. 2, 7, 16). In this verse, it is set in parallelism with the phrase *in (the) midst of (the) years,* characterizing the time in which this prayer of Habakkuk is to function. It is a time of disturbance and agitation, a time when foundations shall be shaken. God's own people shall go into exile. Trembling shall characterize even the most stable of human institutions.

In such a circumstance, the prophet prays that the Lord will remember to be merciful. For nothing but the undeserved mercy of God will prove sufficient to sustain people under such stress.

So the petitions of the prophet are threefold: that the Lord will preserve life, that the Lord will provide understanding, and that the Lord will remember mercy. Only the initiative of divine grace will prove sufficient under the calamitous circumstances which the believing shall face.

B. THE PROPHET ENVISIONS GOD THE SAVIOR COMING IN ALL HIS GLORY (3:3–15)

Having offered his petition, the prophet now turns his eyes toward the past and the future, where he sees the Lord coming in all his glory. He envisions salvation coming amidst the cataclysmic phenomena associated with theophany.

But why is it that salvation should be his theme? Judgment from God on Judah (1:5–11) and on Babylon (2:6–20) had been the message inspiring the original awe in the mind of the prophet.

It is true that judgment had been central to Habakkuk's dialogue with the Almighty. But the whole point had been salvation for God's own in the context of judgment. The righteous would live, he would survive the crumbling of empires and peoples about him.

Does Habakkuk talk about the past or the future as he describes God's coming in all his glory? Without doubt he drew from a number of the past manifestations of God's glory in the history of Israel. But is he rehearsing the past to remind of the way God had previously acted or is he predicting what shall occur in the future by employing language descriptive of the past?

Various exegetes have made strenuous efforts to resolve this question. Keil notes the imperfect form of the initial verb of the section ("Eloah *comes* [or will come] from Teman," v. 3), but concludes that the futuristic perspective of this verb "does not describe what is future, as being absolutely so, but is something progressively unfolding itself from the present onwards, which we should express by the future tense."[1] Rudolph attempts to distinguish between past and future references on the basis of the prophet's experience of the vision itself, which already had occurred, in contrast with the reality of the event which yet lay in the future.[2] But these kinds of fine distinctions press the text beyond the point of reasonableness. The same kind of assessment also must apply to the effort to identify precisely at every point the specific historical deliverance to which the prophet refers.

A collage, a collecting of many images to convey an impression both of past experience and of future expectation is the medium of the prophet. Moses' song, Deborah's song, David's song blend to provide a framework for anticipating the future. By such a method, Habakkuk does not dehistoricize the reality of God's coming for salvation. Instead, he colors the reality of the expectation of God's future manifestation by recalling the many con-

1. Keil, pp. 97–98.
2. Rudolph, p. 241.

crete instances of his intervening in the history of the past. He does not place the coming of God in the realm of timelessness, but forces his readers to appreciate the magnificence and the imminence of his appearing again.

Has the prophet departed from the realm of prayer by turning to this description of the coming of God in all his glory? No, for the reality of God's coming in past and future provides the basis for faith that assures life as he prays and waits. Rather than leaving his petition barely uttered, the prophet provides a framework of faith which will sustain him as well as all those suppliants that would join him through the ages. The Lord has come, and the Lord is coming. Therefore all who wait patiently for him shall live.

The central portion of the prayer may be divided into two sections: (1) The glory of the Lord in his coming (vv. 3–7); (2) Dialogue with the Lord at his coming (vv. 8–15). This division follows the natural distinction in the text, in which the prophet first refers to God in the third person, and then addresses the Lord in the second person.

1. The glory of the Lord in his coming (3:3–7)

3 a *Eloah*
    b *from Teman*
      c *comes,*
  a *and the Holy One*
    b *from Mount Paran.*
              Selah[1]

  a *His splendor*
    b *covers*
      c *(the) heavens*
  a *and his praise*
    b *fills*
      c *the earth.*[2]
4 a *And his brilliance*
    b *is as the light;*
  a *horns*
    b *(proceed) from his hand.*
    There

1. The *selah* occurring three times in this poem of Habakkuk appears only here outside the Psalms. The precise function of the term is still unclear. But it does indicate that Habakkuk's poem was incorporated into the worship of Israel.

2. The parallelism corresponds to the Hebrew, but the word order has been changed to conform to English mode of expression.

        (is) the hiding of his strength.[3]
5 *a* *Before him*
    b *goes*
       c *a plague;*
       c *and a burning pestilence*
    b *goes forth*
  a *at his feet.*
6 *a* *He stands*
    b *and measures*[4]
       c *(the) earth.*

  a *He looks*
    b *and startles*
       c *(the) nations.*

  a *They are shattered—*
    b *the everlasting mountains;*
  a *they bow down—*
    b *the eternal hills.*

    (But) his goings (are) eternal.
7 *a* *Under distress*[5]
    b *I see*
       c *the tents of Cushan;*
       c *the tent curtains of the land of Midian*
  a *are trembling.*[6]

In a most dramatic fashion, the prophet depicts the actual process of the coming of the Lord in all his glory, and the awesome effects this coming has on nature and nations. As the Lord in his glory draws nearer and nearer, the effects of his presence become more and more dramatic.

3a Remarkable is the point from which God begins his approach. It is not in heaven, but at very concrete locales on earth. He comes from *Teman* and *Paran* to display his glory.

    3. The verse reads literally, "And his brilliance as light shall be; horns from his hand (are) to him; and there (is the) hiding of his strength."
    4. Keil, p. 101, rejects the concept of God's "measuring" with his eye. He suggests instead that the verb *mādaḏ* or *mûḏ* is a variant form of *mûṭ,* indicating that God sets the earth in a reeling motion.
    5. The term translated "distress" (*'āwen*) most frequently means "iniquity." But in a passage like Prov. 12:21 ("no *trouble* shall happen to the righteous"), it clearly cannot mean "sin." In the context of Hab. 3:7, "distress" is the better option.
    6. The order of the last two lines has been reversed for the sake of better communication in English.

The poem begins by referring to God as *Eloah,* using an ancient poetic form of the name of God.[7] But when the prophet begins to dialogue with God rather than to observe him in his coming, he addresses him as *Yahweh* (v. 8), the God of the covenant. Upon reaching a final resolution of the struggles of his faith, the prophet speaks of *Yahweh Adonai* (v. 19), expressing his submission to the lordship of this great God who has proven his covenantal faithfulness.

The stunning revelation about this God is that he actually *comes* (*yābô'*). By this expression, Habakkuk reflects on the substance of the earlier vision granted to him in response to his complaint. He had been told that despite overwhelming calamities he must wait for the appointed time of the revelation, for *coming it would indeed come* (*bō' yābō'*, Hab. 2:3c). But this expectation of the "coming" of Yahweh refers back even further to the ancient words of Moses as he reflected on the glories of God's manifestation at Sinai. Moses began his prophecy concerning the tribes of Israel by noting:

> The Lord came from Sinai *(missînay bā')* ...
> He shone forth from Mount Paran. (Deut. 33:2)

The emphasis on the coming of God himself as the source of hope for the Lord's people appropriately finds its consummate expression in the new covenant Scriptures. Suffering believers are encouraged to hold fast their profession, since he who is coming will come, and will not delay (Heb. 10:37). Through all the ages only the coming of the Lord himself can provide genuine hope for his people.

According to Habakkuk, the Lord comes from *Teman* and *Mount Paran.* By these designations, the prophet traces back along the steps by which God led Israel into the possession of the land. The two locales designate roughly the boundaries of the journey of Israel in the desert. *Teman* is associated generally with Edom (cf. Obad. 9; Amos 1:12), although it may refer to the "south" in more general terms (Josh. 12:3; Isa. 43:6; Zech. 9:14). *Paran* designates the desert area about Sinai and Egypt (cf. Gen. 21:21; 1 K. 11:18; Deut. 33:2), although it may refer to Kadesh (Num. 13:26) or to territory near the southern border of Judah (1 Sam. 25:5). In any case, Habakkuk depicts God in movement from Sinai through Edom on the way to the possession of the land for his people. Habakkuk recalls Israel's past experience as a means of anticipating the intervention of the Lord in the future.

But now in Habakkuk's day Israel itself suddenly stands in the way

---

7. *Eloah* occurs 41 times in the book of Job and 16 times in the rest of the OT, including once in Hab. 1:11.

of God's movement to provide salvation for his people. Since Israel has acted persistently in unrighteousness, they must be removed from the way of God's realizing his redemptive purposes.

As Habakkuk says, the God of Israel is *the Holy One*. It is this *Holy One* who comes from Mt. Paran. Essential to his character is his refusal to be a respecter of persons in tolerating evil. In a great expression of faith, Habakkuk earlier had addressed the Lord as "my Holy One," the One who assured him that God's people would not die despite the appearances of injustice in the earth (Hab. 1:12). As the Holy One, he would maintain justice with perfect impartiality.

At Sinai, Israel had been told that they must be holy, for the Lord was holy (Lev. 11:44–45; 19:2). Because he had separated them from all the other peoples of the earth, they must be holy (Lev. 20:26). At a later time of covenant renewal, Joshua had told Israel that they could not serve the Lord, for he was a holy God who would turn and consume them if they forsook him (Josh. 24:18–20).

Now Habakkuk sees the righteousness and holiness of God in action. With impartiality he shall strike down first the ungodly in Israel, and then the heathen Babylonian. In such a manner he will be established as the Coming Holy One.

How awesome must have been the new covenant words of Peter when he declared to his generation of Israelites: "you denied the Holy and Righteous One" (Acts 3:14). By the rejection of Jesus Christ the "Coming One" (*ho erchómenos*—Matt. 11:3), Israel sealed its fate for the experience of a destruction more awesome than the devastations wrought by the Babylonians.

The remainder of this section (vv. 3b–7) develops the extensiveness (v. 3b), the intensiveness (v. 4), and the effects of the glory of God (vv. 5–7) as he comes to provide salvation for his people.

3b As the prophet envisions the coming of the Lord in glory, he first sees the magnitude of that glory from afar. The majesty of God blankets the heavens above, and his splendor permeates the earth.[8] The prophet does not refer to the glory of God which naturally is reflected in the creation (cf. Ps. 19:2 [Eng. 1]). Instead, he speaks of the particular glory radiating from the theophany of God as he comes to deliver his people. Particularly at those crucial points in history when God intervenes to save his own, his glory is

---

8. The passage says lit., "His praise fills the earth." In this case, it is not literally activities of praise that are filling the earth. Instead, the word *praise* is referring to the attributes of God worthy of the spontaneous praise of all his creation. Cf. Exod. 15:11, which speaks of God as "fearful" in (attributes worthy of) praises."

manifested. The spectators of that deliverance witness the permeation of the whole of the created universe by his glory.

These past manifestations on a limited scale may be regarded as anticipations of the great final epiphany of the glory of God, when the Son of Man shall come in the clouds, accompanied by lightning shining from the East to the West (Matt. 24:27). Then every eye shall see him, and the vision of Habakkuk shall receive its finalized fulfillment.

4 From a distance, the prophet saw the glory of God filling the whole of the earth. Now as the Almighty draws closer, he can see those points of concentration in which the essence of God's glory is located.

In view of the limitations of human language and experience, the indescribable glory of God can be depicted only in terms of relative value. Only in a limited sense may the infinite be comprehended by the finite.

The purest, the most brilliant element of the created universe is light itself. So the prophet declares that God in his coming is as the essence of light. Earlier David had used this same imagery to depict God's coming in brightness to destroy all his enemies (2 Sam. 22:13). As the sun's rays penetrate with their brilliance into all the earth, so God in his coming radiates a glory like the purest light.

"God is light," say the new covenant Scriptures (1 John 1:5), and so this same tradition continues to communicate the perfections of the divine glory. With an identical metaphor, the Scriptures of the new covenant exalt the glories of God, describing him as dwelling in unapproachable light (1 Tim. 6:16).

Yet this glorious God approaches man. As he approaches, the concentration of his glory is seen in the *Horns* or "rays" that *(proceed) from his hand*. The *horn* naturally symbolizes the concentration of power, whether literally in terms of the horn of the charging beast, or figuratively in terms of a ray of light emitted from its source.

Habakkuk's allusion to the past traditions of Israel is quite clear. He depicts the coming glory of God in terms of the past glory associated with the theophany of Sinai. As Moses descended from the mountain, his face "horned," which is the only other place in Scripture where this particular term is used to describe the shining of rays of light (cf. Exod. 34:29–30, 35). The connection of Habakkuk's imagery with the manifestation of God's glory at Sinai is further seen by a more detailed comparison with Deut. 33:2:

a Yahweh
  b from Sinai
    c came *(bā᾽),*
    c and dawned

<blockquote>
b from Seir
a unto them.
</blockquote>

<blockquote>
He shone forth
   from Mount Paran,
and he came (*'āṯâ*)
   with myriads of his holy ones.
From his right hand (went)
   a fiery law
      for them.
</blockquote>

The phrase translated "fiery law" which went from the hand of God is uncertain in meaning.[9] But the parallels with Habakkuk are clear in God's coming from Sinai and Seir, his "shining forth," his manifestation of holiness. In this context, the reference to something, whatever it may be, proceeding from the "(right) hand" (*yāmîn* in Deuteronomy; *yāḏ* in Habakkuk) of Yahweh adds one further point of comparison.[10]

In any case, the concentration of power and light in the *hand* of God at the time of his coming emphasizes his readiness to move into action for his people. He does not appear simply as a brilliant specter which ought to inspire awe among all who witness his appearance. He comes as an active person, powerfully and awesomely working to establish his supremacy among the nations.

By the use of a remarkable imagery, the poet has stretched the human imagination in depicting the effects of the power and glory of God. *There (is) the hiding of his power!* he exclaims. Rays of unapproachable glory stream from his hand; what then must be the nature of this power and glory hidden in his clenched fist!

The exclamation *There!* appears frequently in Hebrew poetry to designate a spot vividly captured by the imagination (cf. Ps. 14:5; 36:13 [Eng. 12]; 48:7 [Eng. 6]; 66:6; Hos. 6:7; Zeph. 1:14). There is his hand, the spot from which those glorious rays proceed—there the unlimited power of the Almighty resides.[11]

This power, this glory, must be *hidden,* because of the limitations of finite human beings. Just as one cannot stare directly into the brilliance of

---

9. The Hebrew phrase is obscure. BDB, p. 206, identifies the term *dāṯ* as a word used "only in (the) Persian period."

10. This light which beams from the hand of Yahweh could be lightning bolts. Or the reference could be to the rays of light which shine across the heavens at sunrise.

11. The Hebrew phrase could also be translated "where is the hiding of his power," as in the NIV. But the more dramatic rendering fits the context better.

the sun, observing only with caution the shining of its glory, so also the glory and power of God must be veiled. For he dwells in light unapproachable (1 Tim. 6:16).

5 Having depicted something of the glory of God in its essence as he comes to deliver his people, the prophet now describes the effects that accompany the manifestation of God's glory. Significant is the fact that this radiating source of light is on the move. As God comes as personified light, he brings with him the penetrating, destructive force of divine judgment. Even before the Lord arrives, the land is scarred by plague.

References to *plague* in the OT cluster especially around the events of the Exodus and the prophecy of Jeremiah. In the latter case, the prophet announces the destruction of Judah because of their persistence in sin (cf. Jer. 14:11–12; 21:6, 9; 24:10; 27:8, 13). In declaring this coming scourge of the land, the prophet only echoes the curses of the covenant as threatened earlier (cf. Lev. 26:25; Deut. 28:21–22). The vengeance of the covenant comes in the form of a plague that devours God's enemies together with all their possessions.

So Habakkuk, in choosing to express himself in terms of the ancient curses of the covenant, gives evidence that he has reconciled himself to the rightness of God's devastating his own people, as had been revealed to him by the initial response of God to his complaint (Hab. 1:5–11). This acceptance of the just appointments of God finds fuller expression in the final verses of the poem (3:17–19).

The advancing theophany leaves a trail of destruction behind it. If the plague precedes him, the *burning pestilence* marks the path he has followed. The term for *burning pestilence (rešep)* has the basic meaning of "burning"[12] and may suggest the imagery of sparks springing up as the Lord's feet strike the earth. In any case, the coming of the Lord is an awesome sight to behold. The closer he comes, the more fearful appear the consequences of his approach.

6 Now the Lord actually arrives. Manifestations of his approach had first been seen from a distance in terms of the radiance of his glory filling the earth. But now that the Almighty has arrived, it becomes evident that he is not simply a phenomenon to be observed.

Like a great colossus towering over the mountain peaks, the Lord God *measures the earth,* claiming the right of domain inherent in himself as Creator. With a glance of his eye, he manifests his sovereignty in apportioning territories (cf. Ps. 60:8 [Eng. 6]).

---

12. Rudolph, p. 234, notes this basic meaning, but opts for the translation "pestilence."

His glance *startles (the) nations.* As a grasshopper springs suddenly with his disproportioned legs, so entire nations leap with fright when they suddenly become aware that the Lord has come (cf. the use of the same term in Lev. 11:21). Judah, Babylon, and Babylon's successors shall forever remain subject to the Lord's will.

In underscoring the cosmic significance of the coming of the Lord, Habakkuk depicts the effect of his arrival on the most fundamental masses of creation. First to arise out of the watery abyss were the *everlasting mountains,* which still serve as the stabilizers of the world (cf. Gen. 1:9). Ever since the dawn of creation, they have stood resolute, binding together the earth even until today. They say to the ocean's depths, "you may go this far, but no farther" (Ps. 104:9). But at the Lord's appearance, these massive structures *are shattered* as though smashed by a gigantic sledgehammer; they prove to be as fragile as a clay pot. The *eternal hills* grovel in the dust, flattened before the Lord's majesty.

In contrast with the proven temporality of the foundational structures of the present creation is the everlasting stability of the Lord himself. The prophet deliberately sets one *eternal* back to back with another: the *eternal* (*ʿôlām*) hills bow down, but (even) the goings of the Lord are *eternal* (*ʿôlām*). The Lord's movements take on an unchanging character, due to the permanency of their effect.

Elsewhere the psalmist speaks of the "processions" (*hᵃlîkôt,* lit., "goings") of "my God, my King" in describing actions of the Lord as he proceeds to smash all his enemies (Ps. 68:25 [Eng. 24]). His pattern of activity has been consistent throughout the ages. Without partiality he appears at the right time to establish justice in all the earth. He sees, he measures, he comes to enforce his sovereign will.

The images employed by Habakkuk come to fullest realization in a new covenant perspective. Not only will the hills bow at his glory; the most essential elements of the universe will dissolve in fervent heat (2 Pet. 3:10). The Lord himself shall descend in the glorious splendor of the clouds, and every eye shall see him (Rev. 1:7). The impartiality of his judgments shall be manifested throughout eternity.

7 Now the prophet becomes much more specific in his description of the effects of God's arrival. First he had spoken of the sinking of mountains at his appearance, and the stunned response of nations in general (v. 6). Now he envisions the concrete effect on particular nationalities which Israel had confronted in the past.

Basically two possibilities exist with respect to the identification of *Cushan* and *Midian.* The reference might be to two nomadic tribes associated in a general way with the Sinai peninsula and God's self-manifestation in that environment. Or the allusion could be to two of the early oppressors of Israel after their settlement in the land of Canaan.

Cushan might be understood as an expanded form of the name "Cush," similar to the expansion of "Lot" to "Lotan" in Gen. 36:20. Consequently "Cushan" might refer to the land of Ethiopia. This interpretation is supported by the LXX rendering of Cushan as *Aithiopōn* (Ethiopia).

On the other hand, "Cush/Cushan" might refer to a bedouin tribe of the Sinai peninsula which would have been neighbor to the "Midian" mentioned in Exod. 3:1. In this respect, it may be noted that the Midianite wife of Moses (Exod. 2:21; 18:2) is apparently called a Cushite in Num. 12:1.[13]

The major problem with this second identification of Cush with Midian is that it violates the progression depicted in the coming of God *from* Sinai to Palestine. The whole point of the previous verses has been to trace the progress of the theophany as its glory moves from the peaks of Sinai. God now has finally arrived, and has begun his awesome deeds of meting out judgment on the nations.

Although the term *Cushan* does not appear by itself outside Hab. 3:7, it does appear in the compound phrase "Cushan-Rishathaim" in Judg. 3:8–11. In that context, Cushan arises as the first of the oppressors of Israel, sent by God to chasten them because of their sin. For this reason, a reference to Cushan-Rishathaim in the framework of Habakkuk's expectation is quite appropriate. The very problem which Habakkuk had to face was the prospect of a chastening invasion by a foreign power. So now as he anticipates this gloomy future, he may be encouraged nonetheless over the fact that ultimately the Lord came to provide relief from oppression for his people. It furthermore may be noted that this nation in Judges is identified as coming from the land of Aram-Naharaim, "Aram of the two rivers." This identification has some significance because in the very next verse Habakkuk poses the rhetorical question, "Did Yahweh rage against the *rivers?* Were you angry with the *rivers?*" The putting of the question in this precise fashion could intend to recall the ancient conflict of the Lord with "Cushan . . . of the two rivers."

The reference to the *tent curtains of the land of Midian* might intend to echo a distinctive aspect of the confrontation of the Lord with the invading Midianite oppressors in the days of the Judges. As may be remembered, Gideon overheard one Midianite telling another about his dream in which a loaf of barley bread tumbled into their camp and struck the tent so that it collapsed (Judg. 7:13). The *trembling* tent curtains of these oppressing invaders

13. This view is supported by Rudolph, p. 244; Keil, p. 102; Laetsch, p. 346.

underscores the transitoriness of the pain they may inflict on God's people, whatever it may be. They may be here today, but gone tomorrow.

This particular confrontation with Midian became the framework for prophetic utterances predating Habakkuk (cf. Isa. 9:3 [Eng. 4]; 10:26; 60:6). This fact adds further support to the idea that it was this particular Midian that most likely was the frame of reference for Habakkuk's prophecy.

The prophet's placing of the anticipated chastisements of Israel in terms of Israel's past experience with Cushan-Rishathaim and with Midian indicates that Habakkuk finally had accepted the fact that a chastening judgment of the severest type must come on Israel for their persistence in sin. But he never lost hope that the remnant would survive. For he had been given the sign that "the justified (by faith) would live by his steadfast trust." No matter how awesome might be the terrors inflicted by the Babylonian invaders, Habakkuk had been led to a point of hope that could not be shaken. The structures of all oppressive kingdoms would quake and come *under distress*. But he had citizenship in a kingdom that could not be shaken (cf. Heb. 10:29–30).

2. Dialogue with the Lord at His Coming (3:8–15)

8 *Is it against the rivers*
    that Yahweh rages?
Toward the rivers
    (is) your anger?
Toward the sea
    (is) your wrath?

      that you ride
        on your horses,
        your chariots of salvation?
9 *You fully unsheathe your bow;*
battle rods are sworn by oath.
        Selah.

With rivers
    you cleave the earth.
10 *The mountains*
    see you—
    they flee.
Tempest of waters
    overflows.
The abyss
    gives its voice;
    it lifts its hands high.

11 *Sun, moon*

> *stand in their lofty abode;*
> *at the light of your arrows*
they flee,
> *at the radiance of your gleaming spear.*

12 *a In indignation*
> *b   you march through the land;*
a in wrath
> *b   you thresh the nations.*

13 *You go forth*
> *for (the) salvation of your people,*
> *for salvation with your anointed.*

You crush
> *(the) chief of (the) household of (the) wicked (one),*
> *laying bare*[1] *(from) the foundation*
> > *up to the neck.*
> > > *Selah.*

14 *You pierce with his (own) rods*
the chief of his throngs.[2]

> > *They storm in*
> > > *to scatter me.*
> > *Their rejoicing (is)*
> > > *as one who devours the poor in secret.*

15 *You tread*
> *on the sea*
> > *with your horses*
> > *(amidst) the heap of many waters.*

8 The transition from God's coming to God's actually being present is made apparent by the prophet's addressing God initially in the third person and then in the very next phrase in the second person: "Is it against the rivers that *Yahweh* rages; towards the rivers is *your* anger?" He continues by addressing God as "you" until the end of this section (v. 15).

Why is it that the prophet envisions the manifestations of God's glory

---

1. *ʿārôṯ* is a rare form of the Piel infinitive absolute from *ʿārâ*. Cf. GKC, § 75n.

2. The horde-like character of the enemy in Habakkuk is represented by the term *pᵉrāzāw*. Although some of the ancient translations rendered the term as "warriors" or "dynasties" (Vulgate, LXX), the use of related terms points to the multitudes who lived in tents on the open plains, in distinction from the more restricted number who lived in walled cities (Deut. 3:5; Judg. 5:7, 11; 1 Sam. 6:18; cf. Ezek. 38:11).

by its effect on *rivers* and the *sea*? Is he intending to depict a recurrence of God's ancient struggle with the chaotic abyss?[3] The absence of reference to *rivers* in sections of Scripture which supposedly allude to this original conflict argues against understanding the prophet to be thinking in this direction. Instead, the concentration on the theme of salvation for God's people indicates that the intervention of God is not directed toward mythological battles with chaos but with the real enemies faced by his people.

The reference to *the rivers* and *the sea* constructs a collage of past deliverances to depict God's action in the future. A river often serves as a territorial border. Therefore to smite rivers suggests movement toward a fuller possession of God's promises. The Lord had smitten the Red Sea, the Jordan River, and the river Kishon. In each case, he had moved his people closer to the full possession of the promises concerning the land.

It may be the river Euphrates that is envisioned as the future object of the wrath of God. As the Babylonian comes to heap judgment on God's people, he may expect an awesome retaliation from the same One who has smitten rivers and sea in the past.

The conglomerate of words employed to depict the *wrath* of God enforces the solemnity of this hour. Over 170 times the *anger ('ap)* of God is mentioned in the OT. His *wrath ('ebrâ)* heaps vengeance on his enemies. Yahweh *rages (ḥārâ)* at times because of simple sins such as complaint or jealousy (Num. 11:1, 10; 12:9).

The consummate manifestation of the wrath of God shall occur at the end of time, when God's angelic messengers shall pour out the bowls of the wrath of God on the "sea" and the "rivers" once more (see Rev. 16:3–4). The springs of water shall be turned to blood (16:4), and the river Euphrates shall be dried up (16:12). In the context of Revelation, the anticipated judgments of God are described in images reminiscent of God's wrath as it was manifested against Egypt and Babylon. He shall show his wrath against *sea* (Egypt) and *rivers* (possibly including Babylon) by turning the waters to blood (Egypt), and by drying up the Euphrates (Babylon). In any case, the book of Revelation has depicted the same judgmental interventions founds in the prophetic anticipations of Habakkuk. God's redemptive acts of the past provide the basis for an expectation concerning the future.

Noteworthy is the fact that Habakkuk has now blended images of judgment and salvation in his anticipation of the future. Even though it is Israel itself that will be a major object of the forthcoming judgment of God, the prophet has regained his balance and come to understand that even in this

---

3. Cf. Rudolph, p. 244.

terrible event the Lord shall be advancing his purposes of redemption. God rides on his horses, his chariots, for *salvation.*

that you ride on your horses, your chariots of salvation. This dramatic imagery of God's riding as a mighty warrior on horses and chariots to conquer his enemies appeared regularly in Israel's traditions. Its roots have been traced by some to the imagery of Baal riding in the clouds in Ugaritic materials.[4] Although some connection with the extrabiblical imagery is possible, the permeation of this concept throughout the various literary pieces of the OT suggests that by the time of Habakkuk the concepts behind the imagery had their own distinctive function in the framework of Israel's theology.

Particularly in the period of Israel's monarchy, God's appearance on horses and chariots became a characteristic imagery. After long years of frustrating confrontations with the kings of Israel, the divinely sent chariot and horses of fire swept Elijah the prophet up to heaven (2 K. 6:14, 17). Part of David's preparation for the dwelling of God in Israel's midst included a collection of gold "for the model of the chariot, even the cherubim, that spread out their wings" (1 Chr. 28:18, NASB). God's agents of intervention stood ready with vehicles capable of the fastest and most effective means of transport.

4. Various efforts have been made to relate this material to a mythological background. J. L. Crenshaw, "Treading on the Heights of the Earth," *CBQ* 34 (1972) 50, 52, asserts that the Ugaritic background is pronounced in at least one point, but feels that the mythological language is simply metaphorical. W. A. Irwin, "The Psalm of Habakkuk," *JNES* 1 (1942) 30, concludes that the present text of Hab. 3 is characterized by "unmitigated imbecility, and all translations that follow it arrive just there." In "The Mythological Background of Habakkuk 3," *JNES* 15 (1956) 48–49, he argues against the view that Canaanite myth serves as the primary background for this chapter, and posits instead that it is the Babylonian myth of Enuma Elish that explains the chapter. In response to W. F. Albright's critique that his "drastic emendations and forced interpretations yield a text which does not conform to any known Hebrew dialect or literary form, and that his innovations can safely be dismissed" (*JBL* 61 [1942] 121), Irwin expressed frustration that he could get no "bill of particulars," and notes that "the most I could get from him was that this was nothing to what he might have said" (p. 47). A sample of Irwin's suggested changes in the text may be seen in his proposal that the phrase "feasting on the poor" of 3:14 must be reversed so that it indicates that the poor (Jew) is to feast on Tiamat, the slain mythological monster (Irwin, "The Psalm of Habakkuk," p. 32).

An impressive defense of the MT may be found in J. H. Eaton, "Origin and Meaning of Habakkuk 3," *ZAW* 76 (1964) 144–71. So far as the mythological background of the poem is concerned, such allusions may be acknowledged as based on a possible but unestablished hypothesis. Nothing in the language of the chapter requires that a source be found outside the historical traditions of Israel, and it appears much more natural to identify the frame of reference in terms of the great saving acts of the Exodus, as noted by R. K. Harrison, *Introduction,* p. 936.

In the Psalms and the Prophets God is also depicted as having at his disposal horses and chariots to enforce his sovereign will (Ps. 18:11 [Eng. 10]; 68:18 [Eng. 17]; Isa. 66:15; Jer. 4:13; Ezek. 1:15ff.; Zech. 6:2–3, 6). This imagery echoes the ancient blessing of Moses (Deut. 33:26), and was extended naturally to describe the armaments of the messianic king, who was expected to "ride prosperously" in majesty on behalf of truth, meekness, and righteousness (Ps. 45:5 [Eng. 4]).

As Habakkuk faces devastations by an alien army, he depicts the greater wrath and the greater power found in Yahweh's own horses and chariots of salvation. No nation shall be able to stand against him when he comes to accomplish salvation for his people.

It was indeed a step of great faith that enabled Habakkuk to affirm an expectation of *salvation* in view of the revelation he had received. The greatest calamities imaginable must come on the Lord's own people in the form of the Babylonian invasion. Yet now faith had taught him that God's purposes of salvation would be advanced by these very circumstances.

In a similar fashion, Jesus Christ warned of the increasing tribulation that would afflict his own people as the end of the age approached. But even in those circumstances they must be encouraged to expect his appearance in the clouds, like lightning, with the accompaniment of the militant hosts of heaven (Matt. 24:30).

9a This innocent-looking verse has been subjected to an unending number of interpretative contortions. Over a hundred different explanations have been offered.

You fully unsheathe your bow. The emphatic conjoining of a noun and a related verb to describe God's laying bare his bow dramatizes this action by which the divine Warrior readies himself for attack against his enemies. The positioning of the noun (ʿeryâ) before the verb (tēʿôr) strengthens the thought. Sometimes the Lord unveils his power in a modest fashion (cf. 2 Sam. 22:36; Ps. 113:6–7; Isa. 57:15). But now his ire has been aroused, and he acts with the full force of his destructive powers. As David saw the angel of the Lord with sword drawn, so Habakkuk envisions the Almighty as ready to heap vengeance on his enemies.

In the lament of Jeremiah over Jerusalem's destruction, the prophet personalizes the attack of the Lord against his own people. God has bent his bow and set his own people as the mark of his arrow (Lam. 2:4). But now it is the enemies of the Lord who are the objects of his attack. His arsenal of weapons shall be focused on them (cf. Ps. 7:13–14 [Eng. 12–13]).

The difficulty of the next phrase is that each of the three Hebrew words (šᵉbuʿôt maṭṭôt ʾōmer) could have more than one meaning, and the precise grammatical relation of each to the other is not clear.[5] Most plausible is the interpretation offered by Delitzsch, "massively argued" and supported by others.[6]

Battle rods (or spears, staves) *are sworn by oath* captures the flavor of the context and suits the basic meaning of the words. God had enlisted weapons and pledged them on oath for the destruction of his enemies. The recurrence of the plural form of *rods (maṭṭāyw)* just five verses later in a context which demands that a weapon of conflict be envisioned supports this understanding.

In the oath of the covenant as recorded in Deut. 32:40–43, the Lord swore by lifting up his hand to heaven that his sword and arrows would consume his enemies, avenging the blood of his servants and rendering vengeance on his adversaries, while having mercy on his land and his people. Habakkuk now discerns that the hour in which that oath shall be fulfilled has come.

9b–10 Now it becomes plain that this warrior for righteousness is no ordinary personage. His weapons of offense include the primeval elements of the creation. It is hardly likely that any earthly enemy will be able to withstand his assaults.

with rivers you cleave the earth suggests a sudden and awesome rainfall. But it is not an ordinary thunderstorm that is being depicted. For the cosmic waters of the deep emit their gurgling roar. A *tempest of waters overflows* so that even *the mountains . . . flee.*

The reference to the *abyss (tᵉhôm)* reflects on the depths of waters that originally covered the entirety of the earth (Gen. 1:2). So it is no wonder that the mountains seek to escape the coming deluge. Not only at creation, but at the flood the abyss *(tᵉhôm)* of waters rose up to cover the earth (Gen. 7:11). In his assault on his enemies, the Lord shall employ the most basic elements of his created order. The mention that the abyss *lifts its hands high* draws on the imagery of waves that stretch their foaming whitecaps heavenward, reaching ever upward to enclose more of the world within their domain.

The collage of images of the past which now are employed by the prophet to anticipate God's future act of judgment also includes the triumph

---

5. *šᵉḇuʿôṯ* could be "oaths," "those sworn," or with a modification of pointing *(sᵉḇēʿôṯ),* "spears." *maṭṭôṯ* could be either "tribes" (that are sworn), "rods," "lances" (that are sworn), or more specifically "rods (of chastisement)" (that are sworn). *ʾōmer* could be "a word," "a decree," or "a speech."

6. J. H. Eaton, "Origin and Meaning of Habakkuk 3," *ZAW* 76 (1964) 151. See also Laetsch, p. 348.

of God over Pharaoh at the Red Sea. For there the deeps *(tᵉhōmōṯ)* covered them (Exod. 15:5). The flowing waters stood up like a heap, and the deeps *(tᵉhōmōṯ)* were congealed in the heart of the sea (v. 8).

Although calamity and judgment certainly are central to the theme of Habakkuk's poem, he also places these judgments in the framework of God's ongoing program of redeeming a people for himself. Yes, even Israel may be devastated by the impartiality of God's righteous judgments. But the fact that the Babylonians in their turn shall also undergo devastation indicates that God has a purpose for continuing his work in the world. And if it is true that "the justified shall *live* by his steadfast trust," then reason for continued hope throughout out all these calamities has a solid foundation on which to build.

11 A further manifestation of nature's response to divine judgment is seen in the dramatic *Sun, moon stand in their lofty abode.* Despite the objections of some, it appears most likely that this phrase intends to reflect the "long day" of Joshua, in which the sun and moon stood still *(ʿāmaḏ)* allowing Joshua to complete his work of judgment on the Lord's enemies.[7] This allusion adds further imagery in terms of God's bringing all of nature in subservience to his purposes of redemption.

In this awesome array of spectacular phenomena in nature, the prophet will not let the reader forget that it is the personal Lord himself who is behind all these events. It is *you* that the mountains see, inspiring their cringing retreat (v. 10). *Your* arrows and *your* gleaming spear cause the mighty rulers of day and night first to freeze and then to flee in terror (v. 11).

This descriptive language finds its closest parallel in Ps. 77:17–21 (Eng. 16–20), as has been noted by several commentators. According to the psalmist, the waters, the deeps, saw and trembled. The clouds poured out waters, and the Lord's arrows flashed here and there.[8] Worthy of note in the light of this parallelism is the psalm's ending by reflecting on the fact that the way of the Lord was in the sea, and God's leading his people like a flock by the hand of Moses and Aaron (v. 21 [Eng. 20]). This conclusion underscores the fact that these descriptions of cataclysmic events relate primarily to God's work of redemption. Through these activities, the Lord carries forward his plan to deliver his people.

---

7. The term *zᵉḇulâ* refers to an "exalted dwelling place" for the sun and moon. Keil, p. 108, rejects the idea that the phrase could refer to Joshua's long day, since he concludes that this term cannot refer to standing still in the sky. But the preceding phrase specifically describes "sun" and "moon" as "standing still."

8. The "arrows" apparently refer to lightning. Cf. 2 Sam. 22:15; Ps. 77:19 (Eng. 18); Zech. 9:14.

12 Now the answer finally begins to emerge in response to the earlier question. Is God's anger against the rivers and the sea (v. 8)? Does an irrational anger against his own creation explain the disturbance among mountains and deep, sun and moon? No, it is in response to the wickedness of the nations that the Lord unleashes his *indignation.* As a judgment for evil he comes in all his awesome glory to *march through the land.*

The vivid imagery of God's marching through the land implies that the Lord has what may be called *presence.* Three, yea, four things are stately in their march: the lion, the greyhound, the goat—and the king against whom there is no rebelling (Prov. 30:29–31). Obviously this proverbial encapsulating of reality applies to the march of the King of Kings.

The nations have attempted to overthrow the yoke of the Lord's reign. But all their efforts are in vain. For when the Lord acts, it immediately becomes apparent that the earth hardly can bear his presence, trembling under the weight of his footsteps. Note other instances of the earth's shaking at the march of Yahweh in Judg. 5:4; Ps. 68:9 (Eng. 8).

in wrath you thresh the nations. The Lord's threshing *(dûš)* of the nations moves even closer to the specific point of his theophanic manifestation. This imagery of God's threshing a nations' populace for its iniquity finds historic expression in the case of Gideon's treatment of the princes of Zebah and Zalmunna for their failure to aid his men as they pursued the Midianites. In fidelity to his word, Gideon returns and threshes *(dûš)* their flesh with thorns of the wilderness (Judg. 8:16). Noteworthy as a prophetic parallel to this declaration of Habakkuk are the words of Micah a century earlier:

> Rise and thresh, O Daughter of Zion,
>   for I will give you horns of iron;
>   I will give you hoofs of bronze
> and you will break to pieces many nations. (Micah 4:13)

13a The alternation of tenses in this context does not contrast past activities of God with interventions that may be expected in the future. Instead, the prophet uses this grammatical device to suggest that the ways of God's working in the past may be understood as anticipating the ways in which he shall work in the future. It is for this reason that the verbs, whether in the Hebrew perfect or imperfect form, have been translated by the English present tense.

This verse reminds the reader again that the overall setting of this poem is in terms of God's coming to his people, manifesting his glory in creation as he comes, and always with the ultimate intent of bringing salvation. *for salvation . . . for salvation* the verse repeats. God does not destroy the wicked

236

simply for the sake of destroying the wicked. He destroys them for the sake of his people. God has a special people, and he saves them from their enemies.

The sudden introduction of a reference to *your anointed* in this seventh-century prophet must be recognized for its distinctiveness. Contrary to what many assume, the OT uses the term *messiah* to refer to a future deliverer in only a very few instances.[9] Indeed, the term appears in only one other text from the prophetic writings.[10]

It is not surprising therefore to discover that the *anointed* in Hab. 3:13 has been interpreted as a plural, referring to Israel corporately as the people of God.[11] This interpretation is supported by the parallelism of the verse. God goes forth for the salvation of his people, for the salvation of his anointed (ones). However, several factors argue against this modification of *your anointed.* The Hebrew text is singular rather than plural, and interpretation must begin in that light. Nowhere else in the OT are the people of God called the *anointed* of the Lord. In addition, some notice must be given to the introduction of the Hebrew word *'et* ("with") in this second line of the parallelism. Although the term could be taken as the sign of the direct object, this interpretation does not explain why it is introduced in the second line and does not appear in the first.

A better interpretation is that the term means "with," and is presenting God's "anointed" as having a different relation to salvation from that of the *people.* God's salvation is *for* his people, but it is accomplished *with* his anointed.

But who is this *anointed* that is to serve as the agent by which the Lord accomplishes his salvation? Possibly the prophet could be anticipating the appearance of an ideal "David" of the future. Since the contemporary descendants of David hardly measured up to the requirements of a deliverer from God, the prophet would have been forced to set his hopes on a future, more perfect anointed one.[12]

Yet another interpretation should be acknowledged as a possibility. The only other passage in the prophets using the term *messiah* refers to Cyrus as God's servant when he devastates the Babylonians (Isa. 45:1). God will "subdue nations before him," overcoming kings.

---

9. The clearest instance is Ps. 2:2. 1 Samuel 2:10 is another possibility. Isaiah 61:1 uses the verbal form of "to anoint" in referring to the servant of the Lord. Other OT uses of the term *messiah* referring to a future individual are scarce.

10. Isaiah 45:1 denotes Cyrus as "messiah."

11. Some LXX mss. read "to save your Christ." But others have the plural, "your christs."

12. Rudolph, p. 245.

Of course, the identification of Habakkuk's "anointed one" with Cyrus would raise insurmountable problems in the mind of anyone already committed to a view which required that Isaiah's reference to Cyrus must come after the king of Persia had appeared on the scene of history.[13] But given the absence of a single use of the noun *messiah* in the prophetic books in reference to the ideal David,[14] and working with the external testimony of the textual evidence of the corpus of Scripture as it presently stands, it would appear quite possible that Habakkuk would be echoing this earlier prophetic reference to an "anointed one." Furthermore, the circumstances of this reference in Habakkuk conform rather closely to the role that Cyrus fulfilled in redemptive history. Habakkuk has been led to recognize that after God had judged his own people by the hand of the Babylonians, he would then raise up another power that would execute just judgment on Babylon for their excesses of cruelty. Habakkuk finally arrives at a satisfactory resolution of his troubled state of mind in the hymn of ch. 3 after receiving the assurance that the justified by faith would continue to live throughout these calamitous times in which God would be working out his righteous ways.

Because of the vital role that the monarch Cyrus would play in rounding out these events, it would not be surprising if Habakkuk should call attention to his role in the working of God. The possibility of such a reference would presuppose the prior existence of the Cyrus prophecy of Isaiah. But if the presuppositional difficulties commonly associated with such a fore-naming may be set aside, this interpretation suits the context of Hab. 3 very well.

At the same time, the identification of the messiah of Hab. 3:13 with Cyrus does not inherently exclude a reference to the realization of this "salvation" in terms of the coming of the final messianic king-deliverer of God's people. Isaiah already had intertwined with his presentation of Cyrus the servant-deliverer (Isa. 44:24–45:7) a development of the Suffering Servant motif (Isa. 42:1–4; 49:1–6). These two deliverers and their deliverances are intentionally layered so that the one must be understood in relation to the other. As one anointed servant restores the people in a limited politico-geographical sense, so the other anointed servant restores the people in the fullest redemptive setting.

13. It should also be noted that perceiving Isaiah's mention of Cyrus as originating after he appears on the scene of history contradicts the central theme of these chapters of Isaiah, which centers on the idea of challenge to prophecy.

14. Claus Westermann asserts that in the OT the term *messiah* is never used except of a reigning monarch (*Isaiah 40–66*, OTL, tr. D. M. G. Stalker [Philadelphia: Westminster, 1969], p. 159). But he has minimized the usage in a passage like Ps. 2.

13b Now it becomes evident that the prophet is not speaking purely on a hypothetical basis. Even though his language is saturated with recollections of past deliverances, he looks to a specific action of the future. God shall *crush the chief* (lit., "head") *of the household* (lit., "house") *of the wicked (one) (rāšāʿ)*.

laying bare (from) the foundation up to the neck. This portion of the verse has been subjected to a variety of interpretations. What is this *foundation* that is laid bare? What is the meaning of laying bare a foundation *up to* (or down to) the *neck?* Puzzlement over this image forces a reexamination of the reference to the *chief* of the *household.*

The language of crushing "the head of a house(hold)" might be interpreted by attaching it to the figure of the laying bare of a foundation. In this construction, the *head* of the house most naturally would refer to its roof, in contrast to the house's foundation.[15]

However, scriptural usage of the phrase "the head of the house" points in another direction. The phrase occurs rather frequently in reference to the head of a family (Exod. 6:14; Num. 7:2; 17; 18; Josh. 22:14; 1 Chr. 5:24; 7:7, 9). Further support for this interpretation is found in the very next verse in Hab. 3, which uses the same term *(rōʾš)* to refer to the *chief* or leader of the wicked.

So the prophet envisions a *household* of *the wicked* which has a *chief* established for the purpose of leading this household in its opposition to the people of God and the Lord's redemptive purposes. This *chief* is the prime object of the Lord's offensive. God crushes this principal leader of the throngs of the wicked (v. 14) in the same way in which the star of Jacob was to smite the corners of Moab (Num. 24:17), and Jael smote Sisera (Judg. 5:26), and Messiah would smite through the head of many (Ps. 110:5–6).

Of the approximately 250 times in which the adjective *wicked (rāšāʿ)* occurs in the OT, it seems always to modify persons rather than things. It is not the leader of the "land of wicked*ness*" (NIV) that the Lord smites but the leader of the *household of the wicked one* or "wicked people."[16]

Standing in contrast to the *anointed one* who goes forth to accomplish salvation for his people (v. 13a) is this *chief* of the wicked who oppresses God's people (v. 13b). As in so many cases in Scripture, the singular anointed

---

15. See Rudolph, p. 246; Keil, p. 110.

16. The singular may refer either to a single individual or to a body of people which may be characterized as "wicked," as in Hab. 1:13; cf. Gen. 18:23. The NIV is apparently reading *rešaʿ* as "wickedness," in distinction from the MT *rāšāʿ*.

hero wins the victory over the single chief of the wicked, and so accomplishes victory for all God's people.

This victory is described in terms of a *laying bare (from) the foundation up to the neck. The foundation* appears to refer to the legs upholding the body, and the neck to the portion of the body upholding the head. The *laying bare* or exposing of the foundation suggests the undercutting of all supportive strength. The extension of this assault to the neck indicates the thoroughness of the destruction.[17]

14 The irony of the whole process of the destruction of this enemy is amplified by the intimation of self-destruction. *with his (own) rods* the enemy destroys itself. In his distinctive way of working, the Lord sees to it that the enemies of his people suffer from the severest of humiliations—they destroy themselves with their own weapons.

Often God's people find themselves severely disturbed because they see no visible power as strong as their enemies. But the prophecy of Habakkuk encourages the faithful to assume a strange perspective. They must look at the strength of the enemy as the very source of their own protection. The stronger the enemy, the more sure its own self-destruction. For as God sovereignly raises up powers and brings them down again, he turns the strength of the enemy against itself. Haman hangs on his own gallows (Esth. 7:10). Daniel's adversaries perish in the very den of lions into which they had cast him (Dan. 6:25 [Eng. 24]). He who digs a pit to entrap the righteous falls into the same ditch that he has made (Ps. 7:6 [Eng. 5]). Abimelech and Shechem, conspiring rebels in the days of the Judges, are cursed with the curse of self-destruction (Judg. 9:19–20). Facing a mighty coalition of enemy nations, Judah under Jehoshaphat must stand still and see the salvation of the Lord (2 Chr. 20:17). When God's people look across the wilderness, they see a vast array of the corpses of their enemies, for the Lord had set them against one another (2 Chr. 20:24). Characteristic of the last great conflict will be a warfare in which each of the Lord's enemies shall eat the flesh of his own arm (Isa. 9:19 [Eng. 20]; cf. Ezek. 38:21; Zech. 14:13). Rather than being terrified at the strength of their enemies, God's people ought to rest confidently in the assurance that the strength of the enemies' power only displays their capacity to destroy themselves.

Set as a poetic counterpoint to the Lord's destruction of his enemies

---

17. Keil, p. 110, treats the reference to "foundation," "neck," and "head" as expanding on the imagery of a "house." From this perspective the "head" refers to the gable of a roof. While this approach to the verses is possible, it lacks the support of the use of this imagery elsewhere in Scripture.

is the description of the ferocity of the alien's attack. They *storm in to scatter me;* they gloat *as one who devours the poor in secret* (v. 14b).

But who is the *me* who suffers the brunt of this tempestuous assault? Is the prophet envisioning himself as the distinctive object of the enemy's wrath? To this point, the prophet himself has played a prominent role throughout this poem. He is the one who personally has heard the report of the Lord (v. 2). He himself saw the vision of the trembling tents of Cush (v. 7). He offers his personal response to this theophanic vision in a first person form (vv. 16–19). Only twice does he speak of God's "people" in a corporate sense in this chapter (vv. 13, 16).

In this light, it seems rather appropriate to regard the *me* of v. 14 as referring expressly to the prophet himself. He is not caught up in the ecstatic moment of this glorious vision of the coming of the Lord so that he removes himself from the awful interlude in which the enemy assaults the people of God. No! He senses that he too must bear the brunt of the enemy's ferocity. Perhaps as the messenger of righteousness and judgment, he sees himself as the special object of their wrath, in accord with the experience of every generation of prophets. As the point man in the confrontation of truth and error, he knows that he cannot be exempt from their fury. Like the swirling sirocco of the desert, the enemy tears at the prophet, wrenching him from his moorings, scattering his possessions, threatening his slender hold on life itself.

The fiendishness of the enemy is seen in their gloating, their glee over the destruction of the righteous. What sort of savage soul would take delight in victimizing the helpless? As a wild animal lurks and then drags and devours its prey in secret, so this ruthless oppressor assaults his victims.

15 But the newborn faith of the prophet encourages him to remember the great salvation provided by the Lord from the hands of the oppressor in ages past. Disdaining the strength of the enemy, the Lord treads on the sea with his horses, raising like a dust cloud the heap of many waters. In a clear allusion to the deliverance of the Israelites at the Red Sea, the prophet reminds himself and his contemporaries of the saving strength inherent in the Lord's coming. As one humble preacher has noted, the only way to pass through a bog is to seek out the "solid places."[18] God's great deliverance at the Red Sea clearly provides one of those points of solidarity to which the tried faith of God's people may return over and over.

So the prophet has depicted God the Savior coming in all his glory (vv. 3–15). The faith that gives life must look to the glorious appearing of the

---

18. D. Martyn Lloyd-Jones, *From Fear to Faith* (London: Inter-Varsity, 1953), p. 27.

great God and our Savior. He shall come, and he shall devastate all his enemies. But in the interim, judgment must begin with the house of God.

C. THE PROPHET RESOLVES HIS STRUGGLE BY TRIUMPHANT TRUST (3:16–19b)

Having heard the Lord's response to his complaint (2:2–20), and having seen a vision of the Lord drawing closer and closer in his approach to intervene by the destruction of the wicked and the salvation of the righteous (3:3–15), the prophet now records his reaction to this awesome interchange (3:16–19b). His reaction includes three elements: (1) a response of stunned awe (v. 16); (2) a recognition of coming loss (v. 17); and (3) a resolution of joysome entrustment (vv. 18–19b).

1. A Response of Stunned Awe (3:16)

> 16   *a* *I heard*
>   *b* *and my belly*
>   *c* *trembled.*
>   *a* *At the Voice*
>   *b* *my lips*
>   *c* *buzzed.*
> *Rottenness has come into my bones,*
> *and beneath me I tremble,*
>   *because I must wait quietly*
>   *for the day of adversity,*
>   *for the coming up of the people*
>   *who will invade us.*

The dialogue scheme that has run throughout the book prevails to the very end. The prophet's note that he has *heard (šāmaʿtî)* the response of the Lord to his complaint echoes the opening acknowledgment of the chapter that he had "heard the report" *(šāmaʿtî šimʿaḵā)*.

But this time the prophet is speechless. He finds himself totally unable to respond. By a patient rebuttal that never swerved from his point, the Lord has shut up his servant to a position of passive acknowledgment of the rightness of his ways. Habakkuk earlier had set himself to "answer his rebuke" (Hab. 2:1). But now his speech is paralyzed.

The expression of the prophet concerning the effect of the Lord's speech on him ought not to be taken merely as a dramatizing literary device. He describes instead an actual physical experience which he underwent as the full weight of the significance of his vision dawned on him. His solar plexus convulses. His feeble effort to maintain a dialogue with the Almighty results in an uncontrollable buzzing of the lips. His bones give the sensation of suddenly rotting away. His legs quake beneath him.[1]

Rather than despising the prophet for an excessive emotionalism, the reader should honor him for his sensitivity to the import of the message he has received. The more godly the person, the greater his fear of the Lord.

Four times in this single chapter reference is made to a response of *trembling* to the manifestation of God's truth and glory (vv. 2, 7, 16). Even as at the Exodus the nations of the earth "heard" and "trembled" at the report of God's mighty works (Exod. 15:14), so now the news of judgment inspires a similar trembling. The day of God's judgment on the Transjordan nations inspired trembling among the peoples of the earth (Deut. 2:25). But now, sadly, God's own people must tremble at the judgment coming on themselves.

Particularly *the Voice* that is the occasion of the prophet's trauma should be noted. His response to the speaking of God reminds of Israel's poem about the Voice:

> The voice of the Lord is upon the waters. . . .
>
> The voice of the Lord is powerful, . . .
>
> The voice of the Lord breaks the cedars. . . .
>
> The voice of the Lord hews out flames of fire.
> The voice of the Lord shakes the wilderness. . . .
>
> The voice of the Lord makes the deer to calve.
> (Ps. 29:3–5, 7–9, NASB)

Using the imagery of a ferocious thunderstorm as it sweeps across Palestine, the psalmist has captured something of the majesty of the revelation that comes from the Lord.

But precisely what is it in his vision that has brought the prophet to this point of extreme convulsiveness? Has not the Lord predicted the judgment of Israel's enemies and the vindication of the righteous?

The last portion of v. 16 directly explains the reason for the prophet's stunned awe. It is *because (ʾašer)* of the terrible devastation that God's own people must undergo prior to their full possession of the promises that the prophet trembles from head to toe.

---

1. The trembling "beneath" the prophet could refer to tremors of the earth. But in this context of the description of the somatic effects of the Lord's message, the reference more likely is to the trembling of the legs "beneath" him.

Some problem in interpretation appears because of the rather unusual usage of the verb *wait* or *rest (nûaḥ)* in this context. Is the prophet actually saying that he is upset because he must *wait quietly?* Because of this apparent tension, some commentators have suggested a textual emendation, reading "I moan" rather than "I rest" (*'eʾānaḥ* instead of the Massoretic *'ānûaḥ).*[2] However, this problem may be more imagined than real. The prophet is upset because nothing will stop the inevitable tragedy of Israel's being invaded by the chastening forces of the Babylonians. He must *wait quietly* for the day of adversity, for the assault of the invading armies.

Habakkuk's distraught body shudders to consider that he must live with the constant anticipation of God's coming judgment. Although deliverance is certain, it will come only after judgment.[3]

At a later date, when the remnant of faithful Israel was reduced to a single individual, a similar circumstance developed. Alone in the garden, peering now into the awesome abyss of hell, the Lord Jesus himself sweated great drops of blood (Luke 22:44). Even though he was assured that the Lord would not leave his soul in hell (Ps. 16:10; cf. Ps. 42:6, 12 [Eng. 5, 11]; 43:5), yet the reality of the agonies that he had to endure before his deliverance overwhelmed him. His soul was exceedingly troubled *(perílypós estin hē psyché mou,* Matt. 26:38), and his body responded with awesome signs of sympathy.

2. A Recognition of Coming Loss (3:17)

17 *Even though*

> *a   the fig tree*
> *b   shall not blossom;*
> *b   and no fruit (shall be)*
> *a   on the vines;*

> *a   shall fail*
> *b   the making of the olive;*
> *b   and the fields*
> *a   shall not make food;*

---

2. W. H. Ward, p. 28: "For the inappropriate [Massoretic] *'nwḥ* it might be hazardous to conjecture *'eʾānaḥ,* meaning *I moan in view of the day of trouble,* but nothing better occurs." Cf. also BDB, p. 628. G. A. Smith, *The Book of the Twelve Prophets,* Expositor's Bible (Garden City, NY: Doubleday, Doran, & Co., 1929), 2:156, leaves the phrase untranslated.

3. *leʿam yeĝûdennû,* "for the people (who) will invade us," anticipates the assault of the Babylonian army against Judah.

> a   *shall be cut off from the fold*[1]
> b   *the flock;*
> b   *and no cattle*
> a   *(shall be) in the stalls.*[2]

The word that introduces this verse *(kî)* could be regarded as setting up only a hypothetical possibility: "*If* the fig tree should not blossom. . . ." But the context demands more. The passage describes a series of facts that shall transpire. These dreadful things shall happen.[3]

But they shall not occur as a consequence of drought or a plague of locusts. Instead, the ravages of war shall leave the land desolate. The senseless rapacity of the invading army shall consume all that is worthwhile on the face of the earth. The consequent disruption of the basic structures of the family and other social orders shall eventuate in an unproductive land.

The prophet's rehearsal of items that shall be denied the inhabitants of the land is arranged in the form of three poetic stanzas of four lines each (see the translation above). The *a-b-b-a* interchange of subject and verb is perhaps the most typical of Hebrew poetic parallelism.

Within this formal structure, a double triad of objects may be noted, moving from the optional to the essential items for human survival. The *fig tree,* the *fruit,* and the *olive* represent the choicest products of the land as seen in passages such as Joel 1:7; Hos. 2:12; Mic. 4:4; 6:15; Deut. 6:11; 8:8. The grain of *the fields* and the *flock* and *cattle* encompass the necessities of bread, milk, and meat. The absence of these items means no fig cakes, no wine, no anointing oil for the sunbaked lady. No cereal, no vegetables, no milk, no mutton, no wool—none of these needs or pleasures shall be available to the prophet and his people.

In sharpest contrast with the spirit of complaint and unbelief manifested by Israel in the desert, Habakkuk openly recognizes the coming loss of all these luxuries as well as life's necessities, but believes nonetheless. The promised mercies of God to his people extend well beyond all material losses. The entire present world order may pass away, but God's grace to his people shall endure.

Perhaps part of the explanation for the prophet's willingness to accept this severe chastening at the hand of the Lord is to be found in the ex-

---

1. *miklâ,* "fold," is apparently a variant of *miklā'.* Cf. BDB, p. 476.
2. The term for "stalls" *(rᵉpāṭîm)* occurs only here in the OT, and its meaning is uncertain. But it is probably related to postbiblical Hebrew *repet,* "cattle shed, stall."

plicit warnings of the ancient Mosaic legislation. If Israel would not hearken to the commandments of the Lord, but instead would despise all his chastenings, then he would punish them seven times more for their sin, and the land would not yield its increase (Lev. 26:18, 20; cf. Deut. 11:17). But the prophet's faith encompasses broader options than suffering for sin. For he himself, along with the remnant who perseveres in faith, also shall endure all these deprivations. His entrustment of all things into the hands of the Lord anticipates a later faithful one who declared, "I suffer the loss of all things" (Phil. 3:8).

3. A Resolution of Joysome Entrustment (3:18–19b)

18   Yet I—
      a   in Yahweh
        b   I shall exult;
        b   I shall rejoice
      a   in the God of my salvation.
19 Yahweh my God (is) my strength.
      a   For he will set my feet
        b   like hinds' (feet);
        b   and on my high places
      a   he will make me walk.

Finally a resolution of the conflict that began the book appears. The prophet now understands through divine revelation the justice of the ways of God with men, and the inevitable judgment that must come even upon the faithful remnant of Judah. Even the prophet himself shall suffer the deprivation of all things necessary for the sustaining of life.

Yet he shall live! He shall rejoice! He shall mount to the highest peaks of the earth!

Is it resurrection faith that comes to expression in these final words of the prophet? Is he speaking of an expectation of life after the last enemy has done his worst? Certainly his faith is not far from that point. Despite all the anticipated tragedies, he actually can rejoice in his confidence that the vigor of life shall be his. For "the justified (by faith) shall *live* by his steadfast trust" (see the exposition of 2:4 above).

Notice that it is in the person of Yahweh himself that the prophet rejoices. He now has learned that he may be deprived of all material benefits, comforts, and blessings—yet he can rejoice because of his faith in Yahweh.

18 He calls the Lord the *God of my salvation*. By such a designation, the prophet expresses his confidence that the Lord ultimately shall accomplish deliverance for him. From an OT perspective, this *salvation* cannot be perceived as a purely spiritual reality in contrast with his loss of all material possessions. Instead, *salvation* must include all the material blessings that life can offer, along with the wholeness of a soul united to God.

The transition from the complaining prophet to the rejoicing prophet surely must be seen as a work of God's sovereign grace. Nothing else could explain how a person could be happy and contented in face of the calamities Habakkuk had to undergo. May the Lord himself continue to provide the grace of life to people of this generation by the faith that justifies.

19a, b The only way by which the prophet could make such an assertion is in view of the fact that he can affirm: Yahweh is "*my* God, *my* strength." How otherwise could he anticipate ultimate triumph and live in the mere hope of victory beyond devastation?

Like a female sheep, he shall mount with swift surefootedness to the heights of the mountains. The prophet echoes the words of David's psalm of triumph when the Lord delivered him from all his enemies: "He makes my feet like a doe's feet, and on my high places he makes me stand" (Ps. 18:34 [Eng. 33]). Surefooted, untiring, bounding with energy, the Lord's people may expect to ascend the heights of victory despite their many severe setbacks. The heights of the earth, the places of conquest and domain, shall be the ultimate possession of God's people. As spokesman for God's people in this song to be celebrated through the ages, the prophet displays the magnificence of a victorious faith. Even the most horrifying setbacks cannot break the confidence in ultimate victory.

So before our very eyes the message of Hab. 2:4 finds fulfillment. Habakkuk lives—by faith. He keeps on trusting God, despite the utter chaos and absolute calamity of the Exile. As a consequence, he lives.

Throughout the ages all who set their trust on the Prophet par excellence shall live. They may fall asleep in death—but they shall not "die" in the ultimate sense. The sting of death has been removed by the power of the Resurrected One. Joyfully we live by faith in him.

SUBSCRIPTION (3:19c)

To the chief musician on my stringed instruments.

It is impossible to determine whether this final notation originated with Habakkuk himself or represents an addition by a later editor. In either case, the tradition appears very ancient that this psalm of submission was to be celebrated in the congregation throughout the generations. It was not merely a personal resolution of faith achieved by the prophet for himself alone. Intentionally placed in the first person, it effectively draws each participant into the experience of yielding to God in a way that corresponds to his own personal trials. A very common dimension of tragedy is that it tends to set a person alone with a grief he himself must learn to bear.

To the chief musician is the most common rendering of *lamnaṣṣēaḥ,* the obscure first term. The word occurs fifty-five times in the Psalms as a superscription, but only here as a notation at the end of a poetic composition. The root of the word *(nṣḥ)* can mean "be preeminent" or "be enduring."

The LXX normally translates "unto the end" *(eis tó télos).* But it is not clear whether the intent of the Greek translators was to provide some instruction to the choir director ("perform this psalm 'unto the end,' " whatever that might mean), or to offer a comment on the character or content of the psalm ("a psalm about the end!" i.e., one of an eschatological nature). In this particular case, the LXX reads, "that I may conquer in his song" *(tou nikēsai en tḗ ōdḗ autoú).* But the use of the second term also as a musical notation of sorts ("on my stringed instruments") argues against this rendering.

The final reference to *my stringed instruments,* or "my songs," *(binᵉgînôṯāy)* is paralleled in a distinctive passage reflecting the same kind of triumph in song. In Isa. 38:18–20 King Hezekiah celebrates the extension of his life beyond the earlier sentence of death. "All the days of our living we will play my songs on stringed instruments *[nᵉgînôṯay]* in the house of the Lord," says the rejoicing king (Isa. 38:20). For "the living, the living— he is the one who praises you" (v. 19).

In similar fashion, Habakkuk's message is all about life—the life of faith despite many calamities. Integral to such a life is the singing of songs praising the redeemer and sustainer of life.

So a book beginning with complaint and distress ends in joy. Faith triumphs in life despite many calamities. Songs in the night anticipate the glad arrival of the eternal dawn in which the faithful shall receive their ultimate vindication.

The Book of
ZEPHANIAH

SUPERSCRIPTION (1:1)

1 *The word of Yahweh which came to Zephaniah*
   the son of Cushi,
      the son of Gedaliah,
         the son of Amariah,
            the son of Hezekiah,
   in the days of Josiah son of Amon king of Judah.

The text presents itself as the word of the covenant God of Israel, and not
merely the word of Zephaniah the prophet. By this opening phrase, the
prophet sets himself in the stream of those servants of God, from Moses to
Jesus Christ, who were prophetic mediators of the covenant. Inspired of God
so that their words were identical with God's words, these instruments of
divine revelation mediated a confrontation with God too terrible for the
people to endure on their own (cf. Deut. 18:15–17).

As the role of Israel's prophets is explained in Deuteronomy, their
words were to substitute for God's own awesome presence. To mishandle a
prophetic utterance is to abuse the very presence of God himself.

As this phrase *the word of Yahweh* now stands, it encompasses the
whole of the book under consideration in its present literary form. Conceiv-
ably the phrase may have introduced originally a smaller unit of Zephaniah's
words. But no extant manuscript evidence provides objective support for this
hypothetical possibility.

The superscription claims this document to be heir to the divine
authority invested in the original covenant documents which were essential
to the maintenance of the covenant relationship established at Sinai.[1] As the
Lord of the covenant dictated to Moses terms for covenant life, so now he

---

1. Cf. M. G. Kline, *The Structure of Biblical Authority* (Grand Rapids:
Eerdmans, 1972), pp. 27–39. Kline indicates the significant role of the original
covenant documents as written testimonials to the binding character of the covenant.

inspires his prophetic mouthpiece to record against his own people their covenant violations and the fearful consequences of such transgression. Because these consequences were to stretch over the decades to come, the prophet had to record his declaration in order that future generations might attest to the truth or falseness of his words (cf. Deut. 18:22).[2] Zephaniah's contemporary Jeremiah had been directed to record his every prophetic utterance over a twenty-two-year period, and to re-record those utterances after they had been mutilated and burned by the arrogant Jehoiakim (cf. Jer. 36:1–2, 23, 27–28). In similar fashion, Zephaniah was directed to preserve his utterances for the generations to come so that they might see God's word of judgment and blessing actually coming to pass.

Zephaniah means "he whom Yahweh hides" or "hidden of Yahweh." No convincing relationship of the prophet's name with the message of his book can be found. On one occasion the book mentions the possibility that God's people may be "hidden" from the terrors of his wrath (2:3). But another Hebrew root is used rather than the one found in Zephaniah's name (*str* rather than *spn*). Although other "Zephaniahs" are mentioned in Scripture, none can be identified with this prophet.[3]

Zephaniah is designated as *son of Cushi.* A variety of conclusions may be reached on the basis of this distinctive name of the father of Zephaniah.[4] But they all fall in the realm of speculation which has inadequate foundation in fact that can be substantiated.

The superscription traces Zephaniah's lineage through *Gedaliah* and *Amariah* back to the prophet's great-great-grandfather *Hezekiah.* The recording of this extensive genealogy is unique in the prophetic books. Eight of the prophets have no family history recorded, which is appropriate to the prophet's distinctive role as "voice" (cf. Isa. 40:3; John 1:23). Six of the prophets have only the names of their fathers recorded, and Zechariah is identified by reference to his father and grandfather.

---

2. Note the useful contribution of G. von Rad, *Old Testament Theology,* 2 vols., tr. D. M. G. Stalker (New York: Harper & Row, 1962–65), 2:40–45, in indicating the significance of the prophets as writers.

3. According to 1 Chr. 6:21 (Eng. 36), a certain "Zephaniah" appears in the priestly line. Note also the priest named "Zephaniah" mentioned as contemporary to Jeremiah in 2 K. 25:18; Jer. 21:1; 29:24–25, 29; 37:3; 52:24. In Zech. 6:10, 14, mention is made of "Josiah son of Zephaniah" who came from Babylon. No positive relationship may be determined to the prophet mentioned in Zeph. 1:1 in any of these cases.

4. See the discussion of Rudolph, p. 259. A. Bentzen, *Introduction to the Old Testament,* 2:153, stretches the evidence a bit in his suggestion that Zephaniah may have been a Negro slave in the service of the temple.

But why should Zephaniah's lineage be traced through four generations? Some reason for this extensive detailing of ancestry must exist. As
J. M. P. Smith has suggested: "when only one of sixteen prophetic books ex-
hibits a striking variation, the probability seems to be on the side of that variation having been deliberate rather than accidental."[5]

It might be suggested that this fourth-generation genealogy is intended to relieve Zephaniah from the stigma and the sanctions associated
with a Cushite ancestry. For the Egyptian (at times equivalent in Scripture to
the Cushite) was excluded from the assembly of Israel until the third generation (Deut. 23:7–8). The obvious problem with this suggestion is the positioning of Cushi in Zephaniah's genealogy. He does not stand in the third (or
fourth) position, but in the first position in relation to the prophet.

More probable is the suggestion that this genealogical tracing reaches
back to the fourth generation because of an intention to focus on the last-
named individual: *Hezekiah*. Very possibly Zephaniah's genealogy intends
to indicate his royal origins. Good King Hezekiah was the most recent of
Judah's monarchs to manifest the covenantal fidelity essential for the well-
being of the nation. This relationship of the prophet with the monarchy in Israel could have provided him with ready access to the royal court, as well as
offering some position by which he could lend additional weight to the radical reforms promoted by young King Josiah.

It was *in the days of Josiah son of Amon king of Judah* that the word
of the Lord came to Zephaniah. Josiah was the last good king of Israel, with
a reign dating approximately from 640 to 609 B.C. His radical reform of the
religious and social practices of Judah are described in 2 K. 22–23 and 2 Chr.
34–35.

Can it be determined more specifically when in the days of Josiah
Zephaniah prophesied? Did Zephaniah prophesy prior to the discovery of the
law book in the temple in approximately 622 B.C.? Could he have contributed
to the earlier efforts toward reform mentioned in Chronicles during the
twelfth year of Josiah's rule (cf. 2 Chr. 34:3ff.)?[6] Or was it after the discovery
of the law book that Zephaniah prophesied, showing something of the limitations of Josiah's reforms?

5. J. M. P. Smith, p. 167.
6. The distinctions between the record of Josiah's reform in Kings and in
Chronicles must not be exaggerated. Some type of reform almost certainly would
have preceded the discovery of the law book if a process of temple cleansing had been
begun. It then should be expected that further reform would follow the reading of the
book.

Appeal to Zephaniah's reference to God's determination to cut off the "remnant" of Baal (1:4) is inconclusive in resolving this question. Although the removal of a "remnant" could imply some previous purging, the phrase might mean simply that God would remove the worship of Baal down to the very last bit.

The fact that Zephaniah anticipates a purging of those bowing down on their housetops and worshiping the starry host (1:5) supports the locating of Zephaniah's prophecy prior to the thoroughgoing reform of Josiah which came as a consequence of his discovery of the law book. This particular consideration has led most commentators to conclude that Zephaniah's material must have dated before 622 B.C.

However, one consideration especially points in another direction. As the material of Zephaniah is studied carefully, the wealth of phraseology paralleling expressions in the law book of Deuteronomy is quite remarkable. These parallels relate not merely to single words, but to larger phrasings of thought. Particular phrases include the following:

1. "And they shall build houses, and they shall not dwell (in them)" (Zeph. 1:13)

   "And a house you shall build, but you shall not dwell in it" (Deut. 28:30)

2. "And they shall plant vineyards, but they shall not drink their wine" (Zeph. 1:13)

   "Vineyards you shall plant and you shall serve, but (their) wine you shall not drink, and not shall you glean" (Deut. 28:39)

3. "A day of constraint and distress" (Zeph. 1:15)

   "In the constraint and in the distress by which your enemy will distress you" (Deut. 28:53, 55, 57)

4. "A day of darkness and thick darkness, a day of cloud and thick cloud" (Zeph. 1:15)

   "(The mountain) . . . (with) darkness, cloud, and thick cloud" (Deut. 4:11)

5. "And they shall walk as blind men" (Zeph. 1:17)

   "And you shall be groping . . . as a blind man gropes" (Deut. 28:29)

6. "And in the fire of his jealousy all the earth shall be consumed" (Zeph. 1:18)

   "They have provoked me to jealousy . . . fire is kindled in my wrath, and it shall consume the earth and its produce" (Deut. 32:21–22)

7. "Yahweh (is) righteous . . . he will not do iniquity" (Zeph. 3:5)

   "A God . . . who does no iniquity, righteous and just (is) he" (Deut. 32:4)

8. "He will rejoice over you with singing" (Zeph. 3:17)

   "As he rejoiced over you to do you good . . . Yahweh will rejoice over you to destroy you" (Deut. 28:63)

   "Yahweh will return to rejoice over you for good" (Deut. 30:9)

9. "And I shall set them for a praise and for a name" (Zeph. 3:19)

   "For I shall set you for a name and for praise among all the peoples of the earth" (Zeph. 3:20)

   "And to set you high above all the nations which he has made for a praise and for a name" (Deut. 26:19).

Other comparisons between Zephaniah and Deuteronomy deserve attention. Note the reference to God's threat that he will "bring distress" on Israel (Zeph. 1:17; cf. Deut. 28:29); the concentration on God's inspiring "fear" in Israel, often by the manifestation of his righteous judgments (Zeph. 3:7; cf. Deut. 4:10–11, 13; 5:29; 6:2, 13; 13:11; 14:23; 17:13, 19; 19:20; 21:21; 31:9–13); the description of the exiles as the "scattered ones" (Zeph. 3:10; cf. Deut. 4:27; 28:64; 30:3); the distinctive concentration on the "love" of God for Israel (Zeph. 3:17; cf. Deut. 4:37; 7:8, 13; 10:14–15; 23:6 [Eng. 5]); and the representation of God as the King, the Lord, a Mighty Hero (Zeph. 3:17; cf. Deut. 10:17).

What implication does this material have on the question of the dating of the prophecy of Zephaniah? Two possible options may be suggested.

First, it might be concluded that Zephaniah prophesied before the discovery of the law book, and that his materials affected the production of the book of Deuteronomy. This analysis of the evidence would support the critical theory that Deuteronomy was the literary product of a prophetical group functioning in the days of Josiah, and that the Mosaic origins of the book of Deuteronomy were invented at the time of its "discovery" to establish the authority of the document in the context of seventh-century Israel.

However, reaching this conclusion as a consequence of the parallels of phraseology between Zephaniah and Deuteronomy creates more problems than it solves. For if Zephaniah in his prophesying had anticipated quite distinctively the actual phraseology of the book of Deuteronomy, grave suspicions concerning the supposedly "Mosaic" origins of Deuteronomy would have been created in the minds of Zephaniah's contemporaries. How could it be explained that Zephaniah had anticipated so extensively the very phraseology of the book of Deuteronomy without having had access to the book? If Deuteronomy was to be presented as a product of Zephaniah and his contemporaries, no such problem would exist. But if Deuteronomy was to appear as the product of Moses the lawgiver, Zephaniah would not want to anticipate the phraseology of this document prior to its public appearance.

A second and much more likely explanation for the parallels of phraseology between Zephaniah and Deuteronomy may be found in the supposition that Zephaniah prophesied *after* the discovery in 622 B.C. of the book of the covenant that promoted Josiah's reform. As a consequence of the revelation of Israel's true status before their covenant God, Zephaniah addressed his contemporaries. Under this construction, Zephaniah appears as a prophetic helper to advance the reform instituted by Josiah. Such a perspective offers a much more realistic picture of the progress of reform under the young king.

It should not be supposed that a people committed to the worship of idolatrous gods would give up their practices very easily. Judah's return to its former habits within the brief three-month reign of Josiah's successor establishes that fact rather definitively (cf. 2 K. 23:32–33).

The description of Josiah's reforms in the book of Kings appears as something of a blitzkrieg. But even if his major policies were instituted in a relatively short period of time, he still would have needed the strong supporting confirmation of a contemporary word from the Lord to make his policies even remotely acceptable to the public. Very possibly this supporting word came from Zephaniah the prophet. Incorporating into his message the very phrases of the recently discovered book of the covenant, he addressed the people as God's contemporary mouthpiece, applying God's ancient word to the current situation.

So it may be proposed that Zephaniah prophesied in the days of Josiah, and more specifically in the days immediately following the discovery of the book of the covenant approximately in 622 B.C.

The superscription more specifically identifies Josiah as *son of Amon king of Judah.* Both of these phrases underscore the perilous situation in which Zephaniah prophesied. For Amon had been assassinated in an action of political intrigue by his own officials (2 K. 21:23). Despite many situations of peril which had been faced by the southern kingdom of Judah, it had been spared such self-destructive conspiracies except in very rare cases.

Stability was maintained in this dangerous situation by the intervention of the "people of the land" who executed Amon's murderers and secured the eight-year-old Josiah as Davidic successor (2 K. 21:24). But the occurrence of such an assassination of a Davidic monarch reveals something of the explosive character of the political situation.

That Josiah should be identified as *king of Judah* also attests to the threatening character of the day in which Zephaniah prophesied. Not only had schism occurred so that David's descendant did not reign over the whole of the kingdom; the northern kingdom of Israel was no more.

The discovery of the law book coincided with the one hundredth anniversary of the captivity of the northern kingdom. Judah had survived. But the rediscovery of the law book must have forced them to ask whether they might expect continued survival.

It is a sign of the persistence of God's grace in redeeming a people to himself to note that Amon, Josiah, and Josiah's son Jehoiachin are mentioned in the genealogy of Jesus Christ, the ultimate successor to the throne of David (Matt. 1:10–11). Despite many perils and many failings on the part of God's people, the purposes of God could not be thwarted.

I. COSMIC COVENANTAL JUDGMENT COMES WITH YAHWEH'S GREAT DAY (1:2–18)

The "Day of Yahweh" may be seen as that theme which unifies the entirety of the book of Zephaniah. Certainly in the first chapter Yahweh's Great Day binds together the message of the prophet. The destruction of the cosmos, judgment on God's own people, the sacrificial feast of Yahweh, and the terrors of a finalizing theophany relate to "the Day."

A. CREATION REVERSED (1:2–3)

2 *I shall wipe out completely*[1]
    everything on the face of the earth,
        declares Yahweh!

1. The Hebrew phrase *'āsōp 'āsēp* has been explained in a variety of ways. Fairly certainly it intends to employ the common Hebrew idiom of intensification by joining an infinitive absolute with a finite form of the verb. Although these conjoined forms normally derive from the same root, instances do occur in which differing roots are employed. (See GKC, § 113w n.3, although questions may be raised about the three examples given.) *'āsōp* would be understood as a Qal infinitive absolute of *'āsap*—"to gather (for removal)"; and *'āsēp* as the Hiphil imperfect first person singular of *sûp*, "to sweep away." In this instance, the author would have added to the force of his expression by the assonance of these two particular forms.

This explanation of the opening phrase of Zephaniah's prophecy is the most

3 *I shall wipe out*
  man and beast;
I shall wipe out
  the birds in the sky,
  and the fish in the sea—
  and the stumbling blocks with the wicked.
Particularly man I shall exterminate from the face of the earth,
  declares Yahweh!

2 Stunning are the opening words of the prophecy of Zephaniah. With the thud of a mighty kettledrum the prophet startles his hearers into a recognition of the solemnity of the hour. Everything on the face of the earth shall be utterly wiped away.

By a number of poetic devices, Zephaniah intensifies the impact of his message. By repetition of phraseology, by parallelism of members, by allusion to past revelation, the prophet confronts his audience with the crucial nature of the impending calamity. Particularly distinctive is the echoing of the provisions of God's earlier covenant commitment to Noah as it in turn reflected the ordering of God's creation. To Noah God had said he would wipe away "from upon the face of the ground" man and beast and bird (Gen. 6:7).

3 The order in which items are listed for destruction is precisely the reverse of the order in which they appear in the creation narrative.[2] First man, then beasts, birds, and fish are designated as the objects of God's consuming judgment. Originally it was fish, birds, beasts, and man that God created.

But how could it be that God would violate the provisions of the

---

satisfactory. But other possibilities have been proposed. GKC, § 72aa, proposes reading *ʾōsēp* as a Hiphil imperfect first common singular form of *ʾāsap,* instead of the Massoretic *ʾāsēp.* This analysis is supported by J. M. P. Smith, p. 191. Cf. also T. H. Robinson. and F. Horst, *Die Zwölf Kleinen Propheten: Hosea bis Micah,* HAT, 3rd ed. (Tübingen: Mohr, 1964), p. 190. However, *ʾāsap* does not follow the vowel pattern of the distinctive *pe-aleph* verbs.

A third option is proposed by A. S. Kapelrud, *The Message of the Prophet Zephaniah* (Oslo: Universitetsforlaget, 1975), p. 21. He suggests reading *ʾāsōp* *ʾeʾēsōp,* "I will utterly sweep away," assuming that the Massoretic reading must have arisen from a scribal error. L. Sabottka, *Zephanja: Versuch einer Neuübersetzung mit philologischen Kommentar,* BibOr 25 (Rome: Pontifical Biblical Institute, 1972), pp. 6–7, proposes a wordplay on the two homophonic roots *ysp,* "add," and *ʾsp,* "gather (for removal)," meaning "I shall again sweep away."

2. Cf. M. DeRoche, "Zephaniah 1:2, 3: The 'Sweeping' of Creation," *VT* 30 (1979) 106.

solemn covenantal bond with Noah? Had not the Creator indicated that he would not again destroy all flesh from the face of the ground (cf. Gen. 8:21)?

Perhaps in Zephaniah's mind resolution may have been found in his concept of this great day of destruction as the *final* day. God's promise to Noah was valid only "so long as the days of the earth" continued (Gen. 8:22). But now those days were to come to their end. Even refuge for the fish of the sea would fail.

The reference to the destruction of the *stumbling blocks with the wicked* combines once more the idea of judgment on the created universe with judgment on humanity in its wickedness. Various efforts have been made to emend the term *stumbling blocks (hammaksēlôt),*[3] but the word itself makes very good sense in context. Beasts, birds, and fish, representative of the whole of creation, have become for humanity an occasion of stumbling. Because of his wickedness, humanity has twisted the good things of creation into a cause for sin. The prophet's reference may be to idols shaped after the form of created things, or to the various other ways in which the creation may have become an occasion for stumbling. One instance of the former may be seen in King Ahaz's sacrificing to the gods of Damascus in the hope that they would prove to be a help to him: "but they were to him for his cause of stumbling *[lᵉhakšîlô]* and for all Israel" (2 Chr. 28:23).

While either man or beast may be characterized as "stumbling blocks," only man can be *wicked.* He alone has the responsibility of living according to the moral law of God. So the message of universal judgment concentrates on the devastation of humanity. Particularly humanity in its wickedness shall be destroyed in a coming universal calamity.

Quite remarkable is the appearance of this striking combination of *stumbling blocks with the wicked* in the NT (Matt. 13:41). Jesus interprets to his disciples a parable of universal judgment, which suits precisely the context of Zephaniah's prophecy. At the end of time God shall send his angels, who will "gather together [*syllégō;* cf. Zephaniah's *ʾāsōp*] everything that makes stumble and the doers of lawlessness *[pánta tá skándala kaí toús poioúntas tḗn anomían].*"

By this apparent allusion to Zephaniah, Jesus transfers the coming cosmic judgment described by the prophet from the devastation associated with judgment on old covenant Israel to the devastations associated with his final return. Jesus thereby indicates that the ultimate application of the pro-

---

3. For suggested emendations, see Rudolph, pp. 261–62. The Greek equivalent for "stumbling block" occurs in the Washington papyrus of the LXX, but is lacking in other Greek mss.

phetic threat of Zephaniah still is outstanding. The cosmic judgment that will reverse the creation is yet to come.[4]

B. COVENANT PEOPLE CUT OFF (1:4-7)

4 *More specifically, I shall stretch out my hand*
  against Judah
  and against all the inhabitants of Jerusalem;
  and I shall exterminate from this very place
  the remnant of Baal,
  the name of the Chemarim with the priests;
5 *those who worship the host of heaven on (their) rooftops;*
  those who worship
    by swearing to Yahweh
    while swearing by their "King";
6 *those who turn back from following after Yahweh,*
  who do not seek
    Yahweh
  and do not inquire
    of him.
7 *Hush!*
  Before Yahweh the Lord;
    for near is the Day of Yahweh.
    For Yahweh has prepared a sacrifice,
    he has sanctified his guests.

4 After announcing the cosmic character of God's imminent devastation, the prophet specifies a more exact object of judgment. Not just the world in general, but those who have been identified as God's own people in particular shall experience the consuming judgment of the Almighty.

Zephaniah's methodology of spiraling from an outer rim to an inner core in depicting the object of God's judgment compares closely to the technique of Amos (cf. Amos 1:6–2:16). In an elaborately structured oracle, this earlier prophet of Israel began with a word of judgment against each of Israel's neighbors that must have been applauded by his contemporaries. But he climaxed his word of judgment by denouncing God's own people residing in Israel.

---

4. Recognition that Matthew's Gospel probably intends to refer to Zephaniah is found in D. Hill, *The Gospel of Matthew,* New Century Bible Commentary (repr. Grand Rapids: Eerdmans, 1981), p. 236. Cf. A. H. McNeile, *The Gospel of Matthew* (London: Macmillan, 1938), p. 201.

Most stunning is the fact that the favored tribe of *Judah* and the supposedly inviolable city of *Jerusalem* should become the object of God's consuming judgments. The scepter never was to depart from Judah (Gen. 49:10). God had sworn that he never would remove a lamp from Jerusalem for the sake of his servant David (1 K. 11:13, 36; cf. 15:4; 2 K. 8:19; 19:34; 20:6). It was unthinkable to a Judean that somehow the place of God's own enthronement on earth could ever fall. Yet Zephaniah is unequivocal in his declaration: Jerusalem shall be devastated.

Two graphic words describe the coming judgment on God's own covenant people. God says, *I shall stretch out my hand [wᵉnāṭîṭî yāḏî]* against them, and *I shall exterminate [wᵉhiḵratî;* lit., "cut them off"] them.

A "hand stretched out" symbolizes a person's moving into action with all the force at his disposal. In God's case, he "stretches out his hand" when he intervenes dramatically, employing means "beyond what is common."[1] Particularly in the plagues of Egypt, God "stretched out" his hand to accomplish miraculous judgmental interventions (cf. Exod. 7:5; 15:12; note also the "stretching out" of the hand of Moses and Aaron as a means of inaugurating the various plagues in Exod. 7:19; 8:1–2, 12–13 [Eng. 5–6, 16–17]; 9:22; 10:12, 21–22; 14:16, 21, 26–27). In an awe-inspiring manner God liberated Israel with a "mighty hand and a stretched-out arm" (cf. Deut. 4:34; 5:15; 7:19; 9:29; 11:2; 26:8). But now this same power shall operate against Israel, because of a new adversary relationship.

The awesome character of this prophetic pronouncement must be appreciated. Who is it that does not have the potential to err with Israel in their sin? Because they knew themselves to be the favored of the Lord, they judged themselves exempt from his righteous indignation. But the hand of God's judgment may be directed as well against those who have been called by his name as against those who have not known him in the fulness of the truth.

The LXX renders this phrase *ektenố tền cheírá mou,* "I shall stretch out my hand." The same concept appears in the NT when Christ works a miracle of healing by stretching out his hand (Matt. 8:3; Mark 1:41; Luke 5:13). Elsewhere Jesus interprets his supernatural interventions as the work of the "finger of God" manifesting the arrival of the kingdom of God on the earth (Luke 11:20). His interpretation of these events suggests that the "stretching forth" of his hand was probably intended not merely as a means of making physical contact but as a means of symbolizing a direct connection with those ancient occasions in which God stretched out his hand in salvation. This *gracious* character of these new covenant interventions displays

---

1. Calvin, p. 191.

the extent of God's mercy toward the undeserving in Jesus' day, but does not nullify the ultimate fulfillment of the judgment motif involved in this symbolism as anticipated by Zephaniah.

Five objects of God's exterminating activity within Judah and Jerusalem are indicated by the prophet's use of the sign of the direct object in Hebrew (*'e*ṯ). Each of these itemized practices displays various corruptions in Israel's worship. Later the prophet will denounce the sins of the people against one another, such as deceitfulness and violence. But he begins appropriately with an exclusive concentration on the sins committed directly against God in the worship practices of the people.

Too often a broad tolerance toward worship is promoted even within the framework of those generally professing faith in the God of the Scriptures, even though immoral actions such as violence and deceit may be roundly condemned. But this true prophet of God perceived the lie embedded in this moralistic approach to religion. Only as the fountainhead of devotion to God is purified by the truth will the concrete actions of man conform to the law of God concerning love of neighbor.

The first two items to be cut off are *the remnant of Baal* and *the name of the Chemarim with the priests.* No small number of commentators have interpreted the reference to the destruction of the *remnant* of Baal as indicating that Josiah's reform already must have been in progress.[2] Already a significant portion of Baal-worship had been removed by the earlier reforms of Josiah. But now Zephaniah prophesies that the Baalism which still was left would be removed.

Paralleling the removal of the remnant of Baal is the obliteration of the *name* of the heretical priests. So thoroughgoing will be this coming judgment of the Lord that even the names of the false priests will be forgotten.

In both these expressions, the emphasis falls on the elimination of every last association with Baal and its worship in Israel. Whether or not one may infer that a purging of Baalism already has begun, the destruction of the remnant of Baal emphasizes the thoroughness of God's consuming judgment.[3]

For how could it be otherwise? Either Yahweh is God or Baal is God. Either one or the other must function as Lord over the people and their land. Either history proceeds in a purely cyclical pattern according to the orderings of nature ill-conceived, or history receives its direction from God the Creator and moves toward a consummate goal of redemption according to the sovereign purposes of God the Redeemer. The God who created in health

2. Cf. among others Keil, p. 128.
3. Cf. S. R. Driver, p. 112; Rudolph, p. 262.

and redeems in wholeness cannot be joined to a God who fertilizes the earth through sacred prostitution and who claims his portion by child sacrifice.

The Chemarim (RSV "idolatrous priests") are joined to the priests of Baal as elements involved in the purging of Judah by Josiah in 2 K. 23:5, 8. The precise meaning of the term *Chemarim* is uncertain.[4] Adequate evidence is lacking to establish the theory that the term refers to "idolatrous" priests as over against another (nonidolatrous?) classification of priests. Neither is it clear that *Chemarim* was a term that described a nonlevitical priesthood in Israel,[5] since the normal term for "priests" is used also for the nonlevitical functionaries destroyed by Josiah at Bethel (cf. 1 K. 13:33–34).

God established a priesthood to mediate oneness with his people. The very existence of priesthood implied weakness in humanity and a need for compassionate understanding in maintaining the way of access to God for the sinful. But under the corruptions of Baalism, the priesthood apparently offered the defenseless infant as a sacrifice. Instead of providing for the removal of sin, the priesthood instigated depravity of the worst sort.

At the time of the establishment of the rival altar in Bethel, an unnamed prophet had declared that a man named "Josiah" would defile that very altar by sacrificing the serving priests and by burning the bones of the dead on its surface (1 K. 13:1–2). Zephaniah in his turn predicted the utter devastation of the priests who followed in this corrupted practice, and perhaps saw with his own eyes a partial fulfillment of his prophecy. For his contemporary King Josiah was the very one who sacrificed priests and burned the bones of the dead on the altar of Bethel (2 K. 23:20).

But Zephaniah's primary concern was with the corrupted priesthood now entrenched in Jerusalem itself. He declares that the purging of God would remove altogether the erring priesthood *from this very place.*

Jerusalem was Judah's worship center because God had established his dwelling in the midst of that city in a unique sense. For that reason, its purity had to be maintained. The judgment of the Exile had the effect of terminating Israel's "itch after idolatry."[6] But the ultimate purging of every remnant of false worship awaited the full transformation of the cosmos associated with Zephaniah's first word concerning the coming judgment (vv. 2–3).

4. Cf. the discussion of KB, p. 442.

5. Keil in C. F. Keil and F. Delitzsch, *Commentary on the Old Testament*, vol. 3: *I & II Kings, etc.,* tr. James Martin (repr. Grand Rapids: Eerdmans, 1950), p. 483.

6. Jonathan Edwards, *The History of Redemption* (repr. Evansville, IN: Sovereign Grace Publishers, n.d.), p. 132.

After dealing with the corrupt officialdom of Judah's worship (v. 4b), the prophet declares the inevitable extermination of all those who participate in improper worship practices (vv. 5–6). The fact that the people have been led into these practices does not exempt them from the judgment of God.

5 The first group denounced is *those who worship the host of heaven on (their) rooftops.* A form of this superstition has found its devotees in almost every ancient culture, and is manifest today in believers in the modern horoscope.

Zephaniah's frame of reference may be found in two passages from the law book uncovered by Josiah. According to Deut. 4:19, Israel is warned specifically not to "worship" (*hištaḥᵃwîṭā*) the sun, the moon, and the stars, "all the host of heaven" (*kōl ṣᵉḇāʾ haššāmayim*). For Yahweh has displayed his unquestioned sovereignty over these great phenomena by apportioning them among all the peoples of the earth. Deuteronomy 17:3–7 prescribes the death penalty for any man or woman found worshiping (*wayyištaḥû*) the sun, moon, or stars.

Jeremiah subsequently indicates that particularly the women of Israel succumbed to the temptation of worshiping the heavenly host. Even after Israel's devastation, those in Egypt insisted on offering their sacrifices to the host of heaven (Jer. 44:19).

Worshiping *on (their) rooftops* suggests in part the idea of an individualized, domestic control of worship.[7] The epitome of the abuse of the principle that all Israel was a "kingdom of priests" (Exod. 19:6) may have been found in this practice. On the private housetop, each person could worship in a manner that pleased only himself. The deuteronomic legislation intended to counter just such a depraved tendency in its requirement that any such practice in Israel would be brought to the attention of the community by the mouth of two or three witnesses (Deut. 17:4–7). The Law and the Prophets combine to condemn the idea that a person's worship may be left to the dictates of his own conscience.

The next phrase of the prophet focuses on the syncretistic aspect of the worship of Baal in Israel. Zephaniah assures the utter devastation of *those who worship by swearing to Yahweh while swearing by their "King."* The

---

7. Private control of worship practices performed "on the rooftops" could have been exercised even though some evidence is available in cuneiform texts from Ras Shamra describing "a ritual to be used when offerings were made on rooftops to astral deities and celestal luminaries" (R. K. Harrison, *Jeremiah and Lamentations,* Tyndale Old Testament Commentaries [Downers Grove, IL: InterVarsity Press, 1973], p. 112). This degree of regulation would not exclude a nightly individualized practice in the private circumstances provided by worshiping "on the housetop."

subtle distinction between swearing *to* Yahweh while swearing *by* another who is called their "King" is not always brought out in translation.[8] But it manifests precisely the damnable syncretism plaguing Israel's worship. What could be more satanic than a religion that took to itself the name of the true God while at the same time professing devotion to his chief rival? By this method, a person could practice the proud imaginations of his own heart undisturbed. The *"King"* who is set in tandem with Yahweh in this verse is apparently Baal, regarded as divine monarch by his devotees.[9]

The very nature of worship involves a person in a posture of oath taking. Only if a person functions purely as a spectator can he avoid solemn commitments of loyalty to the God he professes, which in essence involves a vow.

Once again, the denunciation of Zephaniah echoes the legislation of Deuteronomy. Israel had been commanded explicitly to fear Yahweh, and "by his name" to swear (*bišmô*—Deut. 6:13; 10:20). Yet the nation now was attempting to retain the best of two antithetical worlds by invoking both the name of Yahweh and the name of Baal. Thus human beings display all the resources of their depraved ingenuity (cf. Matt. 23:16–22).

The self-destructive contradictions implicit in syncretism may be seen in Zephaniah's subsequent exposé of the attitude of his contemporaries. Although they vow allegiance to Yahweh, they simultaneously assume that Yahweh actually "can do neither good nor ill" (v. 12). Even the most devoted worshiper of God in a syncretistic framework will ultimately deny all power to the true God. For no one can serve two masters.

6 In his last specification of the causes for God's annihilating judgment, the prophet turns from the sins of "commission" to the equally heinous sins of "omission." Devastation shall come on those who do not follow after Yahweh, who do not inquire after him.

It is difficult to maintain a distinction between the words used for *seek (bqš)* and *inquire (drš)*. The second term may contain more the idea of seeking guidance in a perplexing situation. But both words refer essentially to a concentration of devotion directed toward their God. The combination of terms underscores the fact that worshiping the true God requires a conscious and directed effort. This intensity in devotion cannot be regarded as an op-

---

8. The LXX makes no distinction, translating both *l* and *b* by *katá*. The NIV also makes no difference in its rendering of the prepositions.

9. Kapelrud, *Message of the Prophet Zephaniah*, p. 3; Rudolph, pp. 265–66. The proposal that MT *malkām*, "their 'King,'" should be read "Milcom" (a Canaanite deity) is possible, and could be effected without consonantal modification. But the context does not suggest that this would be the place for the introduction of a reference to the chief Ammonite deity.

tion reserved for a pious minority. Failure to seek after the Lord is a sin which shall bring an exterminating judgment.

The prophet further specifies that the people *turn back from following after Yahweh*. This same condemnation, cited in the NT to establish the universal judgment of God on the whole of mankind (Rom. 3:9), leads to the same fearful silence before Yahweh as commanded by Zephaniah. Every mouth is stopped (Rom. 3:19; cf. Zeph. 1:7).

7 *Hush! Before Yahweh the Lord.* Stop your vain protestations. Your syncretistic insincerities only intensify the basis for condemnation. A limpid response to the truth only multiplies the causes for condemnation.

Some sign of hope and grace in this bleak situation may be found in the record of the reform of Josiah. For the young king turns to "inquire of the Lord" when quickened by the reading of the law book (2 K. 22:13, 18). Josiah did exactly what the sinful nation had failed to do.

The sovereignly victorious grace of God finds its ultimate expression in the declaration that he would be found even of those who "did not seek him" (Isa. 65:1). This priority of grace finds programmatic, historic realization in the aftermath of the judgment experienced by Israel under the old covenant as it is now being anticipated by Zephaniah. He too predicted the dawning of a day beyond devastation when the Gentiles, those heathen peoples who did not seek Yahweh, would be found by him (Zeph. 2:11; 3:9; cf. Rom. 10:20).

Ultimately it was because of the coming *Day of Yahweh* that the recipients of the prophet's message were to stand in hushed awe. This solemn summons to silence by the prophet implies the imminence of the Lord himself. Standing before his awesome majesty on his great day inspires the most humble and reverent demeanor.[10]

The significance of the materials in Zephaniah for the subject of the "Day of Yahweh" has been recognized quite generally.[11] This one theme permeates the book and constitutes a major organizational motif.

---

10. Note the appearance of the term in Hag. 2:20; Zech. 2:17 (Eng. 13); Neh. 8:11. The suggestion of Rudolph, p. 266, that the use of the term implies a cultic call is a possibility. But it is questionable that this framework is adequate to explain the origins of the "Day of Yahweh."

11. Note the comment of Gerhard von Rad, "The Origin of the Concept of the Day of Yahweh," *JSS* 4 (1959) 102, that the material in Zephaniah "certainly belongs to the most important material at our disposal concerning the concept of the Day of Yahweh." Again, in his treatment of *yôm* in *TDNT*, 2:945, he states: "Alongside the powerful depiction of the day of Yahweh in Isaiah, Zephaniah contains the most comprehensive proclamation of this day of judgment."

Evidence in Zephaniah indicates that research into the concept of the Day of Yahweh cannot be limited to those passages which explicitly use this phrase. In a context clearly unified by the theme of the coming Day, Zephaniah speaks not only of the "Day of Yahweh." He also uses as equivalent phrases "on the day of the sacrifice of Yahweh" (1:8), "in that day" (vv. 9–10); "at that time" (v. 12); "the great Day of Yahweh" (v. 14). It need not be concluded that every time one of these phrases appears elsewhere in Scripture it must refer to the Day of Yahweh. But the terminology of Zephaniah argues rather strongly against a methodology which would limit research too pointedly to those passages where the precise phrase "Day of Yahweh" occurs.[12]

Particularly with reference to the question of the origin of the concept of the Day of Yahweh, Zephaniah has much to contribute. A variety of suggestions has been proposed concerning the origin of the Day of Yahweh in Scripture. But none of the options adequately assimilates all the various data in Scripture concerning the origin of the Day.[13] .

12. Some lack of consistency exists between the "earlier" and the "later" von Rad on this subject. In his 1935 article on the Hebrew term *yôm* in *TDNT*, 2:946, von Rad notes that Jeremiah never speaks of the "Day of Yahweh" by this specific phrase, but that he frequently refers to "those days" and "that time," explaining that "in Jeremiah this seems to have essentially the same meaning as *yôm yhwh* in other prophets." He also employs other passages to elucidate the concept of that Day which do not use the exact phrase, such as Zech. 12:1ff.; 13:1ff.; 14:8; Mal. 3:2. But in his later article of 1959, he insists that investigation must not be tempted into going beyond the material evidence which mentions the Day of Yahweh expressly, although he does recognize that broader concepts were associated with the Day ("The Origin of the Concept of the Day of Yahweh," *JSS* 4 [1959] 97).

Von Rad eliminates some of the key passages at the outset in this later article, "as they do not provide the interpreter with any sure exegetical basis" (p. 97). He notes that a broad base of passages exists in the prophets, but because of a number of totally heterogeneous ideas, the "only correct method" is to narrow the sphere of investigation (ibid.). In view of his initial elimination of the larger framework of the concept, the source of these heterogeneous ideas is unclear.

13. For discussion and interaction with the various theories that have been proposed, see L. Černý, *The Day of Yahweh and Some Relevant Problems* (Prague: University of Karlova, 1948); Kapelrud, *Message of the Prophet Zephaniah*. Discontent with von Rad's treatment is expressed by M. Weiss, "The Origin of the 'Day of the Lord' Reconsidered," *HUCA* 37 (1966) 40; Černý, *Day of Yahweh*, p. 59; Kapelrud, *Message*, p. 82.

Limitations also surface in the various other suggestions concerning the origin of the Day. Either the proposals lack adequate support within the text of Scripture, or they are not comprehensive enough to embrace the broad dimensions of the data, or they are so broad that they lack adequate particularizing significance.

Černý, *Day of Yahweh*, p. 45, severely criticizes Mowinckel's tracing of the

In the context of this ongoing discussion, Zephaniah may have something distinctive to offer. The general agreement that the *Day of Yahweh* involves a theophany in which God manifests his powers may serve as a useful starting point for comprehending the origins of the Day. But how may this theophanic manifestation be defined more precisely?

The first chapter of Zephaniah's prophecy presents in sequence three connected images. The first depicts the reversal of the order of the cosmos as sustained by the provisions of the covenant with Noah (vv. 2–3). The second describes a sacrificial feast connected with the curses symbolized in the covenant-making procedure manifested at the time of the establishment of the Abrahamic covenant (vv. 7–8; cf. Gen. 15). The third presents a frightful image of God's appearance with darkness, thick darkness, cloud, and trumpet, reflecting the theophany associated with the establishment of the Mosaic covenant (Zeph. 1:15–16). These last two images will have to be explored in greater detail subsequently. But in the meantime, it may be noted that the Day of Yahweh in Zeph. 1 is associated with the establishment of the successive covenants made with Noah, Abraham, and Moses.

The Day of Yahweh therefore may be seen as the Day of his Covenant. On this day, he establishes his sovereign lordship over men. Either by instituting the covenant or by enforcing the provisions of the covenant, Yahweh manifests his lordship on that Day. No other day may be so fittingly designated as belonging to him than the Day of covenant establishment and enforcement.

This covenantal perspective on the Day of Yahweh may assist in relating the coming of the Day with the coming of the kingdom. According to L. Černý, "This day will make a definite end of all the previous history of the whole world, and from this day onwards in the new world there begins an everlasting Kingdom of Yahweh never experienced anywhere before."[14]

---

prophetic Day of Yahweh to a Babylonian *akîtu* festival. Suggestions concerning the cultic origins of the Day as found in G. W. Ahlström, *Joel and the Temple Cult of Jerusalem,* VTSup 21 (Leiden: Brill, 1971), p. 63, do not deal adequately with the historical dimension of the prophetic Day. Note von Rad's comment, *TDNT,* 2:944, that the concept of the Day of Yahweh developed "in striking alienation from the world of the cultus." The idea in Černý, *Day of Yahweh,* p. 79, of "a fateful day decreed by Yahweh" is simply too broad a concept to be helpful. The suggestion of Weiss, *HUCA* 37 (1966) 46, that the Day relates essentially to God's action without dealing specifically with the question of time contradicts the emphasis on the imminence of the Day. Kapelrud's idea of a "great annual feast" in which God determined the fate of humanity does not possess adequate roots in biblical evidence (*Message,* p. 86).

14. Černý, *Day of Yahweh,* p. 84. Note von Rad, *TDNT,* 2:944, who indicates that it would be quite natural for Yahweh's kingship and the Day of Yahweh to be interrelated.

God's lordship throughout the world finds its meaningful structure in the coming of the great Day when he enforces the provisions of his covenant.

A covenantal perspective on the Day of Yahweh also may assist in integrating other concepts in Scripture associated with the coming of the Day. As conquering Suzerain, Yahweh goes forth in war to subdue all his enemies beneath his feet, and to bind them to himself in covenantal loyalty. As the Great King and Maker of all, Yahweh possesses the power to overturn the cosmos. Judgment on God's enemies climaxes on the Day of Yahweh as a consequence of the sworn curses of the covenant.[15]

In this context of the presentation of the Day of Yahweh in connection with covenant inauguration and enforcement, Zephaniah declares that *Yahweh has prepared a sacrifice* and *sanctified his guests* (Zeph. 1:7). Both of these actions are closely associated with the establishment of the covenant in the traditions of Israel.

In a text of acknowledged antiquity, Abraham divided animals and set their parts opposite one another in preparation for the "passing through" of a theophany (Gen. 15:9–18). The action symbolized a self-maledictory pledge to covenantal curse. The attempt of the ravenous birds of prey to devour the exposed carcasses vividly displayed the final horrors of covenantal curse.

Zephaniah's contemporary Jeremiah indicates the continuing significance of the patriarchal symbolism in his explicit allusion to the ancient covenant-making procedure precisely at the time when God was bringing covenantal devastation on Jerusalem through his "servant" Nebuchadrezzar (Jer. 34:18–20). In several other passages, Jeremiah refers to the covenantal curse associated with the devouring of exposed carcasses by birds of prey (cf. Jer. 7:33; 16:4; 19:7).[16] Particularly in describing the destruction of the army of Pharaoh Neco at Carchemish, Jeremiah employs the language of covenantal sacrifice in depicting "that Day":

> For that Day
> is for Lord Yahweh of hosts
>
> a Day of vengeance,

15. Note D. R. Hillers, *Treaty-Curses and the Old Testament Prophets,* BibOr 16 (Rome: Pontifical Biblical Institute, 1964), p. 531, who concludes that in the instance of Isa. 34, "the prophet pronounces doom on a nation in terms which occur as a curse in a treaty."

16. For a fuller exposition of the significance of this concept of covenantal curse as a unifying factor in Scripture, see my *The Christ of the Covenants* (Grand Rapids: Baker, 1980), pp. 124–42.

for the avenging of his enemies.
The sword shall devour and be satisfied,
   quenching its thirst with their blood.

For a sacrifice
  is (set) for Lord Yahweh of hosts
    in the land of the North
    on the river Euphrates. (Jer. 46:10)

This imagery of covenantal sacrifice relating to the enforcement of
the curses of the covenant supplies the perspective from which the prophet
Zephaniah views God's imminent judgment on Judah. Because they had
been bound in covenantal oath of self-malediction, they must experience
devastation on the Day that the Lord of the covenant enforces his sovereignty.

Other passages in the prophets develop the imagery of a sacrifice offered by the Lord in depicting his judgments on the nations. Two passages
may be summarized as follows:

On the Day of Yahweh's revenge, his sword will be bathed in the
blood of Edom. For the Lord will offer a sacrifice in Bozrah and will
execute a great slaughter in Edom. (Isa. 34:5–8)

Every kind of bird together with all wild animals must assemble. For
the Lord is preparing for them a great sacrifice. They will eat the flesh
and drink the blood of the mighty men of Israel. (Ezek. 39:17–20)

Alluding to this ancient collage of prophetic images, the new covenant book of Revelation depicts the final devastation of God's enemies. On
that day, all birds flying in midair shall be summoned to "the great supper of
God," where they may eat the flesh of kings and mighty men (Rev. 19:17–
18). In that last great Day, prophetic anticipations of covenantal judgment
will realize their consummate fulfillment.

The sacrifice which Yahweh has prepared in Zeph. 1:7 must be Judah
and Jerusalem. For they have already been specified as the objects of God's
judgment (vv. 4–6). This awesome announcement should not have caught the
people by surprise. For they had pledged themselves by the self-maledictory
oath of the covenant.

Yahweh also has *sanctified [hiqdîš] his guests* in preparation for the
feast of the great day of Yahweh. These *guests* may be wild birds and beasts
of the field who sup at the table of covenantal condemnation. Or they may
be the heathen nations which would serve as the instruments of God's judgment on Israel. In either case, the sanctification of these objectionable *guests*

270

for the sacrificial banquet would be essential to the maintenance of the holiness of God in his role as host.

This purification of guests may be compared to the sanctification of Israel for three days in preparation for the covenantal encounter at Sinai (Exod. 19:10). The covenantal bond established at Sinai was consummated when representatives of the people "ate and drank" in the presence of God (Exod. 24:11; cf. 1 Sam. 16:5). A further connection with the sanctification of guests at a covenantal meal may be seen in the Lord's consecrating *(hiqdaštî)* all the firstborn of Israel at the time of the Passover. They could participate in the covenantal meal of the Passover only because the Levite had been "offered" *(hēnaptā)* in place of the firstborn who had been "sanctified" *(hiqdaštî)* to the Lord (Num. 8:15–17).

Zephaniah's message from the Lord is not merely descriptive. It is declarative. For the prophet announces unequivocally that *near is the Day of Yahweh.* This announcement means that the Day is both inevitable and imminent.

Nowhere in this oracle does the prophet suggest a course of action that might turn aside the fury of Yahweh's Day. Not even in subsequent oracles calling for repentance does he suggest that the judgment of the Day might be cancelled. Only "perhaps" the pious remnant "may be hid" upon the arrival of the Day (Zeph. 2:3b).

The nearness of the Day indicates that it could arrive at any moment. Time had run out for Judah. Now they must prepare for devastation.[17]

The finality of cosmic overthrow associated with the coming of Yahweh's Day in the fullest sense never came in the context of events associated with the old covenant. It is not surprising, therefore, to find in the NT both passages which suggest an arrival of the Day of Yahweh in events current in NT times as well as passages looking to a future arrival of the great Day. Both of these perspectives must be kept in mind for a proper understanding of the contemporary significance of the coming of the Day.

When John the Baptist calls for repentance in view of the imminence of the coming judgment of God, his message parallels Zephaniah's announcement concerning the nearness of the Day of Yahweh (Matt. 3:1–12; Luke 3:1–18). John's preaching underscores the arrival of the kingdom of God in

---

17. Von Rad, *JSS* 4 (1959) 108, speculates that the outcry concerning the nearness of the Day of Yahweh could be "the old stereotyped call with which the troops were summoned to take the field in the holy war, or a cry with which they went into battle with Yahweh." His proposal lacks adequate supporting evidence. Cf. Weiss, *HUCA* 37 (1966) 36.

association with those purging fires of God's judgment. It is not to be supposed that the coming of the kingdom is identical with the arrival of the Day. But the interrelation of these two idea-complexes suggests that the Day of Yahweh serves to inaugurate the kingdom. Only as the purging judgment of God sweeps the earth will the kingdom come.

When Christ deliberately parallels the tearing of his own flesh as covenantal sacrifice with the substitutionary death of the Passover lamb, he is interpreting his own death in the familiar terms of covenantal malediction (cf. Matt. 26:26–29; Luke 22:14–22). The fury of God's wrath, that wrath that is epitomized in the outpouring of covenantal curses on the Day of Yahweh, falls on him. Eating his flesh and drinking his blood by faith introduces the participant into the sacrificial feast of Yahweh, offered only to consecrated guests.

The outpouring of the Spirit, accompanied by supernatural signs of a down-drafting wind from heaven, marks the arrival of the "last days," of the "great and glorious day of the Lord" (Acts 2:17–18, 20).[18] Now the kingdom inaugurated by the arrival of the Day has come, because the Lord the King has come. Having ascended to his throne of glory, he pours out his Spirit on all his subjects.

In a certain sense, the Day of Yahweh has come. But distinctive to the Day is the characteristic of finality. In a sense the Day came in association with certain events surrounding the advent of Jesus Christ. But in another sense the Day is yet to come. And as Zephaniah prophesied, it is *near.*

The old covenant Scriptures manifest a variety of phrases by which the coming Day of Yahweh may be designated. Zephaniah speaks in terms of "the Day," "that Day," "the great Day," "the Day of Yahweh," and "the Day of the overflowing wrath of Yahweh" (1:7–10, 14–15, 18). In similar fashion, the new covenant Scriptures employ a variety of phrases in referring essentially to the same phenomenon. The Day of Yahweh may be designated as the "day of judgment" (Matt. 10:15; 11:22, 24; 12:36; John 12:48; 2 Pet.

---

18. The signs mentioned in Acts 2:20 that were to precede the coming of the "great and glorious Day of the Lord" include the items listed beginning at v. 17 and running through v. 21. Peter specifically declares that "wonders and signs" have occurred, starting with the ministry of Jesus (v. 22). The "coming" of the "Day" therefore does not await the arrival of a day associated with "wonders" and "signs." Some might propose that it is necessary to have a literal turning of the moon into blood before the arrival of the Day. Yet the fulfillment of the other signs in connection with the coming of Christ in his birth, ministry, death, resurrection, ascension, and outpouring of the Spirit would suggest strongly that at least the first phase of the arrival of the day has been realized.

3:7), the "last day" (John 6:39, 40, 44, 54; 11:24; 12:48), the "day of the Lord" (Acts 2:20; 1 Cor. 5:5; 2 Cor. 1:14; 1 Thess. 5:2; 2 Thess. 2:2; 2 Pet. 3:10), the "day of the Lord Jesus Christ" (1 Cor. 1:8), "the day" or "that day" (Matt. 7:22; Luke 10:12; 21:34; 1 Cor. 3:13; 1 Thess. 5:4; Heb. 10:25), the "day of Christ Jesus" (Phil. 1:6), the "day of Christ" (Phil. 1:10; 2:16), the "day of God" (2 Pet. 3:12), the "eternal day" (2 Pet. 3:18), the "great day" (Jude 6), the "great day of their wrath" (Rev. 6:17), and the "great day of God the Almighty" (Rev. 16:14).

All of these passages deserve careful consideration when attempting to determine matters related to the consummate fulfillment of the Day of Yahweh as prophesied by Zephaniah. Suffice it to say that the cosmic judgment associated with a dramatic theophany now may be understood in terms of the glorious return of Jesus Christ. On the day appointed he shall consummate all things.

C. CONSUMPTION OF ALL CONCERNED (1:8–14a)

8 *On the day of the sacrifice of Yahweh:*
  a I shall inflict punishment
  b on the leaders,
  b on the sons[1] of the king,
  b and on all who are clothed with foreign garments.
9 *a I shall inflict punishment in that day*
  b on all who leap over the threshold,
  b who fill the house of their lords with violence and deceit.
10 *In that day, declares Yahweh, there shall be:*
  a A voice pleading
  b from the fish gate;
  a howling
  b from the second quarter;
  a a tumultuous crashing
  b from the hills.
11 *Howl, you inhabitants of the Pounding Place:*
  a For utterly devastated
  b are all the people of Canaan;
  a utterly exterminated
  b are all the dealers in silver.

---

1. The LXX translates "sons" as "house." Cf. Rudolph, p. 267, who concludes that the term refers to all members of the king's household rather than to the sons of the reigning king.

12 *At that time:*
> *I shall search out Jerusalem*
>> *with candles;*
> a *I shall inflict punishment on the men*
> b *who settle on their haunches,*
> b *who say in their heart,*
> *"Yahweh will do no good, nor will he do evil."*

13 a *Their wealth will be*
> b *dissipated;*
> a *their houses*
> b *pillaged.*

> a *They will build houses*
> b *and never live in them,*
> a *they will plant vineyards*
> b *and never drink their wine.*

14a *Near*
> *is the great Day of Yahweh!*
> *Near*
> *and coming with great haste.*[2]

This section continues to expand on the theme of the Day of Yahweh and the devastating consequences of the judgment associated with the arrival of that Day. Explicit usage of the phrase *Day of Yahweh* brackets this material (vv. 7, 14), and three different phrases substitute for "Day of Yahweh" in the intervening verses: "On the day of the sacrifice of Yahweh" (v. 8), "in that day" (vv. 9–10), and "at that time" (v. 12) all introduce the permeating theme of the Day of Yahweh.

These verses narrow the object of judgment even more specifically than had been done in the previous section. Originally the scope of God's judgment had been indicated as including the entirety of the cosmos (vv. 2–3). Then Judah and Jerusalem were specified (vv. 4–6). Now particular Judeans are designated (vv. 8–9, 11), as well as specific districts within the targeted city of Jerusalem (vv. 10–11). The section also offers a more precise cataloguing of the consequences of the judgment soon to come, which may be described generally as despair, devastation, and frustration (vv. 11, 13).

An extensive use of poetic parallelism marks this section, as has been

---

2. The term *mahēr* probably represents an abbreviation of the Piel participle *mᵉmahēr* (cf. Rudolph, p. 263; GKC, § 52s). But it may be an adjective, modifying "day," that developed out of an adverbial usage of the infinitive absolute (cf. Keil, p. 135; von Orelli, p. 266).

indicated by the layout of the translation above. This literary device increases the effectiveness of the message involved.

8 The opening of this verse illustrates the rather common abruptness in alternation between first person and third person material in Zephaniah. "On the day of the sacrifice of *Yahweh* [third person reference to Yahweh] *I* shall inflict punishment [Yahweh now speaks in the first person]." This kind of variation occurs repeatedly throughout the book, and should be considered as a characteristic literary device for vivifying the Lord's own involvement. The changes are too frequent and too obvious to be regarded as the considered editing of a later hand.[3]

By a fourfold use of the Hebrew preposition *ʿal* ("on"), the prophet indicates the specific objects of the punishing hand of Yahweh (vv. 8–9). The first two categories of personages set for judgment relate to the leadership of Israel. The *leaders* and the *sons of the king* God himself shall punish (v. 8).

Because the term *prince* in the English language is virtually equivalent to a *son of the king,* it is best to render this first term *(śār)* as *leader* in order to distinguish individuals from the "sons of the king" mentioned in the next line. The first in dignity, honor, office, and leadership shall be first to receive judgment.

But what about the *king?* Why should he not be the object of divine wrath? If Zephaniah's prophetic ministry was founded on the law book recently discovered by Josiah, the answer is not difficult to discover. Since the king was manifesting the kind of commendable character appropriate for a sovereign serving as vicegerent under Yahweh, he would not receive the same kind of treatment accorded the disobedient. Zephaniah, it must be remembered, does not deal in categories of possible punishments. He announces the inevitable. Judgment on the king's *sons* is inevitable.

A complication arises when it is recognized that at the time of Josiah's discovery of the law book his two oldest sons would have been ten and twelve years of age (2 K. 23:31, 36). This fact, along with other considerations, has led some commentators to conclude that the phrase *sons of the king* refers to the royal court in its broader dimensions, rather than to the king's sons specifically.

But despite all the problems involved in relating the phrase *sons of the king* directly to Jehoahaz and Jehoiakim, the specific nature of the phraseology, as well as the subsequent developments in Judah's history, point precisely in that direction. The most convincing explanation for the omission

---

3. Rudolph, p. 264, concludes that the change in speakers indicates the secondary origin of the materials.

of reference to the "king" as an object of judgment is that the person of Josiah was excluded intentionally. This specificity suggests also specificity with regard to the *sons* which the prophet had in mind. Unique to patterns of succession in Judah's history is the fact that no fewer than three of Josiah's sons ultimately ruled in the place of their father.

The first two sons of Josiah had different mothers but the same father, which may provide some insight into a circumstance by which Zephaniah perceived the direction that the sons would inevitably pursue. If the prophet was of the royal line himself, being the son of "Hezekiah" (1:1), he may have had special awareness of the situation prevailing in the royal palace.

The third category of personages condemned are *all who are clothed with foreign garments*. Keil's suggestion that this phrase condemns those who were willing to wear the styles of foreign peoples because of political considerations does not appear adequate to the context. More likely is the possibility that the phrase refers to those who dressed distinctively as priests of foreign gods. Some significant weight must be given to the incident of Jehu's purging of the priests of Baal. In order to effect a total annihilation of these foreign priests, Jehu instructed the "keeper of the wardrobe" to bring out vestments *(lᵉḇûš)* for all the servants of Baal (2 K. 10:22; cf. *lōḇᵉšîm* in Zeph. 1:8). In the vast throng assembled for sacrifice, recognition of the priests of Baal in distinction from the priests of Yahweh may have hinged on a difference in clothing (10:23). A reference to the "keeper of the wardrobe" is found also in a passage describing the situation contemporary to Josiah (22:14), during the time of Zephaniah's ministry.

It should be noted as well that Solomon had brought many "foreign women" *(nāšîm noḵrîyôt)* to Jerusalem, and had allowed them to set up their own worship centers on the "hill of abominations" across the valley from the temple area (1 K. 11:1, 7–8; cf. *malḇûš noḵrî* in Zeph. 1:8). Very likely each of these foreign centers of worship possessed its own priesthood with its distinctive vestments. In the decades that ensued, the inhabitants of Jerusalem must have become accustomed to seeing the distinctly clad priests of various foreign gods parading their streets. Possibly Zephaniah addressed himself to this type of corruption.

Some significant parallelism of phraseology may be found in this description by a comparison of the LXX translation of this phrase and a passage in the Gospel of Matthew. In the context of Matthew's Gospel, Christ cites several OT texts which declare judgment against Israel. First, he applies the imagery of the unproductive vineyard of Isa. 5 (Matt. 21:33). Second, he relates the rejection of the "chief cornerstone" by Israel's leadership in Ps. 118 to the nation's current response to his ministry (Matt. 21:42). Then Jesus tells the parable of the king's wedding feast prepared for his son. In a section unique to Matthew (Matt. 22:11–13), one guest appears without a proper wedding garment. This audacious guest must be cast into outer darkness, where there will be weeping and gnashing of teeth.

The parallel expressions are:

Zephaniah condemns those who are "clothed with foreign garments" *(endedyménous endýmata allótria).*

In Matthew the king orders his attendants to cast out the one who is "not clothed in a wedding garment" *(ouk endedyménon éndyma gámou).*

Of course, this parallelism of expression could be altogether incidental. One passage speaks of priestly garments, the other of wedding garments. But the context in Matthew suggests the possibility of an intentional allusion to the prophecy of Zephaniah. In both contexts, judgment on Israel is the major theme. This particular parable of Jesus falls in a Gospel framework intent on depicting Israel's rejection in terms of the fulfillment of OT predictions. Particularly if *all who are clothed with foreign garments* in Zephaniah refers to devotees of foreign gods functioning in the assemblies of Israel, a parallelism with Jesus' parable may be quite likely.

The difference in context may be explained by the fact that Jesus depicts a situation in which God's lordship over his kingdom already has been displayed by the actual assembling of guests for the wedding feast, while Zephaniah still awaits the coming judgmental intervention of God. As a consequence, Matthew sees pretenders to the kingdom in a decided minority, while Zephaniah must contend with a situation in which those *clothed with foreign garments* are still a majority.

9 The final object of God's punishment introduced by the preposition *on ('al)* in this series is described as *all who leap over the threshold.*[4]

---

4. The idea that the phrase means leaping *upon* the threshold rather than *over* the threshold is grammatically possible (see J. G. Frazer, *Folk-lore in the Old Testament* [New York: Macmillan, 1927], p. 313n.2). But would that imply a blatant contradiction of the sacred practices of Israel's Philistine neighbors? A syncretistically inclined Israel would hardly exert itself deliberately in such a manner. The alternative understanding of the phrase to mean "leap over" in the sense of "do violence to," referring to the breaking in of houses, is also possible (cf. Keil, p. 132). But the text indicates that it is in the "house of their lords" rather than in private homes that this violence is done, as seen by the absence of an additional conjunction which would separate the latter portion of the verse from the former. Because it appears rather strange to speak of violently breaking into public houses of worship, this interpretation should be rejected.

This phrase is best understood by reference to the superstitious practice of the Philistines in stepping over the threshold of their temple. "To this day," according to the writer of 1 Samuel, this custom was practiced by the priests of Dagon (1 Sam. 5:5).

The irony associated with the importation of such a pagan superstition is found in the next phrase. While gingerly leaping over their temple threshold, the people of Judah nonetheless *fill the house of their lords with violence and deceit.* They observe the minutia of a senseless pagan law, but then run rampant over the basic ordinances of God in his own house.

Once the earth was filled with *violence (ḥāmās)* that led to its destruction in the days of Noah (Gen. 6:11, 13). Now the temple of God itself is filled with *violence and deceit,* which must eventuate in its destruction.

Zephaniah's contemporary Jeremiah also complained about the people's making the house that bears God's name a "den of robbers" (Jer. 7:11). They had the audacity to claim safety for themselves as they chanted, "The temple of the Lord, the temple of the Lord, the temple of the Lord is this." But all the time they oppressed the alien, the fatherless, and the widow, shedding innocent blood in God's holy place (7:4, 6). Jesus found the same practices of violence and deceit within God's house in his own day (Matt. 21:13). He exercised God's prerogative of judgment by cleansing the temple.

10–11   The next two verses turn from specifying classes of people set for judgment to indicating the consequences of judgment for the various sectors of the city of Jerusalem. Pleading, howling, devastation, and destruction shall result from the infliction of divine punishment.

10   The *pleading* and *howling* arising from the areas of the *fish gate* and the *second quarter* of Jerusalem give expression to the utter despair of a people who have lost all hope in life. The judgment of God has now entered their own private district of town. The *fish gate* apparently refers to an entrance on the north of the city of Jerusalem, which normally would be the first place attacked by an invading army.[5] The *second quarter* is mentioned in 2 K. 22:14, paralleled by 2 Chr. 34:22, and possibly in Neh. 11:9. It could allude to the newer portion of the town added by Manasseh when he extended the wall of the city to the north.[6] But the location of this section of town is not certain.

The *tumultuous crashing from the hills* may describe the breaking down of the idols located on the hills surrounding Jerusalem. Jeremiah alludes to the "humming (of busy activity) on the mountains" *(hāmôn hārîm),*

5. Rudolph, p. 268.
6. Cf. Smith, p. 199.

the "lie (which comes from) the hills" *(laššeqer migg^{e}bā'ôt)* (Jer. 3:23). All this busy activity, set in contrast with "the Lord our God" as Israel's trust, may have been an audible phenomenon to the inhabitants of Jerusalem. But Zephaniah now announces that this busyness will be replaced by a *tumultuous crashing.* In one great cacophonic calamity, all the idols shall be destroyed.

11 Various suggestions concerning the identity of the *Pounding Place (maktēš)* have been offered.[7] The grammatical change in the expressions of this verse from an indicative to an imperative in comparison with the previous treatment of districts within Jerusalem suggests that *maktēš* should be handled differently. Possibly the term refers to the whole of the city rather than to one particular district. Encircled by higher hills, Jerusalem itself may be compared to a mortar, a pounding place. God in his judgment shall grind the whole of the city as though it were encased in a mortar.

Pleading, howling, wailing in the Day of Yahweh. Utter and absolute despair shall wrack the hearts of all the inhabitants of Jerusalem. This Day is coming soon.

The remainder of the verse extends the description of the effect of the judgment on Jerusalem. The Day shall bring devastation for all merchants and businessmen of the city. Industry, initiative, and enterprise will pay off in frustration and personal ruin. The reference to the *people of Canaan* must be interpreted in the light of the phrase with which it is set in parallelism: *the dealers in silver.* Because of their reputation as tradesmen, the name of the Canaanite populace became equivalent to "merchant."[8] The cutting off of *all the dealers in silver* meant that the city as a center of culture, trade, luxury, beauty, and craftsmanship would come to an end. If any life were left in the city, it would consist only of groveling for the most meager of existences.

Thus far the prophet has specified political, religious, and commercial leadership as the objects of the coming judgment of the Day of Yahweh. None of these noble employments shall avail to deliver from devastation.

12 Zephaniah indicates furthermore that a thoroughgoing *search* shall be made throughout the whole city. None shall escape the scrutinizing eye of God. This carefulness in ferreting out every single inhabitant may be compared to the searching out for judgment described in Amos 9:2–4. Neither the grave nor the sky nor the peak of Carmel nor the pit of the sea shall conceal the objects of God's scrutinizing judgment.

---

7. Cf. Driver, p. 117. The term literally means "mortar."
8. Note the parallelism found also in Isa. 23:8; Hos. 12:8 (Eng. 7). Cf. Driver, p. 117; Rudolph, p. 263.

Particularly the uninvolved, the indifferent, and the skeptical are selected for condemnation. The *men who settle on their haunches* shall receive punishment from the Lord. The spiritually skeptical who have convinced themselves that *Yahweh will do no good, nor will he do evil* may be compared to the dregs *(šimrêhem)* which thicken *(haqqōpeʾîm)* in uselessness, as the phrase reads literally. Although they whisper these insults about God *in their heart,* they will not go undetected.

13 As a consequence of their audacious insults against Yahweh, *their wealth will be dissipated, their houses pillaged.* In the immediately preceding phrase, these men had expressed their judgment that Yahweh could do neither good nor evil. Now it is declared that they will be able to accomplish nothing.

In its broader dimensions, the term translated *their wealth (ḥêlām)* includes the idea of strength, power, or riches. Earlier Israel had been warned that when they came into the land, they must beware of saying, "my hand has gotten me this wealth *[haḥayil hazzeh].*" They were to remember that it was Yahweh who gave them the ability to produce wealth and so confirmed his covenant (Deut. 8:17–18). But now they must forfeit all the blessings of the covenant.

So *They will build houses and never live in them, they will plant vineyards and never drink their wine.* Absolute frustration is the consequence of this curse of the covenant. All the labor of their hands shall be for nothing. Adam had been cursed originally in the labor of his hands. But at least he was assured that he would eat bread (cf. Gen. 3:19). Under the gracious provisions of God to Israel earlier, they were to enjoy houses, wells, cities, and vines that they had not produced. All these treasures would be given them freely. But to stand under God's curse meant something altogether different. Overrun by an invading army, their *houses* were to be pillaged. All their possessions were to be ripped from them (Deut. 28:30, 39).

14a Twice the prophet underscores his certainty that this awesome Day of Yahweh is *Near.* Sooner than any of his contemporaries might imagine, all the devastations he has described shall become realities. Going beyond his previous announcement concerning the Day (v. 7), Zephaniah now characterizes the coming calamity as the *great* Day of Yahweh which is *coming with great haste (mahēr meʾōd).*

Once more a theme of Zephaniah is underscored in the law book of Deuteronomy. God had repeatedly assured Israel that if they departed from his law, they would perish "quickly" *(mahēr)* from the land (Deut. 4:26; 7:4; 11:17; 28:20). Human beings may need a long period of preparation to accomplish their intentions. But "God has no need of much preparation, for His own power is sufficient for Him when He resolves to destroy the wicked."[9]

This concept of the "nearness" of the coming Day of judgment receives repeated emphasis under the new covenant administration as well. "He is near, at the very gates" (Matt. 24:32–33). The Lord is "near," and the time is "near" (Phil. 4:5; Rev. 1:3; 22:10). Rapid progress toward the coming of the Lord is seen in the fact that "our salvation is nearer now than when we first believed" (Rom. 13:11).

Zephaniah's contemporaries saw with their own eyes the terrible fulfillment of these words of prophecy. Since that day each new generation must face the possibility of experiencing the consummate fulfillment of this prophetic announcement.

D. THE TERRORS OF THEOPHANY (1:14b–18)

14b *The voice of the Day of Yahweh:*
  A bitter crying—
  there is a mighty hero!
15 *A Day of overflowing wrath*
  is that Day.
A Day
  of adversity and distress;
a Day
  of destruction and desolation;
a Day
  of darkness and thick darkness;
a Day
  of cloud and thick cloud;
16 *a Day*
  of trumpet blast and battle shout
  against the fortified cities
  and against the highest corner towers.
17   *For I will bring distress*
    on man,
  and they shall walk
  as blind men.
    For against Yahweh they have sinned.

  Their blood
    shall be poured out

9. Calvin, p. 221.

> *as dust*
> *and their entrails[1]*
> *as dung.*
> 18 *Neither their silver*
> *nor their gold*
> *shall be able to deliver them*
> *in the Day of the overflowing wrath of Yahweh;*
> *for in the fire of his jealousy*
> *all the earth shall be consumed.*
>
> *For he will make a complete end;*
> *indeed, a shocking end he will make*
> *of all the inhabitants of the earth.*

These verses continue the theme of the Day of Yahweh which first had been mentioned specifically in v. 7. Now the concentration on this theme reaches the level of saturation. No less than ten times in these five verses is the Day explicitly mentioned.

The day is now characterized as a terrifying theophany in which the overflowing wrath of God is unleashed. Drawing heavily on the description of the awesome events of Sinai, the prophet anticipates another manifestation of God's terrors in which the curses of the covenant will be inflicted, not merely inscribed. Now covenant enforcement replaces covenant inauguration.

14b The prophet introduces this section by a vivid description of the effect of the Day. See the *mighty hero?* He shrieks bitterly as a consequence of the coming of the Day. The *voice,* the sound that characterizes this tumultuous Day, is the hopeless crying of the once-mighty warrior. At the original theophany of Sinai, attention was focused on the voice of God *(qôl ʾĕlōhîm)* declaring his lordship over the people (Deut. 4:12, 33, 36; 5:19–23 [Eng. 22–26]); 8:20; 18:16). But now attention centers on a voice which responds to Yahweh's self-manifestation on his great Day. It is a voice of bitter despair on the part of the warrior who has been overwhelmed. This Day will be "so horrible that the mighty man, the warrior of many battles, accustomed to blood-curdling scenes and horrifying destruction, will shriek in abject terror at this unprecedented devastation."[2]

---

1. The term *lᵉhummām* is difficult. BDB, pp. 535–36, says it "perhaps" means "intestines, bowels"; hence the proposal "entrails." The LXX translates "their flesh" *(tás sárkas),* assuming the root to be *lehem.* This interpretation is supported by Driver, p. 120. But as he indicates, it is not the usual word for flesh.

2. Laetsch, p. 363.

15–16   The *Day* is mentioned seven times in the next two verses. Five couplets poetically arranged characterize the Day and describe its accompanying phenomena.

The prophecy of Zephaniah may fittingly be called a treatise on the wrath of God. The dominant characteristic of this Day is that it is *a Day of overflowing wrath* (yôm ʿebrâ; cf. v. 18). From this verse apparently arose the inspiration for the thirteenth-century song written by Thomas of Celano, which may have been translated into more languages than any other hymn:

That day of wrath, that dreadful day
When heav'n and earth shall pass away!
What pow'r shall be the sinner's stay?
How shall he meet that dreadful day?

When, shrivelling like a parched scroll,
The flaming heav'ns together roll;
When louder yet, and yet more dread,
Swells the high trump that wakes the dead;

O on that day, that wrathful day
When man to judgment wakes from clay,
Be thou the trembling sinner's stay,
Though heav'n and earth shall pass away.[3]

The series of five couplets in the text of Zephaniah employs extensively the poetic device of paranomasia. Zephaniah joins together words with similar sounds to add emphasis. The second word of each of these pairs generally is stronger than the first.

The commonness of expression with Deuteronomy's description of the theophany at Sinai indicates the prophet's intention to depict the Day of Yahweh in terms strongly reminiscent of the establishment of the covenant with Israel mediated through Moses. Now those terrors from which Israel cringed shall be displayed again. But this time no mediator shall shield the nation from the consuming force of God's righteous judgments.

Extensive parallelism also may be noted between the expressions of Zephaniah and those found in the prophecy of Joel as he describes the coming Day of Yahweh:

---

3. Translated from the Latin by Sir Walter Scott, as found in *The Trinity Hymnal* (Philadelphia: Great Commission, 1961), No. 242.

Zeph. 1:15	**Joel 2:2**
"A day of darkness and thick dark-ness"	"A day of darkness and thick dark-ness"
"A day of cloud and thick cloud"	"A day of cloud and thick cloud"

Zeph. 1:16	**Joel 2:1**
"A day of trumpet blast and shout"	"They shall blast a trumpet in Zion and they shall shout in my holy mountain"

Similar expressions are found in Amos 5:18, 20, a third passage of principal importance dealing with the subject of the Day of Yahweh. The clustering of these distinctive phenomena about the subject of the Day of Yahweh in three different prophets of Israel indicates a common tradition among them. Most likely each of these prophets drew from an older tradition which was readily available in Israel. The ancient covenant-making tradition associated with Sinai provides just such a common source of ideas. Darkness, thick darkness, cloud, and trumpet blast all characterized the appearance of God at Sinai.

Once more Zephaniah has associated the coming Day of Yahweh with ancient covenantal manifestations. Noah's covenant (Zeph. 1:2–3), Abraham's covenant (vv. 7–8), and Moses' covenant (vv. 15–16) provide the framework for understanding the appearance of Yahweh on his great Day. Phenomena related to past covenantal establishment will be echoed in future covenantal enforcement.

The first couplet declares the Day to be one of *adversity and distress.*[4] Pressures leading to utter despair shall mark the day of God's assault on his own people.

Second, the Day shall be a day of *destruction and desolation.*[5] The land shall be left in absolute ruin.

Third, the Day shall be a day of *darkness and thick darkness.* That "thick darkness" (*ʾapēlâ*) of the ninth plague in Egypt which isolated and immobilized its victims shall characterize all the inhabitants of the land on the Day of Yahweh (cf. Exod. 10:22).

Fourth, the Day shall be a day of *cloud and thick cloud.* Numerous passages associate God's theophonic appearance in the old covenant with

---

4. *ṣārâ ûmᵉṣûqâ.* Both terms suggest the idea of an extremity of pressure which constrains its victim.

5. *šōʾâ ûmᵉšōʾâ.* KB, p. 572, calls the second term an "artificial [*sic*] amplified form of *šōʾâ.*"

dense cloud (cf. Exod. 20:21; Deut. 4:11; 2 Sam. 22:10; 1 K. 8:12; Ps. 18:10 [Eng. 9]; Ps. 97:2).[6]

This same association of cloud and theophany is found in the context of the new covenant. A thick cloud enveloped the one designated as Son of God at the time of his transfiguration (Matt. 17:5). His ascension to glory was in clouds, and his return in glory shall be with clouds (Acts 1:9, 11; cf. Matt. 24:30; 26:64; 1 Thess. 4:17; Rev. 1:7; 14:14–16). The consummating Day of Yahweh will involve the manifestation of his glory in the clouds of heaven.

Fifth, the Day of Yahweh shall be a day of *trumpet blast and battle shout.* Fortified cities with the highest of corner towers shall crumble before him on his great Day. Even as Jericho tumbled before the trumpets announcing the presence of Yahweh, so every human defense against the Lord will crumble on that great Day.

17 The consequences of the coming Day of Yahweh are specified more particularly in the verse following this series of couplets. Humanity as the principal object of the wrath of God shall be devastated.

Both the fact that God will *bring distress* and the fact that the people *shall walk as blind men* may represent ideas arising out of the curses of the covenant as described in Deuteronomy (cf. Deut. 28:28–29). God's smiting of Israel with blindness finds a most dramatic fulfillment in Nebuchadrezzar's treatment of Zedekiah, the last of Judah's kings and the third of Josiah's sons to reign on the throne (note the prophet's earlier indicator of a coming punishment for the "sons of the king" in v. 8). After murdering his sons before his eyes, the king of Babylon blinds Zedekiah so that the last sight he had to remember is the destruction of his line of descent (2 K. 25:6–7).

The undeserved favor of God is fully manifested elsewhere in the prophetical promise of the removal of this curse of blindness (Isa. 61:1). It was in the framework of this promise of gracious deliverance that Jesus chose to inaugurate his ministry (cf. Luke 4:18). From that point on, the recovery of sight for the blind was interpreted as a sign of the coming of the kingdom (Matt. 11:5; cf. 9:27–28; 12:22; 15:30–31; 20:30; 22:14).

Sandwiched between descriptions of the awful consequences of God's judgment on Judah is a simple statement of the reason for this devastating destruction at the hand of God: *For against Yahweh they have sinned.* Some have interpreted the abruptness and brevity of this condemnation as a

6. According to J. M. P. Smith, pp. 204–5, "This is a characteristic frequently connected with theophany in the Old Testament; the word 'cloud' occurs no less than 58 times in such connections."

sign of its secondary character. But an appreciation of the heinousness of sin should provide sufficient basis for seeing this short statement as an adequate explanation of the judgment that was to come. The people of Judah had violated the personal trust involved in a covenantal relationship. For this reason, all the curses of the covenant must fall on them. On a previous occasion, the whole of the nation had been devastated because of one man's sin (cf. Josh. 7:11). Since all Israel now stood guilty, it should not be surprising that the whole nation should be condemned.

The two following phrases describe with realistic vividness the coming judgment on Judah. God had indicated that he never would set aside his judgment of the nation because of the innocent blood that Manasseh had shed (2 K. 24:4). Because blood defiles the land (Num. 35:33), the vengeance of the covenant had to come to expression. Now the *blood* of the inhabitants of Judah would be of no more value than the *dust* of the ground.

Speaking even more vividly, the prophet announces that *their entrails* would be poured out *as dung*. The poetic parallelism indicates that the same verb is to be supplied for the second figure. The vital organs of the victims of God's judgment shall be poured out on the ground as though they were of no more worth than dung.

18 The prophet proceeds to describe the hopelessness of any possibility of escape from the overflowing wrath of the Day of Yahweh. Customarily an invaded nation could buy off its conqueror. By paying adequate tribute, some semblance of national integrity could be maintained. But when Yahweh comes on the terrible Day of his conquest, nothing can deter his purposes. In establishing perfect justice, he shall utterly devastate the wicked. Sin inevitably evokes the *overflowing wrath of Yahweh*. His longsuffering and patience over many years, decades, and centuries must not be misrepresented as complacency or lack of commitment to render a just punishment to the transgressor.

for in the fire of his jealousy all the earth shall be consumed. The essence of God himself is involved in this burning jealousy. For the Lord, whose name is Jealous, is a jealous God (Exod. 34:14). Whenever his people worship other gods, they evoke this essential jealousy within the Lord. Particularly as God manifested himself at Sinai, he showed himself to be a consuming God who will not clear the guilty.

In its description of the devastation of Jerusalem that occurred shortly after the prophecy of Zephaniah, the book of Lamentations emphasizes the "fire" of the Lord that consumed Jerusalem:

"From on high he sent down fire" (1:13)

"He has burned in Jacob like a flaming fire that consumes everything around it" (2:3)

"He has poured out his wrath like fire" (2:4)

"He kindled a fire in Zion that consumed her foundations" (4:11).

These verses indicate the historical outworking of the wrath of God anticipated by the prophet.

Yet the context of Zephaniah's prophecy points to a more total consumption of the earth. For in the fire of his jealousy, *all the earth shall be consumed.* There is some ambiguity as to whether this consumption extends only to "the whole land" (of Judah) or to the "entire earth."[7] The immediately preceding context clearly has been speaking of the destruction which is to fall on the nation of Judah.

But the broader context of this unified discourse on the Day of Yahweh suggests a cosmic conflagration. In his opening verses, the prophet had spoken in terms of a worldwide judgment which would reverse the entire order of creation (vv. 2–3). Now at the end of this material, he returns to this broader theme of the total destruction of the world. If his own covenant people are to be destroyed, it can be expected that the whole of the universe will be consumed with them.

This broader interpretation of the "land" involved in God's consuming fire finds support in the closing phrases of this chapter. The theme of universal judgment will find explicit development in subsequent portions of the prophecy (cf. particularly 3:8 and its reference to the consuming of the whole earth in the fire of God's jealousy). But the point seems to be made here also. In a most startling fashion God shall bring judgment on *all the inhabitants of the earth.*

Summary

The prophecy of Zephaniah clearly presents itself as a treatise on the wrath of God. The great Day of Yahweh is coming soon. On that Day, the God who has pledged himself repeatedly and in various contexts by the oath of the covenant shall devastate all who have broken the covenant. This terrible judgment is inevitable and unavoidable. The Day is coming soon.

7. Rudolph, p. 270, feels the weight of the "all," and inclines toward interpreting this judgment as universal. But he proposes that a later hand after the Babylonian invasion has added the phrase, or that this verse actually belongs after 3:8, where "land" clearly means "earth."

Zephaniah's Day of Yahweh, in which the wrath of God was to be poured out on Judah, found expression in the destruction of Jerusalem by the Babylonians. But the "day of wrath" is yet to come (Rom. 2:5). This "great Day of his wrath" (Rev. 6:16–17) is as certain to come as was the devastation of Jerusalem. With eschatological finality, all who are not found by faith to be united in him shall be consumed from the face of the earth (cf. Matt. 3:7; 1 Thess. 1:10; Rev. 11:18; 14:10; 16:9; 19:15).

II. THE CALL TO REPENTANCE SOUNDS BEFORE THE ARRIVAL OF GOD'S GREAT DAY (2:1–15)

The call to repentance which follows the prophet's solemn announcement of the coming of the Day of Yahweh must not be misinterpreted. This call does not imply that somehow the arrival of the Day may be turned back, or even delayed. Already the time has been set, and it cannot be altered. However, some possibility exists that protection may be provided for the repentant at the arrival of the Day. This slim hope the prophet holds out as his primary motivation for urging the people to turn from their sinful ways (vv. 1–3).

The second motivation for repentance is more fearsome in its perspective. In considering the coming devastation of other nations, Judah may find adequate reason to accept the pealing of the death knell that has sounded for them also (2:4–15). In this section, the prophet does not remind of past judgments that already have fallen on other nations. Instead, he exercises his prophetic powers to announce other coming judgments whose justice should be apparent to his contemporaries. If they can see that the God of all the earth shall do right among other nations, then they may be led to see their own status as a condemned people, and so be brought to repentance. Yet in this case, they will have to repent without any expectation of escape from divine chastening.

It is quite amazing that modern people, with all their accumulated sophistications, cannot read the signs of the times. After God has displayed his judgments on the nations of the earth so dramatically, people still convince themselves that the evil day is always distant from them.

Particularly appalling are the contortions of religionists of the Judeo-Christian heritage who blunt the cutting edge of the announcement of impending judgment found in the prophetical writings of Holy Scripture. Shall the appeal to a fictional and unproven principle of prophecy *post eventum* continue to lull the unbelieving until that final Great Day itself has arrived to consummate all that the prophets have said? Zephaniah's condemnation of all syncretistic tendencies may have something to say directly to the mass of modern biblical scholarship.

A. SEEK NOW, FOR PERHAPS YOU MAY BE HID IN THAT DAY (2:1–3)

1 *Gather yourselves together like stubble,*
yes, gather together like stubble,
　O nation that has no shame;
2 *a Before*
　　　　b the decree gives birth
　　　　　　(like chaff the day passes over),
　　a before
　　　　b the burning of the wrath of Yahweh
　　　　　c shall come on you,
　　a before
　　　　b the Day of the wrath of Yahweh
　　　　　c shall come on you.
3 *Seek Yahweh*
　all you meek of the land
　　who do his justice;
　seek righteousness,
　seek meekness.
　Perhaps you shall be hid in the day of the wrath of Yahweh.

The form of this section stands in direct contrast with the previous portion of the prophecy. Grammatical considerations underscore this contrast. The first section (1:2–18) was declarative in form. It made known to the hearers in no uncertain terms the realities associated with the Day of Yahweh. But this section comes in the form of an *admonition.* As a matter of fact, these three verses contain five admonitions. These five admonitions are joined by three temporal clauses to emphasize the urgency of the admonition being directed to Judah (v. 2).

The section concludes with a statement of the possible outcome if the people of Judah will hearken to the word of admonition. The possibility still exists that they may be hid in the Day of Yahweh.

1 The first verse begins with a coupling of admonitions that have created many problems for interpreters. The first two words of this section build on the word *stubble (qaš).* As a verbal form, the root concept conveys the meaning of "gathering stubble." It is used with this meaning in passages describing the gathering of straw or stubble by the Israelites in Egypt (Exod.

289

5:7, 12), the gathering of stubble on the sabbath (Num. 15:32–33), and the widow's gathering of stubble in Elijah's day (1 K. 17:10). The first term is reflexive in form (Hithpolel), and therefore conveys the idea of *gather yourselves together like stubble,* or possibly "gather together stubble for yourselves." The second imperative in the verse builds on the same root, and has the effect of intensifying the concept being presented.

But what is the significance of this unique imperative, *gather yourselves together like stubble?*[1] This admonition follows a lengthy description of the inevitability of the judgment that must fall on Judah. It looks toward the faint "perhaps" of protection at the arrival of the Day of Yahweh.

Understood in this context, the admonition may be interpreted as a form of derogatory address. Judah is worth no more than stubble. Its populace ought to bunch together in a manner that acknowledges this utter worthlessness. Let them stand as sinners worthy of judgment.

Although quite unusual in its imagery, this expression communicates rather effectively the message of self-abasement needed by a self-confident nation. The figure employed finds an echo in Mal. 3:19 (Eng. 4:1) that "the Day comes . . . and all the proud . . . shall be stubble" *(wᵉhāyû . . . qaš).* Zephaniah's reference in the next verse to the day's passing "like chaff" also may lend some support to this understanding of the prophet's imagery.

How typical it is that a people most self-confident would be most ripe for judgment. With the relative weakening of the Assyrian empire, Judah must have begun to sense a new confidence concerning its own future. But either they must humble themselves to the dust, or they must expect the hum-

---

1. The AV renders the phrase: "Gather yourselves together, yea, gather together." J. Gray, "A Metaphor from Building in Zephaniah 2:1," *VT* 3 (1953) 404, characterizes this rendering as "quite a feasible translation from a purely grammatical point of view," although he proceeds to offer his own unique interpretation of the figure. Cf. J. M. P. Smith, pp. 211–12.

Numerous other interpretations of this controverted phrase have been offered. Laetsch, p. 365, suggests that the people are being told to take to themselves the humblest task, echoing their enslavement in Egypt. But this particular method for serious self-humiliation seems rather peculiar. Driver, p. 121, suggests the changing of two letters, so that the phrase reads, "get you shame, and be ashamed" *(hiṯbôšᵉšû wābôšû).* But J. M. P. Smith, pp. 211–12, rightly observes that it would be difficult to explain how such a simple reading evolved into such a difficult one. Gray, *VT* 3 (1953) 407, suggests "Stiffen yourselves and stand firm, O people without cohesion"; but the reasoning that leads to this rendering is not quite convincing. Rudolph, p. 271 n. 1, suggests a solution based on an Arabic root which he admits does not appear in Hebrew. With all the difficulties involved in the unique figure of "gather together like stubble," it offers the most straightforward and convincing solution.

bling of God. Either they reckon rightly concerning their own worthlessness as servants of a holy God, or they must expect to be gathered and burned as the stubble.

The various proud peoples of the earth today would benefit by taking heed to the admonition of the prophet of old. This phrase indeed is offensive to the self-esteeming person. But it provides the exclusive way to a slight glimmer of hope for sinners.

This solemn call to self-abasement is addressed to a *nation that has no shame*. This particular phrase also presents serious difficulties in interpretation. The verb employed has the basic idea of "to become pale" *(kāsap)*. Elsewhere in Scripture it indicates becoming pale through longing (Gen. 31:30; Ps. 84:4 [Eng. 3]) or through hunger (Ps. 17:12). Paleness effected by desire is a part of the significance of the word. This root meaning is reflected in the AV translation: "O nation not desired." Although possibly a proper rendering, this understanding does not suit any of the various meanings proposed for the first portion of the verse.

A related meaning would be "O nation not paled (by shame)." This understanding of the phrase is reflected in the RSV ("O shameless nation"), and in the NIV ("O shameful nation").[2] Judah is to gather itself together as though it were worthless stubble, although in pride it currently is a nation that "knows no shame." Not even a blush rises on its cheek from an awareness of its guilt before God.

Only a nation blinded to its own sin could feel no shame in the midst of such guiltiness. Tottering on the brink of utter destruction by the righteous judgments of God, the nation goes blithely on its own way, oblivious to the calamities staring it in the face. But it was to just this situation that the prophet was sent. His responsibility was to declare God's coming Day, and to summon the nation to repentance. Perhaps the living word of God would quicken in the people an awareness of their sin.

2 The prophet now casts his admonition in a framework of urgency. Only a narrow space of time stands between the people and their utter devastation, for once the Day arrives they will have no future opportunity for repentance. The sinner must not wait until the Day arrives in order to humble himself before the Lord. Only in the interval of time sandwiched between the declaration of the prophet and the dawning of the Day can any meaningful

---

2. Cf. J. M. P. Smith, p. 212, who says: "The idea of 'shame' is associated with this root in Aramaic, in late Hebrew and in colloquial Arabic. This furnishes a good meaning in this place and, in default of anything better, may be adopted." Note the similar conclusion reached by BDB, pp. 493–94.

readiness be achieved. Waiting to see if the prophet's evaluation has validity will prove fatal. Action must be taken now.

By the threefold use of the temporal term *before (beṭerem)*, Zephaniah strengthens the urgency of his admonition. The additional negative *(beṭerem lō')* intensifies the need for urgency in action.[3]

The solemn warning concerning the brevity of time available for rectification of wrong in heart and action applies equally to the need to assemble in self-abasement (v. 1) and to seek the Lord (v. 3). It is not necessary to decide between a connection of these three phrases with the admonition that precedes or succeeds them.

A further underscoring of the shortness of time available occurs with the parenthetical phrase: *(like chaff the day passes over)*. The imagery of chaff presents too insubstantial a picture to stand for the solid realities associated with the Day of Yahweh itself. That Day does not "pass over like chaff." But it suits ideally the brevity of the time now remaining for repentance. Chaff hovers momentarily, floating in the air. A gust of wind swirls about, and it is gone in an instant. Because of its lightness, the chaff is easily and quickly blown away.

In just such a manner, the time intervening between the present moment and the descent of the fierce wrath of Yahweh passes away in an instant. No time remains to dillydally before that Day. Now or never a turning of the ways must be effected. Who knows when the wind will stir and sweep away forever this last hope for deliverance on the Day?

A further figure of speech is employed in the discussion of the Day. It has been established as a *decree* that *gives birth (leḏeṭ ḥōq)*. God has solemnly pronounced that the Day of his wrath shall intersect with human history. This decree, this fixed ordinance that cannot be altered, shall *give birth* to numerous phenomena. The violent wrenchings associated inevitably with the birth process shall characterize the coming of Yahweh's Day.

This Day shall give birth to the burning of the wrath of Yahweh which shall consume those who have broken covenant with him. This vivid description of God's anger occurs no fewer than 33 times in the OT.[4] The concept of a "burning wrath" *('ap ḥārôn)* in Scripture applies exclusively to God, with perhaps only one or two exceptions.

Collect yourselves together like stubble to be consumed in the burning wrath of Yahweh. Melt before the heat of his fierce indignation. With the

---

3. Cf. GKC, § 152y; Keil, p. 139.
4. J. M. P. Smith, p. 214.

suddenness of the arrival of the pangs of childbirth, his burning anger shall consume all those who are not properly prepared for his great Day.

Insight into the essence of this coming day is dramatized by the parallelism in this verse. This second phrase alters only one word of the first phrase, so that instead of reading "the *burning* of the wrath of Yahweh," it reads "the *Day* of the wrath of Yahweh." The Day of Yahweh is nothing more nor less than the occasion of the fierce burning of his wrath.

3 Against this solemn backdrop, the gently phrased admonition of the following verse takes on much deeper significance. The only adequate refuge from the consuming wrath of Yahweh may be found in Yahweh himself. So the prophet informs the people that they must *seek Yahweh.* The arrival of the Day of Yahweh will be a terrifying experience to all except those who previously have found their refuge in him.

Three times the prophet admonishes the people to *seek (baqqᵉšû).* Earlier, judgment had been declared because of a failure to seek the Lord (1:6). Now seeking is presented as a necessary response to the threat of judgment. This mild-sounding admonition implies a wholehearted pursuit after God. Genuine seeking involves persistence until success is realized. It inevitably includes an unshaken trust in that which is being sought.

Subsequently, in a letter filled with passionate concern for those who had been carried into captivity by Nebuchadrezzar, Jeremiah conveys the same message: "You will seek me and find me when you seek me with all your heart" (Jer. 29:13). The Lord's mercies do not fail; but neither do his requirements for seeking him.

The concentration of the prophet on this particular term indicates his understanding that the destinies of life hinge more immediately on the commitment of the heart rather than on a feverish round of activity. Concreteness of action inevitably will follow, as the specific admonition to *seek righteousness* indicates. But the primacy in determining destiny goes to the solemn committal of the heart.

Since this admonition is plural in form, it underscores the idea of a corporate and communal questing after Yahweh. As such, it may be regarded as a summons to worship. For only as the assembled community solemnly pledges the submission of its will to the will of Yahweh may a meaningful "seeking" of the Lord be achieved. As his binding word of the covenant is rehearsed, as the sacrifices of praise and adoration are offered, the Lord may be found.

This admonition to seek the Lord is addressed specifically to *all you meek of the land who do his justice.* Perhaps the prophet intended to offer some encouragement to those who had chosen the path of righteousness, that they might continue despite their many discouragements. Perhaps he sensed their need to be roused to greater ardor than they had manifested previously.[5]

Worth further exploration is the possibility that these *meek of the land* (*ʿanwê hāʾāreṣ*) addressed by Zephaniah may have been identical with the "people of the land" (*ʿam hāʾāreṣ*) who played a significant role in the political developments of Judah at this juncture in the nation's history.[6] The "people of the land" had been responsible for setting eight-year-old Josiah on the throne at the assassination of his father Amon (2 K. 21:23–24). Possibly they had contributed to the upbringing of this impressionable youth, and therefore had played a direct role in the early development of his piety. Perhaps these people particularly needed a word of encouragement to stir them up to continuation in pursuing the Lord.

Those admonished to seek the Lord also are designated as those *who do his justice (mišpāṭô pāʿālû)*. This *justice* may be understood as defined by his will as revealed in the ancient covenants of Israel. At an earlier time, the Lord had revealed to Abraham his intentions to destroy Sodom and Gomorrah because the patriarch had been chosen to direct his children by doing "righteousness and justice" (*ṣᵉdāqâ ûmišpāṭ*) (Gen. 18:19). Now in the context of a revelation concerning the coming judgment of the Lord on all the nations of the earth (Zeph. 2:4–15), the Lord speaks to the heirs of the covenant practicing *justice (mišpāṭ)* and admonishes them to seek *righteousness (ṣedeq)*.

In addition to seeking righteousness, this faithful remnant is to *seek meekness*. Zephaniah several times condemns pride and extols meekness (cf. 2:15; 3:4, 12). Only the grace of meekness gives adequate recognition to the reality of God. Even in the Lord himself may be found that meekness he demands of his creatures. When David sung praise to God at the defeat of all his enemies, he extolled the source of all his triumphs:

> You gave me your shield of victory
> and your meekness has made me great
> (*waʿᵃnōtᵉkā tarbēnî*). (2 Sam. 22:36)

How striking to find this same underscoring of meekness in himself even as Jesus claims for himself a knowledge restricted only to deity. No one could know the Father except the Son. Yet because of his humility even in his greatness, all may learn from him that he is meek and lowly in heart, and so find rest for their souls (Matt. 11:28–30).

---

5. Both of these suggestions are found in Calvin, pp. 235–36.
6. For the literature, see B. Oded's references in *Israelite and Judaean History*, ed. J. H. Hayes and J. M. Miller, OTL (Philadelphia: Westminster, 1977), pp. 452, 457–58.

Seek meekness as you contemplate the nature of God and his Son. Only in such a manner will rest for the soul be found.

The prophet rounds off his admonition on a rather tendentious note. He encourages his hearers, but he provides no blanket assurance of deliverance. The term *perhaps (ʾûlay)* employed by Zephaniah generally expresses an expectation that falls short of absolute assurance. Sarah hopes that "perhaps" she may obtain children through Hagar (Gen. 16:2). Hezekiah prays that "perhaps" the Lord will intervene to save Jerusalem (2 K. 19:4; cf. also Exod. 32:30; 1 K. 18:5, 27; Job 1:5).

Often commentators follow the lead of the LXX by its translation of this word as "in order that" *(hópōs).* Seek the Lord "in order that" you may be hid. This interpretation places the character of a confident assurance on the prophet's *perhaps.*[7] But the ambiguity of the text must prevail. Perhaps, that "ominous little word," must retain the sting of ambiguity.[8] For not the slightest possibility remains that the Day of Yahweh's wrath shall be turned back. It shall burn like fire among Israel, consuming all. The entirety of the universe shall be overturned. Even the meek of the earth must undergo this purging judgment.

But *perhaps.* Possibly in the coming of the Day, the meek may be hid. As the fire burns, the Lord's meek may be preserved.

Of course the purposes of the Lord shall be established. None of these attached to him by faith shall be lost. They already have passed through the judgment of God. Yet God's holiest people may undergo the severest of chastening judgments. They may suffer alongside the rebellious. The exile of Judah carried in the stream of its displacement the pious Jeremiah along with an unrepentant remnant.

This *perhaps* of the prophet still speaks. For who knows the seasons of the Lord's judgments? Who can say when he will determine that the grossness of iniquity has become full? Now is the time to seek the Lord with all your heart. You *may* be hid on the Day of his appearing.

---

7. Cf. also Calvin, pp. 238–39; Rudolph, p. 274.

8. Cf. Kapelrud, *Message of the Prophet Zephaniah,* p. 88. Kapelrud goes so far as to conclude that "not even righteousness and humility could make a man or a group sure of becoming part of the remnant." The question is not, however, whether a person may be part of the remnant, but whether the remnant will be spared the coming judgment of God. Zephaniah is using cosmic categories to describe the historical event of the approaching judgment of the nation. At the same time he anticipates the final calamity itself. The remnant certainly will be spared in the final judgment, but it was not clear at all that they would be spared the calamities associated with the historical destruction of Judah and Jerusalem.

B. SEEK NOW, FOR CONSIDER THE DEVASTATION OF NATIONS (2:4–15)

The second incentive for repentance is found in God's word of judgment on the nations.[1] A mixture of motivations for repentance in Judah arises from this announcement of the coming calamity for their various neighbors. On the one hand, the Lord's devastation of other nations should make his people realize that they shall not escape his righteous retribution. On the other hand, the blessings accruing to Judah from God's judgment on their neighbors should inspire them to walk in righteousness before him. From still a third perspective, participation in the blessings of the Lord by the Gentiles should move Israel to a jealousy that will lead them back to the only true and living God. All of these elements are found in the present section.

Zephaniah covers the four directions of the compass in his review of the nations to be judged. He announces the devastation of Philistia to the west (vv. 4–7), Moab and Ammon to the east (vv. 8–11), Cush to the south (v. 12), and Assyria to the north (vv. 13–15).

The particular reason for this order is not clear. Assyria may be reserved for last because of its role as the most formidable of Judah's contemporary enemies. A crisscross pattern moving to opposite extremes of the compass may be a part of the scheme, in a manner reminiscent of Amos's earlier oracular structure (Amos 1:3–2:16). Further rationale for Zephaniah's arrangement is difficult to determine.

1. To the West: Philistia (2:4–7)

4 *For*

> *Gaza will be abandoned,*
> *Ashkelon devastated;*
> *Ashdod—at noontime they will drive her out;*
> *Ekron will be uprooted.*

5 *Woe to the inhabitants of the territory of the sea,*
> *nation of the Cherethites.*

---

1. Rudolph, p. 279, asserts that 2:4–15 does not connect with 2:1–3. He judges that it is plain that the "for" which connects v. 4 with the previous section is secondary, since the presentation of coming judgment on the nations has nothing to do with the Day of Yahweh. It is true that the Day of Yahweh is not explicitly mentioned in this section, in contrast with the manner in which it permeated the first section. But it should be remembered that Israel was unique in its relationship as the covenant nation of Yahweh. Since Zephaniah is presenting the Day as the time of covenantal enforcement, quite naturally this theme would be more prominent when he was dealing with the Israelite nation.

> *The word of Yahweh is against you,*
> *Canaan, land of the Philistines:*

> *"I shall destroy you*
> *so that there is no inhabitant. "*
> 6 *The territory of the sea shall be*
> *pastures with caves for shepherds,*
> *with walled fences for flocks.*
> 7 *The territory shall be*
> *for the remnant of the house of Judah.*

> *Upon them they will find pasture;*
> *among the houses of Ashkelon*
> *in the evening they will lie down.*

> *For Yahweh their God will visit them,*
> *and will return their captivity.*

This section does not possess the extensive parallelism of expression found in previous portions of the book. But this word of judgment on the nations opens with a very interesting illustration of paranomasia. Words sounding alike are used to dramatize the effect of the oracle.

4 Of the four cities of Philistia mentioned in this verse, the first and the last are coupled with words of a similar sound. Commentators have puzzled over the failure of the second and third Philistine cities to be joined with verbs having a similar sound.[1] It may be that the four phrases are to be viewed in a chiastic arrangement, as presented in the translation. In this analysis some paranomasia may be seen in the names of the second and third Philistine cities, *Ash*kelon and *Ash*dod. The Hebrew could then be arranged to show the parallelism and paranomasia:

a *kî ʿazzâ ʿᵃzûḇâ ṯihyeh*
b *wᵉʾašqᵉlôn lišmāmâ*
b *ʿašdôḏ baṣṣohᵒrayim yᵉgorᵉšûhā*
a *wᵉʿeqrôn tēʿāqēr*

This particular analysis provides the most convincing arrangement of the words.

1. D. W. Thomas, "A Pun on the Name of Ashdod in Zephaniah 2:4," *Exp-Tim* 74 (1962) 63, argues that since Prov. 19:26 seems to support the idea that *šāḏaḏ* may have the sense of "to drive away," perhaps this connection may explain the usage of *gāraš* with Ashdod. If the connection was with the idea of "to drive away," however, it may be asked why Zephaniah would not have used *šāḏaḏ* instead of *gāraš*. Thereby both similarity of sound and sense would have been established.

The order in which the Philistine cities are mentioned begins with the southernmost city of *Gaza* and moves northward along the coast to *Ashkelon* and *Ashdod*. The inland city of *Ekron* is mentioned last. Gath, the fifth city of the Philistine pentapolis, may have been under the control of Judah at this point.[2]

Gaza, Ashkelon, and Ekron will be *abandoned, devastated,* and *uprooted*. The diversity of terminology, as well as the cumulative impact created, has the effect of underscoring the totality of the destruction envisioned.

The prophet breaks the cadence of his grammatical orderliness by his interjection concerning the third of the cities: *Ashdod—at noontime they will drive her out*. This reference to a *noontime* expulsion could be interpreted in a variety of ways. Since the noontime hour regularly introduces a siesta break in tropical countries, an attack under those circumstances might suggest the idea of suddenness and surprise.[3] Although this interpretation is possible, the context emphasizes the idea of utter devastation more than surprise in conquest.

Noontime expulsion could suggest that the conquest would be completed in half a day. Esarhaddon the Assyrian monarch boasts on one occasion: "Memphis, his royal city, in a half day, with mines, tunnels, assaults, I besieged, I captured, I destroyed, I devastated, I burned with fire."[4] This sudden collapse of the city would stand in dramatic contrast with the twenty-nine years in which Psammetichus I of Egypt besieged this same city of Ashdod from 640 to 611 B.C.[5] If the historical record of this assault is correct, it would have been in progress at the time of Zephaniah's prophecy.

However, the greater likelihood is that a *noontime* devastation refers to the absolute superiority of the forces driving out Ashdod. These invaders will have no need to take advantage of the element of surprise afforded by an early-morning or a late-evening attack. They simply shall storm the city and overwhelm it in broadest daylight.

Neither as single cities nor as united community shall Philistia withstand the assaults of Yahweh's judgments. The mighty God's authority

2. Suggested as a possibility by Rudolph, p. 279. Keil, p. 140, proposes that Gath was omitted simply because the parallelism of clauses allowed for the mention of only four cities.

3. Cf. Driver, p. 123, who compares this midday assault with the assassination of Ishbosheth while he was napping at noontime (2 Sam. 4:5).

4. D. D. Luckenbill, *Ancient Records of Assyria and Babylonia* (New York: Greenwood, 1927), 2:227, no. 580.

5. See J. M. P. Smith, p. 216.

over the nations of the world is not reduced simply because the territory of his own chosen community has shrunk as a consequence of his chastening judgments. His righteousness shall prevail among all the peoples of the earth, with or without a continuing "Israel."

5 This woe oracle pronounces doom on Philistine territory. First the area had been identified by reference to its noteworthy cities (v. 4). Now it is defined by reference to its position among the peoples of the world. They possess the *territory of the sea,* which represented the western extremity of the land promised to Israel (Exod. 23:31; Num. 13:29; 34:6; Deut. 3:27; Josh. 1:4). As *Cherethites,* they hail from Crete, having been assigned their coastal territory by the providential orderings of God (Ezek. 25:16; cf. Deut. 2:23; Amos 9:7; Jer. 47:4).[6]

As *Canaan,* their land had been promised to God's people.[7] As *Philistines,* they were the long-standing enemies of Israel, particularly at the time the nation was attempting to establish its monarchy. God originally had given Philistia its territory, assigning its bounds "according to the number of the sons of Israel" (Deut. 32:8–9). They possessed territory bordering Judah's so they might be of service to God's own nation. The wild beasts of the field must not overrun this land. But now the *word of Yahweh is against* them. This specific word comes to expression in a first person utterance of the prophet as he represents the Lord: *I shall destroy you so that there is no inhabitant.*

Will the people of Judah now learn from the Lord's treatment of their Philistine neighbors to the west? God had previously warned his people that if they did not remain faithful to him, he would *destroy (ʾāḇaḏ)* them just as he had *destroyed (ʾāḇaḏ)* the nations who inhabited the land before them (cf. Deut. 8:19–20). God would rejoice over his people to destroy *(ʾāḇaḏ)* them even as he had rejoiced over them to do them good (Deut. 28:63). The solemn oath of the covenant had been taken: God had called heaven and earth to witness that his people would be destroyed *(ʾāḇaḏ)* from the land if they should forsake him (Deut. 4:26; 30:18–19).

Now the prophetic decree goes forth. The Philistines will be driven from the land. Cannot Judah see in the Philistines' fate the awesome premonition of their own fate?

6 The prophet expands on his description of the effects of the devas-

---

6. Cf. KB, p. 458; BDB, pp. 504–5; J. M. P. Smith, p. 216; Rudolph, p. 280.

7. Rudolph, p. 277, adopts the conjectural emendation proposed in the 3rd ed. of *Biblia Hebraica* (1937): *ʾaḵnîʿēḵ,* "I will humble you." But despite his objections, "Canaan" is quite appropriately used to designate that portion of the coastal area which particularly concerned Judah.

tation of Philistia. Instead of continuing as a commercially favored territory through which the major trade route connecting three continents perpetually passed, this seacoast will be reduced to open pastureland, totally void of commercial enterprise. All the agelong endeavors of the Philistines to establish and maintain this flourishing commercial center will be in vain.

The problems associated with this verse are particularly difficult. The term *territory (ḥebel)* is normally masculine in gender, but here it occurs with a feminine form of the verb "to be" *(hāyᵉtâ)*. The phrase *pastures with caves for shepherds (nᵉwōt kᵉrōt rōʿîm)* has been subjected to numerous emendations.[8] The term *caves (kᵉrōt)* is found only here in the OT.

The grammatical relationship among the various words is difficult. But in the end, the problems associated with the text as maintained by the Massoretes are less than those created by the numerous, bewildering, and hypothetical substitutions. As Kapelrud has indicated: "The good state of the unit, its regular metre, its choice of words and its whole scope give strong evidence that we have here the original words of a prophet."[9]

7 Now a new perspective on the judgment of Philistia is introduced. A new motivation for repentance on the part of the nation of Judah also emerges. For the first time the prophet mentions explicitly the expectation that a *remnant* shall remain. After the judgment of God has passed through, some community shall be left.

To this remnant shall be granted the full possession of the land of promise, including the *territory* of the Philistines. The blessing of the law book of Deuteronomy shall be renewed, for they shall dwell in houses they had not built. As a flock under the protection of the Almighty, *among the houses of Ashkelon in the evening they will lie down*. Neither wild beasts nor marauding bands shall threaten their security.

---

8. *nᵉwōt* is a plural construct of "pasture" *(nāweh)*. *kᵉrōt* may be either a plural construct of "cave" *(kārâ)* or an infinitive construct of "to dig" *(kārâ)*. Keil, p. 141, renders "pastures of the excavations of shepherds," rejecting the possibility that *kᵉrōt* could be a noun form, and favoring the infinitive construction. The LXX, reflected basically in the NIV, renders "and Crete shall become a habitation for shepherds and a fold for flocks," reading *kᵉrōt* as a reference in singular form to the "Cherethites" *(kᵉrētîm)* that had been mentioned in the previous verse. This interpretation involves a reversal of the original word order. Driver, p. 124, says "the text cannot be correct." J. M. P. Smith, p. 218, suggests that "caves" *(kᵉrōt)* is a "corrupt dittograph" of the immediately preceding word *(nᵉwōt)*. By omitting this supposed corruption, the simple reading "pastures of shepherds" is obtained. John S. Kselman, "A Note on Jeremiah 19:10 and Zephaniah 2:6, 7," *CBQ* 32 (1970) 581 n.13, analyzes *kᵉrōt* as a feminine by-form of *kārîm*, "hollows."

9. Kapelrud, *Message of the Prophet Zephaniah*, pp. 34–35.

The prophet does not further identify this remnant that shall survive the devastating judgment of God. Apparently they are the "humble" that have "sought the Lord" as described earlier (cf. 2:3).

The meek shall inherit the earth (cf. Matt. 5:5). This possession shall come as a gift of the Lord, even as the original possession of the land was a precious grant. Although many sad calamities would have to be undergone before the territory of Philistia would be possessed, the assurance of the Lord's word must have provided significant encouragement for the "humble" to "seek humility" (Zeph. 2:3).

Earlier the prophet had spoken of the "visitation" of God in terms of his coming judgment (1:8–9). Now he speaks of "visitation" in terms of future salvation. When the Lord moves into action on behalf of his people, he shall revive lost blessings.

The last phrase of this verse may be read either *return their captivity (šāḇ šeḇîṯām)* or "restore their fortunes" *(šāḇ šeḇûṯām).*[10] This concept of restoration is rooted in the legislation of the deuteronomic law book. The code of the covenant had indicated that after all the blessings and the curses of the covenant had come to pass, if the nation would return to the Lord, he would return their captivity (Deut. 30:1–3). As judgment would come in fulfillment of the curses of the covenant, so restoration would come in fulfillment of the conditions of the covenant. Judah's neighbor to the west would be devastated without hope. But for God's people restoration would arise after devastation.

2. To the East: Moab and Ammon (2:8–11)

8 *I have heard*
> *the reproach of Moab,*
> *and the taunts of the sons of Ammon,*

> *in which*
>> a *they have reproached*
>> b *my people,*
>> a *and magnified themselves*
>> b *against their border.*

9 *Therefore as I live, declares Yahweh of hosts, God of Israel:*
>> a *Moab*
>> b *will be*

---

10. J. M. P. Smith, p. 220, favors "turn their captivity." For a fuller discussion, see Keil, p. 142; J. M. P. Smith, p. 224. The LXX reads *apéstrepse tén aichmalōsían autōn,* "he shall turn away their captivity." Note also Ps. 68:20 (Eng. 19); Jer. 15:2; Eph. 4:8; Rev. 13:10.

  c *as Sodom,*
 a *and the sons of Ammon*
  c *as Gomorrah—*
      d *a possession*[1] *of nettles,*[2]
      d *a pit of salt,*
      d *a desolation forever.*

 a *The remnant of my people*
 b *will plunder them,*
 a *that which remains of my nation*
 b *will inherit them.*
10 *This (destiny) shall be theirs*
   in place of their pride.
      For they have reproached and magnified themselves
      against the people of Yahweh of hosts.
11 *Yahweh will be fearful among them,*
   for he will make lean all the gods of the earth.
      They shall worship him,
         every man from his own place,
         (even) all the islands of the nations.

This second pronouncement of judgment on neighboring nations introduces several new perspectives. Now the prophet speaks against blood-relatives of Israel instead of aliens set against Israel. In this denunciation, reasons for the coming judgment are delineated, in contrast with the absence of specification of crimes in the first judgment oracle. The remnant theme is enlarged so that God's preserved people shall participate actively in the spoiling of their enemies. Finally, the message now sounds forth for the first time in Zephaniah that worship of the living God shall extend to the uttermost extremities of the earth.

The distinctives involved in this second oracle of judgment broaden

---

1. The term *mimšaq* occurs only here in the OT, and thus its precise meaning is uncertain. J. M. P. Smith, p. 227, finds no light from the versions or cognates. The LXX translates "and *Damascus* shall be left as a heap on the threshing floor"; cf. Gen. 15:2, where Abraham speaks of *ben-mešeq bêtî,* "The son-of-possession-of my house," i.e., the main possessor of my house, who is "Eliezer of Damascus" *(hû' dammešeq 'ĕlî'ezer).* BDB, p. 606, judges the text of Zeph. 2:9 to be probably corrupt and the word *mimšaq* to be "very dubious"; but such a conclusion only dismisses the problem rather than solving it. The context here and in Gen. 15:2 supports the idea of "possession."

2. *ḥārûl* refers to a weed associated with desolate areas; cf. Job 30:7; Prov. 24:31.

the horizons of expectation concerning the coming of God. Salvation begins to play a role as significant as devastation.

8–9   This oracle begins in the first person. Yahweh himself declares the judgment that will fall on Moab and Ammon. Much of the phraseology in these verses echoes the narrative of the destruction of the very valley in which Lot the father of the Moabites and Ammonites formerly dwelt. God once more has *heard* of gross sins deserving a radical judgmental intervention (cf. Gen. 18:20–21). He has not become deaf to outcries of injustice and oppression in the world.

8   This time the transgressors are the inhabitants of *Moab* and *Ammon.* Both these nations were blood-relatives of Israel, descendants of Lot's incestuous acts committed in a cave with his two daughters (cf. Gen. 19:30–38). Both nations in Zephaniah's day resided near the rim of that area which had been consumed by the conflagration sent on Sodom and Gomorrah.

Both the Moabites and the Ammonites had a long history of acrid animosity against the people of God. Moab's king Balak hired Balaam to curse a defenseless Israel as they came out of Egypt (Num. 22:3). He received in return only the prophetic assurance that a star and a scepter would rise out of Israel which would crush his own forehead (24:17). This ancient warning now receives prophetic reinforcement by the words of Zephaniah.

Ammon relentlessly pursued the goal of shaming Israel. Nahash the Ammonite king ignored every concession by the inhabitants of Jabesh-gilead, pressing on with his intent to humiliate the people of God (1 Sam. 11:1–2). He would have nothing less than the crude pleasure of blinding the right eye of every inhabitant of the Israelite city. Hanun, son and successor to Nahash, pursued this same tradition. He humiliated David's messengers of compassion by shaving half their beards and baring their buttocks (2 Sam. 10:1–4). Again, Tobiah the Ammonite found his chief pleasure in mocking Nehemiah's wall building; it was to him a flimsy farce that even a fox would break down (Neh. 4:3; cf. 2:10, 19; 4:7). Still further, Baalis the king of Ammon could not be satisfied with the utter ruin of Judah effected by Nebuchadrezzar. He commissioned Ishmael to assassinate Gedaliah the provisional governor, thus bringing even greater havoc to a people already devastated (Jer. 40:14).

Rather ironical is the fact that a people born of incest should be so determined to humiliate their neighboring relatives. This kind of consistent insensitivity cuts deeply into the hearts of God's people. As Calvin rightly observes: "There is not so much bitterness in a hundred deaths as in one reproach, especially when the wicked licentiously triumph, and do this with the applauding consent of the whole world; for then all difference between good and evil is confounded, and good conscience is as it were buried."[3]

Reproach for the righteous seems unavoidable. The psalmist is led almost to despair over his sufferings at the hands of the wicked. A band of evil men has encircled him. They have pierced his hands and feet (Ps. 22:17 [Eng. 16]). They gloat over him, dividing his garments among them, casting lots for his clothing (vv. 18–19 [Eng. 17–18]). He is scorned by men, mocked by all who see him (vv. 7–8 [Eng. 6–7]). "Let the Lord deliver him, since he delights in him," they chant (v. 9 [Eng. 8]).

In the minds of the Gospel writers, something more than coincidence brought Jesus to a similar point of public mockery and reproach, so that even his crucified companions taunted him (Matt. 27:44; cf. vv. 35, 39, 46, 48). The reproaches of those that reproached the Lord himself fell on him (Ps. 69:10 [Eng. 9]; cf. Rom. 15:3). It was this reproach that broke his heart (Ps. 69:21 [Eng. 20]).

This scorn for God's own people arises out of the exaggerated self-esteem and pride exemplified in the attitude of the Moabites and Ammonites. They have *magnified themselves* against the border of Israel. Both Isaiah and Jeremiah note the broadly reputed conceit of Moab (Isa. 16:6; Jer. 48:29–30). This arrogance has led these nations to violate the providential establishment of national boundaries for Israel by intruding on *their border*. In pursuing its rapacious conquests, Ammon has been guilty of "ripping open the pregnant women of Gilead in order to extend his borders" (Amos 1:13). Satanically attacking simultaneously the divine promise to Israel concerning their land and their seed, Ammon attempts to devour the inheriting seed of Israel in order to possess their land (cf. Gen. 3:15; John 8:44). The heinousness of this sin is increased by Israel's care over the centuries not to violate Ammon's borders, in accord with specific divine command (Deut. 2:19; Judg. 11:14–28).

9 But even as God had sworn that all nations in Abraham would be blessed, so now he swears that Moab and Ammon, having made themselves Israel's enemies, shall be cursed. When this precise formula *as I live (hay-°ānî)* is taken into the mouth of the Lord, it assumes a particularly ominous significance. Of the approximately twenty times in which it appears in the OT, it always involves the invoking of divine curses, with two possible exceptions (Isa. 49:18; Ezek. 33:11). So far as existence locates in God, so far goes the certainty of the utter devastation of Moab and Ammon.

So far as existence locates in God! He is the source of all life. Nothing exists apart from him.

---

3. Calvin, p. 246.

This unchanging God, *Yahweh of hosts,* delights to identify himself as *God of Israel.* Although his own nation will be subjected to a most devastating judgment, he nonetheless is their God.

The living Lord, Yahweh of hosts, God of Israel, swears that *Moab will be as Sodom, and the sons of Ammon as Gomorrah.* The tradition of this holocaust must have lived on vividly among the Moabites and Ammonites, since they lived on the rim of the Dead Sea, and had opportunity to see constantly the effects of God's judgment on Sodom and Gomorrah. Their origins traced back over twelve hundred years to this past event of divine judgment. All their intervening generations had lived within the vicinity of this awesome calamity.

Now their future fate, settled irreversibly by divine oath, is declared to be the same as the utter destruction of those cities. Their whole territory will become just as Sodom and Gomorrah once had been characterized in the deuteronomic law: "a burning waste of salt and sulfer—nothing planted, nothing sprouting, no vegetation growing on it" (Deut. 29:22 [Eng. 23]). Just like Sodom and Gomorrah, they shall be *a possession of nettles, a pit of salt, a desolation forever.*

Striking is the fact that the very land which is left a scoured desolation will become the possession of the remnant of Judah. Why would Judah want such a possession? Some resolution of this tension might be achieved by suggesting that the *people* of Moab and Ammon are spared in distinction from the *land,* which is abandoned in its sterility.[4] But more likely the prophet simply has mixed his imagery. For if a destruction along the proportions experienced by Sodom and Gomorrah had taken place, neither people nor possessions would be left to pillage.

Now the prophet introduces a new perspective on the future for the remnant of his people. At last the patience of Abraham shall be rewarded. As a stupendous act of faith, he had surrendered his claim on the choicest portion of the land specifically promised him by the Lord (Gen. 13:8–17). But now the land claimed by Lot's descendants shall revert to its rightful heir.

An earlier prophet in Judah had assessed the depravity of God's own people by noting:

> Unless the Lord Almighty
>   had left us some survivors,
> *we* would have become like Sodom,
>   *we* would have been like Gomorrah. (Isa. 1:9)

---

4. Cf. J. M. P. Smith, p. 227.

Unless the sovereign and undeserved grace of God had intervened, the fate of the entirety of Judah's populace would have been no different than the fate of Moab and Ammon.

The devastating judgments of God manifested in history and prophecy do not end with the administration of the old covenant. For the true purpose of God in the destruction of the wicked cities of Sodom and Gomorrah is fully realized only as it is seen as mirroring the final reality of divine judgment. It shall be more tolerable in that Day for the inhabitants of Sodom and Gomorrah than for those who reject the emissaries of the Christ (Matt. 10:15). Only the undeserved grace of God today preserves a remnant of Jews and Gentiles from the fate of Sodom and Gomorrah (Rom. 9:29–33). Not temporal but eternal fire shall descend on all those who continue in their ungodly ways (Jude 7; cf. 2 Pet. 2:6). Let not the most religious arrogantly suppose they cannot be threatened with such terrors, for the last "Sodom" to be mentioned in the Bible is none other than the city in which the Lord was crucified (Rev. 11:8).

10   Now the prophetic pronouncement shifts from having God himself speak in the first person to having the prophet speak about the Lord in the third person. The verse emphasizes the breaking of the pride that has characterized Moab and Ammon for so many centuries.

Pride as a distinctive aspect of Moab's reputation is underscored by the prophet Isaiah:

> *We have heard* of Moab's pride—
>> her overweening pride and conceit,
>> her pride and her insolence—
> but her boasts are empty. (Isa. 16:6)

Jeremiah repeats this same theme, possibly by alluding to the words of Isaiah:

> *We have heard* of Moab's pride—
>> her overweening pride and conceit,
>> her pride and her arrogance,
> and the haughtiness of her heart. (Jer. 48:29)

This same widespread reputation is reflected in Zephaniah's similar *I have heard* (v. 8). Moab had become internationally repugnant for her arrogance.

Isaiah the prophet had indicated that within three years of his prophecy Moab would be humbled for her arrogance (Isa. 16:13–14). But apparently this earlier chastening by the Lord had not proven effective in breaking the nation's insolence in despising the people of the Lord, making Israel the object of their ridicule, treating Israel as though she had been caught among thieves, shaking her head in scorn every time she spoke of Israel (Jer. 48:27).

Will God's people of Zephaniah's day hear the message of the prophet? If such utter devastation should fall on Moab and Ammon for their sin of pride, can Judah expect to escape the Lord's judgments apart from obeying the prophet's admonition to "seek humility" (v. 3)? Only among the meek of the earth would any hope of survival be found. This remnant must earnestly quest for even greater meekness. Their worth was no more than the stubble which would be consumed by a single spark from the fire of God's wrath (v. 2). Let them assemble themselves with such a frame of mind. Then, "perhaps" they would be hid in the coming Day of God's wrath.

With all the warnings emblazoned in the prophetic records of the past, modern people fail to see the significance of humility in survival before God. Scorn and contempt continue to be poured on all who possess a "meek and quiet spirit," which is "in the sight of God of great price" (1 Pet. 3:4).

In presenting himself as the Messiah sent of God, Jesus spoke of the alternatives his presence placed before all people. Either they must break themselves before him, or they would be broken. Either they must fall on the rock, smashing the pride and self-conceit within them, or that same rock would fall on them, grinding them to pieces (cf. Matt. 21:44).

11 Now the prophet touches on the source of the problem in the lives of these neighbors to the east of Judah. Ultimately a religious problem lies at the root of Moab's and Ammon's pride.

The announcement that *Yahweh will be fearful* [or awesome, *nôrā'*] *among them* suggests the occasion of a theophany. For the very essence of God is captured in this concept of awesomeness. His greatness so far exceeds human imagination that the manifestation of his true nature can only inspire fear and awe.

In assuring Israel originally of his intention to make them possessors of the nations, the Lord admonished them not to fear the other nations, for he was a "great and fearful God" *('ēl gāḏôl wᵉnôrā')* who would drive them out before his people (Deut. 7:21). They were to fear only him, for as possessor of heaven and earth he was God of Gods and Lord of Lords, the great God, "the mighty and the fearful" (*haggibbōr wᵉhannôrā'*—Deut. 10:17).

Now as the Lord renews his commitment to bring their national neighbors to the point of submission, he reiterates the awesome character of his nature. The humbling of the nations will be accomplished by the Lord's manifestation of his fearful essence among them.[5]

---

5. Worth noting is the fact that this same characterization of God is found in two prophets describing God's self-manifestation on the Day of Yahweh (Joel 2:11; 3:4 [Eng. 2:31]; Mal. 3:23 [Eng. 4:5]).

In this manifestation, the Lord will *make lean [rāzâ] all the gods of the earth*. Incapable of making the territory God has devastated ever to produce again, these gods of the Moabites and Ammonites shall "starve to death." The land will produce nothing which might be offered to the idolatrous gods. They will wither to nothing for lack of attention.

When the gods of the nations are humbled, the peoples of the earth will have no choice. *They shall worship him, every man from his own place.*

Now a remarkable picture emerges. After the devastation of both Judah and the surrounding nations, a turning in adoration to the living God occurs. Earlier the prophet had indicated that a "remnant" would be preserved from his people who would possess the territory of the nations (vv. 7, 9). But now he introduces a new concept. The peoples of the world also shall acknowledge the supremacy of Yahweh. Wherever they are found, they shall offer their sacrifices to the Lord.

Most striking is the concept that the nations of the world will *worship* the Lord in their own locale.[6] The more common imagery of the prophets had depicted a pilgrimage of the nations to Jerusalem (cf. Isa. 2:3; 66:23). But now Zephaniah sees the worship of the true God spreading outward to the ends of the earth. Every nation shall become sacred as a center for the worship of the Lord.

Zephaniah was not the first to suggest this radical perspective on the worship of Israel's God by the nations. Isaiah earlier had foreseen not only the flow of the nations to Jerusalem; he also described a day in which there would be "an altar to the Lord in the heart of Egypt" (Isa. 19:19, 21). The Assyrians would pass through Israel to worship Yahweh in Egypt, and the Egyptians would pass through Israel to worship Yahweh in Assyria (Isa. 19:23).

Neither would Zephaniah be the last to suggest this perspective on the coming Day. Malachi spoke of the Day in which incense and pure offerings would be consecrated to the Lord in every place. From the rising of the sun to its setting he would be adored (Mal. 1:11).

Zephaniah's distinctive imagery of each person worshiping in his own place anticipates a central aspect of the worship perspective provided by Jesus. No longer would the debate rage as to whether the Lord was to be worshiped in Samaria or Jerusalem. Wherever the Spirit and the truth were found, people would worship the living God (John 4:21–23).

The uttermost extremities of the earth were to participate in this extension of genuine worship. *all the islands of the nations (kōl 'îyê haggôyim)* refers to the most distant habitations of people on the earth. Originally these

---

6. This interpretation is disputed in Keil, p. 145. But cf. Rudolph, p. 282.

territories were populated by the seed of Japheth (Gen. 10:5). Subsequently, Tubal, Javan, and Tarshish, all descendants of Japheth, are specifically marked as the inhabitants of the "islands of the nations" who shall worship Yahweh (Isa. 66:19).[7]

So Zephaniah joins the grand prophetic tradition in announcing the coming day in which God's judgment on the nations will have its final issue in their adoration of the true and living God. These expectations find their fulfillment currently when the gospel of Christ is proclaimed among the most distant island populations. For now the glorious day has come in which the sun never sets on the worshipers of the true God.

Yet more shall come in fulfillment of these words. For we do not now see with absoluteness either the devastation of the wicked or the purification of worship.

3. To the South: Cush (2:12)

> 12 *Also you, O Cushites—*
> *slain of my sword*
> *are they!*

Several features of this oracle set it apart in this series of judgment pronouncements. The subject is addressed as *Cush* rather than the more formidable "Egypt," as might have been expected if a representative foe to the south of Judah were to be designated. The extremely abrupt alternation of persons is also distinctive. *you* Cushites instantly become *they* who are to be slain.

Most striking is the disproportionate brevity of the oracle in comparison with the other three in this series. Why should the prophet offer so little detail regarding the devastation of Cush? Why should he not elaborate on the devastation of land as well as people?

The abrupt change of person in this brief oracle may function as an intentional literary device. The swift sword of the executioner has found its victim immediately upon the Lord's uttering the name of the Cushites: *And you, O Cushites—slain of my sword are they!* The language also underscores the direct involvement of the Lord himself in bringing about this judgment. The Lord's own personal sword, wielded by his own hand, strikes the deathblow for the Cushites.

---

7. Of the 38 times in which the "distant islands" are mentioned in the OT, 17 appear in Isaiah. These occurrences primarily describe the worship of the true God by the most distant heathen. It is unnecessary to attribute this concept of a worldwide worship of Yahweh to a later writer (as Driver, p. 127, does).

This sword of the Lord makes its awesome presence known at many points in Scripture. In concluding the covenant renewal ceremony with Israel in the plains of Moab, Moses the prophet had spoken as the mouth of God:

> I lift my hand to heaven and declare:
> As surely as I live forever,
>   when I sharpen my flashing sword
>   and my hand grasps it in judgment,
>   I will take vengeance on my adversaries
>   and repay those who hate me.
>   I will make my arrows drunk with blood,
>   while my sword devours flesh—
>   the blood of the slain and the captives,
>   the heads of the enemy leaders. (Deut. 32:40–42)

Bound by the oath of the covenant, the Lord must employ his *sword* to slay all the wicked. This sword of the Lord appears readied in the hand of the captain of the Lord's host as Joshua contemplates his attack on Jericho (Josh. 5:13). It became the central feature of Gideon's battle cry against the Midianites (Judg. 7:20). In the apocalyptic visions of the Revelation of John, the one whose name is the Word of God brandishes a sharp double-edged sword that strikes the nations (Rev. 1:16; 2:12, 16; 19:15, 21). This eschatological sword joins the "iron scepter" of the messianic king as an instrument for subduing the nations (Rev. 19:15; cf. Ps. 2:9).

If the avenging sword of the covenant reaches down to Cush, Israel's southernmost enemy, can Judah expect to escape? Will the specter of the chastening hand of the Lord lifted against other nations awaken God's own people to the judgmental terrors awaiting an unrepentant nation? The Israel of Zephaniah's day must remember that once in David's day the sword of the Lord had been turned against his own beloved Jerusalem (2 Sam. 24:16–17). Should they not now be awakened to see the potential threat against them in that awesome sword of the Lord stretched against the Cushites?

4. To the North: Assyria (2:13–15)

13   *a*   *Let him stretch out his hand*
      b   *against the north,*
  a   *let him destroy*
      b   *Assyria;*
  a   *let him set*
      b   *Nineveh*
         c   *for destruction,*

      c dry as a desert.
14 *a There shall lie down*
      b in her midst
        c herds,
        c every wild beast[1] constituting a nation.

        c Also the vulture
        c as well as the screech owl[2]
      b among her decorative columns
  a shall roost.

      a A voice cooing
      b in the window,
      a destruction
      b in the doorway;
        for her cedarwork is laid bare.
15 *This (is)*
      the ecstatic city,
      the one living in security;
      the one saying in her heart:
      "I[3] alone am,
        and there is no[4] other."

Astounding![5]
She exists for desolation,
  a dwelling place for the wild beast.

1. The word *ḥaytô* has the old genitive case ending, as does the same word in Gen. 1:24 (cf. GKC, § 90a; BDB, p. 312). The unusual "every beast of a *nation*" appears in the LXX as "every beast of the *earth*" *(thēría tēs gēs)*. Driver, p. 128, says the text cannot be in order.

2. Kapelrud, *Message of the Prophet Zephaniah,* p. 60, regards the *qā'aṭ* as a "vulture" and the *qippōd* as probably an owl. Other suggestions include pelican and porcupine (Driver, p. 129) and pelican and hedgehog (Keil, p. 147). BDB, p. 891, suggests that *qippōd* is porcupine, in the light of the possible derivation of the word from the verb *qāpaḏ,* "roll together."

3. E. Stauffer in *TDNT,* 2:343, notes that the "I"-style "is solidly established in divine proclamations in the ancient East."

4. The term *'epes* is essentially a poetic equivalent of *'ên,* suggesting the idea of nonexistence (BDB, p. 67; GKC, § 152s). The termination *î* here is probably paragogic (but cf. Keil, p. 148, who regards the ending as a sign of the first person pronoun). Here the LXX has *Egō eimi, kaí ouk éstin met' emé éti:* "I am, and there is no other with me." *'epes* is used to declare the unique self-existence of Yahweh in Isa. 45:6, 14; 46:9.

5. The term *'êk* derives from Heb. *'êkâ,* "How," and as an interjection expresses the idea of "How could it be!," in terms of joy, surprise, or lament.

Everyone who passes her
    will hiss
    and dismiss her
        with a wave of the hand.

The last of Israel's neighbors to have the prophetic pronouncement of doom declared over them is Assyria, Judah's most threatening enemy. This nation's power had been weakened by the days of Josiah. But it still maintained resources sufficient to level Judah at any moment.

13 The prophet begins by narrowing the object of judgment from the north country in general to the city of Nineveh in particular. *Let him stretch out . . . let him destroy . . . let him set.* Each of the verbal forms expresses a wish of the prophet *(weyēṭ . . . wîʾabbēḏ . . . weyāśēm).* Now the desire of God's spokesman unites with the decree of the Lord. This more specific personal involvement may arise from the extent of the brutality witnessed by the prophet himself that habitually marked the conquests of the Assyrians.

Almost unbelievable is the description of desolation which is to characterize the cultural metropolis of *Nineveh.* This city shall be *dry as a desert.* The greatest city of an era shall have no remnant to mark its existence. So in about 401 B.C. Xenophon passed the site of Nineveh and found not a trace of its existence in the shifting desert sands.[6] The judgment of the prophet found a most literal fulfillment.

14 The utter finality with which Nineveh shall be destroyed is seen in the inhabitants that shall move in to take over the territory. The sophisticated metropolis shall be inhabited by *herds* and *every wild beast constituting a nation.* Joel designates the locusts invading Israel as a "nation" *(gôy),* alluding in part to their rigidity in organization (Joel 1:6; cf. 2:7–8). Zephaniah describes these sundry beasts that have overrun the site of Nineveh in similar fashion. Although representing the wide divergence found among the various beasts of creation, they are knit together as an organized community that is determined to resist expulsion.

The entire imagery depicts a reversal of creation's order. Humanity originally had been given the responsibility for exercising dominion over the whole of creation. But now the creation seizes power from the greatest of human empires and transforms it into a bestial wilderness. Organized chaos has supplanted civilization.

Some significant effort has been spent attempting to determine the

---

6. Cf. Xenophon, *Anabasis* 3.4.8–12.

specific creatures inhabiting the decorated capitals on the columns left standing after the city's destruction. John Calvin's restraint on the subject is commendable: "As to their various kinds, I make no laborious research; for it is enough to know the prophet's design."[7]

vulture. The first-named creature is a bird of some kind, since the designation occurs in two other passages in a list of birds (Lev. 11:18; Deut. 14:17). More significant is the fact that each of these lists names those birds designated unclean. The ceremonially defiled shall make their residence in the ruins of Nineveh.

Both the windows and the doorways of the ruins shall possess signs of their desertion. Very frequently a *doorway* or threshhold *(sap)* is noted as having keepers or guards to maintain it night and day (2 K. 12:9; 22:4; 23:4; 1 Chr. 9:19; Esth. 2:21; 6:2; Jer. 35:4). But now the rubble bars the doorway. The entire community has fallen into total neglect.

cedarwork is generally a sign of luxuriant living. David and Solomon lived in palaces of cedar (2 Sam. 7:2, 7; 1 K. 5:6, 8), and Jehoahaz (Shallum), son of Josiah, was condemned for squandering resources on the building of a new cedar palace while ignoring the religious and social crises of his day (Jer. 22:14–16). But all such luxuries shall be disregarded in the devastation of Nineveh. Beautiful cedar workmanship will be neglectfully exposed to the ruining forces of the elements.

15 Three features characterize Nineveh before its destruction: ecstasy, security, and self-sufficiency. A city rejoices when everyone prospers, when the economy is good, when the arts flourish, and the populace has time for leisure. No overburdening sense of responsibility and care oppresses the people.

Assyria in the height of its glory revelled in these experiences of prosperity. She suffered no external threats from her neighbors. Plundering the wealth of all the nations, she lived in pleasure and prosperity.

All this prosperity led Nineveh to a single conclusion. She assumed her own self-sufficiency. Even the divine attribute of self-existence she attributed to herself: *I alone am, and there is no other.* The Assyrian capital blasphemously assumed to herself all the prerogatives belonging only to God. The city owed her existence to no one, and needed no one to maintain her.

But "God cannot endure the presumption of men, when inflated by their own greatness and power. . . ."[8] So Assyria only seals its own fate by

7. Calvin, p. 255.
8. Calvin, p. 257.

313

its blasphemous assertion of its own deity. *Astounding!* How can it be? Mocking her own sense of self-sufficiency, the Lord affirms that her actual *raison d'être* is only for *desolation*.

Two gestures reflect the scorn heaped on this once-glorious city. A *hiss* from the mouth and a *wave of the hand* express contempt for the humiliated heap that once was a mighty city. Not always is such scorn justified. Sometimes the faithful servant of God witnessed the merciless mockery of the godly. All who saw him jeered, tossing the head and sneering (Ps. 22:8 [Eng. 7]). All those who passed by the crucified King of the Jews blasphemed him, shaking their heads in scorn (Matt. 27:39). But Assyria's scorn was deserved. Because this nation exalted itself to the highest heaven, it must be brought to the lowest hell.

Conclusion

So this second major section of the prophecy shows the Lord's involvement with all the nations of the earth. Wherever unrighteousness is found, it shall be punished. The announcement of judgment on the nations also functions to summon Judah to repentance. Little time remains before the arrival of the Day of Yahweh. Judah must seek the Lord. Humility may make it possible for them to be hid on the Day of Yahweh's wrath. Let them consider the Lord's dealings with their national neighbors. Let them be moved by fear and by jealousy to turn to the Lord. The Day cannot be turned back. But they may be among that remnant that shall be saved for the enjoyment of the plundered nations.

III. GOD RECONSTITUTES HIS PEOPLE WITH THE ARRIVAL OF THAT GREAT DAY (3:1–20)

After having dealt with Philistia, Moab, Ammon, Cush, and Assyria, the prophet now focuses on Jerusalem (3:1–8). In the midst of his denunciation, he recalls the judgments the Lord has inflicted on other nations (v. 6), which should remind his hearers of the word of judgment just spoken against their neighbors in every direction (2:4–15).

This coming judgment on the rebellious city of Jerusalem shall occur in association with the arrival of *the Day* (3:8). The Day of Yahweh will bring not only destruction for the unrepentant, but purification of the remnant (vv. 9–13). This glad occurrence will occasion mutual rejoicing among God and his people (vv. 14–20).

A. GOD WILL FINALLY JUDGE THE REBELLIOUS (3:1–8)

1 *Woe*

    for the rebellious,[1]
    the polluted,
    the oppressing city.

2 *a* *She has not hearkened*
    b *to the Voice;*
  a *she has not accepted*
    b *correction.*

  a *In Yahweh*
    b *she has not trusted;*
  a *to her God*
    b *she has not drawn near.*

3 *a* *Her princes in her midst*
    b *(are) roaring lions;*
  a *her judges*
    b *evening wolves;*
     they leave no gnawing for the morning.

4 *a* *Her prophets*
    b *(are) reckless,*[2]
    b *men of deception;*
  a *her priests*
    b *have profaned the holy place;*
    b *they have done violence to the torah.*

5 *Yahweh is righteous*

    in her midst;
  he will never do evil.
    Morning by morning he will bring his justice to light;
    he shall never fail.
     But the evil know no shame.

6 *I have cut off*

    nations;
    their corner towers are destroyed.
  I have devastated
    their streets

1. The term *mōr^e'â* apparently derives from the verb *mārâ,* "to rebel," and demonstrates the manner in which the final ' sometimes replaces the final *h.* Cf. GKC, § 75rr. The LXX, understanding the root meanings of the words differently, translates "glorious and ransomed" *(epiphanés kaí apolelytrómenē).*

2. The term *pāḥaz* means essentially to be "unrestrained" or "insolent." Cf. BDB, p. 808; KB, pp. 757–58.

> so no one passes by;
> their cities are laid waste[3]
> so no one dwells there.[4]

7 I said:

> Surely she will fear me,
> she will receive correction
> so her refuge will not be cut off,
> (because of) all the punishment I have inflicted on her.[5]
> But alas!
> They rose early,
> they acted corruptly
> in all their doings.

8 Therefore:

> Wait for me,
> declares Yahweh,
> for the Day when I rise to testify.
>
> For my determination (is)
> a   to gather
> b   nations,
> a   to assemble
> b   kingdoms,
> to pour out on them

3. *ṣādâ* is a *hapax legomenon* in the OT, and apparently means "to lay waste." Cf. BDB, p. 841.

4. J. M. P. Smith, p. 242, rejects the authenticity of v. 6 because of its message concerning foreign matters: "Statements concerning the nations are wholly alien to his context, which is concerned solely with the relations between Yahweh and Judah." The rather arbitrary use of such subjective criteria in determining authenticity is seen by a further statement in the same paragraph in which he defends the inclusion of "streets" even though he acknowledges some logic to the argument that "streets" would hardly be mentioned before "towns": "The prophets were not fettered by logical strait-jackets."

5. The relation of the phrase *kōl ʾašer-pāqaḏtî ʿāleyhā*, lit., "all I have inflicted on her," to the rest of the sentence is difficult. This infliction probably is not to be understood as additional punishment beyond the chastening described earlier in the verse. The verb *pāqaḏtî* is a first person perfect form, and has no *waw* consecutive. It therefore lacks the construct connection with the imperfect form of the preceding verb. Keil, p. 153, following Ewald, suggests that *kōl* functions as an "accusative of manner." But the AV reads "howsoever I punished them," meaning that despite all the Lord's punishments, they shall not be cut off completely. Although possessing its own difficulties, the best construction understands this phrase to be explanatory of the expectation voiced in the first portion of the verse: "Surely . . . her refuge will not be cut off . . . (*as a consequence of*) all the punishment I have inflicted on her."

> *my fury—*
> *all my burning wrath.*
> *For in the fire of my jealousy*
> *all the earth will be consumed.*

References to "the city" (v. 1) permeate this section. Although never explicitly named, this "city" is Jerusalem, as indicated by the fact that this place alone fulfills the role of the unique dwelling place of God (v. 5). A series of verbs and personal pronouns in the feminine singular refer back to "the city" *(hāʿîr)* mentioned in the opening sentence of the chapter (v. 1; cf. vv. 2, 3, 4, 5, 7). Neighboring nations previously have been declared fit for God's judgment, but now it is Jerusalem's turn to stand before the Lord's scrutinizing eye.

A distinction in the prophetic form of address employed in these verses divides the material into two sections. First, the prophet speaks about the city (vv. 1–5); then Yahweh himself addresses the city in the first person (vv. 6–8).

1 Three participles characterize the city over which the prophetic *Woe* is pronounced: *rebellious (mōrᵉʾâ)*, *polluted (nigʾālâ)*, and *oppressing (hayyônâ)*. The grammatical positioning of *rebellious* and *polluted* first in word order stresses the indictment contained in these words. This stress may be assumed to carry over to the third adjective, even though it follows the subject of the sentence. These three terms indicate that it is a people in covenant with Yahweh against whom this prophecy is spoken. A relationship must exist against which the city revolts. The people defiantly and obstinately have refused to do Yahweh's will. Privilege has become the occasion for greater sin.

polluted also suggests an uncleanness which disqualifies a person from performing a sacred task or maintaining a distinctive relationship. Certain individuals after the Exile were "polluted" and as a consequence were excluded from the priesthood (cf. Ezra 2:62; Neh. 7:64). But Zephaniah declares the entire populace to be disqualified from any service to God.

Subsequently, even the nations recognized Israel's pollution as a consequence of the fall of Jerusalem. None of the kings of the earth could believe that enemies could enter the gates of the holy city (Lam. 4:12). But because of the shedding of innocent blood by prophets and priests, the citizenry is utterly polluted with blood. No one dares touch their garments (Lam. 4:13–14). Even the heathen treat them as leprous, crying "Go away, you are unclean; you can stay here no longer" (Lam. 4:15; cf. Num. 35:32–33; Lev. 13:45).

This pollution of Jerusalem's population is not the kind of ceremonial defilement that functioned in Israel only for its value as a teaching model.

317

Instead, it is moral pollution infesting the people. Brutal crimes associated with the shedding of blood have defiled the land.

Because Israel was a stranger in Egypt, they were commanded specifically never to *oppress* a stranger (Exod. 22:20 [Eng. 21]; Lev. 19:33). Brothers and slaves alike were to be free from oppressive treatment (Lev. 25:14; Deut. 23:17 [Eng. 16]). Yet now the prophet declares the whole of this city to be *oppressing* in its very essence. The totality of the populace stands guilty of mutual maltreatment.

A city should be that place where neighbor assists neighbor in service to God and man. But the closeness of the population has become the occasion for cruelty and oppression.

2 From the time of humanity's creation, has so wonderful a thing ever occurred? Has any other nation actually heard the *Voice* of God speaking (cf. Deut. 4:32–33)?[6]

This one city is unique. She has heard the voice of God. Nineveh has not had such a privilege. Neither have the cities of Cush, Moab, Ammon, nor the Philistine cities of the Pentapolis. This city alone has heard. But *she has not hearkened to the Voice.* Ten times in the wilderness, the people would not hearken to God's voice (*lōʾ šāmᵉʿû bᵉqōlî,* Num. 14:22). So the Lord swore that none of them would ever see the land he had promised on oath to their fathers.

How many times has this city refused to hearken to the *Voice?* Had not the curses of the covenant been decreed for all who would not listen to God's voice (*kî-lōʾ šāmaʿtā bᵉqōl yhwh,* Deut. 28:45, 62)? The burial of the law book under the rubble of the temple would not excuse this people's sin in refusing to hearken to God. For the living word continued to be heard through the prophetic mouthpiece. *Woe* to this city for the appalling stubbornness of its resistant will.

This city also *has not accepted correction.* Did she think the calamities that came on her had nothing to do with God's hand of chastening judgment? How could she fail to interpret correctly the providential disciplines which the Lord lovingly brought to her? Certainly she did not think her hours of distress during the reigns of Ahaz, Hezekiah, and Manasseh had come because the gods of the Assyrians were mightier than the God who had brought them out of Egypt, did she? Or did she!

There it is! The greatest indictment of all. This glorious city, beautiful for situation, the joy of all the earth, the locale chosen of God for his

---

6. Although the "voice" is not specified to be God's by Zephaniah, the text of this utterance as well as parallel references in Scripture point in that direction.

dwelling place—this city *has not trusted* in Yahweh. Zephaniah serves his indictment for the sin of unbelief against the whole of the city. From this corrupted fountain of distrust has issued the whole polluted stream of the city's sins. The rebellions against God, the bloody oppressions, the stopping of the ear, and the hardening of the heart all have arisen out of failure to trust in Yahweh.

Often trusting God rather than worrying over a situation is seen as a psychological function which provides benefits to the believer. Failure to believe is not always understood as a gross sin, an act of shameful treason which merits the curse of God. But unbelief is "the mother of all the evil deeds by which men willfully wrong and injure one another."[7]

Sins of unbelief may be committed individually or corporately. From the prophet's perspective, it is the *city* as a corporate community that has not trusted in Yahweh. So the city as a whole falls under the censure of the prophetic *Woe.*

This city also is guilty because *to her God she has not drawn near.* The concept of "drawing near" to God very frequently is associated with worship in the OT.[8] Approaching the Almighty must always include adoration. Approach to God may be for the purpose of making petition, seeking counsel, offering a gift, or expressing praise. But in each case, the act of drawing near must involve worship and adoration. If he is God, every approach to him must be made worshipfully.

Every other deity may find its adherents in the cosmopolitan center of Jerusalem. But approaching Yahweh in association with any other deity only insults the one true God.

This neglect of true worship evokes the prophetic *Woe.* No one can expect blessing in this life apart from a total commitment expressed in acts of purest worship. Although the act has no merit in itself, it seals the faith of the trusting believer.

3–4   Having delivered his indictment against the whole populace of the chosen city, the prophet now specifies his charges against the various elements of leadership which are primarily responsible for this wholesale degeneration. Princes, judges, prophets, and priests each receive their writ of condemnation. Zephaniah deals first with civil officials (v. 3), and then with religious leaders (v. 4).

---

7. Calvin, p. 264.

8. BDB, p. 898, indicates that the phrase functions as a technical expression for worship about 158 times. Particularly significant is the great assembly of Sinai, when Israel "drew near" to God.

3 The nation's real representatives exercise brute force to devour the poor. Rather than shepherding the people, these *princes* feed on the flesh of those whom they govern.

The *judges* responsible for upholding the law of the Lord with impartiality display the temperament of a night-prowling wolf. Furious with insatiable hunger, they lunge on their helpless victims under cover of darkness. So ferocious are their appetites for the innocent that *they leave no gnawing for the morning.*[9]

4 The *prophets* sin most grossly when they presume to speak in the Lord's name. Such arrogance deserved death (cf. Deut. 18:20). For in Israel when God spoke to his people, the nation was obliged to obey without equivocation. No other human utterance carried the same weight of authority as the declaration of the prophets.

The false prophets are not only *reckless* in declaring God's word when he has not spoken. They also are *men of deception.* They act and speak under cover, using their office as a means of achieving their own designs.

Throughout Israel's national history, conflict centered on the struggle between true and false prophets. Particularly as the nation's history moved toward the tragedy of expulsion from the land, the tension among prophets increased. This intensification of the struggle is seen in Jeremiah's use of the term *prophet* approximately ninety times, while in Isaiah the term occurs only seven times.

Zephaniah lashes out against his contemporaries. A single prophet dares to condemn the many. But as John Calvin comments, "no union formed by men can possibly lessen the authority of God."[10] In every age, one with God is a majority.

The *priests* in Israel performed multiple tasks, all of which affected profoundly the spiritual and social welfare of the nation. Among their duties was the responsibility to distinguish between the holy and the common (cf. Lev. 10:10). By this distinction, the people were kept from confusing the Creator with the creation. Through a proper maintenance of this distinction, the holy God was kept distinct from the temporal and material substances of

---

9. The term *gāram* probably means "to gnaw or to crush bones" (cf. *gerem*, "bone"). This meaning is supported by Num. 24:8, where the phrase "he shall devour the nations his enemies" (*yōʾkal gôyim ṣārāyw*) is paralleled by "their bones are crushed" (*ʿaṣmōṯêhem yeḡārēm*). The idea of "not gnawing in the morning" suggests that these ravenous wolves, prowling in the night, leave no morsel for the morning. Rudolph, p. 284, translates, "which before the great beast *[Grossvieh]* do not shrink back."

10. Calvin, p. 267.

his creation. But at the same time, the remarkable fact was communicated that God could be known among his creatures.

But these priests of Judah *have profaned the holy place.* Even the holy place itself lost its significance to the people as the locale of God's dwelling. Inevitably a disorientation of the whole of life had to follow. "Sacred" prostitution, and the "offering to God" of infants as whole burnt sacrifices naturally arose when priests eliminated the distinction between the common and the holy.

The priests of Israel also sat as the chief justices of the land. If a lawsuit proved too difficult for the common court system, the priests in conjunction with a principal judge of the land would decide the case (cf. Deut. 17:8–9). Their decision was designated as *torah,* and bound all parties to obedience. Anyone showing contempt for this office must die (Deut. 17:10–12).

But the priests of Zephaniah's day *have done violence to the torah.* Not only have they brought havoc in the lives of these who have been bound by their decisions. Their assault has been against the law of God itself. Only violence against God's law could explain the perversions promoted by the priests of Judah. If the citizen who disputed the decision of the *priestly torah* must die, what would be the fate of the priest who brutalized the *divine torah?*

Stories concerning ministers who promote immorality in God's name only indicate the continuation of this same corruption within humanity. As T. S. Eliot has phrased it dramatically in *Murder in the Cathedral:*

> Sin grows with doing good. . . .
> Servant of God has chance of greater sin
> And sorrow, than the man who serves a king.
> For those who serve the greater cause may make the cause serve
>   them,
> Still doing right. . . .[11]

Eliot's last phrase may concede too much to Zephaniah's contemporaries. Any resemblance of right in their deeds was despite their intent.

The prophetic "Woe" spoken over this city finds a solemn echo in the sevenfold "Woe" that Christ spoke over the scribes and Pharisees of his day (Matt. 23:2, 13–36). His denunciation concludes as well with a vivid description of the ruin of Jerusalem (Matt. 23:37–39).

5 In contrast with the injustice run rampant among all the inhabitants of Jerusalem, the prophet depicts Yahweh in their midst as always

---

11. T. S. Eliot, "Murder in the Cathedral," in T. S. Eliot, *The Complete Plays* (New York: Harcourt, Brace and World, 1967), p. 30.

doing right! Remarkably, the prophet asserts that *Yahweh* is still *in her midst.* He can do no evil, nor can evil corrupt him. The Lord's presence in the midst of this city clearly indicates that Jerusalem is the place under discussion, even though it is not specifically mentioned. Only Jerusalem possesses such a distinct privilege.

The characterization of God as *righteous* and as one who *will never do evil* may be compared with the declaration of the nature of God at the beginning of Moses' song of the covenant: He is "a God of truth who does no evil; just and righteous is he" (Deut. 32:4). People, princes, judges, prophets, and priests all may be corrupt. But the Lord remains righteous. He cannot do wrong.

But is God fully aware of the horrors being perpetrated in Judah? Can the toleration of these circumstances be continued and righteousness be maintained?

The never-failing righteousness of the Lord must not be doubted: *Morning by morning he will bring his justice to light.* The phrase *morning by morning (babbōqer babbōqer)* expresses the daily regularity of certain sacrifices offered in Israel (Exod. 30:7; Lev. 6:5 [Eng. 12]; 2 Chr. 13:11; Ezek. 46:13–15), of the manna collected in the wilderness (Exod. 16:21), of the freewill offerings brought for the construction of the tabernacle (Exod. 36:3). In one context speaking of the judgment of God, those who make a covenant with death and reject the tested cornerstone laid in Zion shall be overwhelmed by a scourge morning by morning, by day and by night (Isa. 28:19).

In similar fashion, the Lord will bring his justice to light morning by morning. Despite the appearance that corruption prevails on every side, the Lord daily manifests his righteous judgments. Even the faithful remnant, suffering under the oppressive tyrannies of a depraved leadership, must acknowledge the daily realities of the Lord's justice.[12] As faithfully as the Lord provided daily manna for his people during their trial period in the wilderness, so in the chaotic last days of Jerusalem the Lord's righteousness was coming to light.

In this difficult circumstance, the Lord's dependability is seen in the assertion that *he shall never fail (lōʾ neʿdār).*[13] Even as the light of each new

---

12. The context is not satisfied by the suggestion that justice "comes to light" merely in the proclamations of the prophets. The situation demands that the actual enactment of justice be involved.

13. The term *ʿādar* refers to that which is missing or left behind (cf. 1 Sam. 30:19; 2 Sam. 17:22; Isa. 34:16; 40:26; 59:15). Nothing is "lacking" in God's administration of justice.

day surely will dawn, so God himself can never fail. Through all the difficult moments in this era of Judah's history, while every human institution is proved to be corrupt, the Lord is unfailing. He is just. Never on a single day will he do evil.

But the evil know no shame. Even Almighty God shows concern that people understand his righteousness. He daily manifests his justice. But the wicked have sold themselves into sin. They cannot be shamed. Their hearts are utterly hardened.

6 Before announcing the inevitability of God's destructive judgments on these corrupted sinners, the Lord rehearses the numerous expressions of his patience in the past. Now the Lord speaks in the first person.

National integrity violated, avenues of commerce stilled, once-busy cities laid waste. Does the experience of other nations teach nothing to Judah? The *corner towers,* the most strongly fortified points of walled cities, lie in ruins. No one ventures on the broad *streets* of these nations. Cities once teeming with the corporate activities of people now lie in worthless rubble.

The Lord injected these judgments into a stream of history that otherwise might have been expected to flow undisturbed. He did it not only because of the unbearable arrogance and corruption of the population of these cities, but he did it also because of his tender mercies toward his own people. By bringing such staggering devastation on heathen cities "before the time," the Lord intended to startle his own wayward community into turning from their complacency in corruption.

7 Now the Lord explicitly indicates his intention in devastating other nations as well as chastening Judah. These manifestations of his righteous judgments would hopefully instill a godly fear in his people. Then they would be spared absolute devastation. *Surely* they will *fear* him.

According to the legislation of Deuteronomy, simply the reading of the law should have instilled fear in the hearts of Israel. Every seven years, the consequences of covenantal violation were to be read. This solemn ceremony of covenant renewal was intended to provoke fear of the Lord (Deut. 31:9–13). In addition, various individual offenders of covenant law were to be put to death for their transgressions so that all Israel would hear and learn to fear the Lord (Deut. 13:11; 14:23; 19:20; 21:21).

Law-reading became neglected over many decades. Offenders were not discouraged from their crimes. As a consequence, the Lord went to the extreme of inflicting calamities on Judah. Certainly now they would learn to fear him and turn from their corrupted ways. Even during Israel's wilderness wanderings, that rebellious generation would seek the Lord "whenever he slew them" (Ps. 78:34).

The Lord's ultimate goal in inflicting Judah was that their *refuge will not be cut off*. Although his chastening might bring many distresses on the nation, they were calculated to preserve a place of salvation.

Startling is the reaction of the nation to this patient yet increasingly severe treatment by the Lord. Speaking anthropomorphically, the Lord had thought that his chastenings finally would bring them to their senses. *But alas!* They became even more eager in their pursuit of evil. *They rose early* to accomplish their schemings, even while the Lord was "rising early" and sending his prophets to warn them of their folly (cf. Jer. 7:13, 25; 11:7; 25:3; 26:5; 29:19; 32:33; 35:14–15; 44:4).

Moses had declared he knew that after his death the nation would become "totally corrupt" (*hašḥēṯ tašḥiṯûn,* Deut. 31:29). Now the Lord declares fulfillment of this expectation. They have *acted corruptly [hišḥîṯû] in all their doings.* As in the days before the flood, a time had come once more in which all flesh had corrupted *(hišḥîṯ)* its way before the Lord (Gen. 6:12).

8 The consequences of such corruption had been proven once in the destruction of the flood. The reappearance of this same type of circumstance would inevitably evoke the abrupt arrival of the Day of Yahweh.

After the immediately preceding verses, it might be expected that the prophet would focus his announcement of judgment specifically on Jerusalem. This recalcitrant city has resisted every approach of God in his goodness and his severity. But instead the prophet depicts an assembly of all nations. God shall pour out his wrath on the entire earth. The persistent rebellion of Jerusalem will lead to the destruction of all peoples, not merely to the punishment of Judah.

This broadening of the dimensions of the objects of God's wrath once more may explain the rendering of the Massoretes: "Wait . . . for the Day of my coming *for the prey*" *(leᵉʿaḏ)* rather than ". . . coming *to testify*" *(leᵉʿēḏ).* If the nations were to serve as witnesses to the trial of Jerusalem at which the Lord himself would provide testimony, the second possibility for the vocalization of this word would make sense. But before whom is the Lord to offer his "testimony" if the entire world is to be brought to trial?

Therefore, some support may be found for understanding the phrase to mean the Lord will come "for the prey" *(leᵉʿaḏ).* Like a ravenous beast, he shall come to consume all nations. However, this figure of God's coming "for the prey" is quite foreign to the present context. Nothing explains why this particular imagery should now be introduced.

More probably this phrase may be understood as declaring God's coming *to testify (leᵉʿēḏ).* This interpretation has some problems in view of the universal character of the judgment being depicted. Before whom would the trial be held if the nations as well as Judah were being charged?

One possible solution might be to alter the consonantal text slightly so that it affirms that God will assemble the nations that he may pour out his wrath on *you,* the residents of Jerusalem, rather than on *them,* the inhabitants of all the earth.[14] So God would be assembling the nations that they might hear his "testimony" (*ēd)* at the trial of Judah.

But such an emendation of the text actually is not necessary. For at other places in Scripture when the Lord comes to "testify" no third party is present to hear this awesome Witness. Zephaniah's contemporary Jeremiah announces that the Lord will be witness against Israel's sin (Jer. 29:23). Malachi announces that on the Day of Yahweh's coming, he will be quick to testify against sorcerers and adulterers, against those who defraud laborers of their wages and who deprive aliens of their justice (Mal. 3:3–5).

Who shall be able to endure this Day of his coming? Who shall stand when he appears? Zephaniah, speaking for the Lord, says that on that Day, *in the fire of my jealousy all the earth will be consumed.*

Jerusalem indeed shall be included in this Day of destruction. But when the city of God itself is judged, the final day for all the nations will have come. Universal calamity must accompany the devastation of this city.

When Jesus presents the terrors of God's coming judgment, he intertwines the destruction of Jerusalem with the end of the age so that the two aspects of his prophetic declaration cannot be separated. When armies surround Jerusalem and its desolation is near, then the "time of punishment in fulfillment of all that has been written" will have arrived (Luke 21:20–22).

The destruction of Jerusalem in A.D. 70 anticipated that great Day of Yahweh which shall consummate the Lord's judgments, even as did the destruction of Jerusalem in 586 B.C. Even as in Zephaniah's prophecy, so also in Jesus' prophecy, the judgment of God on Jerusalem inevitably anticipates the final devastation of the nations.

This fearful judgment on Jerusalem has occurred. The hour for the final inbreaking of Yahweh's Day presses at the door. If it were possible to speak of an event's being more or less "imminent," then the appearance of the Day of Yahweh is now "more imminent" than ever before. With unmeasurable suddenness the Day of Yahweh's open witness against every secret transgression shall arrive.

The prophet says *Wait!* Wait for the Day! Zephaniah does not mean

---

14. Cf. Rudolph, p. 290, who suggests the change from "on them" (*ʿalêhem*) to "on you" (*ʿalêkem*).

the wait shall be long and tedious. He means that people must wait in trust
(*ḥakkû*) that the Day shall arrive.

Do not entertain any doubts. When you observe the persistent refusal
to fear Yahweh even on the part of those who have Yahweh dwelling in their
midst, trust in the fact that the Day is near. He never does wrong. He never
shall fail. His justice cannot be questioned. Morning by morning it comes to
light. On the rightly appointed Day, he shall come to testify even against those
who bear his name.

B. GOD WILL ULTIMATELY PURIFY HIS REMNANT (3:9–13)

9 *For then*
> *I shall convert the nations*
>> *so that they speak with a purified lip,*
>>> *that they all may call on the name of Yahweh,*
>>> *to serve him with a single shoulder.*

10 *From beyond the rivers of Cush*
>> *my suppliants,*
>> *the daughter of my dispersed people,*
>>> *will bring my offering.*

11 *In that day*
> *you will not be ashamed*
>> *for all your deeds*
>> *by which you have sinned against me.*

> *For then*
>> *I shall remove from your midst*
>>> *those among you who pridefully rejoice.*
>> *You will not exalt yourself ever again*
>> *in my holy mountain.*

12 *But I shall leave in your midst*
> *a humble and poor people,*
> *who will seek shelter in the name of Yahweh.*

13 *The remnant of Israel*
>> *will not do*
>>> *evil,*
>> *will not speak*
>>> *a lie;*
>>> *a deceitful tongue*
>> *will not be found in their mouth.*

> *For they*
>> *will feed*

> *and lie down,*
> *and none will make afraid.*

Now the prophet introduces a new dimension into his message. In this anticipation of circumstances beyond God's judgment, he never suggests that the terrors of the Day somehow may be avoided. The consuming fires of Yahweh's wrath must fall.

In the immediately preceding section, Zephaniah had depicted the final assembly of nations on the Day. Because of his own nation's stubborn resistance to every summons to humility, they too would be among those judged in that awesome assembly.

But now speaking out of the framework of an assumed scattering of his own people in judgment, the prophet depicts the formation of a new community of holy people. This restored remnant shall consist not only of a purged and forgiven group from Israel (cf. 3:11–13). The converted from the nations shall join with his people in the worship and service of the one true God (3:9–10).

But how can the prophet speak of the salvation of a remnant both from the nations as well as from Israel? Already he had declared that the entirety of the universe was to be overturned on a scale comparable to the destruction that occurred with the flood in Noah's day (1:2–3). The fire of Yahweh's wrath would consume the entire earth (1:18; 3:8). If the Day would bring this cosmic destruction, what is the meaning of the reference to a fresh start for humanity?[1]

To deny the authenticity of these words of the prophet on the basis of this tension is to ignore the close similarity of ideas found in this very section when compared with earlier portions of the prophecy. Zephaniah simply does not resolve explictly the tension that might be felt among various aspects of his message. He saw a destruction in judgment beyond any proportions that the world had experienced previously. He saw also a wondrous conversion among the nations of the world as well as among the scattered people of Israel. He does not explain how cosmic judgment and far-reaching salvation coordinate, but he faithfully proclaims both elements.

From the vantage point of the present historical situation together with the further revelation that has come since Zephaniah's day, some reconciliation of these various elements may be perceived. The nations of Philis-

---

1. According to J. M. P. Smith, p. 248: "At this point, an editor, actuated by more kindly and generous feelings toward the nations than are reflected by the foregoing threats, has inserted a section expressing his own sentiment."

tia, Moab, Ammon, Cush, and Assyria all have experienced the devastations anticipated by the prophet. This fact should not be attributed simply to the principle that all nations ultimately must fall, but to the providential ordering of circumstances in fulfillment of the prophetic word. The city of Jerusalem also has experienced the utter devastations promised by the prophet, both in 586 B.C. and in A.D. 70.

These awesome destructions in turn have become the basis for an extension of subsequent prophetic anticipation concerning cosmic devastation, particularly in the intermingling of the then-future destruction of Jerusalem with the final cosmic conflagration in the teaching of Jesus (Matt. 24:3–44). In the meantime, a holy remnant both of Jews and Gentiles continues to be assembled. This development coordinates quite appropriately with the message of salvation presented by the prophet.

9 When the prophet reports the Lord as saying, *I shall convert the nations,* he underscores the necessity of God's immediate involvement in this momentous activity. None but the Almighty could perform this kind of task on such a massive scale. The hardening of the human heart to the point that it could not find repentance had been declared as the occasion for cosmic condemnation. Any turning of the nations must clearly be attributed to the sovereign grace of God.

The Lord's special gift to these nations is that *they speak with a purified lip.* The singular form of the term *lip (śāpâ)* in Scripture often means "language" (Gen. 11:1, 6, 7, 9; Ps. 81:6 [Eng. 5]; Isa. 19:18; Ezek. 3:5–6). But the idea of a "purified language" confuses imageries. The rendering of the phrase so that it reads "they will speak pure Hebrew" hardly can be justified.[2]

The significance of this phrase is found in the next statement: *that they all may call on the name of Yahweh.* From among all the gentile nations a people shall arise who will utter with purest lips the most sacred words. They shall call on the name of Yahweh for salvation. This petition of the nations implies a ready acknowledgment of sin, together with a confession that Yahweh alone is God and Savior.

Joel also connects the coming Day of Yahweh with a widespread "calling on the name of the Lord" for salvation (Joel 3:5 [Eng. 2:32]). This prophecy becomes the basis for the apostolic interpretation of the events on

---

2. Cf. the translation of *The Living Bible,* which has been used to explain the revival of modern Hebrew in Palestine today as a fulfillment of Zephaniah's prophecy concerning a "purified lip." This version reads: "At that time I will change the speech of my returning people to pure Hebrew" (Zeph. 3:9).

the day of Pentecost following Christ's resurrection. By the outpouring of the Holy Spirit, the purification of heart and lip was accomplished that led to a widespread calling on the name of the Lord (Acts 2:21).

Not only with their lips, but also with their lives they will serve him. In a most impressive figure, the prophet depicts this mutual service of the gentile nations *with a single shoulder.* Bowing determinedly and unitedly, these converts to Yahweh will express their adoration to their Lord by assuming the rugged task of the lowliest servant. They labor side by side with Israel's Issachar, who will "bend his shoulder to the burden" (cf. Gen. 49:15). The converted Gentile will gladly *serve (leʿābedô)* Yahweh.

10   The sovereign grace of God will reach *beyond the rivers of Cush* in its converting of the nations. Past the southernmost branches of the Nile, deep into the continent of Africa, shall come prayers for salvation addressed to Yahweh alone.[3]

Earlier Isaiah had characterized *Cush* as a "land divided by rivers" (Isa. 18:2, 7), which sent "envoys by sea in papyrus boats over the water" (18:2). He also depicted these distant people as bringing gifts to the Lord Almighty (18:7).

my suppliants. Once in Israel's past history, the pharaoh of Egypt had been beaten down to the point of requesting Moses to "entreat" *(ʿātar)* the Lord on behalf of his bruised and battered land (Exod. 8:4–5, 24–26 [Eng. 8–9, 28–30]; 9:28; 10:17–18). But now Zephaniah envisions the day in which peoples far beyond the borders of Egypt would have their own lips purified so that they themselves would entreat the name of Yahweh. The Lord's *suppliants (ʿatāray)* include these from other nations.

The *daughter of my dispersed people* creates some difficulty in interpretation. "Dispersion" in itself suggests a previous assemblage. Although the gentile nations were grouped about Babel before their dispersion, it is not likely that their loose relation with Yahweh would have inspired Zephaniah to speak of these dispersed gentile nations as "*my* dispersed people."

The deuteronomic law code had threatened dispersion *(pûṣ)* if Israel should not maintain an obedient spirit before the Lord (Deut. 4:27; 28:64; 30:3). By this scattering, Israel's historical experience of serving as a type of the elect of Yahweh would be interrupted. Although not utterly terminating their covenant relation, this dispersion meant that Israel would become once more as Abraham in Ur before God's call—a people who could be saved only by intervention of Yahweh's sovereign election.

3. Cf. J. M. P. Smith, p. 249, who identifies the "rivers" of Cush with the most distant branches of the Nile.

It is therefore not surprising to find Zephaniah binding a scattered Israelite remnant at their restoration ("the daughter of my dispersed people"—v. 10) with converted Gentiles ("the nations . . . that . . . call on the name of Yahweh—v. 9).[4] For the original "Israel" (Abraham) actually was at first no different than the rest of the Gentiles. So it is quite understandable that the prophet envisages a combined Jewish and gentile community serving with a single shoulder and presenting a single *offering*.[5]

11 Now the prophet returns to his treatment of the future expectation awaiting the city of Jerusalem. This fact is indicated by a return to the feminine singular form of the verb and the use of the feminine pronouns.

The introductory phrase *In that day* could be understood simply as an adverbial clause meaning "then." But the broader context of Zephaniah's prophecy as well as the reference to the Day in the preceding section suggest that the phrase refers more specifically to the Day of Yahweh. This great Day shall include the purging of sin from the remnant of Israel as well as the destruction of the wicked. The city *will not be ashamed,* but not because its inhabitants have no guilt. This city which now is free from all shame is the same city that earlier had been rebuked because it knew no shame (3:5; cf. 2:1).

How great will be that day in which all shame will be removed from the community of God's people. Not only will guilt be eliminated; all the crippling psychological effects of sin shall be wiped away. Each person will attain his full potential in service to God because a guilty conscience will not render him incapable of functioning freely in service to God. Even to the last day, the great day of judgment, the entire community of God's people will be freed from shame (cf. Rom. 9:33; 1 Pet. 2:6).

The community may be depicted without shame because God has purged them of all those who are proudly unrepentant. He shall remove all

---

4. The "daughter" of my dispersed people may be regarded as the "offspring" of the dispersed remnant of Israel, even as the "daughter" of Jerusalem is equivalent to Jerusalem's population.

5. Interestingly, the specific offering which these people bring *(minḥâ)* is most often a cereal offering and is generally not used in Scripture to describe an atoning sacrifice. Both Cain's and Abel's sacrifices are designated as *minḥâ* (Gen. 4:3–4). In passages such as 1 Sam. 2:17, 29; 26:19, the term may refer to animal sacrifices. But most generally it was a cereal offering, a gift to God: "God having granted forgiveness of sins through the burnt offering, the worshipper responded by giving to God some of the produce of his hands in cereal offering. It was an act of dedication and consecration to God as Savior and covenant King. It expressed not only thankfulness but obedience and a willingness to keep the law" (G. W. Wenham, *The Book of Leviticus,* NICOT [Grand Rapids: Eerdmans, 1979], p. 71).

those who pridefully rejoice. The city in which the Lord dwells will not be marred by individuals characterized by arrogant self-exaltation. In his *holy mountain,* they will never lift up themselves again.

12 The prophet saw the sin of pride as a chief cause for the inevitability of the destruction of Judah. Thus genuine humility before God had to be a major characteristic of the remnant who were brought through this purging judgment.

This remnant is designated as *humble and poor.*[6] Particularly in the light of the strong emphasis on the removal of guilt and the ending of pride in the preceding verse, these designations should be understood primarily as describing a moral attribute rather than a social status. This remnant, in humble acceptance of the previous admonition, regard themselves as no better than a heap of stubble suited for consumption by the fire of God's anger (2:2). They find deliverance only because they *seek shelter in the name of Yahweh.* They are fully cognizant of their danger and seek refuge in him who is their judge.

13 Now the prophet describes the consequences rather than the causes of the Lord's preserving a remnant. They *will not do evil (lō'-yaʿⁿśû ʿawlâ).* This phrase parallels the earlier description of Yahweh's eschewing of all evil (*lō' yaʿⁿśeh ʿawlâ,* 3:5). The moral character of the remnant conforms to the nature of the Lord who has delivered them. Re-created in true righteousness and holiness, this preserved remnant reflects the image of God in their patterns of behavior (cf. Col. 3:10; Eph. 4:24).

The fact that they *will not speak a lie* is emphasized by an additional phrase: *a deceitful tongue will not be found in their mouth.* The purified lips of the remnant will not be governed by the impulses of a heart that lies. Although descendants of Jacob the supplanter, they finally have all guile removed.

In the last phrases of this section, the prophet employs a common pastoral scene to depict the blessing that shall come on the remnant of God's people. Departing from the imagery of the "city" that has permeated the chapter, he now speaks in terms of a flock adequately fed and protected: *For they will feed and lie down.* The material of this sentence does not seem at first to connect with the thought that has preceded. Certainly it must not be supposed

---

6. While various efforts have been made to distinguish among the basic meanings conveyed by ʿānî, ʿⁿnāwâ, and ʿānāw, no convincing case has been made. Each of these terms derives from the same root, and each can mean either "humble," "meek," or "poor." Context must decide among these options. Cf. Rudolph, p. 297; Keil, p. 159.

that the remnant of the Lord would be motivated by a grovelling materialism to refrain from evil deeds and deceit.

More likely, the idyllic situation envisioned describes the arrival of the theocracy. The covenantal core of "I shall be your God and you shall be my people" becomes a perfected reality in the experience of the restored remnant. They shall be his people, doing his will; and he shall be their God, shepherding them in a restored paradise.

The concept of God's people as a flock "feeding" in abundance and "lying down" in security is associated with the monarchy in Israel. The king must "feed" or "shepherd" the people (cf. 2 Sam. 5:2; 7:7; Ps. 78:71). With the impending collapse of the monarchy, a renewed emphasis emerged, pointing to God himself as the one shepherding his own flock (Gen. 48:15; 49:24; Ps. 23:1; 80:2 [Eng. 1]; Isa. 40:11; Ezek. 34:2–23). The consequences of this intimate relationship are clear to Zephaniah. The people under the care of the Lord will feed abundantly and will lie down in safety.

This idyllic scene is furthered by the expression, *none will make afraid (w^{e}'ên maḥărîḏ)*. Both Jeremiah and Ezekiel employ this same phrase to depict the status of Israel after their return from exile (Jer. 30:10; 46:27; Ezek. 34:28; 39:26). This imagery also describes the restored paradise in which everyone lives securely under his own vine and his own fig tree, where "none shall make them afraid" (Mic. 4:4; cf. 1 K. 4:25). This picture of restoration originated in the promises associated with the covenant. The people were told they would eat all they desired, would live safely in the land, would sleep securely, and "none would make afraid" (*w^{e}'ên maḥărîḏ*—Lev. 26:5–6). Contrariwise, the curses of the covenant are expressed in terms of birds of prey and beasts feeding grotesquely on the carcasses of the condemned, while the righteous shall enjoy the blessings of paradise, for "none shall make them afraid" (*w^{e}'ên maḥărîḏ*—Deut. 28:26; Jer. 7:33; cf. Gen. 15:11).

So the prophet depicts the Day in which Yahweh ultimately will purify his remnant. This divine intervention will mean salvation for gentile peoples as well as restoration for his own. A forgiven, humbled, and purified people will enjoy the ultimate blessings of paradise restored.

This entire complex of ideas finds its fulfillment in the realities of the new covenant. God's ancient people of Israel join with converts from the world's distant climes. They call on the name of the Lord with lips purified by the Holy Spirit, serving him with a single shoulder. This community of the new covenant, heir to all the blessings prefigured in the old, have all shame removed and all pride purged. They manifest the sensitive moral character of a people who will do no evil, who will not lie. They live in safety with no one to terrify them.

The records of the new covenant attest to the fulfillment of all these promises, while at the same time pointing to an ultimate consummation in the future. Only then, in that Day, shall a completed restoration be enjoyed to the fullest.

C. GOD WILL THEN REJOICE WITH HIS PEOPLE (3:14–20)

14 *a* *Sing,*
     b *daughter of Zion;*
  a *shout,*
     b *Israel;*
  a *rejoice and be jubilant with all your heart,*
     b *daughter of Jerusalem.*

15   *a* *Yahweh has removed*
         b *your punishments,*
       a *he has turned back*
         b *your enemy.*

       The King of Israel,
       Yahweh,
         (is) in your midst;
         never will you fear evil again.

16 *In that day*
     a *it shall be said to Jerusalem,*
       b *Do not fear;*
     a *Zion,*
       b *do not let your hands fall limp.*

17   *Yahweh your God (is) in your midst,*
     a mighty hero who saves.

       a *He will delight*
         b *over you*
           c *with joy;*
       a *he will be quiet*
         b *(over you)*
           c *in his love;*
       a *he will rejoice*
         b *over you*
           c *with singing.*

18 *Those who are grieved because of*[1] *the appointed feasts*

---

1. The *min* of *mimmôʿēd* is causal in significance. Cf. BDB, p. 580 (2.e, f); Keil, p. 162.

> *I shall gather;*
> *from you they originated.*
> *A burden on her was reproach.*
> 19 *At that time I shall deal with all your oppressors.*
>   *a I shall save*
>   *b the lame,*
>   *b and the banished*
>   *a I shall gather.*
>   *And I shall give them*
>   *honor*
>   *and fame*
>   *in all the land of their shame.*
> 20 *At that time*
>   *I shall make you return;*
>   *at (that) time*
>   *I shall gather you.*
>   *For I shall give you*
>   *fame*
>   *and honor*
>   *among all the peoples of the earth*
>   *when I return your captivities*
>   *before your eyes,*
>   *says Yahweh.*

One of the most awesome descriptions of the wrath of God in judgment found anywhere in Scripture appears in the opening verses of Zephaniah. The totality of the cosmos shall be consumed in his burning anger. The very order of creation shall be overturned.

One of the most moving descriptions of the love of God for his people found anywhere in Scripture appears in the closing verses of Zephaniah. God and his people attain heights in the ecstasy of love that are hard to comprehend.

Contrary to the tenor of modern critical scholarship, it does make a difference whether these words come from the prophet Zephaniah as a part of the message delivered to his contemporaries before the Exile had actually occurred.[2] This word of hope is intended for a people who are currently

2. A strange by-product of modern canonical criticism may be seen in B. S. Childs's essentially agnostic attitude toward questions regarding the dating of Zephaniah's material. Because of the overriding eschatological perspective of this material, Childs judges that "temporal differences have been transcended." The canonical process "has disregarded historical differences and organized the material theo-

secure in terms of outward circumstances, and does not apply only to the downcast and the devastated.

The authenticity of these verses is questioned more frequently than any other portion of the book. However, their elimination cannot be based on objective manuscript evidence. Only predetermined judgments concerning what would be possible psychologically for a preexilic prophet to say or to think can eliminate this section.[3]

From an alternative perspective, several elements in these verses echo earlier sections of the prophecy. The removal of punishment (v. 15) is not greatly different from the removal of shame and sin (v. 11). Particularly the idea of the end of shame is found in the adjoining section (v. 11; cf. v. 19c). The returning of Israel's captivity (v. 20) parallels the virtually identical phrase found earlier (2:7). The reference to Israel's being given "praise" and "a name" in all the earth (vv. 19–20) derives from a concept developed in the deuteronomic laws in accord with the many other relationships with Deuteronomy present throughout the book of Zephaniah.

No adequate reason exists for eliminating these verses from the prophecy. They therefore should be regarded as a genuine portion of the prophet's material.

14   The prophet opens this final message with a grand summons for the people to rejoice. The prophetic "Woe" had been spoken over the royal city of Jerusalem. Equally with the foreign nations this rebellious community must be destroyed.

Sadness and depression would seem to be the order of the day. Un-

---

logically" (Childs, *Introduction,* p. 460). Peculiar indeed is this disregard for the significance of history in the theology of the OT. Modern-day biblical theology boasts that it has discovered in the OT a theology integrally bound up with history, in contrast with the cyclical patterns of Baalism. But if the genuineness of Yahweh's intentions in history rests on the historical fulfillment of the prophet's word, then of course it matters whether the prophet spoke before or after the event being prophesied.

3. Kapelrud, *Message of the Prophet Zephaniah,* p. 37, rejects the idea that the message of the prophet may serve as a basis for expunging portions of the text: "Words of promise and hope are also found, and we have no right to delete them from the text because of their content." He objects to the textual notes of *BHS* to the effect that the entirety of these verses may be considered as additions to the text, expressing his judgment that "opinions on this question should not have been found in the text *[sic]* apparatus" (p. 40). Driver, p. 108, says that the judgment that some verses represent "later ideas" is difficult to prove, and asks why Zeph. 3:14–20 could not be seen as describing blessings for a purged Israel, and therefore be found compatible with ch. 1. He considers the grounds generally offered for limiting the text of Zephaniah as "sometimes arbitrary, and in other cases insufficient" (p. 108).

relieved lamentation would be expected. But the prophet can look beyond these tragedies. He calls for an unrestrained celebration of joy.

> Sing!
> Shout!
> Rejoice and be jubilant!

By piling up every available expression for joy, the prophet leaps across the vale of gloom into the realm of grace-beyond-devastation. In his confidence about this future glory, he summons the people now to sing this song of celebration.

The prophet does not merely anticipate a day in which the people who have been blessed by restoration will rejoice. He is not satisfied to announce to his contemporaries a joy that belongs to future generations. He exhorts his own contemporaries. Rejoice! Be jubilant! Despite the unavoidability of the coming Day of Yahweh, they must rejoice!

Not with limpid and fainting spirits, but *with all your heart* you must rejoice. Cast aside all cautious reserve. Let down your guard against the possibility of future disappointment. *Shout aloud! Sing! Be jubilant!*

The term employed for *shout (hārî'û)* is frequently associated with the ringing outcry of a battle's commencement. When Israel entered into battle, the trumpet blast was to be accompanied with a "shout" (Num. 10:9). On several occasions the "shout" of Israel at the initiation of battle is recorded (Josh. 6:10; 1 Sam. 17:20; 2 Chr. 13:12, 15). Even the Lord "shouts" victoriously at his Philistine adversary (Ps. 108:10 [Eng. 9]).

Once the "virgin daughter of Zion" had mocked the invincible forces of the Assyrian war machine encamped outside her gates. The "daughter of Jerusalem" had tossed her head in scorn as she anticipated by faith the routing of the adversary (Isa. 37:22). Now the prophet arouses the faith of the *daughter of Zion* once again to claim a victory obviously beyond her own capacity. In the context of the coming Day, the Lord himself would be Israel's enemy. But beyond that Day, he would turn against their enemies to provide a glorious deliverance.

15 The prophet asserts that Yahweh *has removed your punishments.* The unchanging love of God toward his people cannot rest apart from a completed redemption, despite the necessity of punishment for sins.

The *enemy* of Judah also has been *turned back.* The Lord had promised Abraham that he would possess the gate of his enemies (Gen. 22:17). Judah in particular among the tribes of Israel would seize his enemies by the neck (Gen. 49:8). The book of Deuteronomy had included among the blessings of the covenant the scattering of enemies (Deut. 28:7). Now, with the latitudes implicit in an enemy described with "indefinite generality," the prophet asserts that all of Judah's enemies would be turned back.[4]

The assurance of the prophet concerning these blessings is based on the fact that *the King of Israel* is *in your midst*. The concept of Yahweh as King in the midst of his people is at least as old as the assembly at Sinai. The Lord came with thousands of his holy ones, delivered his divine law, and manifested himself as "king over Jeshurun" (Deut. 33:2–5). Balaam could see nothing but blessing in store for Israel, because "the Lord their God is with them, the shout of the King is among them" (Num. 23:21).

This kingship of God among his people eventually expressed itself historically by the establishment of the Davidic monarchy. Through the line of David, God manifested himself as Lord in Israel. Although tensions surrounded the establishment of an earthly monarch to reign in Yahweh's name, the bringing up of the ark to Jerusalem by King David symbolized the merger of Yahweh's kingship with the Davidic throne. Out of this context, eighth-century prophets projected the reestablishment of David's throne beyond the ruining of the present state of Israel (cf. Hos. 3:5; Isa. 9:5–6 [Eng. 6–7]; 11:1–5; Amos 9:11–12; Mic. 5:2). Particularly close to Zephaniah's call to jubilation over the reign of God in Israel's midst is the similar summons of the postexilic prophet Zechariah. This prophet calls the "daughter of Zion" to rejoice greatly, because her king comes to her (Zech. 9:9–10; cf. Matt. 21:4–5).

In this context, the absence of any reference to an action from the line of David in Zephaniah's anticipations is rather remarkable. He sees Yahweh himself as King in the midst of Israel, but he makes no explicit mention of a son of David to sit on Yahweh's throne. Earlier this prophet had pronounced judgment specifically on the "sons of the king" (1:8). Eventually, three of Josiah's sons took their turn on Judah's throne, and each ended his reign by a tragic judgment from the Lord. The last of Judah's monarchs was Zedekiah, son of Josiah. Could it be that Zephaniah simply could not see beyond the utter devastation of the monarchy in Israel? Could he be looking back to the time of Samuel in which Yahweh maintained his lordship over Israel without the intermediary figure of a Davidic king (cf. 1 Sam. 12:12)?

The prophet clearly does not regard God's covenant with David as hopelessly canceled. For it is *Zion* and *Jerusalem* that he reassures with his call for unrestrained jubilation. The maintenance of the Davidic city was as central to God's covenant with David as was the continuance of his royal line. Yet Zephaniah stresses the continuance of the city, while leaving unmentioned the monarchy.

4. Keil, p. 160.

One avenue for the resolution of this problem concerning the apparent absence of a messianism in Zephaniah may be found in the subsequent affirmation that Yahweh would be in the midst of his people as *a mighty hero who saves* (*gibbôr yôšîaʿ*, v. 17). This descriptive title echoes very closely the announcement of Isaiah concerning the coming son of David who is to be designated, among his other glorious appellatives, "God the Mighty Hero" (*ʾēl gibbôr*—Isa. 9:5 [Eng. 6]). The emerging picture of a virgin-born son of David's house called God-with-us (7:14) who also is Father-of-eternity (9:5 [Eng. 6]) gives expression to the only reality by which all human needs and the promises of God may be synchronized. Only a God-man who rules in fulfillment of the promises to the fathers can be King of Israel ruling in Zion as fulfillment of the promises given to David.

It may not be that Zephaniah himself coordinated all these various pieces of the prophetic expectation in the context of Israel's history as people of God. Perhaps a full comprehension of all the implications of his message had to await the coming of the virgin-born son of David, "who as to his human nature was a descendant of David, who through the Spirit of holiness was declared with power to be the Son of God by his resurrection from the dead: Jesus Christ our Lord" (Rom. 1:4).

Interestingly, the words by which Jesus was hailed as king at his triumphal entry according to the Gospel of John declared, "*Do not be afraid, O Daughter of Zion*" (John 12:15). The expression "Do not be afraid" is not found in the section in Zech. 9 from which the remainder of this quotation is taken. But this phrase is found twice in these verses from Zephaniah which so closely parallel the words of Zechariah (cf. Zeph. 3:15–16). It may be that the Fourth Gospel has employed the common NT quotation methodology of conflating OT sources. The inclusion of Zephaniah's words in the greeting to Jesus at the triumphal entry would be particularly noteworthy, since his statement identifies Israel's king so specifically with Yahweh himself. John indicates that only after Jesus' glorification did his disciples realize that these things had been written about him (John 12:16). When Jesus finally was known to be Lord, equivalent to God himself, then his disciples understood the significance of these words.

The consequences of Yahweh's establishing his rule in Jerusalem according to Zephaniah is expressed first by the simple phrase: *never will you fear evil again*. When all of Israel's enemies have been brought under control, and the Lord has set up permanent residence as King in their midst, then they will have no reason to fear any sort of evil again. Neither disease nor rebellion from within will threaten. Invasion from without will be impossible.

What a glorious reason to rejoice! Sing, shout, and be jubilant! God your king shall subdue all your enemies. No fear of any evil ever again shall disturb your peace of mind.

16   The phrase *In that day* connects adverbially with the section that precedes. When God has removed all Israel's punishments and is established as King in their midst, then it shall be said to Jerusalem, *Do not fear.* Total absence of dread and anxiety will be the joyous state of the reconstituted people of God.

Fear inevitably paralyzes. The *hands* that *fall limp* describe in Scripture a despair over circumstances that renders a person unable to function (2 Chr. 15:7; Isa. 13:7; Neh. 6:9; Ezek. 7:17). But the Lord admonishes his people to activity. He delivers them from every enemy, not that they may delight in self-indulgent pleasures, but "that they may, on the contrary, strenuously devote themselves to the performance of their duties."[5]

This pattern of divine discipline which stirs to activity rather than breaks the spirit finds its way into the scheme of the new covenant as well. Those who have the privilege of being confirmed in the love of God by his gracious disciplines are admonished: "Strengthen your feeble arms and weak knees. Make level paths for your feet, so that the lame may not be disabled, but rather healed" (Heb. 12:12–13).

17   Now the prophet moves into the "holy of holies" by a rapturous description of the love of God for his people. This verse is the John 3:16 of the OT.

The love of God for his own people is not a soft, sentimental emotion that has no strength to act on behalf of its object. For this God who loves is *Yahweh.* He is *God.* He is *a mighty hero who saves.* The term for *mighty hero (gibbôr)* frequently refers to a warrior who overpowers his enemies. The Lord goes forth as a "warrior" who marches against his foes (Isa. 42:13). As the God of Gods, the Lord of Lords, the mighty God, the "hero," he defends the orphan, the widow, and the alien (Deut. 10:17).

This *mighty hero* is in the midst of his own people with power to save. Many calamities may befall Israel because of their sin against the Lord. But in the end he shall show his power to save from every enemy. His love acts concretely to deliver his people.

The next portion of this verse may be called a "poem of personal love." Three parallel lines each containing three phrases express the deepest inner joy and satisfaction of God himself in his love for his people. Delight, joy, rejoicing, and singing on God's part underscore the mutuality of emotional experience felt by God and the redeemed.

5. Calvin, p. 303.

That Almighty God should derive delight from his own creation is significant in itself. But that the Holy One should experience ecstasy over the sinner is incomprehensible.

> God breaking out in singing!
> God joyful with delight!
> All because of you.

The mutuality of the loving response of Redeemer and redeemed is seen in the fact that some of the same terms used in the admonition to his people now describe the response of God himself to his people (cf. vv. 14 and 17). Zion is exhorted to sing *(rānnî)*; he rejoices with singing *(rinnâ)*. Jerusalem shall rejoice *(śimḥî)*; he delights over Jerusalem with joy *(śimḥâ)*. The whole scene depicts a grand oratorio as God and his people mutually rejoice in their love for one another.

The middle line of the poetic triad provides some difficulty in interpretation. Several optional understandings have been offered.[6] But the most straightforward is the most likely: *he will be quiet (over you) in his love.* The only essential difficulty with this rendering is found in the vividness of the phraseology. To consider Almighty God sinking in contemplations of love over a once-wretched human being can hardly be absorbed by the human mind. But this understanding is supported by the regular usage of the word employed *(hāraš* in the Hiphil) as well as the poetic structure of the verse.

The Hebrew verb *ḥāraš,* "to be quiet," is intransitive in meaning, with the possible exception of Job 11:3. It describes the inward condition of the subject of the verb rather than depicting a quietness which is conveyed to another. Here God is the subject of the verb, and he is said to *be quiet in his love.*

The parallelism of the verse also suggests this intransitive sense. The first and last lines of the stanza contain the middle member *over you (ʿālayiḵ).* Since it is quite common in Hebrew parallelism to omit a corresponding

---

6. The LXX reads *kaí kainíei se,* "and he shall renew you" (apparently reflecting Heb. *yᵉḥaddēš).* Cf. Driver, p. 139. But T. H. Gaster, "Two Textual Emendations: Num. 24:8; Zeph. 3:17," *ExpTim* 78 (1967) 267, feels this emendation spoils the point, which is a contrast between the "silence" described in this phrase with the "song" in the next. A. Cohen, *The Twelve Prophets,* Soncino (Bournemouth, Hants.: Soncino, 1948), p. 251, notes that Rashi and other Jewish commentators interpret the phrase to mean that God in his love will cover up the sins of his people in silence. But the term *ḥāraš* is not used of the covering of sins. Better is the remark of Keil, p. 161: "Silence in this love is an expression used to denote love deeply felt, which is absorbed in its object with thoughtfulness and admiration."

phrase in one line that appears in another line, this same *over you* may be regarded as belonging also to the middle line of the stanza.

Almighty God, quiet in his love. God the mighty savior, quietly contemplating, contented in his love for you.

If the prophet's mode of expression appears excessive, it must be remembered that God in his very essence is love (cf. 1 John 4:8). As the direct source of all true love, he not only is capable of achieving every depth of salutary love experienced by his creation. He by his very nature may excel every human emotion of true love. If a human being with all the limitations of his nature may revel in the purity of essential love in short, snatched moments, then certainly the Almighty himself may reach even greater depths of love and sustain these depths without restriction of time.

So these considerations would remove any hesitation about understanding the prophet to be affirming that God sinks into contemplative quietness in his love for sinners. This much in the verse's affirmation can be understood.

The real difficulty lies in assimilating personally the prophet's repeated declaration concerning the object of the all-absorbing love of God. *over you* he will delight; *over you* he will rejoice with singing; *over you* will he be quiet in his love. How could the Sovereign Creator concentrate his whole being in the love of a temporal creature of dust? How could the Holy satisfy himself contentedly in the loving contemplation of the unholy?

One stage in the appreciation of this prophetic affirmation may be achieved by accepting in the abstract this proposition to be true. God can and does absorb himself in his love for human beings. But the total message of the prophet demands personalization. *over you* he shall rejoice. In his contemplation of *you* he shall sink into quietness.

This you of the prophet obviously contains the limitation of contextual definition. It is the *you* that is called "Jerusalem," "Zion," "Israel" (vv. 14–16). None other than the elect of God are the objects of such all-consuming love. Them he loves because he loves them (Deut. 7:6–8). Not in them or for anything in them is to be found the reason for his love. In the nature of God himself may be discovered the only explanation of this love.

But not only does the object of this love have the limitation of definition by context. It also has the openness of invitation. Reaching a breadth that stretches "beyond the rivers of Cush," this incomprehensible love of God embraces all "his suppliants" (v. 10). Whoever they are, whatever their ethnic or moral background, wherever they may be located, this same unchanging love of God reaches to "all who call on the name of the Lord" (v. 9).

This global extension of the love of God is not merely a hypothetical possibility. It is a temporal and historical reality. From all the nations a people with purified lips call on the name of the Lord (v. 9). Every single individual who utters this humble call knows for himself this "love of Christ which surpasses knowledge" (Eph. 3:19). So the prophet describes a love of God exceeding all human imaginations.

"Remember the silence of Jesus, and expound this text thereby," says C. H. Spurgeon.[7] Although the great preacher's point may be related more directly to brilliance in homiletical flair than to precise exegetical science in expounding the intention of the prophet, it cannot be dismissed as having no relevance to the verse at hand. For Jesus' silence in trial and crucifixion was rooted in no other soil than in the fertile depths of the love of God for sinners. "Like a sheep that before its shearers is dumb, so he opened not his mouth" (Isa. 53:7). Jesus' silence lent him the opportunity to contemplate the specific objects of his sacrificing love. He "delighted" to do God's will as he presented his "body" which had been "prepared" for sacrifice (Ps. 40:7, 9 [Eng. 6, 8]; cf. Heb. 10:5, 7). His love for sinners was no less than the love of the Father's.

Attempting to comprehend the depths of this love, one may compare the OT version of John 3:16 to a child on the seashore. Digging a sandy trench to the limitless expanses of the ocean, the child stretches out her arms to gather the ocean's depths into her shallow pool. As the poet has expressed it:

The love of God is greater far
Than tongue or pen can ever tell;
It goes beyond the highest star,
And reaches to the lowest hell.[8]

This contemplative quietness in love is complemented by the rejoicing with singing that also characterizes the love of God for his people. God *will rejoice over you with singing.*

Once again the language of Zephaniah reflects rather specifically the mode of expression found in Deuteronomy. Moses declares to Israel: as the Lord once rejoiced over you *(śāś ʿalêkem)* to do you good, so he will rejoice over you *(yāśîś ʿalêkem)* to destroy you (Deut. 28:63). But the nation could take comfort in the fact that ultimately the Lord will return "to rejoice over you for good" *(lāśûś ʿāleykā lᵉṭôb,* 30:9). Zephaniah sees the fulfillment of

---

7. C. H. Spurgeon, *A Treasury of the Bible. Old Testament,* vol. IV (London: Marshall, Morgan and Scott, 1962), p. 737.

8. F. M. Lehman, as cited in *Making Melody* (St. Louis: Bible Memory Association, 1954), no. 237.

this ancient promise in the future manifestation of the love of God for his people.[9]

18 In this final section, the prophet turns to the first person form of address. The voice of God speaks directly to his people.

The opening words are particularly difficult.[10] But the major thrust seems clear. Zephaniah envisions a day in which all the sorrows associated with God's judgment on his people shall be removed.

Those who are grieved refers to the remnant whose heart is set on the worship of Yahweh. By the destruction of the holy city and the deportation of its population, they are deprived of their chief treasure in life. Access has been cut off from the proper place of worship.

Similar in thought to Zephaniah's prophecy is the picture of the maidens of Jerusalem "grieving" *(nûgôt)* while the streets of the city mourn because no one comes to her "appointed feasts" (Lam. 1:4, NIV).[11] The mourning *because of the appointed feasts* anticipated by Zephaniah finds concrete fulfillment in the Exile of the nation, as indicated specifically by Lamentations. All those meaningful celebrations that punctuated the life of the devoted Israelite were denied to him by the devastation of Jerusalem. The celebration of the "passing over" of the angel of death could only foster bitter wailing among a displaced people. The consecration of the firstfruits of harvest could only remind them that they no longer possessed a settled land. Instead of sending the scapegoat into the wilderness, they found themselves expelled from the land of promise.

Not everyone in Israel would grieve over the loss of these solemn feast days. Even as soon as Jeremiah's day, the captives in Egypt found the worship of the queen of heaven more vital to them than celebrating the feasts of Yahweh (Jer. 7:18).

But those whose hearts longed for the "songs of Zion" had a great promise to which they might cling. *I shall gather* those who are grieved because of the appointed feasts, declared the Lord. He would reverse the processes of dispersion, he would gather those who had been scattered.

---

9. Other passages that speak vividly of God's rejoicing in the love of his people include Isa. 62:4–5; 65:19; Jer. 32:40–41. Cf. Luke 15:7, 10. Each of these passages deserves extensive contemplation.

10. "The difficulties presented by the phrase as it stands are insuperable," says J. M. P. Smith, p. 258. "Every clause of v. 18 is difficult," says Keil, p. 162. Rudolph, p. 298, concludes the verse has arisen out of a postexilic situation, in which the diaspora longs for worship in Jerusalem.

11. The verb for "those who are grieved" *(nûgê)* occurs only eight times in the OT, five of which are in the book of Lamentations (Lam. 1:4–5, 12; 3:32–33). In each case, Yahweh inflicts grief on his people.

The prophet first affirms that God will gather those who mourn over the feasts celebrated at Jerusalem. Then he addresses the royal city itself: *from you they originated (mimmēḵ hāyû).* The *you* of this phrase is Jerusalem. These sorrowers had been scattered from "her."[12]

Jerusalem also is the subject of the next clause: *A burden on her was reproach.* The scorn of the nations came in addition to all the other mishaps that befell Jerusalem. Those who truly loved Jerusalem for what she meant in the purposes of God must have suffered doubly in witnessing the mockery of the heathen as their ridicule added to the calamities experienced by the city.

"Behold and see if there be any sorrow like unto my sorrow," grieves the devastated city (Lam. 1:12). The Lord has put her to grief. These words find their echo on a personal level in the garden of Gethsemane. "My soul is overwhelmed with sorrow to the point of death," was Jesus' lament (Matt. 26:38, NIV). He also found himself in exile, separated from the festivals of the Lord. As the last remnant he grieved above all others over the calamities that fell on the holy city (Luke 19:41–44).

But the prophet's message discusses the deliverance that is sure to come beyond the Lord's devastations. All those sorrows shall pass away.

19 Four times in this verse the usage of the first person form of a verb underscores the role of God in working salvation for his people. The Lord shall take the initiative to *deal with* Israel's oppressors.[13]

Israel's "oppressed" status sometimes was associated specifically with their absence from a land which could stabilize them. Abraham's de-

---

12. One of the recurring problems in the interpretation of Zephaniah arises out of the abrupt changes in speaker and subject (cf. 1:2, 7; 2:5, 8–11, 12; 3:5–6, 9, 12). A faulty process of redaction might be proposed as an explanation of the problem. But the alterations are so obvious that it is difficult to imagine that they originally would have been overlooked. Emendation of the Hebrew text may be proposed as a solution to the problem. But adopting such a procedure ignores the evidence maintained by long centuries of careful textual transmission. Following the lead of the ancient versions where they provide early testimony of a resolution to the problem provides one option for overcoming the difficulties. However, the various ancient versions are only secondary witnesses to the original text, and often are representations of the translator's solution to a difficult problem of interpretation rather than a testimony to another textual tradition.

This particular verse represents special problems in the interchange of speaker and subject. But among all the optional ways in which the problem may be approached, the best procedure begins by dealing with the text as it appears in the extant Hebrew mss.

13. The use of the term *ʿōśeh* for the idea of "to deal with" is found elsewhere in Jer. 18:23; 21:2; Ezek. 22:14; 23:25, 29.

scendants were afflicted in a foreign land for 400 years. Part of the buffer from oppression promised to David was the possession of a land that would be Israel's own (2 Sam. 7:10). Now the prophet promises that Israel shall be secure in their land. The Lord shall deal with all their oppressors. He shall secure their borders and deliver them from the curse of being a scattered nation, tossed to and fro among all the peoples of the earth.

The Lord also promises: *I shall save the lame, and the banished I shall gather.* Set in chiastic arrangement these phrases indicate that the prophet is envisioning a return after exile.[14] The laws of Deuteronomy had threatened banishment as the punishment for disobedience while simultaneously giving unqualified assurance that the Lord would return his people (Deut. 30:1, 4). The prophet now confirms this declaration of the law book.

"Gathering" implies more than simply returning the people to their land. They shall be assembled as a reconstituted community of God's people. Particularly striking because of its similarities with the book of Deuteronomy is the final expression of this verse. Instead of being shamed among all the peoples of the earth, the Lord will give Israel *honor and fame* (lit., "praise and a name"). These two elements are combined only in Deuteronomy and in Jeremiah outside Zephaniah (cf. Deut. 26:19; Jer. 13:11). Possibly the two prophets found a common source in the book of Deuteronomy.

The promise of *fame* does not cater to a vain humanity's insatiable desire for recognition. Frequently the getting of a "name" is associated with the defeat of enemies. By triumphing over opponents, a reputation demanding awe and respect spreads quickly. This concept of a famous name applies to Abraham (Gen. 12:2), David (1 Sam. 18:30; 2 Sam. 7:9; 8:13), Abishai (2 Sam. 23:18), and Israel as a nation (2 Sam. 7:23). Even God's name becomes famous as he displays his power over his enemies (Isa. 63:12; Jer. 32:20; Neh. 9:10).

Wherever Israel had been scattered in the shame of their captivity and defeat, they now shall be honored. The prophet does not specifically state that Israel's fame shall arise out of her defeat of these same enemies that once conquered her. But these nations clearly shall stand in awe of this restored nation, marvelling at the stature she has now achieved in the light of her past humiliations.

20 The placing of *fame* before *honor* in contrast with the previous verse provides a simple poetic variation. The more substantial difference lies in the extent to which Israel's fame radiates. Not only among those places to which they had been carried away in shame, but now *among all the peoples*

14. The entire expression may be taken from Mic. 4:6.

of the earth their honor shall be acclaimed. This worldwide recognition of Israel's glory will occur when the Lord returns their *captivities*.[15]

This promise found its immediate fulfillment in the restoration of Israel after their seventy years of captivity. At that time the banished were restored and the remnant of the Lord was reassembled in their land.

However, it is not at all apparent that the little community of the restoration, returning to Palestine by the good graces of the world-conqueror Cyrus, actually became famous throughout the entire earth. The end of all reproaches certainly did not occur in that "day of little things" (Zech. 4:10).

For this reason, the broader implications of land possession on the part of God's people must be considered. The imagery of Israel's possession of Palestine actually builds on the picture of paradise restored. The prophet had spoken in terms reminiscent of the idyllic situation of paradise (3:13). The original promise of the land to the first father of Israel, as well as the assurance of a multiplied seed, actually reflects the original creation mandate concerning humanity's responsibility to multiply, fill the earth, and subdue it (Gen. 1:28). In microcosmic fashion, the possession of the land by the descendants of Abraham depicted the manner in which God would complete his program for the redemption of the earth. *when I return your* [i.e., Israel's] *captivity* anticipates the rejuvenation of the world. For it actually was the "cosmos" that Abraham and his seed were promised (Rom. 4:13).

Zephaniah declares to his contemporaries that this grand restoration would occur *before your eyes,* which creates something of a problem.[16] For neither Zephaniah's contemporaries nor those who lived to see the restoration of Israel to Palestine experienced all that the prophet promised.

However, embedded in the words of the Voice from the bush to Moses was the promise of resurrection. If he still was Abraham's God hundreds of years after the patriarch's death, then resurrection is a necessity. For he is not a God of the dead but of the living (cf. Mark 12:18–27). In Moses' day promises made personally to Abraham were still outstanding concerning the patriarch's own possession of the land.

Before the eyes of Zephaniah's contemporaries, says Yahweh, the unchanging I AM's return to paradise shall occur. As in the case of another

---

15. The plural "captivities" may be compared with the singular in Zeph. 2:7.

16. The suggestion of Rudolph, p. 299, that this expression must have been a contemporizing addition later than the time of the prophet actually does not solve the problem implicit in the text. For not even the postexilic community saw for themselves the full realization of that which the prophet promised.

patriarchal figure, they shall see this rejuvenation with their own eyes, and not through the eyes of a stranger (Job 19:25–27).

So the book of Zephaniah ends where it begins. The prophet opened with a scene of cataclysmic overthrow. The whole order of the cosmos would be reversed in the judgment of the great Day of Yahweh. The prophet closes with another scene of cosmic scope. The earth shall be reconstituted in the glorious new order achieved by a return to the land on a proportion never before realized. The ultimate of blessing in the covenant joins with the ultimate of cursing to consummate the entirety of the historical process.

INDEXES

SUBJECTS

AUTHORS

SCRIPTURE REFERENCES

352

HEBREW WORDS

ʾe ʾᵉsōp	258	gāraš	297	kaḥaš	101
ʾābaḏ	299			kāpîs	192
ʾaddîr	127	dōhēr	104	kᵉp̄îr	96
ʾûlay	295	dûš	236	kāsâ	205
ʾāwen	140, 221	drš	265	kāsap	291
ʾiyê haggôyim	308			kᵉrōʾî	107
ʾēḵ	311	he ʾᵉmin	178-79	kᵉrōṯ	300
ʾēḵâ	311	hôḵēaḥ	167	kᵉrēṯîm	300
ʾāyōm	151	hôḵîaḥ	158, 211	kaśdîm	144
ʾēn	311	hôy	100, 189	kittîm	144
ʾel	72-73	hêḵal	211		
ʾᵉlîlîm	209	hayyônâ	317	lāḇîʾ	96
ʾilleᵉmîm	209	hᵃliḵōṯ	227	lōḇᵉšîm	276
ʾēmâ	151	hāmôn	114	lahaḇ	105
ʾᵉmûnâ	178-80	hammaḵšēlôṯ	259	lᵉhummām	282
ʾsp	258	hēʿārēl	202	lamnaṣṣēaḥ	248
ʾāsap	257-58	huṣṣaḇ	91	lᵉʿēḏ	324
ʾāsēp	257-58	hiqdîš	270		
ʾāsōp	257	haqqōpᵉʾîm	280	mᵉgammaṯ	153
ʾōsēp	258	hārîʾû	336	māḏaḏ	221
ʾap	231			mahēr	274, 280
ʾap hārôn	292	wayyaḇᵉšēhû	66	maḥᵃrîḏ	332
ʾᵃpēlâ	284			maṭṭôṯ	234
ʾepes	311	zᵉḇulâ	235	maṭṭāyw	234
ʾarbeh	124, 126			maḵtēš	279
ʾaryēh	96	ḥebel	300	mᵉlîṣâ	185
ʾeṯ	237	ḥay-ʾānî	304	malkām	265
		ḥîḏôṯ	185	mᵉmahēr	274
baʾēr	168	ḥêlām	280	mimšaq	302
babbōqer	322	ḥayṯô	311	minnᵉzār	126
bāḡaḏ	143	ḥālāl	106	minḥâ	330
bōḡᵉḏîm	142-44	ḥāmās	139, 278	massēḵâ	208
baggôyim	142-43	ḥeseḏ	70	mᵉṣûqâ	284
bᵉḏê	195	ḥāṣîl	124	miqqedem	157
bûq	94	ḥārâ	231	mōrᵉʾâ	315, 317
bᵉṭerᵉm	292	ḥārûl	302	mᵉraqqēḏâ	104
bᵉlîyaʿal	74-75	ḥāraš	340	maśśāʾ	55, 135
bālaq	94	ḥāšaḇ	72-73	mᵉšôʾâ	284
bāqaq	87, 94			māšāl	185
bqš	265	ṭôḇaṯ ḥēn	102	mišpāṭ	294
baqqᵉšû	293	ṭerep	102		
bᵉraq	105			niḡʾālâ	317
		yᵉgōrēhû	163	neginoth	135
gibbôr	339	yᵉḥîṯan	199	nôḏaḏ	126
gôḇ gōḇāy	126	yeleq	124	nûaḥ	244
gᵉwîyâ	106	ysp	258	nôqēm	58
gûr ʾaryēh	96	yāšᵉrâ	176	nôrāʾ	152, 307
gāzām	124			nᵉwōṯ	300
gāram	320	kōaḥ	115	noḵrî	276